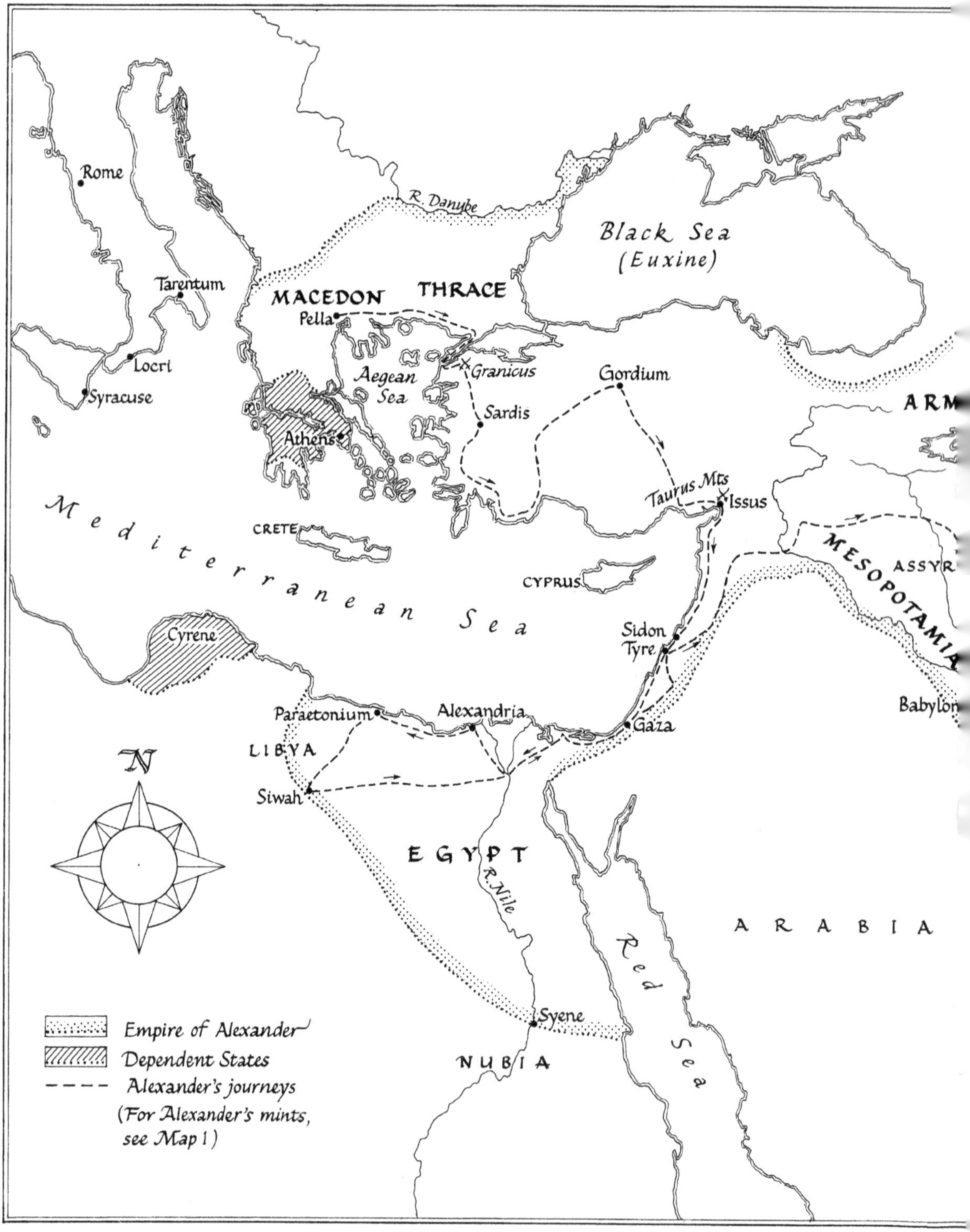
Rome
Tarentum
Locri
Syracuse
R. Danube
Black Sea
(Euxine)
MACEDON
THRACE
Pella
Aegean Sea
Granicus
Gordium
Sardis
Athens
ARM
Taurus Mts
Issus
Mediterranean Sea
CRETE
CYPRUS
MESOPOTAMIA
ASSYR
Cyrene
Sidon
Tyre
Babylon
Paraetonium
Alexandria
Gaza
LIBYA
Siwah
N
EGYPT
R. Nile
ARABIA
Red Sea
Syene
NUBIA
Empire of Alexander
Dependent States
Alexander's journeys
(For Alexander's mints, see Map 1)

The Empire of Alexander the Great
Aral Sea
R. Jaxartes
Caspian Sea
R. Oxus
Samarkand
SOGDIANA
A
e Van
Lake Urmia
BACTRIA
MEDIA
HYRCANIA
Hindu Kush
ugamela
PARTHIA
R. Indus
R. Hydaspes
Susa
R. Hyphasis
ARACHOSIA
uphrates
Alexandria
Persepolis
R. Indus
PERSIS
Persian Gulf
GEDROSIA
Erythraean Sea
0
500 km
0
500 miles

This is the first full study of early Hellenistic coinage to be published. It provides a general history of the coinage of Alexander the Great and his successors, and of the cities of Greece and Asia Minor, over the century and a half 336–188 B.C. Dr Mørkholm gives special attention to the imitative coinages bearing the names of Philip of Macedon, Alexander and Lysimachus which can now, as a result of the work of the great American numismatist Edward T. Newell and subsequent scholars, be confidently attributed to later periods and to different regions in the Hellenistic world.

Dr Mørkholm's original intention was to write a survey of Hellenistic coinage down to the Roman acquisition of Egypt in 30 B.C., but he died with his project only half finished. His survey of early Hellenistic coinage, however, is complete in itself. A short epilogue has been added by Professor Grierson describing the main features of the coinage after 188 B.C.

The book is fully annotated, so that the reader can follow the most recent discussion of each theme, and a select bibliography covers the period down to 30 B.C. The forty-five plates, based mainly on material in the Royal Danish Coin Cabinet and illustrating over 600 coins, include virtually all types struck prior to 188 and a selection of those minted subsequently. Dr Mørkholm's detailed descriptions of the coins will provide a standard work of reference for ancient historians, numismatists and collectors.

EARLY HELLENISTIC COINAGE FROM THE ACCESSION OF ALEXANDER TO THE PEACE OF APAMEA

(336–188 B.C.)

EARLY HELLENISTIC COINAGE

FROM THE ACCESSION OF ALEXANDER TO THE PEACE OF APAMEA (336–188 B.C.)

By the late

OTTO MØRKHOLM

Edited by

PHILIP GRIERSON *and* ULLA WESTERMARK

CAMBRIDGE UNIVERSITY PRESS

CAMBRIDGE
UNIVERSITY PRESS

University Printing House, Cambridge CB2 8BS, United Kingdom

Published in the United States of America by Cambridge University Press, New York

Cambridge University Press is part of the University of Cambridge.

It furthers the University's mission by disseminating knowledge in the pursuit of education, learning and research at the highest international levels of excellence.

www.cambridge.org
Information on this title: www.cambridge.org/9780521395045

First published 1991
Reprinted 1997, 2001

A catalogue record for this publication is available from the British Library

Library of Congress Cataloguing in Publication data
Mørkholm, Otto.
Early Hellenistic coinage from the accession of Alexander to the peace of Apamea (336–188 B.C.) / by the late Otto Mørkholm: edited by Philip Grierson and Ulla Westermark.
p. cm.
Includes bibliographical references.
ISBN 0 521 39504 6
1. Coins, Greek – History. 2. Coins, Greek –Turkey – History.
3. Coinage – Greece – History. 4. Coinage –Turkey – History.
5. Greece – History –To 146 B.C. I. Grierson, Philip.
II. Westermark, Ulla. III. Title.
CJ407.N67 1991 90–1868
737.4938–dc20 CIP

ISBN 978-0-521-39504-5 Hardback

FOREWORD

PHILIP GRIERSON

In 1974 Otto Mørkholm, Keeper of the Royal Danish Coin Cabinet at Copenhagen and one of the most distinguished numismatists of this century, accepted an invitation to write a book entitled *Hellenistic Greek Coins* as a contribution to the Methuen series 'The Library of Numismatics'. His study of the coinage of Antiochus IV, published in 1963, had been the prelude to a doctoral thesis (1966) on the same ruler, and the bulk of his publications during the following decade had been concerned with Hellenistic numismatics. Once the contract was signed he began to systematize his research with a view to producing a general survey, and in the spring of 1977 he spent three months' leave at Princeton and wrote the first of the five sections he had planned. Much of his time over the next few years had to be devoted to preparations for the celebration of the Bicentenary of the Copenhagen Coin Cabinet in March 1981, but he nonetheless managed to achieve a massive output of scholarly articles preparatory to returning to Princeton in the autumn of 1982 for another and hopefully final period of uninterrupted composition.

This was not to be. Shortly after the Bicentenary he fell ill, and in June 1981 he was operated on for cancer. He appeared at first to have made a good recovery and could resume his normal activities, but by autumn 1982 he was again seriously ill. The projected American trip was abandoned, and it was in Copenhagen that, in September, he returned to writing the book. In November he had two further operations, and although he returned to the Coin Cabinet in January 1983 it was plain that he had not much longer to live. His activity in the following months was prodigious, partly devoted to such articles as he thought might be completed in the time left to him, partly trying to get through as much as possible of the book that would sum up his knowledge of the coinage which had been his main interest in the previous three decades. For a time he had two typists turning his material into finished form to be submitted to Margaret Thompson or myself for such revision as the contents or the English might require. But in May he had a serious relapse and on 16 July, twelve days before his fifty-third birthday, he died. He was working on the manuscript and related articles till one or two days before his death, and his last finished paper, published posthumously, was written only a week before he died.

Otto Mørkholm's tragic death in such circumstances and at such a relatively early age was a sad loss equally to Greek numismatics and to his family and many friends. The joint memorial volume for him and Colin Kraay, who died in 1982, is a reflection of the esteem in which his scholarship is held and also of the depth of affection felt for a man who was one of the most widely liked numismatists of his generation.*

By July 1983 Mørkholm was not quite half-way through the projected volume, but the chapters that he left – a general introduction and an account of the coinages down to the Peace of Apamea – were complete in themselves. His literary executors, in association with myself as General Editor of the Methuen series, were faced with the alternatives of either publishing the section as it stood or inviting some other scholar to continue it to 30 B.C., the date envisaged for its ending. Kenneth Jenkins, who had recently retired as Keeper of the Department of Coins and Medals in the British Museum, and who is one of the most eminent scholars in the field, volunteered to provide such a continuation, but he made it clear that other commitments would prevent his starting work at once. Early in 1989 he had to let us know that because of increasing eyesight problems he would have, regretfully, to abandon it.

In view of the length of time that has elapsed since Mørkholm's death we have come to the conclusion that a further delay is unacceptable, and that the manuscript should be published as it stands under a revised title, *Early Hellenistic Coinage*. Such a volume would not easily fit into the Methuen series, and the representatives of this firm have generously renounced their claim to the manuscript so that the work could be published by the Cambridge University Press.

The bulk of the volume – the text of chapters 1–11, the contents of the footnotes, and part A of the Epilogue – are essentially as Mørkholm finished them in 1983. Mørkholm's continuous text ended with what is here chapter 11. What was intended to be the next group of chapters, describing Western coinage in the third century, were never written. He composed, however, a substantial section of the chapter intended to follow these, covering essentially the end of Macedonian coinage, and this has been included here as part A of an Epilogue. Beyond that he had written no more than three pages of typescript on the early second-century coins of Chalcis and Euboea and the origins of the New Style coinage of Athens. These seemed too fragmentary to be worth reproducing, more especially since his views on the dating of the New Style coins are available in a closely reasoned article (Mørkholm 1984b) that appeared after his death. Instead, at the request of the Press, I have supplied a summary sketch of later Hellenistic coinage to round off the volume.

The text of Mørkholm's introductory section (chapters 1–3) has been left unchanged despite being intended for a book originally planned to cover the second and first centuries B.C., since it seemed worth putting on record the author's views on some general aspects of the later coinage even if he did not have time to deal with this in detail. I have, however, altered the arrangement of the chapters, for chapter 3 was originally intended to be chapter 1. Elsewhere my editorial work has been largely confined to changes in words or phrasing, though Mørkholm's

* *Kraay–Mørkholm Essays. Numismatic Studies in Memory of C.M. Kraay and O. Mørkholm* (Studia Lovaniensia 10, Louvain-la-Neuve, 1989). This includes a bibliography of his publications by Jørgen Steen Jensen and an appreciation of him by Margaret Thompson. See also the obituary by Rudi Thomsen in *Det kongelige Danske Videnskabernes Selskabs Virksomhed* 1984–85, 143–9, and the appreciation of his work, particularly for the Coin Cabinet in Copenhagen, by Jan Zahle in the *Nordisk Numismatisk Unions Medlemsblad* 1985, 59–68.

command of both spoken and written English was so perfect that relatively little editing of this kind proved necessary. No attempt has been made to update the text systematically in the light of subsequent research, but I have drawn attention to the views of other scholars, and cited more recent publications, where they seemed of particular consequence. Additions of substance have been put in square brackets to distinguish them from Mørkholm's own text, but it has not seemed necessary to distinguish many minor adjustments in dates made to bring these into line with those in the third volume of N.G.L. Hammond and F.W. Walbank, *A History of Macedonia*, and in the revised Vol. VII, Part I, of *The Cambridge Ancient History*, both published since Mørkholm's death. I have also added lists of rulers, a chronological table of events, a bibliography, and a glossary.

Ulla Westermark's contribution has been of a more creative character. Mørkholm's hope was that the volume should as far as possible be illustrated by material in the Royal Danish Collection, of which he had been Keeper and which now houses his great collection of casts, and this has been done. The arrangement of the plates and the captions are almost entirely her work. She has also supplied the monograms and been consistently helpful in the occasional updating of Mørkholm's text and of the bibliography and in the very necessary revision of my own section of the Epilogue. This has also profited from the comments of Kevin Butcher, for which I am most grateful.

Since the projected book of which this volume forms only a part was intended by Mørkholm as his *opus majus*, summarizing the results of over twenty years of study, it is proper here to thank, on his behalf, the many persons and institutions who actively supported his work: the Danish National Museum, of which the Royal Collection of Coins and Medals forms a part; State Antiquarians P.V. Glob and Olaf Olsen, successive Directors of the Museum; the Carlsberg Foundation and the Rask-Ørsted Foundation, the latter now incorporated in the Danish Research Council for the Humanities; the Numismatic Foundation of Axel and Alfrida Ernst, which made a substantial grant for the plates of the volume; the Institute for Advanced Studies at Princeton and the Fulbright Commission for Educational Exchange between Denmark and the United States; the American Numismatic Society, which enabled him repeatedly to visit New York and work in its Museum in association with Margaret Thompson. It may seem invidious to pick out for special mention any of the many coin cabinets in which he worked for longer or shorter periods, but it should be recorded that the Department of Coins and Medals in the British Museum and the Museum of the American Numismatic Society held a particular place in his affections. He also owed a special debt of gratitude to an individual who played a major role in the planning and writing of this book, his wife Annelis Thygesen Mørkholm, who was for many years his assistant in the Royal Coin Cabinet.

In preparing the book for the press I am grateful for much help and advice to Jørgen Steen Jensen and Martin Price, who have readily answered the many queries I have had to put to them. Ulla Westermark and Dorothy Thompson have been endlessly helpful in the revision of the manuscript, and Richard Ashton has given much advice on the sections dealing with Rhodes. Dorothy Thompson and Professor F.W. Walbank have been of especial assistance in determining matters of chronology, more particularly in relation to the lists of rulers. For the dates of Bactrian kings I have relied on my friend Osmund Bopearachchi of the CNRS in Paris, who has been preparing the catalogue of Bactrian and Indo-Greek coins in the Cabinet des Médailles. The lay-out of the volume owes much to the skilled attention of the staff of Cambridge University Press. I should like to express my special thanks to Ann Johnston, a friend of many years' standing who copy-edited the book for the Press so meticulously as almost to make her a co-editor, to Ted Buttrey, who generously volunteered to check my supposedly corrected proofs while I was in America and put me to shame on my return by the number of errors he had spotted which I had overlooked, and to Mrs Edna Pilmer for her careful initial typing of what was sometimes a difficult manuscript. Ulla Westermark and myself must also express our warmest gratitude to the authorities of the Department of Coins and Medals of the British Museum, the Hunterian Museum at Glasgow, the Cabinet des Médailles of the Bibliothèque Nationale, the Museum of the American Numismatic Society, the Münzkabinett of the Staatliche Museen in Berlin, the Numismatiko Mouseio at Athens, the Institut für Alte Geschichte at Saarbrücken, and the Numismatische Abteilung of Bank Leu AG of Zürich for supplying photographs of the material required for the plates and not available in the Royal Cabinets at Copenhagen or Stockholm.

CONTENTS

Foreword by Philip Grierson	vii
List of maps	xiv
List of tables	xv
List of figures	xv
Summary of plates	xvi
Abbreviations	xxii

PART I GENERAL FEATURES OF THE COINAGE

1	METALS AND WEIGHT STANDARDS	3
	(a) Metals	3
	(b) Weight standards	7
2	COIN PRODUCTION AND USE	12
	(a) Minting technique	12
	(b) Coin production	15
	(c) Coin circulation	19
	(d) The functions of coinage	23
3	TYPES AND INSCRIPTIONS	25
	(a) Types	25
	(b) Inscriptions	29
	(c) Imitations and style	30

PART II ALEXANDER AND THE DIADOCHI, 336–*c.* 280

4	COINS OF ALEXANDER'S LIFETIME	41
5	PHILIP III AND THE EARLY POSTHUMOUS COINAGE	55
6	EGYPT AND ITS NEIGHBOURS	63
	(a) Ptolemy I	63
	(b) Cyrenaica and Judaea	67
7	SYRIA AND THE EAST: SELEUCUS I	71

8 MACEDONIA, ASIA MINOR AND GREECE 77
(a) Demetrius Poliorcetes 77
(b) Lysimachus 81
(c) Lesser dynasts and cities of Greece and Asia Minor 83

PART III THE BALANCE OF POWER: EASTERN HELLENISM, *c*. 280–188

9 THE PTOLEMIES, *c*. 283–200 101

10 THE SELEUCIDS 113
(a) The central region, 281–187 113
(b) The eastern satrapies and the Successor States in the East, 281–*c*. 187 116
(c) Western Seleucid mints 122

11 ASIA MINOR, MACEDONIA AND GREECE 128
(a) The lesser kingdoms of Asia Minor, *c*. 281–188 128
(b) The kingdom of Macedon, *c*. 281–196 132
(c) Posthumous Alexanders and Lysimachi and related coinages 137
(d) Leagues and cities in Greece and Asia Minor, *c*. 280–190 148

EPILOGUE

A The end of Macedonian coinage 163
B Later Hellenistic coinage, by Philip Grierson 169

APPENDICES

LISTS OF RULERS
Kings of Macedon 187
The Seleucids (Syria and the East) 188
The Lagids (Ptolemies) of Egypt 190
The Attalids of Pergamum 191
Kings of Bithynia 192
Kings of Pontus 192
Kings of Cappadocia 193
The Arsacids of Parthia 194
Bactrian and Indo-Greek kings 195

CHRONOLOGICAL TABLE 336–187

GLOSSARY 203

SELECT BIBLIOGRAPHY 209
A List of abbreviations 209
B Regional bibliographies 211
C Principal published collections 212
D Secondary literature 218

PLATES 243

INDEX 267

MAPS

Front endpapers: The Empire of Alexander the Great
Back endpapers: The Hellenistic World, *c.* 200 B.C.

1	The mints of Alexander the Great	*page* 40
2	Ptolemaic mints: Egypt and Syria	100
3	Western and central Seleucid mints	112
4	Eastern Seleucid mints	117
5	Macedonia and Greece	133
6	Western Asia Minor	140

TABLES

1 Eastern Hellenistic coin standards *page* 9
2 Bronze denominations of Ptolemy II 105
3 Bronze denominations of Ptolemy III 107

FIGURES

1 Dies and their use *page* 15
2 Die linkages 16
3 Greek numbering systems 34

SUMMARY OF PLATES

I PHILIP II AND ALEXANDER THE GREAT

Philip II: *Pella* **1–2**; *Amphipolis* **3**; *Uncertain mint* **4**. Alexander: *Aegae* or *Amphipolis* **5–6**; *Amphipolis* **7**, **9**; *Babylon* **8**; *Sardis* **10**; *Uncertain mint* **11**; *Aegae* **12**; *Tarsus* **13**; *Myriandrus* **16**; *Aradus* **17**. Local issues: *Tarsus* **14–15**.

II ALEXANDER THE GREAT AND CONTEMPORARY ISSUES

Alexander: *Byblus* **18**; *Sidon* **19**; *Ake* **20**; *Damascus* **21**; *Salamis* **22**; *Babylon* **27–30**. Local issues: *Byblus* **23–4**; *Egypt* (Artaxerxes III) **25**, (Mazaces) **26**; *Manbog* **31–3**.

III PERIOD OF ALEXANDER THE GREAT AND PHILIP III

Alexander: *Sardis* **34–5**; *Colophon* **36**; *Miletus* **37–8**; *Lampsacus* **39**; *Abydus* **40**; *Citium* **41**; *Alexandria* **42**; *Side* (?) **43**; *Uncertain eastern mint* **44–6**. Philip III: *Babylon* **47**; *Aradus* **48**; *Lampsacus* **49**; *Colophon* **50**.

IV PERIOD OF PHILIP III

Philip III: *Magnesia* **51**; *Sardis* **52**; *Miletus* **53**; *Susa* **54**; *Pella* **55**; *Colophon* **56**. Local issues: *Babylon area* **57**; *Lapethus* (Praxippus) **58**; *Marium* (Stasioecus II) **59**; *Citium* (Pumiathon) **60**; *Paphos* (Nicocles) **61–2**; *Salamis* (Nicocreon) **63–4**, (Menelaus) **65**; *Susiana* (Aspeisas) **66**; *Mylasa* (Eupolemus) **67–8**.

V PERIOD OF THE DIADOCHI

Cassander: *Amphipolis* **69–70**; *Uncertain mint* **71–2**; *Miletus* (?) **73**; *Uranopolis* **74–5**. Lysimachus: *Lysimachia* **76–9**. Antigonus I: *Lampsacus* **80**; *Abydus* **81**; *Aradus* **82**; *Carrhae* **83**; *Tyre* **84**; *Antigonea* **85**; *Corinth* **86**. Seleucus I: *Ecbatana* **87–9**.

VI PTOLEMY I AND CYRENAICA

Ptolemy I: *Alexandria* **90–3**, **96–7**, **99–101**; *Sidon* **94**; *Soli* **95**; *Uncertain mint* **98**. *Cyrenaica:* **102–6**.

VII CYRENAICA AND JUDAEA

Cyrene **107–22, 124–9** (Thibron **108–9,** Ophellas **114–15,** Magas **122**); *Euhesperides* **123;** *Judaea* **130–1.**

VIII SELEUCUS I AND THE EAST

Seleucus I: *Seleucia on the Tigris* **132–4;** *Susa* **135–6, 138–40, 144;** *Ecbatana* **137, 141–3;** *Bactra* **145.** Local issues: *Persis* (Bagadates) **146,** (Oborzos) **147;** *Bactria* or *India* (Sophytes) **148.**

IX SELEUCUS I

Marathus **149–51;** *Laodicea ad Mare* **152;** *Antioch* **153, 160;** *Seleucia Pieria* **154;** *Tarsus* **155;** *Sardis* **156;** *Pergamum* **157;** *Seleucia on the Tigris* **158–9.**

X DEMETRIUS POLIORCETES AND PYRRHUS

Demetrius Poliorcetes: *Tyre* **161;** *Salamis* **162–4;** *Tarsus* **165–6;** *Uncertain mint* (*Caria*?) **167;** *Miletus* **168;** *Ephesus* **169;** *Pella* **170–2, 174;** *Amphipolis* **173.** Pyrrhus: *Pella* **175.**

XI LYSIMACHUS AND PATRAEUS OF PAEONIA

Lysimachus: *Sardis* **176;** *Colophon* **177;** *Amphipolis* **178;** *Lampsacus* **179–80;** *Pella* **181;** *Smyrna* **182;** *Uncertain mint* **183–4.** Patraeus: **185–9.**

XII DYNASTS AND GREEK CITIES

Audoleon of *Paeonia*: **190–1.** Seuthes III of the *Odrysian Thracians*: **192.** Monunius of the *Dardanian Illyrians* **193.** *Dyrrhachium* **194;** *Corcyra* **195;** *Epirus* (Pyrrhus) **196;** (Epirote *symmachia*) **197–8;** *Philippi* **199–201;** *Larissa* **202–3;** *Delphi* **204–5;** *Thebes* **206.**

XIII GREEK AND CRETAN CITIES

Athens **207–11;** *Eleusis* **212;** *Corinth* **213–14;** *Sicyon* **215;** *Elis* **216;** *Gortyn* **217;** *Phaestus* **218–22;** *Knossos* **223–4.**

XIV CRETE AND RHODES

Olus **225;** *Chersonesus* **226–7;** *Stymphalus* (Arcadia) **228;** *Sybrita* **229–31;** *Eleutherna* **232;** *Hierapytna* **233;** *Uncertain mint* **234;** *Rhodes* **235–9.**

XV GREEK LEAGUES AND CITIES

Tenos **240;** *Chalcis* **241–2, 246–7;** *Carystus* **243;** *Histiaea* **244;** *Euboean League* (*Chalcis*?) **245;** *Erythrae* **248–51;** *Colophon* **252–4;** *Ephesus* **255–6;** *Arsinoea* **257–8.**

XVI GREEK CITIES

Samos **259–61**; *Miletus* **262–4**; *Mylasa* **265**; *Cius* **266–7**; *Pergamum* **268**; *Panticapaeum* **269**; *Byzantium* **270**; *Chalcedon* **271**; *Thracian Chersonese* **272**; *Parium* **273**; *Cyzicus* **274**.

XVII ASIA MINOR, DYNASTS; EGYPT AND CYRENAICA

Heraclea Pontica **275–8**; *Amastris* **279–80**; *Sinope* **281–2**; *Gaziura* **283**. Egypt: *Alexandria* (Ptolemy II) **284–5**. Cyrenaica: *Cyrene* (Magas) **286–8**.

XVIII CYRENAICA AND PTOLEMY II

Cyrene, koinon (*c.* 250), **289–90**. Ptolemy II: *Alexandria* **291**, **294–8**, **300**; *Tyre* **292**, **299**; *Sidon* **293**.

XIX EGYPT: PTOLEMY II AND PTOLEMY III

Ptolemy II: *Alexandria* **301–6**; Ptolemy III: *Alexandria* **307–8**.

XX EGYPT, ETC.: PTOLEMY III AND PTOLEMY IV

Ptolemy III: *Alexandria* **309–10**, **314**; *Cyprus* **311**; *Tarsus* **312**; *Ephesus* **313**; *Tyre* **315**. Ptolemy IV: *Alexandria* **316–18**.

XXI EGYPT AND PHOENICIA: PTOLEMY V

Joppa **319**; *Dora* **320**; *Alexandria* **321–3**; *Uncertain Phoenician mint* **324**, **326–29**; *Sidon* **325**.

XXII THE SELEUCIDS: CENTRAL AND EASTERN MINTS

The coins are of *Antioch on the Orontes* or *Apamea* with the exception of **334** (*Ecbatana*). Antiochus I: **330**. Antiochus II: **331**. 'Interregnum': **335**, **336**. Seleucus II: **332–4**, **341–2**. Seleucus III: **337–8**. Antiochus III: **339–40**.

XXIII THE SELEUCIDS: CENTRAL MINTS

Seleucus I: *Antioch* **350**. Antiochus I: *Tarsus* **344**; *Antioch* **349**, **351**; *Carrhae* **354A–B**. Antiochus II: *Tarsus* **352**. Seleucus II: *Nisibis* **355**. Seleucus III: *Simyra* **347**. Antiochus III: *Laodicea ad Mare* **343**; *Tarsus* **345**; *Soli* **346**; *Antioch* **348**, **353**.

XXIV THE SELEUCIDS: EASTERN MINTS

Antiochus I: *Seleucia on the Tigris* **360**; *Bactra* **371–3**. Antiochus II: *Seleucia on the Tigris* **362**. Seleucus II: *Nisibis* **356**; *Ecbatana* **368**; *Hecatompylus* (?) **370**. Molon: *Seleucia on the Tigris* **361**. Antiochus III: *Nisibis* **357–9**; *Susa* **363**; *Ecbatana* **364–7**, **369**.

XXV THE SELEUCIDS AND THEIR EASTERN NEIGHBOURS

Diodotus I–II: *Bactra* **374–5, 380–2.** Euthydemus: *Bactra* **383–7.** *Persis* (Artaxerxes) **376,** (Autophradates I) **377.** *Parthia* (Andragoras) **378–9.**

XXVI THE SELEUCIDS: WESTERN MINTS

Antiochus I: *Sardis* **388–9, 391;** *Magnesia ad Sipylum* **393.** Antiochus II: *Sardis* **390, 392, 395;** *Lysimachia* **394.** Seleucus II: *Sardis* **396.** Antiochus Hierax: *Alexandria Troas* **397;** *Parium* **398;** *Lysimachia* **399.**

XXVII THE SELEUCIDS: WESTERN MINTS; PERGAMUM

Seleucus III: *Uncertain Phrygian mint* **400.** Achaeus: *Sardis* **403–5.** Antiochus III: *Uncertain Phrygian mint* **401;** *Sardis* **402, 406.** *Pergamum:* (Philetaerus) **407–8;** (Eumenes I) **409;** (Attalus I) **410.**

XXVIII LESSER KINGDOMS OF ASIA MINOR

Pergamum: (Attalus I) **411–13.** *Bithynia:* (Nicomedes I) **414–15,** (Ziaelas) **416,** (Prusias I) **417–19.** *Pontus:* (Mithridates II) **420,** (Mithridates III) **421.** *Cappadocia:* (Ariaramnes **422–3**), (Ariarathes III) **424–6,** (Ariarathes IV) **427–8.**

XXIX MACEDON

Antigonus II Gonatas: *Amphipolis* **429–31;** *Uncertain mint* **432.** Antigonus II or Antigonus III Doson: *Uncertain mint* **433–4.** Demetrius II: *Uncertain mint* **435.** Antigonus III Doson: *Amphipolis* **436;** *Pella*? **437.** Philip V: *Pella* **438–40;** *Uncertain mints* **441–4.** Flamininus: *Uncertain mint* **445.**

XXX POSTHUMOUS ALEXANDERS (I)

Argos **446;** *Megalopolis* **447;** *Sicyon* **448;** *Corinth* **449;** *Messene* **450;** *Cabyle* **451;** *Heraclea Pontica* **452;** *Sinope* **453–4,** (*Autonomous types*) **455–7.**

XXXI POSTHUMOUS ALEXANDERS (II)

Parium **458;** *Lampsacus* **459–60;** *Alexandria Troas* **461;** *Cyzicus* (?) **462;** *Sardis* **463–5;** *Chios* **466–70.**

XXXII POSTHUMOUS ALEXANDERS (III)

Rhodes **471–2;** *Samos* **473;** *Miletus* **474;** *Antioch/Alabanda* **475–6;** *Sillyum* **477;** *Aspendus* **478;** *Perge* **479;** *Phaselis* **480.**

XXXIII POSTHUMOUS ALEXANDERS (IV) AND LYSIMACHI; LOCAL ISSUES

Side **481;** *Perge* **482;** *Aradus* **483–5;** *Gerrha* **486;** *Hagar* **487;** *Uncertain Arabian mint* **488–9;** *Aenus* **490;** *Byzantium* **491;** *Chalcedon* **492;** *Cyzicus* **493.**

XXXIV GREEK CITIES

Byzantium **494–5, 498–9;** *Chalcedon* **496–7, 500;** *Athens* **501–2;** *Sparta* **503–8.**

XXXV GREEK CITIES AND LEAGUES

Sparta **509–11;** *Messene* **512;** *Aetolian League* **513–19;** *Acarnanian League* **520–1;** *Epirote League* **522–4.**

XXXVI GREEK CITIES AND LEAGUES; CRETE

Corcyra **525–6;** *Apollonia* **527;** *Dyrrhachium* **528–9;** *Boeotia* **530;** *Elis* **531;** *Achaean League* **532–4;** *Arcadian League* **535–7;** *Gortyn* **538–43;** *Knossos* **544;** *Polyrhenium* **545;** *Arsinoea* **546.**

XXXVII GREEK CITIES

Rhodes **547–56;** *Cos* **557;** *Melos* **558;** *Paros* **559–60;** *Naxos* **561–2;** *Carystus* **563–4;** *Histiaea* **565.**

XXXVIII GREEK CITIES

Ephesus **566, 570;** *Priene* **567, 572;** *Miletus* **568, 571;** *Samos* **569, 573–4;** *Cnidus* **575–7;** *Phaselis* **578;** *Aspendus* **579;** *Selge* **580–1.**

XXXIX MACEDONIA

Philip V: *Amphipolis* **582–3;** *Uncertain mints* **584–7.** Perseus: *Amphipolis* **588–90;** *Uncertain mint* **591.** Regional issues: *Amphipolis* **592–5;** *Thessalonica* (for Amphaxitis) **596.**

XL MACEDONIA AND NEIGHBOURING MINTS

Pella (for Bottiaea) **597–8, 600;** *Amphipolis* (?) (Fulcinius) **599;** *Uncertain mint* **601;** *Amphipolis* (for First District) **602–4,** (Aesillas) **605;** *Thasos* **606,** *Maroneia* **607;** *Samothrace* **608.**

XLI GREEK CITIES; KINGDOM OF PERGAMUM

Athens **609–11;** *Eretria* **612–13;** *Pergamum* (Eumenes II) **614–16;** *Ephesus* **617;** *Cyzicus* **618;** *Cyme* **619.**

XLII KINGDOMS OF ASIA MINOR: SYRIA

Myrina **620;** *Bithynia* (Nicomedes III) **621;** *Cappadocia* (Ariarathes VII) **622;** *Pontus* (Pharnaces I) **623,** (Mithridates IV) **624,** (Mithridates VI) **625;** *Antioch* (Tigranes II), **626,** (Antiochus IV), **627–8.**

XLIII SYRIA AND PARTHIA

Antiochus IV: *Ake-Ptolemais* **629;** *Antioch* **630.** Antiochus VI: *Antioch* **631–2.** Antiochus VII:

Tyre **633.** Demetrius II: *Tarsus* **634.** Cleopatra Thea and Antiochus VIII: *Sidon* **635.** Antiochus VIII: *Ake-Ptolemais* **636.** *Parthia:* (Mithridates I) **637,** (Mithridates II) **638.**

XLIV BACTRIA, ETC.; PHOENICIA, PALESTINE AND EGYPT

Bactria (Eucratides I) **639–40;** *India* (Menander) **641;** *Elymais Susa* (Kamnaskires I) **642;** *Characene* (Tiraias II) **643;** *Aradus* **644;** *Tyre* **645;** *Alexandria* (Cleopatra VII) **646;** *Judaea* (Alexander Jannaeus) **647,** (John II) **648.**

XLV THE HELLENISTIC AGE: REMARKABLE TYPES

Lampsacus **649;** *Mytilene* **650;** *Leucas* **651;** *Ilium* **652;** *Antioch* (Antiochus IV) **653;** *Heraclea Ioniae* **654;** *Cappadocia* (Orophernes) **655;** *Alexandria Troas* **656;** *Ephesus* **657.**

ABBREVIATIONS

The list includes abbreviations used in the text and notes. Abbreviations of catalogues, periodicals, Festschriften and other publications are given at the beginning of the Bibliography (p. 209).

ANS	American Numismatic Society, New York
BM	British Museum, London
BN	Bibliothèque Nationale, Paris
c.	*circa*
d.	died
ed.	editor(s)
edn	edition
g	gramme(s)
illus.	illustrated
mm	millimetre(s)
obv.	obverse
pl.	plate(s)
r.	right
repr.	reprinted
rev.	reverse
var.	variety

PART I

GENERAL FEATURES OF THE COINAGE

At the beginning of the Hellenistic period, which is here taken to start with the accession of Alexander the Great in 336, the Greek world had become accustomed to the use of coinage over a period of about 200 years. The resulting money economy was based on coins of intrinsic value in gold, silver and (sporadically) electrum. In addition, during the fourth century, the use of a fiduciary or token coinage in bronze to supplement the larger denominations in the noble metals had gradually spread throughout the Greek world.[1] In Hellas itself, as well as in most of the colonial areas, coinage played its role, not only in wholesale transactions but also in the ordinary exchange of daily goods in the market place.

Outside the Greek world some of the economically better-developed areas on its fringes had begun to produce coinages of their own. This applies to the southern Anatolian districts from Caria to Cilicia, the island of Cyprus and the important trading centres of the Phoenician coast. Even in Egypt a sizeable production of Athenian imitations and a few issues with local types appeared in the first half of the fourth century.[2] But of the non-Greek peoples in the western Mediterranean only the Carthaginians seem to have started a coinage of their own, and this was apparently restricted to a specific purpose: the payment of mercenaries who were hired to fight the Greeks in Sicily for the possession of the island. This coinage started in the late fifth century, but we must wait until the Hellenistic period before coins were struck for more general purposes at Carthage itself.

---

1 Price 1983, 1979c.
2 Buttrey 1982.

I

METALS AND WEIGHT STANDARDS

(a) METALS

The raw material for coin production in the ancient world – gold and silver for coinages of intrinsic value, copper and tin for token ones of bronze – was ultimately derived from a number of widely scattered mines.[3] Our knowledge of the location and relative importance of these mines is scant and sporadic, but it seems certain that the vast majority of minor coin-producing states had no mines of their own and were thus forced to acquire metal either directly by purchase or through the public income from tolls and dues of various kinds, possibly also in some cases from liturgies of wealthy citizens. The interest in finding new sources of metal is well illustrated by the fact that Alexander the Great, on his expedition into Asia, had on his staff a professional prospector, Gorgos, who is said to have reported on gold and silver mines in India.

The rich gold and silver mines of the Thraco-Macedonian area, which had already supplied Philip II with his financial strength, continued to function under Alexander and his successors on the Macedonian throne. Under Philip V we hear of an increased activity in prospecting for new mines and the re-opening of older ones.[4] After 168 the Macedonian mines were closed down by the Romans for a decade. They were re-opened in 158 and remained productive well into the first century, as is shown by the substantial silver coinages from that period.

In Attica the Laurion silver mines were also being worked, at least to the end of the second century. We hear of revolts involving slaves from the mines around 134 and again in 104/100. But Strabo informs us that in his time, at the end of the first century B.C., the mines were exhausted.[5]

In Asia Minor gold and silver were mined on Mount Ida in the Troad, supplying the kingdom of Pergamum, as well as in the region near Abydus and Lampsacus, accounting for the relatively abundant production of Alexander gold in these two cities. Other mines were found in the mountainous interior, for instance silver mines in Pontus and in the Taurus mountains on the confines of Cilicia and Cappadocia.

3 Healy 1978, 47, 56, 58 (inadequate for the Hellenistic period); Rostovtzeff 1941, II.1170–6; Will 1975.
4 Livy 39.24.2.
5 Strabo 9.1.23 and 10.1.9. For the slave revolts see Ferguson 1911, 379, 427–8.

Apart from the mineral wealth of Asia Minor, the first Seleucid kings could draw upon the resources of the Middle East. River gold and silver mines were present in Carmania according to Onesicritus, one of Alexander's followers.[6] And through the eastern province of Bactria gold from distant Siberia and the Altai mountains may have reached the Seleucid empire. It is significant that after the reign of Seleucus II, when Bactria and Parthia were lost to the Syrian kings, the quantity of Seleucid gold coinage was much reduced.

The Ptolemies had access to the gold mines in Nubia[7] and had at their disposal the very rich copper mines of Cyprus. On the other hand, they had a problem with silver, as they had only insignificant mines in Cyprus directly under their control. Most silver had to be imported into Egypt, but a positive trade balance was sufficient to secure a reasonable flow of this metal into the country. There can, however, be no doubt that the relatively greater importance accorded to coinages in gold and bronze in the Ptolemaic monetary system from *c.* 260 onwards was largely caused by difficulties in acquiring silver.

In the West the most important mines for all the monetary metals were situated in Spain, where mines were scattered from the Pyrenees in the north to Turditania in the south. Both the Greeks in Sicily and Magna Graecia and the Carthaginians derived most of their metal from the Iberian peninsula, the latter developing the mines around New Carthage energetically in the late third century. Gold may also have come to the western Mediterranean from the fabulous Gold Coast in Africa through Carthaginian trade by sea,[8] and it may have arrived at Carthage and Cyrenaica by way of the caravans crossing the Sahara. Another mining district of importance was situated near Aquileia in the territory of the Noric Taurisci. According to Polybius the opening of a new mine in that area during his own times brought the price of gold in Italy temporarily down by one-third, showing the effect of a single lucky find.[9]

The tin necessary for the production of bronze was found almost exclusively in the West. Apart from the Spanish deposits, tin was imported from Brittany and Cornwall by way of Massilia.

Gold and silver were the metals normally used for coinage of intrinsic value. Electrum, an alloy of gold and silver with a silver content of at least 20%, was in the Hellenistic period used only in Sicily and Carthage. In the latter place the gradual increase of the silver component seems to indicate that Carthaginian electrum may actually be regarded as a debasement of an original gold coinage.

During the period from 336 until *c.* 310 a truly bimetallic system seems to have been functioning with the easily calculated ratio of 1:10 between gold and silver. Alexander's control of the Macedonian mines and the Persian treasuries allowed him to maintain this ratio, but from

---

6 Strabo 15.2.14.

7 A famous description of working conditions in the Ptolemaic gold mines by Agatharcides is reproduced in Diodorus Siculus 3.12–17.

8 On Carthaginian trade with the Gold Coast in earlier periods see Herodotus 4.196.

9 Polybius 34.10.10.

about 310 gold apparently rose in value as compared to silver. The fluctuations gave rise to changes in the weight standards of gold and silver coins in Egypt and Cyrenaica. Apparently the ratio of 1:10 gradually gave way to a ratio of 1:12 which was in operation around 290. Later in the third century an official ratio of *c.* 1:12.8 could not be maintained. In commercial transactions a premium or agio was paid on the gold coins which might vary but generally placed the ratio at slightly above 1:13.

While Egypt, undoubtedly prompted by her lack of silver mines, strove to maintain a gold currency, the response of most other Greek states to these fluctuations was to return to a monometallic currency system based on silver. Even in Egypt the unit of account in the third century was the silver stater (tetradrachm). The result was a marked decline in the general production of gold coins after 310, except in a few regions where local circumstances or special demands made their production attractive. Sometimes an economic crisis might necessitate the mobilization of all resources of a state, including the gold. A few of the royal gold issues outside Egypt may have been intended as propaganda, a demonstration of the wealth and power of the issuers. One's general impression, however, is that silver not only provided the common means of exchange but was also regarded as the fundamental measure of value for all commodities including gold.

Coins of gold or silver might in principle be accorded an official value well above the intrinsic value of their metal content. That was done in Egypt, and with the cistophoric coinage in Pergamum. But as the overvaluation was achieved by reducing the weight of the coins while maintaining their official value, the policy was at once apparent to everybody using them. In this way, a category of semi-fiduciary coinage was created which could only function properly when accorded a monopoly as the single official means of exchange within the issuing state.

Another more devious method of raising the profits from the striking of coin was to tamper with the fineness of the metal, a method well known from Roman practices of the Second Punic War and the third century A.D., as well as from later periods. However, during the Hellenistic period this simple way of stretching a given stock of bullion and making an extra profit without informing the public was rarely used. Published analyses of Hellenistic silver coins show in general a silver content well above 90%. Except for local emergencies it was not until the first century that a serious and systematic debasement of silver coinage took place in Syria and especially in Egypt, in the latter case reducing the silver content to below 50%.[10] But other series, as for instance the Athenian New Style coinage, maintained their fineness fairly well until the end.

In addition to official manipulation we have to take account of outright forgeries. The private production of counterfeit coins seems on the whole to have been negligible, although a few specimens are known from hoards. The rare examples on record were often produced by

10 Walker and King 1976, 139–42, 150–2. The average fineness of samples of Egyptian tetradrachms of Ptolemy XII Auletes between 80/79 and 73/2 was found to be 912.8 millièmes; of ones of the same ruler between 68/7 and 54/3 it was 848.6 millièmes; and on ones of Cleopatra VII between 45/4 and 31/30 it was 457.2 millièmes.

plating, a core of some base metal like bronze being covered with a thin envelope of silver. Such counterfeits are usually recognizable by their low weights. As far as is known there are no examples of plated coins being produced by official dies at any established mint.

The production of bronze coinage differed from that of coinages in the noble metals by the fact that the profit to the issuing authority was much greater, the bronze being used as a token coinage of very little intrinsic value. The profit motive behind the issuance of bronze coinage is directly mentioned in an inscription from Sestus of the second century.[11] This explains the eagerness of the cities to obtain the right of issuing bronze coins and the discrimination shown by the kings in according this privilege. It was one of the more important benefactions at the disposal of a ruler in his dealings with cities under his suzerainty.

One of the results of the function of the bronze issues as a token or fiduciary coinage was that their area of circulation was very restricted as compared with the silver. A token coinage can only maintain its official value within the territory under the political control of the issuing authority. This meant that the many city issues in bronze circulated only within the narrow territory of the city itself and perhaps a few neighbouring city states. This fact has greatly helped both numismatists and historical geographers in establishing the location of many minor places. Royal bronze coinages had, of course, a much wider circulation, especially the issues from the great central mints. Seleucid bronze coins of Antioch on the Orontes were predominant at Dura-Europos. And, during some periods at least, the majority of the bronze coins circulating at Susa derived from Seleucia on the Tigris. In both cases distances of about 400km in a direct line were involved.

The determination of the metals of which coins are made is not always easy, but since the Second World War a number of non-destructive methods for metal analysis have been developed. In the context of ancient coins they have been used to answer two questions. One is the straightforward metallic composition, that is to say the fineness achieved in the production of supposedly pure gold and silver coins and the exact proportions of the various components in the fiduciary coinages. The other is that of throwing light on the source of the metal of a given coin series, and if possible of determining from what mines the bullion derived.

The first question is fairly easily answered, and a number of studies have shown for the Hellenistic period in general a surprisingly well-maintained fineness of the coinages in the noble metals, at least down to the beginning of the first century B.C.

The second question is much harder to answer, as it mainly depends on the occurrence of trace elements in the coins. These trace elements then have to be compared with ore samples from ancient mines, and it has to be proved that each special combination of trace elements is peculiar to that mining district and not found elsewhere. In recent years scientists have tended to concentrate on lead isotopes. But I fear that the sceptical numismatist must register a warning. In the first place, the great majority of ancient mines are not located with certainty, so that the sampling of ores still leaves much to be desired. Secondly, all metals in antiquity were so valuable that they were melted down and re-used time and time again, and I personally have

11 The famous Menas inscription (*OGIS* no. 339. 45–6).

no doubt that most of the bullion used for coinage in the Hellenistic period was already mixed from a diversity of sources. The issues of Athens and the mints in Macedonia were probably exceptions, since in each case metal was available from local sources, but it hardly seems worth while spending money and energy in complicated analyses to prove this quite obvious point.

(b) WEIGHT STANDARDS

The study of the ancient weight standards used for striking coins was long dominated by the quest for a common origin of the various standards. This was usually located in Babylonia, and the most complicated arithmetical exercises, leading to quite arbitrary results, were performed in order to derive the different theoretical norm weights from the light or heavy Babylonian *mina*. This highly speculative field of research subsequently came under attack from more pragmatic scholars who preferred to concentrate on the actual weights.[12] Although the pan-Babylonian ghost shows a tendency to reappear at intervals, the pragmatic attitude may now be said to dominate the study of ancient metrology.

Four different methods are available for dealing with the actual weights. In the first place, the average weight of any group of coins may be ascertained. Secondly the median weight, that is the weight of the specimen placed exactly in the middle of a series of coins arranged in a sequence according to their weights, may be used. The third method consists in taking as the norm the heaviest weight of an unbroken sequence of coins arranged by centigrammes, disregarding exceptionally heavy pieces that are separated from the main body of material by breaks in the sequence. Fourthly and finally, the mode of a coin series may be established by the use of a frequency table, where the individual weights of the coins are plotted against a scale with intervals of 0.1g or 0.05g. The interval showing the greatest concentration of weights, the peak of the table, represents the mode.[13]

In theory, when a large body of reliable information is available, the different methods should give the same results. However, in this imperfect world, the frequency table offers the best chance of neutralizing errors. For such a metrological study all coins ought in theory to be weighed under exactly the same conditions on one and the same balance. Normally, however, we have to deal with a very miscellaneous mass of material, weights being culled from different publications or from notes supplied by public collections. Under these circumstances a frequency table, preferably with not too narrow steps, is better suited to eliminate small inaccuracies and mistakes than any of the other methods.

The same considerations apply to the difficulties deriving from the different amount of wear and tear to which the coins have been subjected in circulation. To this must be added the varied effects of soil and climate during the time they were buried. Pierced and broken coins, and those with visible damage, have of course to be excluded, and the same applies to material from hoards which have suffered loss of weight due to peculiar circumstances. The real trouble begins

---

12 See especially Viedebantt 1923, 1–24.
13 Hill 1924; Naster 1975.

when degrees of ordinary wear have to be estimated, and here there is a clear advantage in the frequency table. It allows us to concentrate on the peak, disregarding the large number of light-weight coins that always turn up in a given series. On the other hand, such light coins will have a serious effect on both the calculations of the average and the position of the median.

Even the peaks, however, will not provide us with the original or standard weights. Most of the coins, even apparently uncirculated ones, will have lost some of their weight. To obtain a single figure for the standard weight of an issue we should probably add 1–1.5% to the peak centre for the silver, and *c.* 0.5% for the gold (which circulated less and was more carefully adjusted). The figures in the following survey have been arrived at in this way, whenever a frequency table has been available.

In addition to their fineness, the weights of the gold and silver coins decided their value in international trade. From the preceding period the Hellenistic world inherited a number of different weight standards of which only the most important can be mentioned here.

Owing to the great popularity of the Athenian owls the Attic weight standard was known far and wide. Adopted by Philip of Macedon for his gold and by Alexander for both gold and silver, it rapidly became the dominant weight standard for international trade coinages. All the Diadochi except Ptolemy adhered to it. In Syria, Macedon and the lesser kingdoms of Asia Minor it was used continuously down to the end of their dynastic history. Most cities in Greece and Asia Minor adopted it for their pseudo-royal or autonomous coinages. Its acceptability is clearly demonstrated by the large number of Hellenistic coin hoards which are of a very mixed composition with respect to mints but contain exclusively coins of Attic weight.

The Attic weight standard nevertheless underwent some changes during the 300 years of the Hellenistic period.[14] At the time of Alexander the common trade coin, the silver tetradrachm, weighed 17.28g. By 300 this weight had been slightly reduced to *c.* 17.20g. An examination of the development at the mint of Antioch in Syria, where the material is most readily available, shows that about 172 the weight of the tetradrachm was reduced to *c.* 16.80g. A further official reduction in *c.* 105 brought the weight down to about 16.30g, and the following decades saw a gradual but rapid decline to well below 15.00g, combined with a greater carelessness in the standardization of the individual weights. Elsewhere the development seems to have followed the same general lines. Attic-weight tetradrachms of the second century normally conform to the 16.80g standard, but there are exceptions. It is especially noteworthy that at Athens herself the last issues of Athenian New Style tetradrachms show a weight increase to about 17.00g from the 16.60g/16.80g of the preceding issues.

The weights of the gold issues were always very carefully adjusted. The gold coins of Philip and Alexander, struck on an Attic standard of *c.* 8.64g for the stater or didrachm, show how near to perfection the Greek mints could come in this matter when they so desired.

Another important weight standard in the pre-Hellenistic period was the Aeginetan. It continued to be used in various coinages of central Greece, the Peloponnese and Crete during the early Hellenistic period, with a didrachm slightly above 12.00g. Especially in Crete the

14 Mørkholm 1982a.

abundant coinages of the cities show a tendency already in the late fourth century towards a weight reduction to slightly below 12.00g.

During the third century and the first half of the second very abundant issues of hemidrachms or triobols were produced at various Peloponnesian mints (Argos, Sicyon, Megalopolis, Sparta) as well as by the Achaean and Aetolian Leagues. The earliest of these issues were struck with a weight of *c.* 2.80g, while later the official weight was reduced to *c.* 2.40g/2.50g. There can hardly be any doubt that this weight standard should be called 'reduced Aeginetan'. It has recently been suggested, very plausibly, that the so-called 'Corcyrean' weight system with staters or didrachms of *c.* 10g (Corcyra, the Epirote League) and drachms of *c.* 5g (Elis, Boeotia) is actually identical with the reduced Aeginetan, the common element being the Corinthian drachm of *c.* 2.88g to which the original Aeginetan hemidrachm of 3.0g was first assimilated.[15]

Among the weight systems surviving from the preceding period there was the Persian one, with a stater or double siglos of *c.* 11.2g and a siglos or drachm of *c.* 5.6g. Hemidrachms of this standard were issued at Byzantium and other mints of the Propontis region in the early Hellenistic period. During the third and second centuries it reappears with certain issues of Phaselis in Lycia and Aspendus in Pamphylia. As appears from Table 1, the Persian standard

Table 1. *Eastern Hellenistic coin standards*
(The weights are given in grammes.)

	Tetradrachm	Didrachm	Drachm	Hemidrachm
Aeginetan		12.2	6.1	3.05
Reduced Aeginetan (= Corcyrean)		11.5–10.0	5.75–5.0	2.8–2.5
Persian		11.2	5.6	2.8
Attic	17.3–16.8	8.65–8.4	4.3–4.2	2.15–2.1
Chian	15.6	7.8	3.9	
Ptolemaic	14.3	7.15	3.55	
Rhodian	13.6–13.4	6.8–6.7	3.4	
Cistophoric	12.6	6.3	3.15	

corresponded to a certain phase of the reduced Aeginetan, but the two standards are well separated both geographically and chronologically.

The Chian standard with a tetradrachm of *c.* 15.6g and a didrachm of *c.* 7.8g is another

15 Giovannini 1979, 48–9.

survivor. It was used on the west coast of Asia Minor, on the Aegean islands and on Rhodes. Owing to the economic importance of the last-named island it is often called 'Rhodian', but it seems preferable to reserve this name for the lighter Hellenistic variant described below.

During the Hellenistic period several new standards were introduced. Already about 310 Ptolemy I of Egypt began reducing the weight of his silver tetradrachm from the normal Attic weight to *c.* 15.8g. After an intermediate stage of *c.* 14.9g he finally, around 290, arrived at the weight *c.* 14.3g/14.4g for his tetradrachm, a standard that was maintained, with a minimum weight of *c.* 14.2g, until the early first century. It was very close to the standard used in the great Phoenician trading centres in the fifth and fourth centuries, the unit of which was the shekel of slightly above 7g. This may, however, be a coincidence. It is hard to see why local conditions in Phoenicia some forty years later should have exerted a strong influence on Ptolemy I. The development in Egypt was more probably governed by the wish to retain a workable ratio between gold and silver. On the other hand, the coincidence turned out to be very fortunate indeed. The Ptolemaic standard was regarded by the Phoenicians as their own and became so popular that even the Seleucid kings, beginning with Alexander Balas, had to adopt it for their Phoenician province. And when towards the end of the second century the Phoenician cities became autonomous they all, except Tripolis, continued to strike their civic silver on this standard, the Tyrian double shekel becoming the most acceptable and most abundant coinage of the region. I prefer to call this standard Ptolemaic rather than Phoenician, although the later designation is widely used.

At the beginning of the Hellenistic period the important trading city of Rhodes lowered the weights of its coins. The tetradrachm, originally struck on the Chian standard of 15.6g, was reduced first to 15.2g and then to about 14.9g, apparently before the Ptolemaic reductions. Soon, however, the production of tetradrachms came to an end. They were replaced by didrachms, the first of which weighed about 7.0g, but after a short while a further reduction brought the weight down to *c.* 6.7g/6.8g. In this book the term Rhodian weight is used for this final variant.

Mention, too, should be made of the cistophoric standard, though since it was introduced by the king of Pergamum *c.* 175 it really belongs to a later period. The cistophorus weighs *c.* 12.6g or exactly three-quarters of the Attic-weight tetradrachms of the same period (16.8g). Halves and quarters were also issued, but sparingly. The standard was also used by such cities on the confines of the Pergamene kingdom as Alabanda in Caria and Cibyra in Lycia.

The weights of the bronze coins were generally far less accurately adjusted than the coins in the precious metals, as is only to be expected of fiduciary or token coinages. Moreover, bronze coins normally suffered greater corrosion during burial, with a further differentiation of the weights as a result. Under these circumstances the diameter of different denominations is often a better distinguishing mark than the weight. It also becomes difficult to use frequency tables to establish the norm weights. Often the best we can do is to calculate rough averages. Except in the few cases where the denominations are specifically indicated on the coins, designations in catalogues such as 'unit', 'double' and so forth are only modern speculations.

During the third century, bronze coinage began to play a very special role in the Egyptian currency system. Around 260 Ptolemy II introduced a series in eight different denominations, the heaviest weighing about 92g, the weight of the indigenous Egyptian *deben*. This choice was, of course, not fortuitous, but made in order to facilitate the acceptance of the new coinage by the native population. The government presumably wanted to replace the silver circulation in the rural districts with the heavy bronze. The new coinage was in all probability fiduciary, but it was made attractive to the prospective users by its sheer bulk. The original weights, however, were not maintained. During succeeding reigns several weight reductions were undertaken, making the fiduciary nature of the coinage more obvious.

Very heavy bronzes were also issued sporadically in other Hellenistic kingdoms, for instance in Syria under Antiochus IV (175–164). In this case the Egyptian model was imitated, presumably for similar reasons, namely to replace a silver currency with bronze in order to reap a greater profit for the treasury.

2

COIN PRODUCTION AND USE

(a) MINTING TECHNIQUE[1]

When the fineness and weight of a given coin series had been decided, the blanks or flans for the coins were produced by casting. For gold and silver the flans would have been cast individually to ensure the necessary precision of the weight. They may often have been cast in spherical or lentoid moulds, but during our period flat disk-shaped flans became increasingly popular. The result of this development in the form of the flans was that the diameter of the coins tended to increase. This can be most easily demonstrated by looking at the Alexander and Lysimachus tetradrachms which maintained a fairly steady weight. The thick and lumpy coins of the lifetime issues of Alexander have a diameter of *c.* 25–6mm. The issues from *c.* 280–250 show an increase to about 28–30mm. Issues of around 200 are more variable, *c.* 30–5mm, while the last ones of the period *c.* 190–160 reach diameters of *c.* 35–40mm. There are, of course, local variations, and an increased diameter cannot be used mechanically for dating purposes, although it provides a valuable indication of the relative chronology. Similar broad flans also occur in the many autonomous tetradrachm coinages of the second century. The very thin and spread flans of this period were often hammered along the edge. The purpose of this is not clear. It may have been intended to make the metal denser along the edge, thus strengthening the coin against breaking, for with the increased diameter the edges of the coins were becoming alarmingly thin. Or it may simply have been intended to give greater regularity to the edge.

Flans for the bronze coinage were cast *en chapelet*, as we know from several finds of moulds. Some of these were open with the edge sloping inwards towards the bottom, so that the flans could be easily removed after casting. Coins struck on such flans show a characteristic bevelled edge which occurs very frequently in Syria and Egypt. Ptolemaic bronze coins from Cyprus present a more rounded edge because of the form of the moulds in which the flans were cast.

The moulds, made of stone or fire-clay, were sometimes closed, consisting of two halves with corresponding depressions connected by channels. The two halves were adjusted and joined together, and the metal poured in from above. After cooling, the flans could be separated by being cut loose from the channels. The marks of this method of production often remain visible on the finished coins as a result of negligent trimming. An unusual find from Paphos consists

1 Hill 1922; Hackens 1975.

of two flans still linked by the runner.[2] It is obvious that by this method of production no great precision in the weights of the single flans could be achieved.

On many bronze coins, especially in the Seleucid and Ptolemaic series, there is a small central depression. It has been suggested that this may represent the point of one leg of a pair of compasses used to trim the edge of the coin, but this explanation is disproved by the fact that it is not always exactly in the centre. However this may be, the hole certainly belongs to the flan and not to the die. Another phenomenon concerning the flan is the serrated edge that we find frequently on Seleucid bronzes from Seleucus IV (187–175) down to the reign of Antiochus VI (145–142/1), and on Macedonian coins under Philip V. It was definitely produced during the casting of the flan and is most probably to be regarded as a result of fashion, occasionally employed at certain Seleucid and Macedonian mints and then quietly discarded.

Other methods of producing flans, known from other periods, may have occurred sporadically. The division of a circular rod or bar of bronze by sawing or chiselling is known from a find in the Agora of Athens, perhaps of the Roman period.[3] The cutting out of flans by shears from a metal sheet may have been used for the flans of square Indo-Greek coins. But there can be no doubt that the great majority of Hellenistic coin flans in all metals were produced by casting.

To avoid the difficult and time-consuming production of blanks or flans the mint sometimes made use of obsolete or foreign coins, simply overstriking them with new types.[4] The extent of this practice is difficult to assess, for effective overstriking would cover the original type completely and cause it to disappear without a trace. Consequently only unsuccessful and incomplete overstrikes can be identified, and we are indebted to incompetent and clumsy moneyers for such knowledge as we have of the practice. If the undertype is identifiable, an overstrike becomes important in establishing the relative chronology of different issues. The dispute over the Athenian New Style chronology (see pp. 170–1) depends to a large extent on the interpretation of two crucial overstrikes. Sometimes overstrikes can provide evidence of political changes, as for instance when Demetrius I of Syria (162–150), having defeated the usurper Timarchus, overstruck his coins, or when the bronze coinage of Antigonus Doson (229–221) was overstruck in Boeotia.

Normally overstriking was carried out on coins of the same standard, but Crete provides an interesting example of a weight reduction in relationship to the systematic overstriking of an imported coinage. About 322 a great number of tetradrachms from Cyrenaica were brought to Crete by mercenaries returning home. These coins, weighing *c.* 12.80–13.40g, were cut down by 1–2g and then used as flans for staters of Aeginetan weight (somewhat below 12.00g) struck primarily at Gortyn and Phaestus.[5]

In the Hellenistic period cast coins do not seem to have been produced. Practically all coinages,

2 Nicolaou and Mørkholm 1976, 9–10.
3 *Athenian Agora* (1976), 153 with fig. 78, 258.
4 Le Rider 1975, 46–56.
5 Le Rider 1966, 136–46, 149–51.

even the heaviest bronzes, were struck. Casting was reserved for the fabrication of flans. When these were ready, adjusted with greater or lesser care as to fineness and weight, they were transformed into coins by receiving the impressions of a pair of dies, the obverse and the reverse. Ancient Greek dies were made of iron or bronze. Into a disk of metal the design (types and inscription) was engraved by hand in intaglio. The tools of the die engraver were small chisels, scaupers and burins of various sizes, perhaps also a drill.

There is still some discussion over the practice of hubbing.[6] A hub of hard metal, carrying a positive design of the coin type, could be driven into the softer metal of the die, which would then be hardened. In this way a positive hub could be used to produce a large number of virtually identical dies. The relevance of this form of manufacture for die studies is immediately apparent. In its extreme form the theory of hubbing allows us to assume that coins, apparently sharing the same die, might actually have been produced by different dies deriving from the same hub, perhaps at different places or at widely separated times. The whole basis for the study of die linkage, the assumption that two coins sharing a die were struck at the same place and at approximately the same time, would be called into question.

Modern adherents of the hubbing theory, however, tend to concede that only a rough outline of the type would have been produced by the hub, and many details of both type and inscription would have had to be engraved subsequently by hand. The individuality of the dies and consequently the value of die studies would remain. But the practical advantages of the hubbing would be reduced in proportion to the number of details that were added by the engraver. And for the modern scholar the question of whether hubs were used or not becomes less important if the possibility of identifying the products of individual dies is recognized. I have personally never come across a coin series of the Hellenistic period which showed that hubbing *must* have been used, and I believe that virtually identical designs, e.g. the portrait of a ruler, could have been made quite independently by the same artist without any recourse to mechanical devices. As for the difficulty of engraving a negative and inverse representation freehand, it is enough to cite the achievement of the engravers of gems and seal stones. These contrived such negative designs with excellent results in a material that was much more intractable than the relatively soft metal of an unhardened die.

A phenomenon that does occur with some frequency is the recutting of dies. This was done with the object of repairing dies or in order to change some detail of the designs. Over a period of use, small cracks or flaws might develop in a die and be visible on the coins as small raised knobs or faint lines. These could be removed by recutting the area around the flaw, so that the relief on the coins was higher at this point. The recutting could be done in several ways. Cutting vertically into the die along the edge of the type can enlarge this and render it in higher relief than before; cutting metal away horizontally from the field surrounding the type will make the outline of the type smaller.[7] These different methods of recutting would be used according to

6 Latest survey of the discussion in Crawford 1981.
7 Jenkins 1970, 120–1.

whether the flaw to be removed was situated in the open field or interfered in some way with the type. But the removal of extensive die flaws could lead to a total reworking of the die and result in a new type completely different from the old.

Recutting would be useful notably when applied to inscriptions, monograms or symbols. A privy mark might be added or changed in order to show that a new magistrate had taken over responsibility for production. At Tyre shortly after 300 a reverse die with the name of Alexander was recut to become a die of Demetrius Poliorcetes: the first name was effaced and the second cut into the die at exactly the same place. As is often the case the removal of the first name was not completely successful and traces of it are still visible below the second inscription.

(b) COIN PRODUCTION

When both flans and dies were ready, coins were produced by placing the flans, often still hot from the casting and therefore relatively soft, on the lower (=obverse) die. Then the upper (=reverse) die was put in position above the flan and, by two or three blows of a heavy hammer, the metal of the flan was forced into the negative designs of the two dies. The obverse die was normally embedded in an anvil, while the reverse die was fixed at the end of a punch or trussel that might have slightly different forms (see Figure 1).

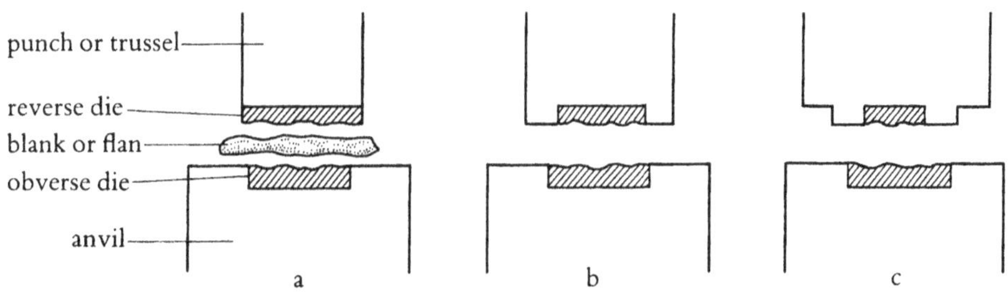

Figure 1. Dies and their use

As the striking was done manually, the free upper die could be placed in any number of different positions in relation to the lower die. Consequently, the orientation of obverse and reverse of the finished coins could be quite random. During the Hellenistic period a tendency towards a more regular die position, most frequently the vertical upright or 12 o'clock position but sometimes the inverted 6 o'clock orientation, spread from the mints of the Levant. The regular upright position was used at the Alexander mints of Salamis on Cyprus and Damascus from their start in 332, and at Citium from *c.* 329/8. The mint of Alexandria also used this position from its beginning in *c.* 326/5. In the western region the only Alexander mint to have used adjusted dies in the upright position is Miletus from *c.* 325. When a new mint was established at Ecbatana by Seleucus I in *c.* 311/10 we find the first systematic use of the inverse or 6 o'clock position. Adjusted dies first occur regularly in Greece proper in an issue of the Euboean League from about 300. Absolute regularity could be achieved by hinging the dies, but the examination of many coin series, including the ones just mentioned, have shown that small variations (e.g. 11 o'clock or 1 o'clock positions instead of 12 o'clock) do occur, indicating that the dies were generally not hinged, but only provided with a notch or a similar mark to help the moneyer keep the punch with the upper die in its proper position.

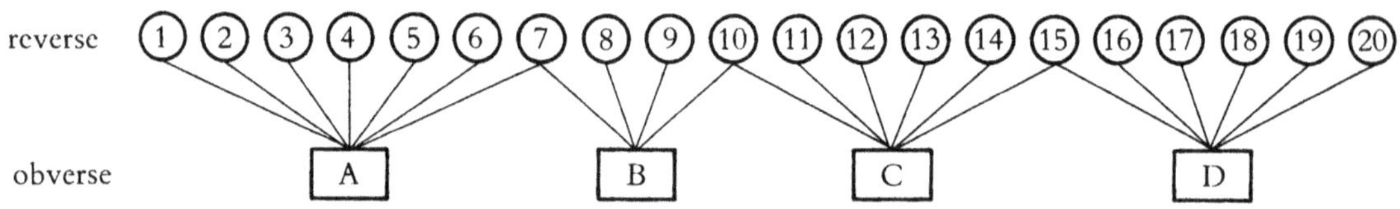

Figure 2. Die linkages

From the study of numerous ancient coin series we know that obverse dies normally lasted much longer than reverse ones, presumably because they were better protected by being placed in an anvil. When sufficient material is available we are able to construct diagrams of coin production, a theoretical example of which is shown in Figure 2. In this case four obverse dies (A–D) were used with twenty reverses (1–20). This ratio is not unrealistic but rather on the low side. For the Athenian New Style coins it has been argued that one obverse die, giving full service, might have been employed with between eight and twelve reverses, and there is a case on record where one obverse was used with seventeen different reverses.[8] By studying the development of die flaws a relative chronology can often be established. The diagram would hold good for a small mint where only one man with one pair of dies was working at a given time. In a larger mint with, for instance, five workers producing coins simultaneously from a common pool of dies, the pattern of die linkage becomes much more complicated.

A study of die linkages, in addition to providing information on chronology, may throw light on the quantity of a given issue. Quantitative calculations are normally based on the obverse dies, simply because they are fewer in number and therefore more manageable, but estimates of the number of coins that could be struck from one obverse die vary considerably. Practical experiments have shown that a production of 10,000 coins per obverse die may be regarded as a safe minimum figure in a series where the obverses were fully used, but very recent research suggests that this number may have to be doubled.[9]

However, before any final quantification can be made, we need to be sure that our material is representative, i.e. how large a percentage of the obverse dies once used are at present known.

8 Thompson 1961, 721–2.

9 Sellwood 1963. Kinns 1983 argues for a minimum of *c.* 23,300 specimens per obverse die.

Here statistics and experience can combine to provide an answer. The important concept is the ratio or index figure between specimens and obverse dies. With the growth of the index figure, i.e. the number of specimens per obverse die, the probability of a complete representation of obverse dies increases. Statisticians tell us that if the average index figure of a given coin series is 5 to 6, the chance of one more obverse die turning up is about 5%. But if the index figure goes up to seven or eight specimens per die, the possibility of finding one new obverse die is reduced to 1%.[10] Practical experience with handling large bodies of material has confirmed the figures of the statisticians, and with a 99% certainty of having a complete record we should be satisfied. On the other hand, we must never forget that the above speculations are only valid under certain conditions. In the first place, they assume that the material studied represents a random sample of the original coin series. The inclusion of dominant lots of material from one or two big hoards can affect the exactness of the total, if some kind of selection was practised in bringing the hoards together. A second assumption is that each full-time obverse die is about equally represented, not necessarily in our material, but by the number of coins in the ground, so that each die has an equal chance of being represented. But if a large part of the coins produced by a particular obverse die was quickly withdrawn from circulation and consigned to the melting pot, this obverse die has less chance of appearing in our coin lists. It is, of course, impossible to estimate precisely the effect of this second factor, but a pronounced unevenness in the distribution, with some obverse dies represented by only one or a very few specimens, may serve to suggest that something is wrong.

The importance of the study of die linkage can hardly be overrated. The observation that two coins sharing a common die must have been struck at the same place at approximately the same time is obviously true in the vast majority of cases and has acquired an axiomatic value. Nevertheless, it may be useful to examine this conception more closely. First the time factor. What does 'approximately the same time' mean? Or, put in another way, for how long could one die remain in use? The obvious answer is that it must depend upon the production rate at the mint in question. Continuous and high production must mean a shorter life span for the dies.[11]

The examination of certain dated coin series allows one to arrive at more specific results. The New Style coinage of Athens provides the advantage that most of the annual issues are dated to the month in which they were produced. This was a busy mint with a fairly continuous production, usually involving the simultaneous use of several pairs of dies. The average working life of an obverse die was three to five months. Only about 4% of the obverses lasted for seven or more months, and in many of these cases there are gaps in the monthly sequence of the material which indicate that the mint may have stopped production for some months.

At other mints the picture is different. The Ptolemaic mints of Salamis, Citium and Paphos on Cyprus, active during the second and early first centuries, were modest establishments with a fairly small production. The coins were dated by regnal years, and although most years saw

10 McGovern 1980.
11 Mørkholm 1982c.

some coinage, quite often their requirements could be met by a single pair of dies. Under these conditions the same obverse die might be used for three, four or even in one case five years in a row. A few dies are known with a life span of seven or eight years, but in these cases special circumstances may have been involved, because there seem to be large breaks in the yearly sequence. At Laodicea ad Mare on the Syrian coast we have several similar examples, one obverse die being used with reverses dated years 24–27 and 30–31 of the civic era, and another with reverses dated years 1–3, 5 and 9 of the Caesarian era used after 47.[12]

The working life of coin dies clearly must stand in inverse relation to a mint's production rate. If mints were inactive for some time, dies may have been able to survive over a much longer interval than the five to nine years suggested above. We have no evidence from the Hellenistic period, but it appears that the dies for Roman imperial medallions, which were struck only on special occasions, might have a working life of up to thirty years.

The other half of the axiom behind the study of die linkage concerns the place of minting: the assumption that die-linked coins must derive from the same mint. This is in most cases undoubtedly true, although exceptions to the rule have long been known. After all, a die engraver might move with his workshop from one place to another and offer his services to a number of city-states, bringing a stock of obverse dies with him. The reverses with the inscription and other marks of identification would be usable only in one place, but an obverse with an attractive head of Zeus or Apollo might appeal to more than one city. Or a die might be sent from one mint to another. If we look at the large territorial kingdoms of the Hellenistic period, where more than one mint was needed for the supply of coinage, we find some cases of the same obverse die being used at different mints. Three possible explanations of this phenomenon may be considered: (1) central production at one single mint; (2) the transfer of an obverse die from one place to another; (3) a travelling or mobile mint.[13]

Travelling mints can be postulated in several cases. They would often have been connected with military undertakings, following the movements of an army and catering to its need for coinage. In Parthia a court mint which followed the king on his tours of inspection was apparently functioning for several decades in the first century. These travelling mints might use the facilities of existing mints whenever it was practical to do so, thereby creating the die links that allow us to infer their existence.

In other cases the first or second explanation must apply, though it may be difficult to make a choice between them. In recent numismatic works the tendency has been to explain such die links in terms of centralized production at one large mint. On balance it seems to me that the Hellenistic coin series offer rather few examples of this kind of die linkage, and that they tend to occur precisely in times of greatly increased production. If coin production in the larger kingdoms were actually concentrated in a few central mints, each using a common stock of

12 Mørkholm 1983b.
13 Mørkholm 1982b.

dies, we would expect far more die links and a more even distribution of them over the series as a whole. I can see no compelling reason for the centralized coin production envisaged by some scholars and find the transfer of dies and/or personnel from one place to the other a much simpler explanation of the material as it is known to us at present.

(c) COIN CIRCULATION

While it is generally possible to ascertain the place and time of any particular coinage with reasonable precision, the fate of the coins after they have left the mint is much harder to determine. For most Hellenistic coins in public or private collections, information on their provenance stops abruptly with the name of a coin dealer or former collector.

Sometimes, it is true, individual coins can tell us a little. We have already mentioned the overstriking of foreign coins. Whenever the undertype is identifiable, it informs us that a coin of city A has been available at city B for overstriking.

Another source of information is provided by the small peck-marks and more elaborate countermarks that are not infrequent in the Hellenistic period.[14] The habit of marking coins with small punches (circles, half-circles, crescents, cross-forms, single letters, and so on) seems to have been widespread in Egypt well down into the reign of Ptolemy II. It occurs already on the issues of the last Persian satraps of Egypt and was undoubtedly unofficial. Private merchants or bankers may have marked the coins in their possession in order to provide them with a personal guarantee, but why this practice should have continued for so long after Egypt must have become well acquainted with Greek coinages is hard to explain. Perhaps these characteristic marks were used only in remoter parts of the country, especially in Upper Egypt. However this may be, the occurrence of such marks on Ptolemaic coins found outside Egypt is conclusive evidence that these coins had, for a while, circulated in Egypt before being exported.

While these punchmarks were in all probability private marks, true countermarks were official. Their function was to provide a coin with a status as legal tender within the area controlled by the countermarking authority. Such official countermarks were placed on both silver and bronze coins, but practically never on gold. Bronze coins are often countermarked by the issuing state itself. The production of fiduciary bronze coins was highly remunerative, and it seems likely that some cities tried to increase their income by periodical demonetizations; the existing bronzes were called in and replaced by a new coinage, naturally at an exchange rate favourable to the public treasury. Under these circumstances a demonetized bronze coin might regain its former status by being countermarked, again of course against a fee. There are, however, instances of countermarking of foreign bronzes. Thus the city of Odessus on the Black Sea countermarked bronze coins of Philip II, Alexander and Lysimachus.

Turning to the silver coinage, we find exactly the opposite situation. Countermarking of a state's own currency is very rare, while the countermarking of foreign silver often occurred.

14 Le Rider 1975, 27–45. On the Egyptian origin of a particular class of countermarks see Newell's view as cited by Zervos 1980, 20.

Although silver coins basically were full value coins, the local issues of a city or a kingdom must have enjoyed a small overvaluation over foreign silver, possibly by only a few percentage points.[15] But there were economic situations when a kind of semi-fiduciary coinage was introduced, with the state trying to profit from a monetary monopoly. In such closed economic systems foreign coins were either sent to the melting pot (Ptolemaic Egypt) or allowed to circulate only after being countermarked. This was the case in the kingdom of Pergamum after the introduction of the cistophorus in *c.* 175. Attic-weight coins, mostly posthumous Alexanders, are known with cistophoric countermarks including the initials of at least nine different Pergamene cities.

A very instructive example of this kind of countermarking has been discussed in detail by Henri Seyrig.[16] In the period *c.* 235–220 the cities of Byzantium and Chalcedon adopted a new coinage of lower weight than their previous Attic-weight issues of posthumous Lysimachi. Once the new coinage, which must have enjoyed a monopoly within these two important trading centres, had been introduced, Attic-weight coinage was banned *unless* it was countermarked by one of the cities. The foreign merchant had either to exchange his silver for local coins or have his coins countermarked against payment of a fee. In Byzantium the episode was short, owing to resistance especially from the Rhodians, but in Pergamum fifty years later the system became a source of profit to the state. This is also the reason why the cistophoric coinage was continued by the Romans.

Foreign silver circulated freely in the Seleucid empire during the third century, provided the coins were of Attic weight. From about 175 to 140 we find, however, a number of official Seleucid countermarks applied to imported coins. To the years *c.* 175–170 we may ascribe the great majority of anchor countermarks as well as a mark showing a facing, radiate bust of Helios, which may belong to the Seleucid mint in Seleucia on the Tigris. One special variant of the anchor countermark seems to be later than the rest. Next in time comes a countermark with a turreted head of Tyche. This has been attributed to Smyrna[17] but in my opinion it is definitely Syrian, being known almost exclusively from a couple of Syrian hoards. Finally, towards 140, the usurper Tryphon placed his own characteristic countermark on a number of wreathed tetradrachms from Asia Minor. This is the latest example of an official Seleucid countermark known to me.

Countermarks were also applied outside the large territorial kingdoms. Those of Byzantium and Chalcedon have already been mentioned. The important trading city of Cyzicus used an explicit countermark in the first half of the second century, and even a small place like Temnus in Aeolis has its own official countermark.

The information on coin circulation provided by countermarks is important, but far more comprehensive evidence is offered by an examination of coin finds. Here a basic distinction has

15 Mørkholm 1982c. In early fourth-century Athens the overvaluation was about 5%.
16 Seyrig 1968.
17 Seyrig 1973, 70.

to be made between single or stray finds and hoards, the latter term implying two or more coins deposited together.[18]

A single coin may have been deposited for a special purpose, e.g. as a Charon's obol in a grave. But the vast majority of single finds consist of coins that were lost accidentally, and bronze coins and small denominations will preponderate. Here lies one of the scientific possibilities in the study of single finds. As bronze coins, especially civic issues, rarely moved far from their mint, the analysis of the single coin finds from a particular site or region can provide evidence on the location of various city mints.[19] Single finds are also absolutely essential for the study of local economic conditions and the day-to-day exchange of goods in the market-places.

Hoards, on the other hand, often consist of the most valuable coins in circulation, gold and silver, especially if they are savings hoards representing the capital accumulated by a person over a number of years. Another type of hoard, emergency hoards, represents the capital that it was possible to hide away in times of acute danger, and here every available denomination may be included.[20]

A few hoards will have been abandoned on purpose as votive offerings. Smaller hoards, for instance the contents of a single purse, may also have been lost by accident, but the great majority were buried by the owner with the intention of later recovery. For our forefathers the earth was the natural safe-deposit box, and sometimes the owner will have been prevented by a diversity of reasons from recovering his fortune.

In modern times most hoards (as well as single finds) are discovered accidentally during farm work or building operations and are usually quickly disposed of without further record. Hoards from archaeological excavations are exceptional, but are important owing to their clear and unequivocal provenance. Many hoards on record have been laboriously reconstituted on the basis of information from dealers and collectors. It is obvious that hoards having this kind of background may have been tampered with, intentionally or unintentionally, and that conclusions from such material must be used with great care. On the other hand, we cannot afford to ignore evidence from such hoards. Another pitfall, especially regarding savings hoards, arises from the fact that a single hoard may contain various components, each constituted at a different time, so that the hoard in the final analysis can be shown to consist of several smaller lots.[21] A very obvious example of this is offered by one of the hoards from Susa, no. 6.[22] In addition to posthumous Alexanders and Seleucid coins running down to 141, it contains one tetradrachm of Characene from 91/90. If the contents were not guaranteed by the archaeologists (all the coins were found in a jar from a Parthian tomb), most numismatists would without any hesitation have regarded the single late coin as an intrusion. In view of all these difficulties it is, therefore, a golden rule never to discuss the circulation of a coin series on the basis of a single

18 A guide to coin hoards is provided by *IGCH*, continued in the periodical *Coin Hoards* published by the Royal Numismatic Society from 1975 onwards. For single finds one has to consult excavation reports.

19 This aspect was emphasized again and again by Louis Robert, most recently in Robert 1982, 315–19.

20 Thompson 1962, 308–10.

21 The phenomenon of composite hoards is noted by Seyrig 1963; see his hoards 1, 5, 6, 16, 26, 28, 30.

22 Le Rider 1965a, 248–9.

specimen recorded from a single hoard. The significance of the presence and absence of issues from hoards can only be discussed with reasonable confidence when a number of sizeable hoards are available so that the danger of individual mistakes can be eliminated or at least diminished.

The analysis of hoard material provides important information on the relative chronology of different issues. For example, the many posthumous Alexander and Lysimachus issues are very difficult to date by themselves, but the publication of a number of large mixed hoards, dated most often by their royal issues, allows us to fix the chronology of many of the posthumous issues within reasonable limits. Successive issues from the same mint may also be arranged in relative chronological order by their different stages of wear. All this is what one might call the internal context of the hoard.

However, the most important evidence derived from hoards concerns the circulation area and economic function of the various coinages. They provide information on trade routes and on the commercial contacts between different states, and are the source of a very substantial part of our knowledge of ancient economic conditions.

For both single finds and hoards it is, of course, important to take into consideration the find context when this is known. Large-scale excavations of important city centres have provided much important information on the circulation and use of coinage, not to speak of the usefulness of coins for the archaeologist in deciding the chronology of the stratification. Aggregates of single finds and hoards from a restricted area have sometimes been termed cumulative finds, for the coins may have been lost or deposited over a long period of time, often over many centuries.

Numismatic material from the excavation of a substantial number of Hellenistic settlements has been published either as chapters in excavation reports or as separate volumes. Since the Second World War there have appeared substantial volumes on the coin finds from Antioch, Dura-Europos, Seleucia on the Tigris and Susa. The last of these[23] provides an especially impressive picture of the political and economic development of the city and the region during the Hellenistic period based largely on the coin finds. It is a masterly demonstration of the contribution that numismatics can make to history when other sources are scarce or non-existent.

23 Le Rider 1965a. The Susa publication well illustrates the nature of site finds, the distribution between silver and bronze coins in hoards and single finds being as follows:

	Silver	Bronze
Twelve hoards	1,847 (10)	384 (2)
Single finds	113	2,527

(d) THE FUNCTIONS OF COINAGE

The classical definition of the use of coins specifies three functions.[24] Coins can serve as a means of exchange, as a measure of value, and as a store of wealth or capital. The first of these has generally been regarded as the most important, deriving from the early days of organized trade. Aristotle[25] supposed that there was a simple development from barter to the use of bullion as a means of exchange, and thence to the introduction of coinage when the volume of trade demanded an easier way of arranging payments for commodities and services. The coin types guaranteed the value of the piece of metal and relieved the merchants of the necessity of measuring and weighing the bullion in each separate transaction.

We are not here concerned with the complicated questions related to the origin of coinage.[26] There can be no doubt that the end of the development as sketched by Aristotle reflected the conditions of fourth-century Athens, and the relationship between coinages in precious metals and international commerce has long been regarded as self-evident. In the Hellenistic period the very large coinages of, for instance, Rhodes and Byzantium can hardly be explained in any other way than as true trade coinages intended primarily for commercial purposes. However, when a coinage had become acceptable and popular on the international market, it might often acquire a commercial value slightly above its intrinsic value, so that a small profit would also accrue to the producer. This profit factor, which was greatly increased for semi-fiduciary and fiduciary coinages, accounts for the astoundingly widespread use of the posthumous Alexanders and Lysimachi as city coinages in the third and early second centuries. When, for instance, Aspendus, Perge and Phaselis and, at a slightly later date, Temnus and Alabanda produced large quantities of posthumous Alexanders for export to the Seleucid kingdom, it must be regarded as a production for profit, the number of coins being out of all proportion to the commercial importance of these cities.

It has often been asserted that Alexander the Great, after the conquest of the Persian empire, stimulated trade and production by putting the enormous amounts of precious metal from the Persian treasuries into circulation. As a description of what actually happened this is undoubtedly correct. It would, however, be anachronistic to ascribe any far-sighted economic policy to Alexander and his administration. It is much more likely that Alexander and the Diadochi simply coined on a huge scale to cover the military and civil expenses which they incurred. With the exception of the Ptolemies and, at a later date, the Attalids of Pergamum, whose interest in coinage must be regarded as exclusively fiscal, the Hellenistic kings coined primarily in order to meet their economic obligations. Owing to the continuous political rivalry between the kingdoms and the numerous wars, military expenses weighed heavily on budgets. It was also part of the royal ideology that the king had to live in style and to spend lavishly on

---

24 All three functions were, of course, already served by the noble metals in the form of bullion before the introduction of coinage.

25 *Politics A*, 1257a.

26 Kraay 1976, 312–28; Price 1983.

benefactions to individuals and cities. I have no doubt that in the kingdoms the prime motivating factor regulating the volume of coinage was the rise and fall in public expenses.

Finally, propaganda and prestige will sometimes have influenced the issue of coinage. In the kingdoms (again with the exception of Egypt and Pergamum, where dynastic feeling was dominant) each new ruler made certain that his own coinage was produced as soon as possible in order to advertise his succession, and because it was felt that a coinage of his own was one of the distinguishing marks of a true king. Similarly, the free and autonomous cities sought to show their status by issuing coins in larger denominations. We have many instances in the Hellenistic period of very small city coinages, sometimes produced by a single pair of dies, which can have had very little economic significance, and which were most probably produced on some occasion when it was found opportune to propagate the fact of the independence and freedom of the city.

Thus commercial considerations, the profit motive, the need to cover state expenditure, prestige and propaganda were all factors that may have influenced the issue of coins. Sometimes more than one factor will have been involved, and under different circumstances one or other of these explanations may have played the dominant role. But it would be wrong to look for one, and only one, answer to a complicated question. The pluralistic approach followed here seems to me to offer a better chance of arriving at the truth regarding the fundamental question: why were coins produced?

3

TYPES AND INSCRIPTIONS

(a) TYPES

As in preceding periods the coin types were predominantly religious. Panhellenic deities together with local heroes, and their various sacred animals and attributes, formed an inexhaustible reservoir from which the authorities and artists derived their inspiration.

The Hellenistic period was essentially one of strong historical consciousness. Literary and historical scholarship flourished and demonstrated an attitude of reverence for the past which often became a substitute for activities that were no longer possible, most notably in the political field. In the choice and execution of coin types this retrospective interest showed itself in a tendency towards archaizing. A good example of this is offered by the second-century tetradrachms of Lampsacus (**649**), where the splendid head of Dionysus on the obverse shows a typical archaization but combining elements of different periods, the archaic-looking curls of hair and beard being joined with a more modern rendering of the facial features, most conspicuously in the treatment of the eye. A phenomenon worth noticing is the occurrence of both archaizing and more modern representations within the same series as, for example, the head of Zeus on some issues of Antiochus IV (**627–8**) and Alexander Balas.[1]

Another aspect of the reverence for the past, combined with an increasing interest in showing full figures rather than heads, is the frequent adoption of cult statues as coin types. A few examples of this practice are known from the Classical period, but it becomes much more common in the Hellenistic age, showing the dependency of the period on earlier achievements. Many of the statues copied and used on Hellenistic coins date indeed from the Archaic age. Examples are the Dionysus of Mytilene (**650**) in the form of a herm, the Amyclean Apollo used at Sparta (**505**), Artemis at Leucas (**651**) and Athena Ilias (**652**), all presenting features derived from venerable *xoana* of remote antiquity.[2]

Another copy of special interest is one of the well-known Artemis Ephesia. During the third and early second centuries the representations of Artemis on coins of Ephesus (**570**) are purely Greek and in a contemporary style. But from about 130 the cult statue appears on the coins, the famous 'many-breasted' Artemis who is identified as an Anatolian vegetation goddess by

1 Mørkholm 1963, 31; Houghton 1982, 154–7.
2 Lacroix 1949, 29–41, 193–4, 328–9.

her dress and ornaments (**657**). A similar figure appears already about 180 on a tetradrachm issue from Pergamum (**615**), and here the statue is designed as a representation of Athena Nikephoros. This goddess had always been regarded as purely Greek, and it is a surprise to see her revealed, by her cult statue shown on the coins, as a syncretistic deity combining the Greek Athena with the Anatolian mother-goddess.[3]

From the very beginning of the Hellenistic period another copy of a work of art becomes quite popular as a numismatic type. This is the fighting Athena, who was probably copied from the well-known and popular representations on the Panathenaic prize amphoras.[4] Here the archaizing features, the most obvious being the stylized 'swallowtail' pattern of Athena's cloak, are already present on the vases. The oldest numismatic representation is on a rare gold stater (**268**) and some silver coins from Pergamum *c.* 325, where the goddess is shown facing in a rigid position and often placed on a base. However, the type became really popular after its adoption by Ptolemy I on his copious silver issues (**92–5**) from *c.* 314 onwards. The goddess is here shown in profile, moving to the right in an energetic stride with her spear poised for attack. Her position balancing on the tips of her toes is one of the indications that a vase painting was being used as a model.

The fighting Athena, sometimes wielding a thunderbolt instead of a spear, was used as a coin type on rare gold issues of Demetrius Poliorcetes (**163**) and later on the silver of Antigonus Gonatas (**430**) and Philip V of Macedon (**438**), as well as on silver and bronze of Pyrrhus at Syracuse. In the second century she appears on the silver issues of the Thessalian League, and even in distant India she adorns the coins of Menander (**641**) and several other kings. The type was used predominantly by kings, and its popularity with them derived from the fact that the fighting Athena was seen as a symbol of an important aspect of ruler ideology: the warrior king acquiring his right to the land, the *doriktetos chora*, by his spear.

An important detail of the representation of the fighting Athena, namely the swallowtail pattern of the cloak, so caught the imagination that it was transferred to other types as well. When Demetrius Poliorcetes in *c.* 300 introduced his coinage with a fighting Poseidon on the reverse (**162**), the god, who was not usually shown in archaistic guise, was provided with a cloak of exactly the same pattern hanging over his extended left arm. This garment contrasts strongly with the muscular body, which is rendered in a quite up-to-date fashion.

The copying of Classical and contemporary statues is much rarer than the copying of Archaic ones. The Apollo of Calamis was used as a model at Apollonia Pontica and the Apollo of Bryaxis, dedicated at Daphne near Antioch by Seleucus I, appears on a special issue of Antiochus IV (**653**).[5] The most famous Classical statue to be represented on coins was, of course, that of Athena Parthenos. Pheidias' masterpiece so impressed contemporary and later artists that it was already copied time and again in the Classical period. In the Hellenistic age the head of the

3 Mørkholm 1984a. Cf. Le Rider 1973b.
4 Havelock 1980; Lacroix 1949, 116–17.
5 Lacroix 1949, 248–9 (Calamis), 319–20 (Bryaxis).

statue was used as the obverse type for the Athenian New Style coinage (**609–11**), as well as at Heraclea in Ionia (**654**) and (in a rather poor derivation) by the Aenianes in Thessaly.[6]

A much more important innovation of the Hellenistic period, as far as coin types are concerned, is the introduction of the ruler portrait. While the reverse type of the royal coinages is often a dynastic badge, like the Ptolemaic eagle on a thunderbolt or the seated Apollo of the Seleucids, the obverse is in many series adorned with the portrait of the king.[7] Although dynastic portraits had appeared in Asia Minor in the late fifth century, the Hellenistic development must be seen as a result of the career of Alexander the Great. It is unlikely that the well-known head of Heracles on Alexander's silver (**9–10**) was regarded as a portrait of the king during his lifetime, but after his death the assimilation of hero and king became a simple matter: on a Bactrian coin of Agathocles, indeed, the head of Heracles is identified by the inscription as 'Alexander (the son) of Philip'. But some of the Diadochi developed personal Alexander representations on their respective coinages in order to stress their connection with the great conqueror from whom they derived their power. It was probably in 321 that Ptolemy of Egypt introduced a new Alexander portrait on his silver coinage, the dead king being shown with a headdress made of an elephant's scalp (**90**). This type was imitated on rare issues of Seleucus I (**137**) who, however, soon preferred a different type: Alexander in a helmet covered with the skin of a leopard and decorated with the horns and ears of a bull (**139**).[8] In *c.* 297 the most popular of the posthumous coin portraits of Alexander was created for the coinage of Lysimachus, with the great king shown wearing a royal diadem and the ram's horns which proclaimed him to be the son of Zeus Ammon (**178–9**).

The first among the Successors to place his own portrait on his coinage was Ptolemy I (**96**), shortly after his adoption of the royal title in 305/4. In about 295 Demetrius Poliorcetes followed his example (**169**). The coin portraits of Demetrius are interesting for two reasons. In the first place, the portrait was adorned with a bull's horns, a clear indication of deification, assimilating the king to Poseidon, the Lord of the Sea. Secondly, the different portraits from a number of mints in Greece and Asia Minor show the opposite tendencies of realism (**172**) and idealization (**173**) that were to continue as separate artistic lines of development throughout the Hellenistic period.

None of the other Successors placed his own portrait on the coins, and after the turbulent period of the first generation after Alexander the use of the royal portrait developed differently in the various kingdoms. In Macedon the excessive egocentricity of Demetrius led to a reaction, and only towards the end of the third century, with the accession of Philip V, was the royal portrait again placed on the coinage. The Ptolemies of Egypt revered the founder of their dynasty, and the portrait of Ptolemy Soter was retained on the most common denomination, the silver tetradrachm. The later Ptolemaic kings and queens did indeed make their appearance,

6 Schwabacher 1953.
7 Newell 1937; Davis and Kraay 1973, esp. 270–7. For Hellenistic portraits generally see Richter 1965, III.
8 This portrait has usually been identified with Seleucus I himself, but see Hadley 1974b.

but only sporadically.[9] Under Ptolemy II a striking new composition was introduced, with the jugate portraits of the royal couple (**297–8**), the *Theoi Adelphoi*, placed on heavy gold octodrachms which on the other side carried a similar double portrait of Ptolemy I and his wife Berenice I. The place of honour in the foreground was, quite naturally, reserved for the kings.

The Seleucid dynasty in Syria showed greater interest in contemporary royal portraits. From Antiochus I onwards (**330ff.**) each king placed his own portrait on the coinage of gold and silver, and frequently also on bronze issues. We have thus a complete gallery of these kings, and a few of their queens, that allows us to trace the history of coin portraiture through a period of more than 200 years. The Seleucid example was followed by the minor kingdoms of Asia Minor with the exception of Pergamum, where the Attalids showed their respect for Philetaerus, the founder of their dynasty, by retaining his portrait (**409–10**) on the coins.

In the eastern Greek world, in Parthia and Bactria, the rulers followed the Seleucid fashion. The most splendid coin portraits in the realistic tradition were in fact created on the very fringes of the Hellenistic world. The Bactrian kings of the years after *c.* 200, Euthydemus and his descendants (**383–6**), are rendered with an artistic brilliance that is not surpassed in the ancient world. Very few works of art of any period can match the brutal realism of the half-Iranian, half-Greek kings of Pontus, the coin portrait of Pharnaces (**623**) being one of the least flattering human representations ever made. As examples of the idealizing trend one can instance the coin portraits of Seleucus II (**332**) from the mint of Antioch and of Orophernes of Cappadocia (**655**), both showing the rulers in youthful glory. Sometimes the same king might be represented in both fashions, as with Antiochus IV of Syria, of whom both realistic and idealized portraits are known (**629–30**). The degree of idealization of this king increases during his reign with the incongruous result that he seems to grow younger as time goes on.[10] The existence of such idealized portraits serves as a warning against trying to use the apparent age of the persons portrayed as a means of establishing the chronology of the issues. Similarly any attempt at establishing the character of a ruler from his coin portraits must be regarded with scepticism. More often than not, it only means that preconceived ideas, whether modern or ancient, are read into the representation.

Hellenistic coin types practically never make direct reference to historical events. The most famous exception to this rule is the representation of the battle between Alexander the Great and the Indian King Porus (**44**) on the heavy decadrachms issued, most probably, by Alexander in commemoration of his Indian campaign. The identifications of the attacking horseman with Alexander and of one of the fighting warriors on the elephant's back with Porus seem to me certain. In spite of its small dimensions the scene reveals the same spirit as the famous Alexander mosaic from Pompeii, where Alexander's opponent is the Great King Darius himself. In both cases the artists have created dramatic unity at the expense of historical truth, as Alexander never confronted either of his two opponents in person on the battlefield.

But the Porus decadrachms are exceptional. If historical events are alluded to, it is generally

9 Kyrieleis 1975.
10 Mørkholm 1963, 57–68.

in a symbolic or allegorical way. A good example is offered by the first coinage of Demetrius Poliorcetes. Here the magnificent Poseidon on the reverse (**162**) is a symbolic expression of the mastery of the sea, which Demetrius could still claim even after his disastrous defeat at Ipsus. On the obverse we see the goddess of victory alighting on the prow of a warship. The reference to Demetrius' great victory over Ptolemy I in the naval battle off Cypriot Salamis in 306 is obvious, although the coins were struck at least six years after the event. More frequently the general nature of victory symbolism does not allow us to connect a coin type of this kind with any specific event. The Nike crowning a trophy on a rare issue of Seleucus I (**139**) is best explained as a general symbol of his acquisition of the eastern satrapies in a fashion which showed him as a worthy successor to Alexander, whose portrait adorns the obverse of the issue. Or perhaps an even broader allusion to the victories of both Alexander and Seleucus over the barbarians was intended.

(b) INSCRIPTIONS

In the Hellenistic period anepigraphic coin issues are very rare, except in outlying areas like Carthage and Etruria. Normally, the main inscription on a coin provided information on the issuing authority, who guaranteed the acceptability of the coinage within the territory under his or its jurisdiction. This authority might be a city-state or a league, a monarchic ruler, or a deity.

As in the preceding period the cities and people organized in leagues issued their coins in the name of the citizen body or people in the genitive plural (e.g. *ΣΥΡΑΚΟΣΙΩΝ*, *ΑΙΤΩΛΩΝ*). The frequent abbreviations must be read in the same way, and with the genitive a substantive meaning 'money' or 'coinage' has to be understood.

The early coinages of Alexander the Great were signed only with his name in the genitive. In about 329 the title of King (*ΒΑΣΙΛΕΩΣ*) was added to the name at Myriandrus (**16**), and from then on the new form of inscription was adopted at different mints, although it never became universal during Alexander's lifetime. The Successors, however, starting with Ptolemy in Egypt, used both title and name on their issues, and this practice was continued by their descendants.

A small but interesting group of coinages bears the name of a deity whose image is also used as the reverse type. In cases where we find both a city name and the name of a deity, as for instance Apollo Smintheus at Alexandria Troas (**656**), the coinage may be regarded as a normal civic issue, expressing the devotion of the population to its main god. But when the deity alone is named, the coinage was most probably struck by a religious organization connected with the cult in question and for a specific purpose, as for instance to be used at the recurrent festivals which were so frequent and played such an important role in the Hellenistic period. The problem has been most thoroughly discussed in connection with the issues of Athena Ilias (**652**) which were once regarded as a civic coinage of Ilium, whereas they were actually struck by a confederation of city-states that had Athena Ilias as their protecting deity and together celebrated her annual festival at her temple near Ilium. For practical reasons the coins were minted at Ilium and the magistrates responsible for the production were Ilian citizens, but the coinage was struck and guaranteed by the confederation.[11]

One issue from Pergamum in the name of Athena Nikephoros (**615**) was undoubtedly struck by order of the Pergamene king but the inscription shows that it was not a normal royal coinage. It was most probably issued in connection with a re-organization of the Nikephoria festival in Pergamum in 181 and must be regarded as a special festival issue, designed to make propaganda for the goddess and advertise her festival to the Greek world.

Most of these coinages in the name of a deity belong to the second century. However, an issue from Perge in Pamphylia (**482**) ascribed *ΑΡΤΕΜΙΔΟΣ ΠΕΡΓΑΙΑΣ* certainly started in the third century and provides the earliest known example of this practice.

In the second and first centuries a number of cities in former Seleucid territory added various epithets to the simple designation of the city. The oldest examples are found in Phoenicia, where under Antiochus IV (175–164) so-called municipal bronze coins were issued at several places.[12] Here, in Semitic characters, Byblus describes herself as 'Holy' and Berytus (re-named Laodicea) as 'the Metropolis of Canaan'. Tyre and Sidon competed with each other, the Tyrian legend 'of Tyre the Metropolis of the Sidonians' being totally outshone by the pompous inscription on some Sidonian coins 'of the Sidonians the Metropolis of Cambe, Hippo, Citium and Tyre'.

After this initial outburst of civic pride a more sensible level was generally adopted. The coin-producing cities in Phoenicia, northern Syria and Cilicia in the late second and early first centuries used the epithet 'sacred' (*ΙΕΡΑΣ*), 'inviolable' (*ΑΣΥΛΟΥ*) and 'independent' (*ΑΥΤΟΝΟΜΟΥ*), either separately or in various combinations. During the first century the designation as 'Metropolis' was also revived.

During the third century most of the royal coinages were inscribed with the name of the ruler and the simple title of king. On posthumous issues of Ptolemy I and Antiochus I the royal title was replaced by the cult name 'Soter', i.e. Saviour (**328**). An Egyptian gold issue of Ptolemy II (**297**) was inscribed *ΘΕΩΝ ΑΔΕΛΦΩΝ*, referring to Ptolemy II and his sister-wife Arsinoe at a time when Arsinoe was dead but Ptolemy himself still alive. Apart from this instance, the use of cult names of kings on their coins was apparently restricted to posthumous issues. The first certain example of a cult name used by a living ruler belongs to the very end of the third century, when coins of Ptolemy V (204–180) from the Phoenician area carry the inscription *ΠΤΟΛΕΜΑΙΟΥ ΕΠΙΦΑΝΟΥΣ* (**329**).

It is, however, with the reign of Antiochus IV of Syria that the fashion of adding cult epithets to the name of the king becomes established. About 172 he adopted the title *ΘΕΟΥ ΕΠΙΦΑΝΟΥ*, 'the God Manifest' (**630**), and a few years later, most probably in 169, the title was expanded by *ΝΙΚΗΦΟΡΟΥ* 'the Victorious' (**627–8**). From that time onwards the fashion spread. It was adopted not only by the Seleucids but by most of the minor dynasties established on former Seleucid territory, the kings of Bithynia, Pontus and Cappadocia in Asia Minor, as well as the Parthians, Bactrians and Indo-Greeks in the far eastern parts of the Hellenistic world.

11 Robert 1966, 18–46; Gauthier 1975, 170–3.
12 Mørkholm 1965a.

It is symptomatic that this practice was introduced at a time when the political power of the Hellenistic kingdoms was being undermined by Rome. Often one gets the impression that the more powerless a king felt, the more he tried to compensate by adopting a string of high-sounding epithets.

Deification (*ΘΕΟΥ*) is not uncommon, while actual identification with one of the Greek deities is rare but does occur: ***ΕΠΙΦΑΝΟΥΣ ΔΙΟΝΥΣΟΥ*** for Antiochus VI. More often the recognized royal qualities or virtues are mentioned: 'victorious' (*ΝΙΚΗΦΟΡΟΥ, ΝΙΚΑΤΟΡΟΣ*), 'just' (*ΔΙΚΑΙΟΥ*), 'pious' (*ΕΥΣΕΒΟΥΣ*) occur very frequently. Dynastic feelings are expressed by epithets like ***ΦΙΛΑΔΕΛΦΟΥ*** ('brother- or sister-lover'), ***ΦΙΛΟΠΑΤΟΡΟΣ*** and ***ΦΙΛΟΜΗΤΟΡΟΣ*** ('father-lover', 'mother-lover'), and ***ΕΥΠΑΤΟΡΟΣ*** ('nobly begotten') or ***ΘΕΟΠΑΤΟΡΟΣ*** ('god-begotten') belong to the same category. Finally, some epithets reveal a political programme: ***ΦΙΛΕΛΛΗΝΟΣ*** ('Greek-lover'), especially popular with barbarians like the Parthians, and ***ΦΙΛΟΡΩΜΑΙΟΥ*** ('Roman-lover'), the pathetic last cry of many of the smaller Hellenistic dynasties.

With city coinages the identification of the place of minting generally presents no difficulties except for such homonymous cities as the older Apollonias and Heracleas and the new dynastic foundations named Antioch, Seleucia, etc. However, some of the leagues and the large kingdoms issued coins at more than one place, and in such cases it may be uncertain where a particular issue was produced. Sometimes initials or monograms may provide the answer: *ΣΙ* on Alexander and Ptolemaic (**293**) coins from Sidon, *ΣΑ*, *ΚΙ*, and *ΠΑ* on Ptolemaic issues of Salamis, Citium and Paphos. Local symbols, often small representations of various objects placed in the field and having no direct connection with the main type, can also be used to indicate places of origin, as for instance the pomegranate of Side or the rose of Rhodes, both of them canting symbols referring to the name of the place (**471–2**). When no initials, monograms or symbols are present, the scholar faces the difficult task of analysing the various series, trying to separate regional styles and distributing the issues in the most logical way. A masterly demonstration of this very complex procedure was provided by E. T. Newell in his work on early Seleucid coinages down to and including the issues of Antiochus III.[13]

In addition to the issuing authority and the place of minting, further information may be provided by the inscription. During the Hellenistic period it became quite common to indicate the magistrates who were directly responsible for each separate issue. City magistrates (who were often elected annually) and royal officials placed their names or initials on the coinage which they controlled. Monograms and symbols were used in the same way by these officials. Names are written in full more often on the civic coinages than on the royal issues and patronymics may even appear on them. An issue from Lampsacus provides the names not only of the father but also of the grandfather of the magistrate in question.

It is tempting to identify the names occurring on the coins with persons known from other sources, since it is natural to assume that the monetary officials were drawn from the same social

13 Newell 1938c (*ESM*) and 1941 (*WSM*), reprinted with additions and corrections in 1977–8.

circles that provided other city magistrates. The occurrence of names found on coins in epigraphical material from the same city is therefore to be expected. The existence of rare names with a strong local flavour makes, of course, an identification easier, although it has always to be remembered that according to Greek usage the same name will tend to re-appear in alternate generations. There has been much discussion of the possibility that the monetary officials performed their duty as a liturgy, paying (in part at least) the expenses at the mint from their own pockets.[14] With bronze coinages there is no need to assume such liturgies, as these brought a considerable profit to a city, but for some of the irregular silver issues of the smaller towns, where civic pride was probably a strong motivation factor, the idea of a liturgy seems quite an acceptable one.

With the royal coinages it is a different matter. Here the identification of moneyers known only through initials or monograms with leading political figures known from the written sources is extremely dangerous, and in most cases should be avoided. The royal officials dealing with the coinage would have been generally quite subordinate persons. Very often they retained their posts during successive reigns, even when these came about as a result of rebellion and war.

During the Hellenistic period there seems to have been an increase of central control. At the beginning one official was generally thought sufficient, but later more complicated control systems, with three or four officials signing each issue, were preferred. The detailed operation of these systems is unknown to us, but we can see from the distribution of initials and monograms that often there was one supervisor, who might be responsible for more than one mint, working together with several subordinate officials. In some cases the initials or monograms may suggest that the production of a mint was divided among different workshops, or *officinae* as they would be termed in the Roman world.

As already mentioned, city magistrates were normally in office for a year. Hence if a list of magistrates is available or can be reconstructed, it may serve as a means of dating the various issues. Magistrates' names introduced by *ΕΠΙ* most probably refer to the eponymous official of the city and are placed on the coins for dating purposes rather than as marks of control. Consequently, a very large and continuous city coinage with names of magistrates should in theory be datable exactly to the year, but the only Hellenistic coinage so far dated by this method is the Athenian New Style coinage. Here the result at present is that, while the relative chronology is more or less agreed upon, there is a conflict regarding the absolute chronology between two systems that are some thirty years apart.[15] It should be kept in mind that the study of die linkages has shown that in city mints two or more moneyers were not infrequently active at the same time.

It is of course much easier when a coinage is dated explicitly by the years of a reign or according to an era (**478–80**), since the identification of the reign and of the era is in most cases

14 For conflicting views see Robert 1973; Gauthier 1975; and Jones 1979, 82–90.
15 For a survey of the latest contributions to the discussion see Mørkholm 1979b, 69–71, and Mattingly 1979.

not too difficult. In the Ptolemaic issues of the second and first centuries we are assisted by the practice of prefixing the sign L for year to the number (see Glossary), indicating without any doubt that a regnal year is meant.[16] On some other coinages, especially those issued by the Seleucids and the kings of Bithynia (**621**) and Pontus (**625**), the dates soon become so high that they are obviously era years.

There is, however, one possible source of error. The Greeks normally used the letters of the alphabet as numerals, with special signs for 6, 90 and 900. If in a given series the officials signed with only the first initial of their name these single letters might be taken as numbers and completely fictitious dating systems worked out, as indeed happened with a coinage of Ptolemy V of Egypt. Another numbering system used the alphabet without any additional signs, using double letters for numbers higher than 24 (the number of letters in the alphabet): *AA* for 25, *BB* for 26, and so on. Such a system, running up to 50, was employed for an Egyptian series in the name of Arsinoe. The letters were long taken to represent a special Arsinoe era, covering the years from 270/69 to 221/20.[17] The latest research (below, p. 103) has shown this to be a fantasy,[18] and we have instead a serial numbering which has nothing to do with annual dates. Figure 3 shows the two different numbering systems of which only the first is used for dating purposes on coins. But numbers from the first system may be used for serial numbering without a strictly chronological significance, as can be proved by a die study of Cappadocian drachms of the late second century.[19]

Sometimes the coins were dated more precisely than to a single year. Seyrig has shown that at Tyre and Sidon a system of dating to the first and second semester of a year was in use for some of their Hellenistic coinages, apparently because the magistrates functioned for six months only or half the civic year. At Aradus certain issues were dated to periods of two months within the year by the use of the first six letters of the Phoenician alphabet (**483**).[20] Even more closely dated coinages are known. At Athens and at Seleucia on the Tigris, at nearly opposite ends of the Hellenistic world, extensive silver coinages were dated by the month. The same is the case with some issues of Mithridates VI of Pontus. At Athens a numerical system like that in Figure 3b was used, the letters *A–M* denoting the twelve ordinary months (**611**) and *N* standing for the 13th month of intercalary years.[21] At Seleucia the tetradrachms of the Parthian kings, beginning with the issues of Orodes II (57–38),[22] bore the names of the Macedonian months in abbreviated form.

Marks of value are rare on Greek coins. For gold and silver, the weights were decisive as soon as the coins circulated outside the area under the direct control of the issuing authority. Most bronze coins were intended for local use only, except in the large territorial kingdoms.

---

16 Seyrig 1950b, 31–5.
17 Mørkholm 1979c, 204.
18 Troxell 1983.
19 Mørkholm 1964b; 1978b, 145–6.
20 Seyrig 1950a, 28–31 (Tyre and Sidon); 1964, 20 (Aradus).
21 Thompson 1961, 608–13.
22 Sellwood 1980, 143, 147, 152.

	a	b		a	b
1.	Α	Α	25.	ΚΕ	ΑΑ
2.	Β	Β	30.	Λ	ΖΖ
3.	Γ	Γ	36.	ΛϚ	ΜΜ
4.	Δ	Δ	40.	Μ	ΠΠ
5.	Ε	Ε	48.	ΜΗ	ΩΩ
6.	Ϛ	Ζ	49.	ΜΘ	À (=ΑΑΑ)
7.	Ζ	Η	50.	Ν	B̀ (=ΒΒΒ)
8.	Η	Θ	60.	Ξ	
9.	Θ	Ι	70.	Ο	
10.	Ι	Κ	80.	Π	
11.	ΙΑ	Λ	90.	Ϙ	
12.	ΙΒ	Μ	100.	Ρ	
13.	ΙΓ	Ν	110.	ΡΙ	
14.	ΙΔ	Ξ	111.	ΡΙΑ	
15.	ΙΕ	Ο	120.	ΡΚ	
16.	ΙΖ	Π	200.	Σ	
17.	ΙΤ	Ρ	300.	Τ	
18.	ΙΗ	Σ	400.	Υ	
19.	ΙΘ	Τ	500.	Φ	
20.	Κ	Υ	600.	Χ	
21.	ΚΑ	Φ	700.	Ψ	
22.	ΚΒ	Χ	800.	Ω	
23.	ΚΓ	Ψ	900.	Ϡ	
24.	ΚΔ	Ω	1000.	͵Α	

Figure 3. Greek numbering systems

With the Seleucids we sometimes find value marks on bronze coins, identifying them as pieces of one chalkous, two chalkoi, four chalkoi and so on. This usage is restricted to a few mints in the East, notably Ecbatana and Seleucia on the Tigris, and it has been suggested that the marks were only added in connection with drastic weight reductions in order to inform the public of the new values attributed to the coins in question.[23] Similarly, the letters *M* and *Π* for 40 and 80 copper drachms on bronze coins of Cleopatra VII of Egypt were most probably intended to notify the public of the official value of the new denominations.

As compared with the Classical period in the West the Hellenistic age provides very few examples of artists' signatures. The extensive use of coinage must have made the die engravers' work seem more a craft than an art. A notable exception is the engraver responsible for some of the earliest portraits of Ptolemy I who included his initial, a diminutive *Δ*, in his new creation.

Sometimes the identity of a deity used as coin type may be specified by an inscription. At Syracuse in the third century we find legends like *ΚΟΡΑΣ* ('Maiden') and *ΣΩΤΕΙΡΑ* ('Deliverer') added to the heads of Persephone and Artemis. We also find legends with a more explicit political message such as *ΔΙΟΣ ΕΛΕΥΘΕΡΙΟΥ* ('Zeus the Deliverer') and *ΔΙΟΣ ΕΛΛΑΝΙΟΥ* ('Hellenic Zeus') used in periods of democracy in Syracuse to identify the head of Zeus on the coins. Direct political propaganda, perhaps expressed as a hopeful expectation, appears with the legend *ΡΩΜΑ ΠΙΣΤΙΣ*, *Roma* and *fides*, on an issue of Locri in southern Italy just before or just after the war between Rome and Pyrrhus.

(c) IMITATIONS AND STYLE

In the preceding sections we have made the tacit assumption that types and inscriptions are directly relevant to the first questions we want to put to numismatic material, namely when and where a given coinage was issued. This is, of course, appropriate in the majority of cases, but we also have to take account of coins that for one reason or another are suspected of being other than what their types and legends proclaim them to be.

I am not here concerned with forgeries, private or official, but with official imitations which have an important place in the study of Hellenistic numismatics. Such imitations were not made with deceitful intentions, but simply to satisfy the need for money in situations when a recognized and popular coinage was not available in sufficient quantity. These imitations are generally of full weight and adequate fineness, and thus very difficult to separate from the original products. Some were produced by barbarian tribes on the outskirts of the civilized world. In such cases the artistic level of the designs, together with mistakes in spelling and awkward letter forms in the inscriptions, may reveal them as barbarous imitations (e.g. **486–9**).

There are, however, other imitation coinages that emanate from the heart of the Greek world. In the third and early second centuries posthumous Alexander and Lysimachus coinages were produced by a large number of city-states in Greece itself and in Asia Minor (see Plates XXX–XXXIII). Although these issues can be separated from the lifetime and early posthumous issues

23 Newell 1938c (*ESM*), 273.

by a number of stylistic and technical details and their dates established by their occurrence in hoards, they are still normally included with the lifetime issues in collections and catalogues. The result is that discussions of the monetary policy and economic importance of many cities in the Hellenistic period are vitiated by the absence of any reference to their most important issues in gold and silver.[24] The reasons for the production of such posthumous issues of Alexander and Lysimachus are various. In the first place, the enormous output of lifetime issues of the two kings had made their gold and silver coins acceptable throughout the Greek world and beyond. By 280 they dominated the monetary circulation, enjoying an immense popularity in international exchanges. It was only natural that some of the smaller states should want to capitalize on this popularity by adopting the Alexander or Lysimachus types and inscriptions for their own coinages.

Public demand was another reason behind the production of these posthumous coinages. It appears, for instance, that the Scythian tribes in southern Russia preferred to trade in gold coins of Alexander and Lysimachus types. It has been very plausibly suggested that the Greco-Macedonian mercenaries who played such an important role in the Hellenistic armies during the third century often demanded to be paid in Alexander coinage, which was known and trusted in international circles.[25] This explanation seems especially appropriate for the Alexander issues from Pergamum, Rhodes and other places which had a normal coin production of quite different types and, in some cases, of another weight standard.

A third reason for their production may be found in the convenient neutrality of these coinages. By 280 Alexander the Great had become a legendary figure. The issue of silver tetradrachms and gold coins was regarded as the prerogative of any free and autonomous state.[26] The position of many of the city states *vis-à-vis* the Hellenistic kingdoms, however, changed repeatedly during the third century. Under these circumstances a city-state, wishing to use its newly acquired autonomy to issue gold or large denominations of silver, might find it expedient not to proclaim its freedom too blatantly for fear of annoying a former suzerain. The Alexander coinage, with the place of minting discreetly indicated by a monogram or symbol, might then appear as a useful diplomatic solution to a problem that might otherwise cause trouble.

In the second century we have an interesting example of the opposite practice. The cistophoric coinage issued at Pergamum and other places in Asia Minor from *c.* 175 onwards is always provided with letters or monograms indicating a city as the place of minting (**616–17**). There is normally no other indication of issuing authority, and until quite recently the cistophoric coinage was regarded as a kind of league coinage issued by various cities in accordance with a monetary convention regulating weight standard and types. All the cities involved, however, were subject to the king of Pergamum, and a recent monograph on early cistophoric coinage has demonstrated beyond any doubt that it must be regarded as a true royal coinage produced

24 E.g. in the Berlin *corpus* (Griechisches Münzwerk) of Byzantium by Edith Schönert-Geiss (1970).
25 Troxell 1971, 61–2, 79; Kleiner 1971, 121.
26 Seyrig 1963, 19–22.

by royal officials from silver provided by the royal treasury.[27] We thus have the interesting paradox that while in the third and early second centuries a number of city coinages appear in the disguise of a royal coinage, an important royal coinage of the second century tries to efface its royal origin and to appear as a coinage issued by a number of cities.

In our discussion of the choice of coin types mention has been made of strongly archaizing tendencies in the Hellenistic period. Even when the style is not archaizing, it is often derivative, feeding upon the Classical tradition as this developed during the fourth century. A certain languid elegance is found in some of the full-figure representations which appear unnaturally slim and elongated. The standing Artemis on the reverse of the coins from Perge provides a good illustration of this. In other cases, especially when naked male figures are represented, we observe a strong and muscular style, reminiscent of the baroque quality of much Hellenistic sculpture. An early example of this is the fighting Poseidon on the coinage of Demetrius Poliorcetes (**162**). The contrast between realism and idealization in portraits has already been mentioned, but even when an idealized representation was preferred, certain stylistic features were often used to emphasize royal qualities such as energy and determination. The bulging brows over deep-set eyes and the prominent chins in many Hellenistic coin portraits probably owe their existence to the conventional ideas of royal physiognomy which resulted in these artistic conventions.

The style of an epoch is, of course, the result of the work of individual artists. During the Hellenistic period the increased production of coinage led to a general decline in artistic level. Gifted and creative artists certainly existed, but their proportion within the total number of die engravers seems to have been much reduced when compared with preceding periods. Thus Head's designations of the periods 280–146 and 146–27 as respectively 'Decline of Art' and 'Continued Decline in Art' are perhaps not unfair in spite of their rather sweeping generality.[28] Of course, we should remind ourselves that even in periods of decline there will be numerous exceptions.

However this may be, stylistic analysis is an important method in the study of coins. It can be dangerously subjective, especially when applied to single coins or only a few specimens. But students who are working on larger coin series often develop an intimate knowledge and understanding of their material which allow the more sensitive amongst them to distinguish the hands of different die engravers or engravers' workshops by following the small and sometimes perhaps unconscious idiosyncrasies apparent on the coins. It is hardly possible to give an abstract definition of similarity and to point out exactly when two dies become so similar that they must be regarded as the work of the same engraver. But the identification of engravers' hands is nevertheless a practical reality and must be accepted. On the other hand, experience has shown time and again that the concept of dissimilarity can hardly be used to separate issues. Two engravers of extremely varying competence were often working at the same time and at the same place, producing the most astonishingly different results within one and the same series of coins.

---

27 Kleiner and Noe 1977, 125.
28 Head 1911, lxii-lxiii.

PART II

ALEXANDER AND THE DIADOCHI 336–*c.* 280

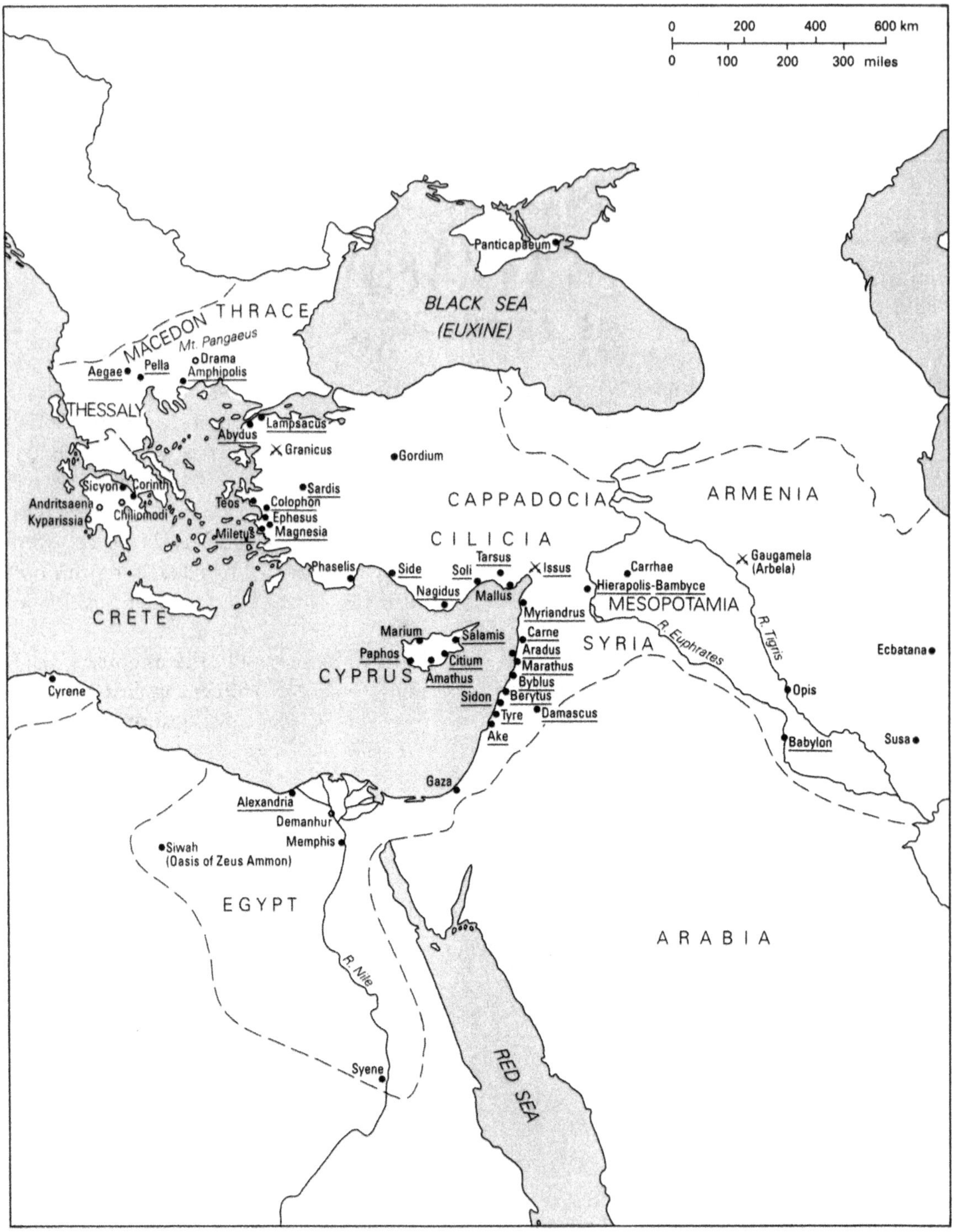

Map 1. The mints of Alexander the Great

Alexander's mints are underlined. Hoards are indicated by hollow dots. For a map of Alexander's empire, see the front endpaper. Its eastern provinces are not shown here, since no mints of Alexander's lifetime seem to have existed east of Babylon, though a travelling mint may well have accompanied his army and struck coin when necessary.

4

COINS OF ALEXANDER'S LIFETIME

When Alexander ascended the Macedonian throne in 336 B.C. the political system of mainland Greece was that recently imposed by his father, Philip II, after his victory over the Greek coalition at Chaeronea two years earlier. Philip's power and influence were based on the military predominance of his Macedonian army, supplemented by his personal skill in diplomatic affairs. As king of Macedon, *archon* of Thessaly, member of the Amphictyonic Council, and *hegemon* of the Corinthian League, Philip wielded an undisputed authority and had used it to organize the Panhellenic campaign against the Persian empire. He was hindered from carrying this out by his murder in the summer of 336. Alexander became the heir to his dominant position as well as to his policy against Persia.

Through the possession of mines in Macedonia and Thrace, especially the important gold and silver mines of the Pangaean region which according to some sources supplied a yearly income of a thousand talents, Philip had been able to issue coins in larger quantities than his predecessors and far beyond the resources of any Greek city-state except perhaps Athens. His main coins had been:

Gold	Stater, *c.* 8.64g (**1**)	
	Obv.	Laureate head of Apollo r.
	Rev.	Nike in chariot drawn by two horses; *ΦΙΛΙΠΠΟΥ*
Silver	Tetradrachm, *c.* 14.52g	
	Obv.	Laureate head of Zeus r.
	Rev.	a. (359–348) Horseman l. with kausia, raising r. hand in salute; *ΦΙΛΙΠ-ΠΟΥ* (**2**)
		b. (348–336) Jockey l. with palm branch; *ΦΙΛΙΠΠΟΥ* (**3**)
Bronze	Unit (**4**)	
	Obv.	Young head with taenia
	Rev.	Horseman; *ΦΙΛΙΠΠΟΥ*

The most remarkable feature of this system was that while the gold, introduced about 345, was struck according to the Attic standard, the silver, coined throughout the reign, followed a local Macedonian standard with a tetradrachm of *c.* 14.52g, taken over by Philip from the substantial silver coinages of Amphipolis and the Chalcidian League. At the beginning of Philip's reign the gold was worth about $13\frac{1}{3}$ times its weight in silver, which meant that eight silver tetradrachms were nearly equivalent to one gold stater. The bronze was a token coinage, its value depending upon the state's guarantee to exchange it against coins of silver or gold. Of the two reverse types for the silver, the second (b: the jockey with palm branch) seems to have been the later, used from about 348 onwards.

The coins of Philip were struck at two or possibly three mints. The certain mints were Pella, the capital, and Amphipolis, the most important trading centre of the kingdom, while the more hypothetical third mint may have been at Aegae.[1]

Immediately after his accession Alexander introduced a new silver tetradrachm in Macedon (**5**). The obverse retains the laureate head of Zeus, while the reverse shows an eagle standing on a thunderbolt with head turned back and the inscription *ΑΛΕΞΑΝΔΡΟΥ*. In the field are two symbols, one of which, common to all surviving coins, is an oriental headdress, the *kyrbasia*, known from the representations of Persian satraps and other officials. The tetradrachms were struck according to the same Macedonian standard as Philip's silver, but the issue was presumably a small one as only five specimens (from three obverse dies and five reverses) plus a few overstruck pieces have survived to the present day. They were issued at Aegae or Amphipolis, and a few months would have sufficed for their production.[2] The eagle type of the reverse was continued, with some variations, on a number of drachms and fractions which certainly belong to the Amphipolis mint (**6**).

After this short interlude Alexander (during the winter 336/5?) carried through a major reform of the Macedonian royal coinage.[3] The main coins of his new system were:

Gold	Distater and stater, 17.28g and 8.67g (**7, 8**)	
	Obv.	Head of Athena r. in crested Corinthian helmet; on bowl, serpent.
	Rev.	Winged Nike standing l. holding wreath in r. and *stylis* in l. hand; *ΑΛΕΞΑΝΔΡΟΥ*.
Silver	Tetradrachm and drachm, 17.28g and 4.33g (**9, 10**)	
	Obv.	Head of Heracles r. in lion's skin
	Rev.	Zeus seated l. on throne, holding in r. hand eagle, in l. hand long sceptre; *ΑΛΕΞΑΝΔΡΟΥ*.
Bronze	Unit (**11**)	
	Obv.	Head of Heracles r. in lion's skin
	Rev.	Bow in case and club; *ΑΛΕΞΑΝΔΡΟΥ*.

1 Le Rider 1977 distributes the coinage between Pella and Amphipolis, but Price 1979b adds a third mint at Aegae. Price ascribes the Philip coins and the Alexander coins of the king's lifetime, which Le Rider followed Newell in giving to Amphipolis, to Pella, and vice versa. See also Price 1979a, 247–9.

2 The Macedonian origin of the eagle tetradrachms was established by Pegan 1968, a specimen having been found overstruck by Patraeus, king of Paeonia. Price 1979b, 239–40, ascribes them tentatively to Aegae.

3 Some have argued, however, that the Alexander coinage was introduced at a later date, 333 or even 331. See the discussion in Zervos 1982 (with comments by Price).

The most important innovation was undoubtedly that the silver coins were now also struck on the Attic standard, used by Philip only for his gold. In this way Alexander made his silver directly interchangeable with the most widely used trade coins of his time, the Athenian 'owl' tetradrachms, and increased its acceptability throughout the Mediterranean world. Within a few decades, thanks to the enormous metal resources at the disposal of Alexander and his successors, this silver currency superseded the Athenian coins as the leading trade coinage of Alexander's empire and far beyond its borders. Moreover, the extensive gold coinage brought about a change in the relation between the two precious metals from about $13\frac{1}{3}$:1 to 10:1, so that a simple rate of exchange could be obtained by striking gold and silver coins of the same or related weights. Five of Alexander's new tetradrachms would thus equal a gold stater in value.

While Alexander's new coinage was introduced throughout the eastern Mediterranean world, the barbarian tribes to the north of Macedon, the Illyrians and the Celts of the Danube region, apparently preferred the types of Philip's gold coins, which were widely imitated in this area. Consequently, in order to maintain the northern trade, Alexander continued to issue posthumous gold coins in the name of his father. This was done at both Amphipolis and Pella, and the issues seem to have continued down to about 328. These coins circulated to some extent in mainland Greece, as well as in the north, but they are never found in Asia Minor or further east. The silver coinage of Philip, on the other hand, seems to have come to a temporary end in 336.[4]

Another interesting feature of Alexander's reform was his choice of new types. The head of Heracles, the mythological ancestor of the Macedonian kings, had a long tradition as a coin type in Macedonia, and the seated Zeus may represent a full-figure version of the god shown on the obverse of Philip's tetradrachms. Whatever the Macedonian connotations, however, one can hardly doubt that these types were also chosen because of their more general appeal. They were, of course, immediately acceptable to every Greek. Heracles was the hero who had earned his way to heaven by fighting robbers and barbarians, and Zeus was the great Panhellenic deity and the common father of gods and men. At a later date these representations turned out, by chance, to be intelligible also to Alexander's oriental subjects, who could identify Heracles with their Melqart or Gilgamesh and find in the seated Zeus the likeness of their local Ba'als or whatever their Supreme God was called.

The types of the gold, on the other hand, are new to the Macedonian coinage. The head of Athena, taken by scholars and artists of the Renaissance to be a likeness of Alexander himself, was most probably a copy or adaptation of that of the colossal bronze statue of Athena Promachos by Pheidias on the Athenian Acropolis, although the serpent on the bowl of her helmet seems to have been added. The Nike of the reverse is an appropriate symbol of the expected victory in the Persian war, but one detail is difficult to explain. The most distinctive feature about her is the *stylis* in her left hand, for a ship's standard is a symbol normally indicating a *naval* victory. Yet great and manifold as they were, Alexander's victories can hardly be said

4 So Price 1979b, 240, and Zervos 1982, 186–8, where the cessation of Philip's silver is dated to 336 but the gold is recognized as having continued after that date.

to include any naval triumph of real significance, and the whole conduct of the Persian campaign in any case provides ample proof that a war at sea never had an important place in his designs. If the *stylis* cannot be explained from anything Alexander did or intended to do, it was presumably copied by Alexander from some well-known original. At Athens, in fact, at about this date, the golden statues of Nike on the Acropolis were being restored, and symbols of victories at sea would have been appropriate for these. Representations on Panathenaic vases show that some of the Nike figures were carrying sea trophies of this kind, and it has been suggested that Alexander, in a spirit of generosity, may have donated to the ancient maritime power one or more of these new statues after he had been elected commander-in-chief of the Panhellenic expedition against Persia and was preparing his campaign.[5] However this may be, it seems quite plausible that Alexander's choice of types for his gold coins was determined by an endeavour to establish a friendly connection with the Greek city that claimed for herself the first place in the centuries-old fight between Greeks and Persians.

Our knowledge of the production of coins by Alexander and the distribution of the various series among the different mints of the empire derives mainly from the analysis of a number of coin hoards buried during his reign or within a decade or so after his death. The fundamental work in this field was done by the American scholar E. T. Newell in a number of publications from the 1910s and 1920s.[6] For the most important coin, the silver tetradrachm, the enormous hoard found at Demanhur in Egypt in 1905 and comprising more than 8,000 specimens provided the basic material. The hoard was buried about 318/17 B.C. and contains practically all issues of any size down to about 319/18 B.C., that is to say the lifetime issues of Alexander plus the first issues of his successors. Newell was able to collect information on nearly 5,000 coins, and his classification of this body of material has become the basis of all subsequent research. It has even proved feasible to draw certain conclusions regarding the relative output of the different mints from the proportion of their coins in the hoard, and a more accurate calculation can be based on the number of dies, especially obverse dies, used for each coinage. The number of obverse dies for Alexander's lifetime and early posthumous issues was carefully listed by Newell, but only a small part of his materials has been published.

Alexander took over the Macedonian mints used by his father (Pella, Amphipolis and Aegae (?)), but now the mint of Amphipolis became by far the most important. Gold and especially silver was coined there in huge quantities and supplied the entire empire with money. Nearly a third of all listed tetradrachms in the Demanhur hoard derived from Amphipolis, and the number of obverse dies known – *c.* 700 down to 319/18 or four times as many as those of Babylon, the next mint in importance – clearly demonstrates the preponderance of Amphipolis

5 Cf. Bellinger 1963, 12–13, and Perlman 1965, 63–7.

6 Newell 1912, 1915 (Cyprus mints), 1916 (Sidon and Ake), 1918a (Tarsus), 1919b (Myriandrus), 1921b (Kyparissia hoard, *IGCH* 76), 1923a (Demanhur hoard, *IGCH* 1664), 1923b (Andritsaena hoard, *IGCH* 83), 1923c (Tyre). A useful survey of Alexander's lifetime coinages is provided by Le Rider in the annual reports of the work of his section in the *Annuaire de l'École pratique des Hautes Études* (Le Rider 1969c, 1970, 1971a).

over all other mints. Moreover, as the Demanhur find was made in Egypt, it also shows that the Amphipolitan silver was exported in quantity from Macedonia to the eastern provinces of Alexander's realm.

In comparison with Amphipolis, Pella was at this time a small mint and its tetradrachms seem to have circulated mainly in Macedonia and mainland Greece. Only 56 Pella coins were listed from Demanhur, while their proportion in hoards from Greece is larger. The coinage ascribed to Aegae is also modest, but is noteworthy for the large proportion of gold coins, including a remarkable number of distaters (**12**).[7] Thirteen obverse dies are recorded for the gold as against ten for the silver tetradrachms.

In the spring of 334 Alexander crossed with his army into Asia Minor and began his Persian campaign. Our historical sources are at pains to stress the financial difficulties of the young conqueror, depicting him as practically broke at the outset of the expedition. His substantial coin production in Macedonia from 336 to 334 is, however, a telling argument against this tradition. Undoubtedly the resources of the Macedonian kingdom, especially from the mines, were still quite adequate both for maintaining supremacy in Greece and for financing the military expedition. This is not to say that Alexander may not have experienced momentary financial difficulties during the first two years of his campaign, but basically his fiscal position seems to have been sound.

During the campaign of 334 Alexander conquered most of western Asia Minor before going into winter quarters. In the area he occupied most of the cities were Greek in culture and whether they submitted voluntarily or had to be taken by force they had, as a consequence of Alexander's own Panhellenic propaganda, to be regarded as liberated from the Persian yoke. They were most probably incorporated in the Corinthian League and seem to have enjoyed the same position as the Greek states of the mainland. Alexander had no reason to establish royal mints in any of these cities at the moment and could still rely on his Macedonian mints for the necessary money for his war.

In 333 a new situation arose. Alexander was at Gordium in the early summer (April/July ?). When (in August ?) he advanced into Cilicia, he apparently felt that the lines of communication with Macedonia had become uncomfortably long and consequently decided to set up a royal mint at Tarsus, the administrative centre of the newly conquered province (**13**). During the preceding period several Persian satraps had used Tarsus as a mint for substantial military issues, so that Alexander would have found all the necessary personnel and installations ready on his arrival. His first issues of tetradrachms show the old die engravers continuing their work for the new master, for the seated Zeus on the reverse is clearly cut by the same hand that had earlier produced a seated Ba'altarz for the last Persian satrap, Mazaeus. The position of the figure shows a few unavoidable corrections to make it conform to Alexander's type, but apart from that all the details of the human body and the throne are identical. Alexander issued coins in all three metals: gold, silver and bronze. Down to about 318 B.C. approximately 70 obverse dies

7 These issues were attributed to Sicyon by Newell and in Noe's monograph (Noe 1950), issues 1–16. See, however, Troxell 1971, 42–4, and, for the attribution to Aegae, Price 1979a, 239–40.

were used for the most common denomination, the silver tetradrachm, which means that the production of the Tarsus mint during this period reached only about 10% of that of Amphipolis.

In addition to the Alexander coinage, the mint of Tarsus also produced two series of local coins: staters or double sigloi struck on the Persian standard and weighing about 11.20g. The first issue (**14**) has been dated *c.* 327 B.C.[8] and clearly imitates the preceding issues of Mazaeus. The obverse type is the seated Ba'al of Tarsus, whose name is inscribed in Aramaic, and the reverse shows an animal group of bull and lion in combat above two lines of city wall. The ear of wheat in the field of the obverse presumably symbolizes the fertility of the Cilician Plain, while the club on the reverse is the weapon of the local god Sandan, who was identified with Heracles by the Greeks. The initials of Tarsus, Mallus, Soli and Issus, the four most important cities of eastern Cilicia, appear in Greek letters on the coins to show that the issue was struck on the authority of, and financed by, these cities. Die links between the specimens reveal, however, that they were struck at one place, undoubtedly Tarsus. Some of the coins show the Greek letter *B* in a prominent position on the reverse. A similar issue of Persic staters was produced *c.* 325/4 for the same four cities. Ba'al of Tarsus remains on the obverse, but without the Aramaic inscription. The reverse type is now a facing head of Athena in a triple-crested helmet. A most interesting specimen (**15**) of this group was issued in the name of Balacrus, the Macedonian satrap of Cilicia from 333 to *c.* 323. The occurrence of this satrapal coin in what is generally regarded as a municipal issue raises some interesting questions concerning the relationship between satraps and cities.

After his victory at Issus in November 333 Alexander quickly became master of northern Syria and Phoenicia apart from Tyre and Gaza. He had to remain for seven months before the walls of Tyre in order to subdue the city, and then had to spend two more months besieging Gaza before he was able to move on to Egypt in the winter of 332. During this period mints proliferated: Myriandrus (**16**) (later renamed Alexandria near Issus, the modern Iskenderun) in Cilicia; Aradus (**17**), Byblus (**18**), Sidon (**19**) and Ake (**20**) in Phoenicia; Damascus (**21**) in Syria, and Salamis (**22**) on the island of Cyprus. In most of these places Alexander was able to take over local facilities already existing, but in the case of Damascus and Ake new mints were opened. The choice of Damascus was perhaps prompted by the accident that here Alexander acquired the rich booty left by Darius after Issus. Ake was presumably a substitute for Tyre and Gaza, which were not allowed to continue as mints after their capture.[9] In the case of Ake we know that the mint was started by transferring workmen and an obverse die from Sidon to the new establishment. At some of the mints (Byblus, Sidon, Damascus and Salamis) the Phoenician practice of using adjusted dies was adopted.

While the majority of Alexander's coins are attributed to the different mints by arranging series of issues according to die linkage and general stylistic considerations, some of the Syro-Phoenician mints identify their coinage by placing the initials of the city on the coins. This is

8 Newell 1918a, 84–5.

9 The coinage attributed by Newell to Ake has been ascribed to Tyre by Lemaire 1976, on which theory see Price 1979a, 241–6.

the case with Aradus (*A* or monogram) and Damascus (ΔA) as also with Sidon (Σ or ΣI) and Ake (Phoenician initials). The issues from Sidon and Ake are especially important for the scientific arrangement of Alexander's coinages by providing us with a series of annual dates. Through a careful analysis of the material, Newell was able to work out the chronology, showing that Sidon started to strike in 333/2, i.e. before October 332. The first issues of Ake were undated, but the use here of one of the obverse dies from Sidon year 333/2 shows that it cannot have started much later and was presumably already functioning during 332. While Sidon used an era of Alexander, dating from the battle of Issus or from his arrival in the town, Ake, when it began to date its coins in 328/7, preferred a local era with the year 347/6 as the starting point, presumably the accession year of some unknown dynast who retained his position under Alexander and the Diadochi. Production was rather small at both mints, Sidon using 24 and Ake 25 obverse dies for tetradrachms down to 319/18. The same applies to other mints of the area such as Myriandrus and Salamis. While Damascus and Byblus had sizeable issues, Aradus boasted an even greater output, using about 150 obverse dies for tetradrachms down to *c.* 318.

In Phoenicia and Cyprus the cities were governed by local kings who were permitted to continue their reigns if they embraced the cause of Alexander, as most did. At Sidon a new king was appointed to replace a ruler with Persian sympathies. The cities were apparently exempted from the direct control of a provincial governor and left with a certain amount of autonomy in their internal affairs. This may explain the use of city initials in this area. At Byblus, Alexander tetradrachms were even marked with the initials of the local king Ainel (**23**), who also issued coins of local types in his own name (**24**). On the other hand, the series of dated gold hemistaters of Pumiathon, king of Citium, who reigned from *c.* 361 to 312, shows a clear break (below, pp. 57–8). During ten years, from 332 to 323/2, their minting was discontinued. The larger denominations of all mints in this area were struck with Alexander's types and in his name. It is therefore hardly proper to make a distinction between 'imperial' mints and 'allied' mints, as Newell was inclined to do. The explanation is rather that, while the other mints were government agencies, the Phoenician and Cypriot city-states under their local kings retained the management of their mints, although they naturally had to operate within the general regulations laid down by the central administration.

Alexander spent the winter of 332/1 in Egypt, where he was received as a liberator by the native population. During the last period of Persian rule, from 343 to 332, the Persian king and his satraps had coined imitations of Athenian 'owl' tetradrachms of good silver and correct weight but inscribed in Demotic (**25**) or Aramaic.[10] They were in all probability struck at Memphis, the seat of the satraps. The last satrap, Mazaces, who governed Egypt for less than a year, has left us only a few coins of Egyptian manufacture (**26**). He turned over his satrapy to Alexander without fighting and was apparently rewarded by being appointed governor of some city or district in Babylonia, where another coin series appears later in his name (below, p. 57).

10 For an issue of Artaxerxes III, struck between 343 and 338, see Mørkholm and Shore 1974. The issues of Sabaces and Mazaces have been published by Nicolet-Pierre 1979. The attempt of Lipinski 1982 to transfer the coinage of Sabaces to the town of Syene (modern Assuan) is hardly convincing.

During the spring of 331 (February ?) Alexander made his famous visit to the oracle of Ammon in the oasis of Siwah. On his way there he made a short stop to found the first and most famous of his colonies, Alexandria in Egypt. Destined to become the largest trading centre of the eastern Mediterranean, Alexandria was in due course to be provided with a mint. There can hardly be any doubt that this was part of Alexander's original plan, but owing to the large scale of the foundation the mint was not ready to start working before a somewhat later date, towards 326/5 (below, p. 52).

In the late spring of 331 Alexander marched north from Egypt along the coast, then turned eastwards to fight the last and decisive battle of Gaugamela (October 331). Shortly afterwards he entered the metropolis of Babylon in triumph. The great city was surrendered without a fight by a high-ranking Persian, the redoubtable Mazaeus, former satrap of Cilicia and Syria, who had been loyal to his master up till now but apparently despaired of further resistance to the conqueror. At Babylon a new mint was established, issuing Alexander coins in great quantity (**27**).[11] Down to *c.* 319/18 about 175 different obverse dies for tetradrachms were used at Babylon, making the mint second only to Amphipolis in output, although its production still amounted only to 20–25% of that of the Macedonian mint. At one point, *c.* 327/6, this mint also struck decadrachms (**30**), heavy lumps of silver weighing more than 40g, with the same types and monograms as the contemporary tetradrachms. These coins were hardly practical to use and the experiment was short-lived. It may be that the issue had a special commemorative function, celebrating Alexander's victories in the East, but this is far from certain.

The rich and important province of Babylonia was placed under Mazaeus, thus advertising Alexander's policy of reconciliation with the Persian nobility. The satrap was also allowed to issue coins in his own name. A series of staters and smaller denominations show the seated figure of Ba'al from Tarsus on the obverse, identified by an Aramaic inscription, while the reverse carries a walking lion above which is the name of Mazaeus in Aramaic (**28**). The staters of this coinage were struck to the same weight as the Attic tetradrachms. After the death of Mazaeus in 328 the series continued down to about 280 but without any satrap's name. At the same time the weights became very irregular, quite a few pieces in good condition weighing below 16.00g. In addition to this local silver a substantial series of gold coins was also struck at Babylon. These double darics (**29**), weighing *c.* 16.80g, together with a few darics, showed on the obverse a royal figure moving right and carrying bow and spear. The incuse of the reverse has a peculiar geometric pattern, and the issues were further distinguished from the earlier Persian coins by various Greek monograms or initials placed on the obverse. The series is generally assumed to have lasted until *c.* 300.

To the years between 331 and 323 we may also ascribe a very odd and definitely 'oriental' series of silver coins with Aramaic inscriptions of rather irregular weights which tend to concentrate between *c.* 8.00g and 8.55g, showing them to be Attic didrachms. The types are often imitated from earlier or contemporary issues from Cilicia and Phoenicia. The legends give the name of *Manbog*, Aramaic for Hierapolis-Bambyce in northern Syria, the great temple-

11 Waggoner 1979a. Her promised full study on the subject never appeared.

state of Hadad and Atargatis who appear in the coin types and legends.[12] An interesting specimen (**31**) shows on the obverse a female facing head with the Aramaic inscription ʿ*Ateh* (= Atargatis). The reverse is a close copy of an Alexander tetradrachm from Tarsus with a plough symbol. The Aramaic inscription reads 'Hadad of Manbog'. We find two further high-priests, ʿAbdhadad and ʾAbyati, signing some coins (**32**), but the greater number were issued in the name of Alexander, as for example a specimen (**33**) showing on the obverse the head of Atargatis and on the reverse a struggle between lion and bull, again copied from Tarsus, with the inscription ʿLKSNDR. There can hardly be any doubt that the famous sanctuary obtained a special privilege for striking these coins and showed its gratitude by placing the name of Alexander on most of the coinage, which will have had a strictly local use. It is impossible to decide whether ʿAbdhadad and ʾAbyati preceded or succeeded the Macedonian conqueror or were contemporary with him.

After the surrender of Babylon Alexander continued his expedition into the eastern satrapies, capturing the huge Persian royal treasures at Susa and Persepolis. At Ecbatana in 330 the Panhellenic expedition against Persia came to an official end, and Alexander continued his campaign in the eastern parts of the Persian empire as king of Macedon and heir, by right of conquest, to the Persian throne. The death of Darius III in the summer of 330 relieved Alexander of a rival and made it possible for him to assume the role of legitimate successor to the Achaemenid dynasty. However, the pacification of the eastern provinces and the following expedition to India covered the next four years, and the march back from the Hyphasis another two years, so that Alexander did not return to Susa until 324. From the numismatic point of view this phase of Alexander's career can be dealt with briefly. Although it has been assumed that some of the double darics and lion staters may have been minted in the eastern satrapies, we have no good evidence that a mint was ever operating east of Babylon during Alexander's reign.[13] Even if some Alexander coins of uncertain attribution should prove to be of eastern origin, there exists no large group of coins unaccounted for that can be assigned to this region, and there is nothing to substantiate the theory that the Persian treasures of precious metal were turned into coin primarily at Susa and Ecbatana, as might have been expected. We are thus faced with a dilemma: either Alexander financed his eastern campaigns, which lasted for six years, with money brought from Babylon or elsewhere, or his soldiers were living off the land without any payment in coin during this long period. Neither explanation looks very satisfactory, but it is hardly possible to argue that a substantial eastern issue of Alexander coins has disappeared without trace.

Prior to 331 Alexander's coinage can be divided among eleven mints. To the three Macedonian ones inherited from Philip eight new ones were added in 333/2, all placed in a restricted geographical area defined by Tarsus to the north, Ake to the south, Damascus to the east and Salamis in Cyprus to the west. Babylon, opened immediately after its capture in 331, was the only Alexander mint east of the Euphrates. In the eastern mints the snake on Athena's helmet

12 Seyrig 1971, 11–21.
13 Bellinger 1963, 70–7.

on the gold staters was sometimes replaced by a running lion-griffin or a sphinx. This innovation seems to date from 331, although the more common bird-headed griffin first appears after Alexander's death.[14]

As already mentioned, Alexander established no new mints in the East during his further campaigns. But while he was away, important developments had taken place in the western parts of his realm.

In about 330 a new mint was opened in Sardis, the capital of the ancient Lydian kingdom and the centre of a satrapy since the days of Persian rule. During the first years mostly gold staters (**34**) were struck, but from *c.* 325/4 a distinctive feature of the mint became its great output of drachms (**35**). While at the mints already mentioned the most frequent silver coin was the tetradrachm, at Sardis the production of drachms soon came to be far more important. Gold was still coined in relative abundance with a marked increase during the years 321 to 318, while the silver tetradrachms are quite rare before *c.* 320.

The same thing happened at a number of other mints, all located in Greek cities in the western part of Asia Minor.[15] In Ionia, Magnesia on the Maeander started to produce Alexander coins, gold staters and silver drachms, around 330 or 329, to be followed by Colophon (**36**) and Miletus (**37, 38**) *c.* 325, and Teos *c.* 324. At the Hellespont, Lampsacus (**39**) began minting Alexander coins around 329 or 328 and a subsidiary mint was opened *c.* 325 in neighbouring Abydus (**40**). In all these mints the silver drachm was by far the most common denomination to be struck. It is difficult to explain this phenomenon in any other way than as a deliberate division of labour, the government reserving the main production of silver drachms for these special mints, while the other imperial mints concentrated on the production of tetradrachms. Hoard evidence shows that the drachms from Asia Minor did circulate throughout the empire, and there can hardly be doubt that the specialization was brought about by a decision of some central authority. During the reign of Alexander and down to *c.* 319/18 Sardis remained the most productive of the mints, followed by Colophon and Lampsacus. The issues of Magnesia, Miletus and Abydus were medium-sized, while Teos was a relatively small mint. Sardis, Miletus, Lampsacus and Abydus struck in addition some tetradrachm issues (**40**), with Miletus and Lampsacus being the most productive in this denomination. All the mints supplemented their silver by substantial issues in gold (**34, 38**), from 323 to 317 sometimes in the form of posthumous staters of Philip II's type (below, p. 57). Gold issues were especially large at Lampsacus and Abydus.

All the western drachm mints, with the exception of Sardis, were located in Greek cities on or near the coast. The cities were presumably exempted from direct control by the satraps and in all probability were members of the Corinthian League. The establishment of royal mints in them would have been legally an infringement of their rights, even if they were allowed to

14 Hill 1923.

15 On the drachm mints of Asia Minor see Thompson and Bellinger 1955. A fuller study is being prepared by Margaret Thompson, but only the first section, on Sardis and Miletus, has appeared (Thompson 1983). On the posthumous issues of Philip II's gold staters see Thompson 1982.

participate in their management and may even have derived some financial advantage from their activity. In any case the opening of these mints testifies to Alexander's change of attitude towards the Greeks. Having become king of Persia, Alexander would have found his position as *hegemon* of the League more of an encumbrance than before, and on several occasions he chose to disregard the charter of the League in order to pursue his own policy. His mints in western Asia Minor provide a further instance of the increasing self-reliance of the king and his growing neglect of outdated political forms as, in this case, the autonomy and freedom from interference guaranteed to the Greek cities by their membership of the Corinthian League.

Returning to the Levant we find that about 329/8 several new mints for Alexander coinage were established in Cyprus. Citium, the neighbour and rival of Salamis, struck a sizeable coinage (**41**) (about 50 tetradrachm obverses down to *c.* 319), while smaller issues were produced at Paphos and Amathus which used 12 and 11 tetradrachm obverses respectively during the same period. At Marium and Soli very limited issues were apparently produced, and the same may have happened at Nagidus or Soli in Cilicia. Small mints also operated, apparently only for very short periods of time, in Syria, where there was a coinage at Hierapolis-Bambyce referred to already, and in Phoenicia where coins were struck at Carne and at Berytus. For all these smaller issues a *terminus ante quem* is given by their occurrence in the Demanhur hoard (*IGCH* 1664), buried in 318,[16] but it is impossible to date them more exactly within the preceding period, so that often we cannot tell whether they were struck before or after Alexander's death.

In this region we also find the earliest examples of an important innovation in the inscription. While the coins, both gold and silver, were originally inscribed *ΑΛΕΞΑΝΔΡΟΥ*, at some date, *c.* 329 according to Newell, the title *ΒΑΣΙΛΕΩΣ*, 'king', was added on the issues of Myriandrus (**16**). The new legend was copied at Citium almost at once (**41**), so closely indeed that the earliest issues in each mint used the spelling *ΑΛΕΞΑΝΔΡ* instead of *ΑΛΕΞΑΝΔΡΟΥ* and placed the two words of the inscription in exactly the same unusual position, with the title in the right field and the name below the seated Zeus. Other mints to pick up the new legend quickly were Amathus in Cyprus and Aradus, both *c.* 328. It is, however, a curious fact that the use of the royal title never became universal, and that in such an apparently important matter a wide measure of discretion should be left to the directors of the various mints. Among the major mints, Amphipolis adopted the title *c.* 325, Babylon *c.* 324 and Tarsus only in 323. Neighbouring mints often followed different practices, and several never used the title at all during Alexander's lifetime. This applies to places like Pella, Damascus, Byblus, Sidon and Ake. The picture becomes even more complicated when we see that, at Myriandrus, coins with and without the title were issued concurrently, while at Amathus the title was adopted quite early, only to be dropped after a few years.

16 Newell 1923a.

About 326/5 two important new mints started striking in the East. Alexandria in Egypt began the production of a very beautiful series of coins (**42**).[17] The Zeus on the reverse of its tetradrachms is represented in a less rigid pose with crossed legs, and the Heracles head of the obverse radiates a human dignity which has led many scholars to assume that the artist was intending an idealized portrait of Alexander himself. Personally I have never been convinced by the argument that Alexander was actually portrayed as Heracles on the tetradrachms during his lifetime, but, if he was, the early issues of Alexandria have the best claim to be regarded as portrait coins. The new style of Alexandria was copied at other mints, the first being Sidon in 325/4. Babylon followed *c.* 323 and Ake in 322/1, but it was not until *c.* 315/310 that the cross-legged Zeus won almost universal acceptance.

The second mint to begin striking coins in 326/5 was situated somewhere on the southern coast of Asia Minor (**43**). Phaselis in Lycia and Side in Pamphylia have both been suggested, but as Side was in the fourth century the more active trading centre of the two, the general probability is in favour of attributing this substantial series to her rather than to Phaselis.[18] In the period from 326/5 to 319/18 approximately 45 obverse dies for tetradrachms are known from this mint, while Alexandria for the same period used only 43.

The considerable increase in the number of mints, especially in western Asia Minor and in the Levant between *c.* 330 and 326/5, reflects a demand for more coins of the imperial type and gives us an indication of the boom in trade which followed Alexander's conquest of the Persian empire. In or around 325 there was a great expansion in output at some of the mints, especially at Amphipolis and Side and at the drachm mints in Asia Minor. It is possible that this increase was partly due to the need to provide money for the Greek and Macedonian veterans and mercenaries, who, being demobilized in great numbers in 324 and 323, were returning to their homes.[19]

One unique and exceptionally interesting coin series remains to be discussed. A few decadrachms (**44**) belonging to it have long been known.[20] They show on the obverse a war elephant with two persons on its back attacked by a horseman carrying a spear charging from the left. The two on the elephant try to stave him off, the *mahout* or driver turning around to defend his passenger. The reverse type is a standing male figure in military dress that includes a Phrygian helmet with a peculiar decoration of upright plumes. He leans on his spear and carries in his extended right hand the thunderbolt of Zeus. The goddess of victory flies towards the right carrying a wreath to be placed on the warrior's head. The coins are anepigraphic except for the monogram on the reverse and the single letter Ξ on the obverse. The coins all *seem* to derive from Mesopotamia or further east, and a hoard discovered near Babylon *c.* 1973 has considerably

17 This is the generally accepted view, but it may be that the Egyptian mint was first established at Memphis, the old capital, and transferred to Alexandria only at a later date. [Cf. Zervos 1967.]

18 The attribution to Side has been questioned by Price 1979a, 249–50, but see Thompson 1981a, 44–8.

19 Thompson 1984.

20 Hill in *BMC, Arabia, etc.*, cxlv–cxlvi (dated 'shortly after Alexander's death'), and Hill 1927, 205–6 (dated 'just after the Indian expedition').

increased our material. In addition to four or five decadrachms this hoard also contained a number of tetradrachms having on the obverse an Indian archer shooting with his long bow and on the reverse an elephant (**45**), with the same monogram and letter as the decadrachms. A single tetradrachm (**46**) from the hoard shows the archer in a quadriga of horses, and, on the reverse, an elephant with two persons on its back.[21] The weights of the tetradrachms are quite irregular and fall well below the Attic standard, resembling in this respect the later lion staters from Babylon which were in some cases used as flans for the new issue.

In spite of the absence of any inscription, the types of the decadrachms are eloquent enough. The obverse clearly depicts a scene from the battle between Alexander and the Indian king Porus which took place in 326 at the River Hydaspes. Here for the first time the Macedonian army encountered war elephants in large numbers and was clearly impressed by them. Although Alexander did not fight personally with Porus, the horseman is undoubtedly intended to represent the Macedonian king. The die cutter took the same liberty as the creator of the famous Alexander mosaic from Pompeii, who confronted Alexander and King Darius in order to concentrate the whole battle in a single vivid and dramatic scene. The figure on the reverse, wearing a Macedonian cloak, a Persian headdress and Greek armour, must be Alexander himself, carrying the thunderbolt in the same way as in the painting of Apelles in Ephesus known to us through literary references.

Where were these interesting coins struck and when? As already mentioned, they derive from the eastern part of the empire, and, as we have seen, Babylon is the only mint known with certainty to have operated in this area during Alexander's lifetime. But around 323 a mint was opened at Susa, where the coinage may also have been produced. This leads to the second, and more important, question: were the coins struck by Alexander himself or by the central government during the first year following his death? The commemorative aspect of the types is obvious, and it might be argued that Alexander had a more immediate interest in celebrating his eastern campaign after his return to Persia and Mesopotamia in 324, when games and festivals were arranged in order to wipe out the memory of the appalling march through the Carmanian desert. What on such an occasion would be more appropriate than a reference to his last major battle, fought in distant India at the boundaries of the known world? The great marriage celebration in Susa or, perhaps even better, the discharge of his Macedonian veterans at Opis, would have been suitable occasions for a commemorative issue to be distributed among the participants as a royal largesse. It therefore seems plausible that Alexander himself was responsible for the issue that glorified his military deeds in India, [though it has recently been argued that the coins were struck not by Alexander at all but by the Indian prince Taxiles, an idea supported by the poor technical quality of the coins and the absence of Alexander's name.[22]] If Alexander

21 Dürr 1976, 43, and 1974; *CH* 1 (1975), no. 38. For the quadriga coin, see Bank Leu 13 (29. iv. 1975), lot 132. There is a detailed study of these coinages in Price 1982a [though Mørkholm did not find it entirely satisfactory, and cf. now Hollstein 1989].

22 [Hollstein 1989.]

were responsible, however, the reverse type of the decadrachms would be a document of crucial importance for the discussion of Alexander's claim to deification, a claim for which we have written evidence from the last years of Alexander's reign.

5

PHILIP III AND THE EARLY POSTHUMOUS COINAGE

With the death of Alexander in Babylon on 10 June 323, his realm passed to his half-brother, Philip III Arrhidaeus, but the succession rights of his posthumous son Alexander, born some months after his father's death, were also recognized. Owing to the mental disability of the new king, power was officially entrusted to a triumvirate consisting of Antipater, viceroy in Macedon, Craterus, a distinguished general who was to act as a guardian for the royal house, and Perdiccas, *chiliarch* or grand-vizier of Asia. Perdiccas, alone of the three, was present at Babylon where the agreement was worked out, and being in charge it was easy for him to acquire full control of the central administration. In the distribution of the satrapies that followed, Ptolemy obtained Egypt and Lysimachus Thrace, while Antigonus the One-eyed (Monophthalmus) was confirmed as satrap of Phrygia, including the neighbouring provinces of Lycia and Pamphylia. There is no need here to try to follow the complicated political manoeuvres and open warfare between Alexander's generals during the next few years except insofar as this is necessary to an understanding of the development of the coinage and its placing in a proper historical context.

In 321 Perdiccas, who was suspected of wanting the throne for himself, was killed during an expedition against Ptolemy, who had refused to submit to the central government. A new arrangement was worked out at Triparadeisus in Syria which left Antipater as head of the government and guardian of the kings. Among the other changes, the most important were that Antigonus, while retaining his satrapy in Asia Minor, received the military command over all Asia, and Seleucus was now appointed satrap of Babylon. When Antipater died in 319 he was followed as regent by Polyperchon, much to the dismay of his own son, the ambitious Cassander, who soon revolted against his father's nominee. The most important event of the following year was the murder of Philip III and his wife in October 317 by Olympias, the mother of Alexander, who acted on behalf of Polyperchon and in defence of the interests of her grandson. With the death of Philip the coinage in his name naturally came to an end, while that with Alexander's name continued. In 316 Cassander was able to recover Macedon and put Olympias to death, securing for himself the boy Alexander, who was recognized as king with a separate reckoning of regnal years that began with the death of Philip. In the east the winter of 317/16 saw the final triumph of Antigonus over the Greek general Eumenes, which left him in a position of undisputed authority over Asia.

About the time of Alexander's death, or during the first years of Philip's reign, some reorganization of coin production in Asia must have taken place. A number of mints in the Levant such as Damascus, Byblus, and the Cypriot mints except Salamis were certainly closed by

319/18. As they issued no coins with the name of Philip some of them may have been closed even earlier. Side in Pamphylia and Myriandrus in Cilicia struck a few issues for the new king before ending production, and as specimens of all their issues were present in the Demanhur hoard they must have been closed by 319/18 at the latest. Similarly, Sardis and Miletus were closed temporarily from 319/18.

Philip III took over the types of his great predecessor without any change for his gold and silver coinage, though with his own name. An indication of the great prestige still attached to Alexander, however, is the fact that coins bearing his name continued to be struck at practically all mints still operating, often concurrently with those of his successor. Some mints even coined exclusively in the name of Alexander, though it is not always easy to be sure whether this refers to the great conqueror or to Alexander IV.

It is in any case impossible to discern any pattern behind the distribution of the two coinages. A survey of the mints shows that the name of Philip appears on coins from Babylon (**47**), Sidon, Aradus (**48**) and Salamis, in addition to those from Side and Myriandrus already mentioned. On the other hand, important mints like Alexandria and Tarsus never used it, and neither did Ake. In Europe a single issue from Pella, presumably struck after 321, when Philip returned to Macedon with Antipater, carries the name of Philip. The huge issues from Amphipolis are all, on the other hand, struck in the name of Alexander. All the drachm mints of Asia Minor (**49–52**) struck for the new king but the extent of their emissions with Philip's name differs greatly. Miletus struck only a few bronzes for Philip (**53**). One might expect that the central government, headed by Perdiccas, would have been eager to have the name of the new king, who was effectively their puppet, advertised as widely as possible, in which case the absence of coins in Philip's name might imply opposition to the central authority and Perdiccas. This explanation, plausible for Alexandria under the authority of Ptolemy, could also cover the situation in Cyprus, where the mints of cities which were allied with Ptolemy against Perdiccas in 321 never struck for Philip, while Citium, which sided with Perdiccas, did strike Philip's coins. Similar considerations might also be applicable to the Macedonian mints under Antipater before 321, but it will not cover all the cases. We have no evidence that the mint of Tarsus, for instance, was under the control of a hostile governor, and the same official would presumably have been responsible for Myriandrus in the same province. And although Sidon and Ake were neighbouring mints, both located in Phoenicia, they followed different paths. Unlikely as it sounds, it would seem that the decision of whether to place Philip's name on the coinage was in many places left to the discretion of the mint directors, rather low-ranking officials, just as was the case with the addition of the royal title to Alexander's name in the 320s.

Simultaneously with the closing of several Levantine mints (*c.* 323–319) two new mints make their appearance. It is hardly surprising that a mint was established around this time at Susa (**54**), the capital of an important satrapy, but the establishment of a new mint at Marathus, so close to the very productive mint of Aradus, is more difficult to explain. In 332, when Alexander arrived in Phoenicia, Marathus was definitely in the possession of the king of Aradus, and the establishment of a mint there *c.* 320 must reflect a change in its political status. Both Susa and Marathus coined in the name of Philip as well as in that of Alexander, but as none of their coins was present in the Demanhur hoard they can hardly have started their production much before *c.* 320. The Philip coinage of Aradus will have started at the same time, as it is also absent from Demanhur.

After 323 important new developments occurred at various mints. In Europe both Pella and Amphipolis resumed the striking of coins in gold and silver with the types and denominations used by Philip II (**55**). At Pella these coins continued to *c.* 315, while at Amphipolis they were produced down to the arrival of Demetrius Poliorcetes in 294. The reason behind these issues was primarily their popularity with the barbarian tribes of the Balkans. At about the same time the drachm mints of Asia Minor, with the exception of Miletus, inaugurated a gold coinage with the types of Philip II (**56**). As these coins were often struck concurrently with silver issues in the name of Philip III, and as both categories were inscribed *ΦΙΛΙΠΠΟΥ* without any royal title, it is tempting to see a reference to the new king in the sudden appearance at several mints of his father's coinage. Arrhidaeus was after all renamed Philip at his accession precisely in order to stress his descent and perhaps also to indicate a political orientation towards the 'Macedonian' programme of his father rather than the more ambitious policy of Alexander, which involved reconciliation and co-operation with Persians and other orientals. By 316/15 the drachm mints of Asia Minor had interrupted their production, with the exception of Colophon and Magnesia. During the following five or six years, indeed, Colophon emerged as the most prolific mint of the area.

To the period 323–316 can also be attributed a number of local issues in the Asiatic parts of the kingdom. Mention has already been made of the satrapal lion staters and double darics of Babylon which continued after Alexander's death. In the same area we also find a series of imitations of Athenian tetradrachms (**57**).[1] Their style is often very bad, but the silver seems to be good and the weights are normal. Most of them carry blundered versions of the original inscription *ΑΘΕ*, but some were struck by Mazaces, whom we have already met (above, p. 47) as the last Persian satrap of Egypt. The provenance of these coins is always Mesopotamia or Babylonia, and their occurrence, in very fine condition, in several mixed hoards of this area suggests that they were minted *c.* 325–315. There can hardly be any doubt that Mazaces issued these coins *after* having come from Egypt to Babylonia with Alexander. Presumably he received the governorship of a city or a district from Alexander as a reward for his peaceful surrender of Egypt in 332.

It is, however, the island of Cyprus which offers the best evidence for the revival of local coinages after 323.[2] Between that date and the Ptolemaic campaign of 315 coins were issued by the kings of Lapethus and Marium. From King Praxippus of Lapethus we have only a few bronze coins (**58**), while Stasioecus II of Marium struck in gold, silver (**59**), and bronze. More important is the series of gold hemistaters (**60**) of Attic weight, issued by Pumiathon of Citium, showing the traditional types of this mint: on the obverse a fighting Heracles, on the reverse a lion bringing down a stag and the king's title and name rendered in Aramaic. These coins are dated by regnal years, and the dates show that after an interruption of nine years the issue was

1 Le Rider 1972a.
2 Mørkholm 1978a.

resumed in year 40, which has been equated with 323/2, and that further issues date from years 46 and 47 (317/16 and 316/15).

At Paphos King Nicocles first asserted his claim to the coinage in a curiously clandestine way. On no fewer than seven obverse dies of the Alexander coinage from Paphos between *c.* 323 and 319 he added his name in minute letters concealed among the tufts of the lion's mane (**61**).[3] The legend is hardly visible to the naked eye and likely to have become indecipherable after a short period of circulation. The careful concealment of the letters gives the impression that Nicocles felt that he was involved in a venture which might have hazardous consequences. The logical date for the issue would be the years around 321, when Paphos together with Salamis, Amathus and Soli joined a coalition with Ptolemy of Egypt directed against Perdiccas. The king of Paphos may well have felt tempted to put his own name on the coinage, but with political conditions so uncertain he was too shrewd and cautious to do so openly and hit upon the idea of signing his obverses in this furtive and clandestine manner, leaving the reverses to show the name of Alexander as usual. At a later date, probably around 315, Nicocles abandoned all subterfuge and issued an Attic tetradrachm in his own name (**62**). The obverse shows a head of Aphrodite wearing a turreted crown, the reverse the figure of Apollo seated on the *omphalos* carrying bow and arrow, all very similar to the representation later adopted by Antiochus I and his successors as the conventional reverse type for Seleucid silver coinage. The reverse legend includes the names of both the king and the city.

The important kingdom of Salamis was from 331 in the possession of Nicocreon, who died in 311/10. On the analogy of Pumiathon of Citium his coins, gold staters of Attic weight and silver didrachms and tetrobols of Rhodian weight, should belong to the period after 323. The gold stater is adorned with two female heads, both representing Aphrodite-Astarte and one identifiable by its turreted crown as a city-goddess (**63**). The silver coins (**64**) show on the obverse the turreted Aphrodite, on the reverse a head of Apollo. Coins of the same type were minted by Menelaus, the Egyptian governor of Cyprus after 311/10 (below, pp. 61–2; **65**).

By 316 the kingdom of Alexander was already, for all practical purposes, divided among a number of his former generals and associates, although the fiction of the unity of the empire was maintained and the young Alexander IV recognized as king, as we know from the dating clauses of Egyptian papyri and Babylonian cuniform tablets. Cassander was in possession of Macedon and the child-king, while the former regent Polyperchon was reduced to some districts of the Peloponnese. In Thrace Lysimachus continued his efforts to control his satrapy, while Egypt was safe in the hands of Ptolemy. But the overwhelming military and economic resources at the disposal of Antigonus the One-eyed made him a danger to his colleagues. After the defeat of Eumenes in early 316 he dismissed and appointed satraps at his will in the eastern satrapies. One of his nominees, Aspeisas of Susiana, put his name on a single issue of tetradrachms from Susa (**66**) but was apparently quickly told to discontinue this practice.[4] In late 316 Seleucus,

3 Newell 1919a; May 1952.
4 Robinson 1921.

the governor of Babylonia, when called to submit his accounts to Antigonus, preferred to leave his satrapy. He appeared at Alexandria as a fugitive, and there he convinced Ptolemy of the threatening designs of Antigonus. At Seleucus' instigation a coalition was formed between Ptolemy, Cassander and Lysimachus, and in 315 war was declared. The fighting went on until 311, when a peace on the basis of *status quo* was negotiated. The independence of Ptolemy, Cassander and Lysimachus was acknowledged, but Antigonus' claims to a superior command over all Asia were recognized. An immediate consequence of the peace was Cassander's murder of the young Alexander IV in 309, though it did not become publicly known till 306/5. The male line of the Temenid dynasty thereby came to an end.

The period of struggle between 315 and 311 may be responsible for a small coinage of Alexander drachms at Mylasa in Caria (**67**).[5] Four different issues are involved, three of which are die-linked. Their production has been connected with the activities of Eupolemus, a Macedonian officer fighting for Cassander against Antigonus in Caria in 315/14. Eupolemus also issued a bronze coinage in his own name (**68**), most probably from Mylasa. The types are strictly military: on the obverse three Macedonian shields, on the reverse a sword in sheath. The bronzes are relatively common and may have been struck over a longer period of time.

During the war Antigonus had acquired the western Satrapies of Asia Minor, but in 312 Seleucus with a small force re-occupied his own former satrapy of Babylonia. He was not included in the peace treaty of 311, but Antigonus proved unable to drive him out of Babylon and gradually lost all the eastern satrapies to his energetic adversary. One of the reasons for Antigonus' failure was the renewal of hostilities by Ptolemy and the fighting with Cassander for control of Greece. The hostilities continued with varying fortunes. In 306 Antigonus' son, Demetrius, later known as Poliorcetes, the 'Besieger', won a resounding victory over Ptolemy off Salamis on Cyprus. He became master of Cyprus, but even more important, Antigonus used the opportunity to proclaim himself and his son kings, thus advertising his claim to the succession of Alexander as ruler of the entire empire. His opponents had to follow his example, and in 305/4 Ptolemy, Seleucus, Cassander and Lysimachus all took the royal title in order to emphasize their independence of Antigonus. A new coalition of the four was formed, and in 301 the battlefield of Ipsus in Asia Minor saw the death of Antigonus. The dismemberment of Alexander's empire was a fact.

During these years of complicated political and military changes the coinage for the most part presents a surprisingly stable picture. Only Ptolemy in Egypt was an innovator, but the changes in the Egyptian coinage are dealt with separately in the next chapter. The other rulers adhered strictly to the well-established Alexander tradition. They continued it after the death of Alexander IV, and Cassander and Antigonus were still minting in gold and silver with the name of Alexander unchanged even after they had assumed the royal title.

In Macedonia the mint of Pella apparently stopped the issue of posthumous coins of Philip II *c.* 315, while the Alexander coinage continued. Amphipolis was still by far the most productive

5 Thompson 1981b.

mint in the area.[6] About 315 a new issue was started, identified first by the Greek letter *Λ* and a bucranium, later by *Λ* and a torch (**69**). The *Λ* and torch issue continued at least to Cassander's death in 297 and possibly even later. Posthumous silver tetradrachms of Philip II were struck with the same identification marks (**70**), showing that at Amphipolis these issues were produced well into the third century. Only the bronze coins were inscribed with the name of Cassander. A series with obverse head of Heracles, reverse seated lion reads *ΚΑΣΣΑΝΔΡΟΥ* (**71**). It dates from between 310 and 305. From 305 to 297 four different series of bronzes were struck (**72**), all inscribed *ΒΑΣΙΛΕΩΣ ΚΑΣΣΑΝΔΡΟΥ*, and there are anonymous bronze coins (**73**) perhaps belonging to Cassander's sons (below, p. 79).

A remarkable series of Alexander tetradrachms can best be fitted in here. All have as a symbol in the field a tall pyramidal structure surmounted by a star (**74**). The same structure is worn as a headdress by Aphrodite Urania, who is represented seated on a globe and holding a sceptre on an issue of small bronze coins (**75**) inscribed *ΟΥΡΑΝΙΔΩΝ ΠΟΛΕΩΣ*, 'of the City of the Uranids'. This city, Uranopolis, was a foundation at or near Mt Athos, on the easternmost promontory of Chalcidice. It was founded between 316 and 300 by Cassander's younger brother Alexarchus, a strange character who called himself Helios, the Sun, and became the *ktistes* of his own Heavenly City. A few silver coins (tetradrachms, didrachms, and a single drachm) with the type of Aphrodite Urania and inscribed *ΟΥΡΑΝΙΔΩΝ* are known, but as the weights of the fractions are erratic their authenticity has been questioned.[7] But the bronze coins of similar types are quite common and are undoubtedly genuine. The tetradrachms seem to form a rather compact issue of short duration, with about 50 obverse dies used for their production. The coinage was presumably made possible by the vicinity of Uranopolis to important silver mines on the Chalcidice. The earliest obverses show a close similarity to contemporary issues of Amphipolis, which undoubtedly provided the first engravers, though a characteristic local style soon developed. The Heavenly City of the religious reformer Alexarchus had but a short existence and presumably came to an end in 297, when Cassander died and left his brother without the military and political support necessary for this utopian enterprise.[8]

The only one of the Diadochi who in 310 still had no mint at his disposal was Lysimachus. Apparently he obtained such coins as he needed from Macedonia. He and Cassander were on good terms and, during the confusion of changing alliances, maintained their co-operation unshaken down to Cassander's death. Lysimachus' first coinage (**76–7**) consisted of silver tetrobols and bronzes (obverse: head of Apollo; reverse: horseman). The types were copied from ones of Philip II, and Philip's name, with *ΛΥ* (for Lysimachus), appeared on the first issue. A second issue (**78–9**) with the same types was inscribed *ΛΥ* or *ΒΑΣΙΛΕΩΣ ΛΥ* only. Lysimachus' distinctive badge, the forepart of an attacking lion, appears as a symbol on all these

---

6 [Cf. Ehrhardt 1976.]

7 Lederer 1931, though the genuineness of the tetradrachms has been defended by Breitenstein 1942, 248–50, and Thompson 1981a, 43–4.

8 This Alexander coinage has been ascribed to Amphipolis by Thompson, 1981a, 40–4, but see Mathisen 1981, 115, who calls attention to the existence of the silver mines in eastern Chalcidice.

coins, which were struck between 306/5 and 301/300 at his new capital Lysimachia, situated on the European coast of the Hellespont.[9]

The pre-eminence of Antigonus among the Diadochi at this period is graphically illustrated by the great number of mints located in his territory. From 310 onwards all mints in western Asia Minor except Miletus were producing coins on his behalf. The largest output of drachms now came from the two Hellespontine mints of Lampsacus (**80**) and Abydus (**81**), while Colophon, Magnesia and Teos had a more normal production, with Colophon as the most prolific of these three. In marked contrast to the period before 317 Sardis, re-opened in 310, now struck very few drachms but large issues of tetradrachms, thus approaching the production pattern of the 'normal' mints outside western Asia Minor. Substantial issues of gold were struck at some of the mints, especially at Abydus and Magnesia.

Further east Antigonus had the use of mints in Tarsus, Aradus (**82**), Marathus, Sidon and Ake. His Alexander coinage from Aradus and Marathus carries a large anchor as a symbol on the reverse. They have therefore often been attributed to Seleucus I, but the careful examination of Newell proved that they belong to the decade or so preceding Seleucus' arrival in Phoenicia after his victory at Ipsus (301), and the anchor has no connection with the Seleucid emblem.[10] In *c.* 310 Antigonus extended his activities to Mesopotamia, where Carrhae became the seat of a mint (**83**). In the following years new mints were opened at Tyre (*c.* 307) (**84**) and Antigonea in Syria, the new capital of Antigonus (*c.* 306) (**85**).[11] In 306 the mint of Salamis in Cyprus came into his possession. Even at this date, and also after Antigonus' and his son's proclamation as kings, all the mints continued turning out the same well-known Alexander coinage. A few tetradrachms of the Alexander type and with Antigonus' name were earlier ascribed to Monophthalmus, but they are now seen to belong to his grandson, Antigonus Gonatas (below, p. 135). The establishment of the mint of Tyre made the neighbouring mints of Sidon and Ake superfluous, and within a couple of years they were both closed. The last Alexander coinages instituted by Antigonus were one or two issues at Chalcis, minted between *c.* 304 and 300, and an extensive series struck at Corinth (**86**) from *c.* 303, when Antigonus and Demetrius, during their desperate fight with the coalition, tried to resuscitate the Corinthian League as a political weapon against Cassander. This series was earlier attributed to Sicyon, but the occurrence of the same markings, monograms and symbols on both the Alexander coins and on bronzes from Corinth makes the ascription to Corinth practically certain.[12] The issue of Alexander tetradrachms, struck from a little over 50 obverse dies, lasted until *c.* 287/6, when Demetrius was mobilizing all his resources for a military comeback in Asia Minor (below, pp. 132–4).

The particular developments at Alexandria in Egypt will be dealt with in the next chapter. Down to 306 Ptolemy had the use of the mint of Salamis in Cyprus, where he continued the coinage of Alexander tetradrachms. His brother Menelaus, who was governor of the island

---

9 Thompson 1968a, 165 and 168.
10 Newell 1941 (*WSM*), 192–4.
11 Newell 1941 (*WSM*), 38–43 (Carrhae) and 84–6 (Antigonea). On Tyre see most recently Merker 1974.
12 Noe 1950, issues 17–19, 22–39. Cf. Troxell 1971, 44–50.

from 311/10, issued a few small gold coins of the same types as Nicocreon (above, p. 58). The one-third stater (**65**) which was his largest denomination bears the Cypriot sign *ba*, for *basileus*, showing that he had assumed the local kingship. The use of the royal title in Cyprus and in Phoenicia at this time did not, of course, constitute any claim to independence.

We left Seleucus reinstated as governor of Babylonia in 312 and engaged, in the following years, in wresting the satrapies east of Babylon from the generals of Antigonus. He thus came to possess the mint at Susa, and in *c.* 311/10 he opened a new mint at Ecbatana, the capital of the province of Media and the former summer residence of the Persian kings. Here an Alexander coinage in gold and silver (**87**) was struck down to *c.* 293.[13] A characteristic feature of Ecbatana was the relative frequency of small silver denominations (**88–9**), hemidrachms, obols, and even hemiobols.

13 Newell 1938c (*ESM*), 162–76.

6

EGYPT AND ITS NEIGHBOURS

(a) PTOLEMY I

We have seen how the production of Alexander coinage continued in most places for many years after both the death of the conqueror and the division of his empire. An exception was Alexandria, where Ptolemy soon introduced a new and significant obverse type on his silver tetradrachms (**90**).[1] While the reverse type of the seated Zeus and the inscription were left unchanged, the obverse now shows the head of the deified Alexander wearing an elephant's scalp with trunk and tusks. Beneath the elephant headdress the ram's horn of Zeus Ammon is visible, and the royal diadem appears above the forehead. The king also wears the *aegis* of Zeus, tied around the neck by two snakes.

The date of the new obverse has to be estimated from its relative position in the sequence of coins from Alexandria. It definitely belongs to the beginning of Ptolemy's governorship, and the years 321 and 319 have both been suggested. Perhaps it can best be related to the events of 321. In that year Ptolemy secured for himself the corpse of Alexander the Great by persuading those who were in charge of its transportation from Babylon to Macedonia to divert the convoy to Egypt, where the body was first buried in Memphis and later transferred to a magnificent tomb, the *sema*, in Alexandria. Later in the same year Ptolemy repulsed the attack of Perdiccas, who was murdered by some of his officers. The resulting settlement at Triparadeisus in Syria left Antipater head of the central government but confirmed Ptolemy, his son-in-law, in his position as governor of Egypt. This chain of events offers the most likely explanation for the new coin type. As possessor of the human relics of Alexander, Ptolemy could establish a state cult of the dead conqueror, undoubtedly in order to enhance his prestige with the Macedonians and attract them to his service. An identical head of Alexander with elephant's scalp and the horns of Ammon is known from sculptures, and it is tempting to see in the new coin type a representation of the very cult statue which Ptolemy must have set up. The relatively high relief of the coin type serves to underline its sculptural qualities. In this way the type would be

1 For Ptolemaic coinage the comprehensive collection of material by Svoronos 1904–8 is still indispensable. For a modern catalogue, arranged by mints, see Kromann and Mørkholm, *SNG Copenhagen*, part 40: *Egypt: The Ptolemies* (1977).

intimately associated with the events of 321, although its introduction on the coins may have waited until the following year.

The first issues of the new coinage show the same markings, symbols and monograms as the latest issues of the normal Alexander coinage. It has consequently been argued that the two series were issued concurrently for several years, but this implies that the marks belong to annual magistrates.[2] If several officials, each with his own mark, were working at the mint at the same time, the whole group may well have been responsible first for the Alexander coinage and later for the new issue, and the transition from one coinage to another carried out at one stroke. The new coinage was of the full Attic weight, as were the gold coins which were still issued with the international Alexander types.

The next change at Alexandria affected the reverse of the silver. After a transitional issue (**91**), which is differentiated from the earlier coins by the conspicuous scaly *aegis* of the obverse type and may be dated *c.* 315, a new reverse type (**92**) was introduced in the following year. The seated Zeus was replaced by a standing Athena, fighting to the right with shield and thunderbolt. The figure of Athena is rendered in an archaizing style, especially noticeable in the drawing of her cloak or *chiton* with its schematic folds arranged in a regular 'swallowtail' pattern. The personal badge of Ptolemy, an eagle standing on a thunderbolt, appears as a symbol on the transitional and following issues. The obverse type is left unchanged, but the high relief with its sculptural quality gives way to a flatter style, more reminiscent of a drawing. At the same time the head becomes larger and tends to fill the surface more completely. The diameters of the coins are also increasing. One of the first issues of the new series shows the interesting legend *ΑΛΕΞΑΝΔΡΕΙΟΝ ΠΤΟΛΕΜΑΙΟΥ*, which may mean either 'Ptolemy's [coin] of Alexandria' or 'Ptolemy's [coin] of Alexander' (**92**). In any case it is the earliest appearance of Ptolemy's name on his coinage. The experiment was short-lived and, after a few coins with the rare variation *ΑΛΕΞΑΝΔΡΕΙΟΝ*, the mint at Alexandria soon returned to the normal short legend *ΑΛΕΞΑΝΔΡΟΥ*.

The existence of an interesting issue of gold staters (**110**) and hemistaters of Alexander types and the normal Attic weight should be mentioned here. They are inscribed ***ΚΥΡΑΝΑΙΟΝ ΠΤΟΛΕΜΑΙΩ***, a perfect parallel to the legend just mentioned, especially if this is taken to mean 'Ptolemy's coin of Alexandria'. Together with this gold, however, goes a silver didrachm with the same inscription but with civic types (**112**), so they can most profitably be discussed in connection with the other civic coinages of Cyrene from this period (below, p. 68).

A few years later an innovation of even greater consequence took place in Egypt. Up to this date, irrespective of their type changes, the coins had been struck on the Attic weight standard. But *c.* 310 the weight of the silver tetradrachms (**93**) was reduced from the Attic 17.20g to *c.* 15.70g, i.e. by just under 9%. At the same time the production of gold staters came to an end. The types of the new reduced tetradrachms were similar to those of the preceding issues. Many overstrikes exist which show that the heavier coins in the treasury were sent back to the mint, reduced to the new standard, and then overstruck by new magistrates in order to secure

2 Zervos 1967.

the speedy transition from one coinage to another.[3] The dating of the change in weights depends partly on the evidence of the Chiliomodi hoard found near Corinth and buried *c.* 304[4] It contained several different issues of reduced weight, so that the weight reduction must have taken place some years before that of the burial. On the other hand, a few issues struck outside Egypt provide the *terminus post quem*. After the battle of Gaza in 312 Ptolemy for a short period occupied Phoenicia and Palestine. At Sidon he struck an issue of tetradrachms (**94**) with his new types (head of Alexander in elephant's scalp/fighting Athena) but of Attic weight. The coin is dated to year 22 of the Sidonian era corresponding to 312/11. To about the same time belongs an Attic-weight tetradrachm of Ptolemaic types (**95**) signed by Eunostus, king of Soli in Cyprus and son-in-law of Ptolemy. At Soli a series of reduced weight was also produced; this issue has the unusual legend *ΠΤΟΛΕΜΑΙΟΥ*. As the two Cypriot issues are only roughly dated, the clinching evidence is offered by the Sidonian dated coins. Ptolemy would hardly have struck Attic-weight coins in Sidon if the reduced standard was already used in Egypt.

During his campaign in Greece Ptolemy occupied Corinth from 308 to *c.* 304 (see below, p. 87). A special issue of Ptolemaic drachms was struck there, no doubt to provide the garrison with the king's money. Most if not all the known specimens seem to derive from the Chiliomodi hoard and they are connected with contemporary Corinthian issues by the occurrence of the initials *ΔΟ* on both series.

In Egypt the reduced tetradrachms continued down to shortly after 300, but the last issues, from *c.* 304 onwards, were accompanied by a new series of gold staters (**96**). The obverse of these shows a portrait of Ptolemy wearing the royal diadem and carrying the *aegis*. The reverse type represents Alexander standing in a quadriga of elephants and holding the thunderbolt. Ptolemy still had an interest in drawing attention to his connection with Alexander and to the cult he had established. The coins are inscribed *ΠΤΟΛΕΜΑΙΟΥ ΒΑΣΙΛΕΩΣ*, showing that they belong to the period after 305/4, when Ptolemy first assumed the royal title. The obverse type is interesting in providing us with the earliest individual portrait of a Hellenistic ruler. In contrast to the highly idealized portraits of Alexander the Great, this head shows an astonishing degree of realism. Very little is done to embellish an energetic face dominated by the heavy chin that juts out defiantly, or the king's long, often drooping nose and characteristic bulging eyebrows with deep-set eyes. On some of the later portraits, especially on the silver, these features are exaggerated to the point of caricature. With this issue the weight of the gold coins was also changed. Instead of the 8.60g of an Attic stater, the new staters of Ptolemy weigh only *c.* 7.12g, a reduction of more than 17%.

Some of the new gold staters (**122**) were struck at Cyrene, a semi-independent dominion of Ptolemy I since 322, together with a series of bronze coins (**127**), showing on the obverse a head of Apollo, on the reverse an eagle with open wings standing on a thunderbolt. A single issue of gold tetrobols of Attic weight, but in the name of Ptolemy and with the royal title, was also issued at Cyrene (**124**). Their transitional character is shown by the types. The obverse has the

3 Emmons 1954.
4 Ravel 1938: *IGCH* 85 (with burial date 306). For the revised burial date of *c.* 304 see Mørkholm 1980b, 156.

diademed head of Ptolemy, while the reverse type is the standing Nike of the Alexander gold coinage. The interrelation of these issues with the civic issue of Cyrene is discussed later.

The final changes in the coinage of Ptolemy were introduced shortly after 300. The same types were now used for all denominations in gold and silver:

Obv. Head of Ptolemy I
Rev. Eagle standing on thunderbolt; *ΠΤΟΛΕΜΑΙΟΥ ΒΑΣΙΛΕΩΣ*.

The tetradrachms in silver (**97**) were first reduced to *c.* 14.9g and then further to the final level of *c.* 14.25g, where they stayed for the next two centuries. In this last stage the tetradrachms were accompanied by pentadrachms (**98**) (*c.* 17.85g) and hemidrachms (*c.* 1.78g) in gold (**101**) and some rare octodrachms (*c.* 28.40g) in silver (**100**). The coinage in the precious metals is paralleled by a coinage of several denominations in bronze. The main denomination (**99**) shows the laureate head of Zeus on the obverse. The reverse has the Ptolemaic eagle on thunderbolt, but the bird is shown with its wings open. These pieces weigh *c.* 16.00g–19.00g and their control marks generally differ from those of the gold and silver. The bulk of the coinage was struck at Alexandria, but towards the end of the reign a few tetradrachms were struck at Tyre, which was a Ptolemaic possession between 294 and 286.

These changes in types and weights, which we are able to follow in the Ptolemaic coinage from *c.* 320 down to about 295, demand some explanation. As far as the types are concerned, this is not too difficult. The changing types reflect the growing autonomy of Egypt under Ptolemy. Step-by-step he moved towards total independence of the Alexander coinage which, as we have seen, was being produced by his competitors in great quantities right down to 300 and, in some places, even longer. The cautious but tenacious policy of Ptolemy, aimed at securing his own independent position, is admirably illustrated by his coinage.

The changes in the weights of the coins are quite different in their implications. By reducing the weights of the silver and gold coins Ptolemy created, from *c.* 310, a separate circulation area, one of the prerequisites for the closed Egyptian economy as we know it from the reign of his successor onwards. Egyptian coin finds show that foreign coins of Attic weight were being freely imported into Egypt down to *c.* 305. After that date Ptolemaic coinage enjoys a complete monopoly, and it has been argued that this was the result of a deliberate attempt, by monetary manipulation, to exclude foreign coins from the Egyptian market.[5] This is known to have been done under Ptolemy II and it may well have started under his father, although we have no explicit evidence from contemporary documents to such an effect.

The establishment of a separate economic area, closed to foreign influences that could not be controlled, was certainly desirable from the point of view of the Egyptian king and a sufficient explanation for the creation of a separate monetary system. But that the reductions took the form they actually did may have another explanation.[6] We have seen that at the time of Alexander, gold and silver stood at a ratio of 1:10. During the last decades of the fourth century

5 Zervos 1976, 52–4; 1978, 53–4; 1980, 28–9.
6 E.S.G. Robinson in Rostovtzeff 1941, III. 1635–9.

the ratio changed gradually to 1:12. In the third century gold became even more expensive, but the final phase of the Egyptian system seems built on the ratio 1:12. In this system a gold pentadrachm of 17.85g equalled 60 silver drachms or 15 tetradrachms of 14.25g each. The gold stater of Attic weight named a *χρυσοῦς* had equalled 20 silver drachms during the reign of Alexander, and therefore the new Ptolemaic gold coin, which equalled 60 silver drachms, albeit of lighter weight, was called a *τρίχρυσον*.

About 295, after more than two decades of experimenting with types and weights, Ptolemaic coinage was established in an enduring form. Gold pentadrachms and silver tetradrachms were the most common denominations, supplemented by a substantial series of bronze to be used locally as a fiduciary coinage. Such a monetary system, using the same types and legend, continued into the reign of Ptolemy II, and at present it is impossible to determine exactly at what point of the sequence of issues Ptolemy II took over from his father.

(b) CYRENAICA AND JUDAEA

In the winter of 332/1 an embassy of the Cyrenaeans met with Alexander the Great at Paraetonium and concluded a treaty of alliance with him. During the years from 331 to 323 the city of Cyrene issued a prolific series of gold staters of Attic weight (**102**) with chariots drawn by four horses on the obverse and Zeus in various positions on the reverse. Some of the seated Zeus figures are clearly influenced by the tetradrachms of Alexander. They are accompanied by gold drachms (horseman/*silphium*) (**103**), hemidrachms (triple *silphium*/head of Athena or with the types interchanged) (**104**), and tenths (heads of Carneius or Ammon/female head, possibly Cyrene) (**105**). The contemporary silver coinage consisted of tetradrachms and drachms of the so-called Asiatic standard, the tetradrachm weighing four-fifths of an Attic tetradrachm or *c.* 13.76g.[7] On the tetradrachms (**106**) appears the bearded head of Zeus Ammon, while the young and beardless Hermes Parammon[8] (earlier identified with Carneius) occupies the obverses of the drachms (**107**). The *silphium*, an aromatic plant only found in Cyrenaica and used for drugs, is seen on the reverses of both denominations. The silver coins are generally slightly lighter than the theoretical weight. Both gold and silver coins were signed by various magistrates or moneyers, some of whom were in office for considerable periods of time.

The silver tetradrachms were brought to Crete in some quantity by returning mercenaries and were used for overstriking, especially at the mints of Gortyn and Phaestus. The sudden influx of silver coins from Cyrenaica to Crete has been plausibly connected with a specific episode in the history of Cyrenaica.[9] From 323 to 322 an adventurer named Thibron, a former companion of Harpalus, the treasurer of Alexander, interfered in a civil war in Cyrenaica and was able to conquer part of the region. He even struck coins during his operations. Two small bronze coins are known with two different obverse types: head of Athena (**109**) or head of

7 The standard works are Robinson, *BMC, Cyrenaica* (1927) and Naville 1951.
8 Chamoux 1959.
9 Le Rider 1966, 144–6. Cf. also Newell 1938b, 9–11; Robert 1955.

Heracles (**108**), while the reverse (from the same die) shows the name of Thibron between a spearhead and a club. Among his troops there were almost certainly a contingent of Cretans, who after the defeat of their leader in 322 by Ophellas, general of Ptolemy I, may have returned home and brought the Cyrenaican coins with them.

The political organization of Cyrene in 322 was based on a very complicated arrangement which left the city nominally free but gave Ptolemy a position as supervisor and guardian of the oligarchic constitution with wide discretionary powers of interference. The autonomous coinage, however, most probably continued unchanged until *c.* 315/14, when we find Attic gold staters (**110**) and hemistaters of Alexander types with the inscription *ΚΥΡΑΝΑΙΟΝ ΠΤΟΛΕΜΑΙΩ* or *ΠΤΟΛΕΜΑΙΟΥ*.[10] With the gold go a few silver didrachms of Attic weight, one of which (**111**) is also inscribed *ΚΥΡΑΝ ΠΤΟΛΕΜ* and a few bronze coins. Another of the silver coins (**112A**) shows on the reverse a standing Athena copied from the Ptolemaic tetradrachms of 315 onwards. Both the use of this type and the occurrence of Ptolemy's name indicate a tightening of Ptolemaic control in Cyrene. This was presumably the cause of a revolt in 313/12. On some silver and bronze coins of these years (**113**) we find the interesting legend *ΚΥΡΑΝΑ ΔΑΜΩ*, stressing the authority of the people, *demos*, over the coinage, probably as a reaction to the greater royal interference which we may infer from the legend of the preceding issues.

In 312 Ophellas was restored by Ptolemy and governed the province until 308. During this period he gradually asserted his freedom of action without apparently committing himself to an open revolt against the Egyptian king. The years from 310 to 308 saw Ptolemy occupied in the Aegean and in mainland Greece, which may explain the relatively independent position of Ophellas. During these years civic issues in gold and silver on the Attic standard were continued together with various bronze series. At the end of the period some unusual types appear which have been connected with Ophellas' growing independence and, more specifically, with his adventurous attack on Carthage in co-operation with Agathocles of Syracuse in 308. A gold hemistater (**114**) shows on the obverse a horseman in military dress who has been identified with Ophellas, and on the reverse, as on some of the silver (**115**), the *silphium* of Cyrene is placed beside a palm tree, which may symbolize North Africa, over which Ophellas hoped to extend his domination. However this may be, his dreams were cut short by his murder in 308 after a quarrel with Agathocles.

After the death of Ophellas, Ptolemy was able to reassert his domination over Cyrene. To the years immediately after 308 we may assign a group of small gold coins (**119**), with divine heads as types, weighing one-eleventh of the Attic stater. To the same period I would ascribe the inauguration of a new series of silver didrachms (**116**). The head of Hermes Parammon adorns the obverses, while the reverse shows the *silphium*. Several different issues are known and the rather extensive coinage may cover the period down to *c.* 295. The weight of these coins shows a concentration around 7.70g. The standard is generally called Rhodian, but actually it is the reduced standard used by Ptolemy in Egypt from *c.* 310 to *c.* 298 for his tetradrachms

10 Mørkholm 1980b, with a different chronology from that of Robinson and Naville.

of *c.* 15.70g. The copious didrachms are accompanied by a few issues of tetradrachms (**117**). Their obverse type is the head of Zeus Ammon and on the reverses we find the ubiquitous *silphium*. The contemporary gold issues consist of Attic tetrobols and obols of the usual civic types. The smallest gold coins now weigh one-twelfth of the Attic stater. The gradual decrease in the weight of these coins from one-tenth to one-eleventh to one-twelfth of the Attic stater reflects the rising value of gold against silver which we have already encountered in Egypt during the same period.

In *c.* 305 the Cyrenaeans again asserted their independence of Egypt and maintained their autonomy until *c.* 300. During these years the civic issues of Attic tetrobols (**120**) and obols in gold were continued. A few silver coins were struck on an uncertain standard. Probably they were octobols and tetrobols of Attic weight, but this experiment was of short duration and the reduced Ptolemaic didrachms soon returned. In addition a few Attic-weight gold staters and hemistaters (**121**) and some silver tetradrachms (**118**) with the type and name of Alexander the Great were produced. The appearance of Attic-weight silver at this juncture points to independence from Egypt, where the Attic weight had been abandoned since *c.* 310. The Cyrenaeans must have felt the need for an international coinage usable outside the Ptolemaic economic area. This is one of the earliest examples of the striking of posthumous Alexander silver by an independent city, motivated undoubtedly by the desire to partake in the advantages attached to a truly international currency which had become popular with the mercenaries of the period.

In or about 300 Ptolemy again recovered Cyrene and entrusted the governorship to his stepson Magas. The return of Ptolemaic suzerainty did not involve any break in the civic didrachm issues, but the gold coinage was now strictly royal. Staters (**122**) were issued with the same types as the contemporary coins from Alexandria: head of Ptolemy on the obverse and Alexander standing with thunderbolt in an elephant chariot on the reverse, which also carries the inscription *ΠΤΟΛΕΜΑΙΟΥ ΒΑΣΙΛΕΩΣ*. These staters were issued at both Cyrene and Euhesperides. At the latter mint a small issue of silver didrachms (**123**) is inscribed *ΒΑΣΙ* instead of the usual *ΚΥΡΑ*. They show the head of Apollo Carneius on the obverse. The weights of the few specimens known suggest that they were struck on a lighter standard than the other didrachms, but the material is too sparse to warrant any secure conclusions. A few royal gold tetrobols (**124**) show on the obverse the head of Ptolemy, on the reverse a standing Nike and the name and title of the Egyptian king. We also now, for the first time, meet an issue of royal bronzes (**127**) (head of Apollo/eagle on thunderbolt), the monogram on which connects them both with the royal gold coinage and with the civic silver.

At a date which we may put somewhere around 295/290 a further general weight reduction affected the silver didrachms. They now weighed *c.* 6.70g–6.90g, undoubtedly a somewhat light variant of the final Ptolemaic silver standard in Egypt, with a tetradrachm of *c.* 14.25g. The obverse type was changed, the head of Apollo Myrtous replacing that of Hermes Parammon, while the *silphium* remained on the reverse (**125**). The issue was small and may have covered about five years, *c.* 295/290 or *c.* 290/285. One of the silver issues is linked by the crab symbol and the monogram  to the last civic gold issue of Cyrene. A unique stater in Paris (**126**) shows a quadriga driven by Nike with *ΚΥΡΑΝΑΙΟΝ* above, on the obverse, and a standing Zeus performing a libation on the reverse. The coin weighs 7.16g, the same weight as the royal staters of the preceding period. The specific occasion for this last civic gold coinage of Cyrene is unknown to us, but it may have been accompanied by a few gold obols.

To the years after 295 belong two prolific series of bronzes, one, with head of Ammon/palm-tree with fruit (**128**) and the other with head of Apollo Myrtous/lyre (**129**). They may well have lasted until 280 or perhaps even longer.

Another province which produced a coinage of its own in the time of Ptolemy I was Judaea.[11] A few coins inscribed 'Yehud' in Aramaic are known from the Persian period and possibly also from the reign of Alexander, but it was a great surprise when, a few years ago, a number of minute silver coins (weights from 0.12g to 0.22g) were discovered with indisputably Ptolemaic types (**130**). Quite recently slightly larger coins, probably hemidrachms of the Ptolemaic standard, have appeared. We find the Ptolemaic eagle on thunderbolt together with a diademed portrait of Ptolemy I. Even more astonishing was the occurrence (**131**) of a female head that on account of its characteristic hairstyle has been identified with Berenice I, the queen of Ptolemy I. The coins are inscribed 'Yehud' or 'Yehudah', the name of the province of Judaea, but now in Hebrew characters. They must be dated *c.* 300–283/2 and provide us with the earliest strictly contemporary portrait of Berenice.

Ptolemy I's policy in monetary matters at this late period in his reign has always been represented as strongly centralizing and aiming at a royal monopoly. The existence of a special silver coinage for the temple-state of Judaea, even if consisting only of the smallest denominations, must in the light of this be regarded as a surprising exception for which no satisfactory explanation has yet been offered.

11 Mildenberg 1979; Meshorer 1981 (hemidrachms); [Mildenberg 1987, 388–90]. Meshorer suggests that the coins may belong to the early years of the reign of Ptolemy II.

7

SYRIA AND THE EAST: SELEUCUS I

We saw in chapter 5 that Seleucus I, soon after his recovery of Babylon in 312, took possession of the eastern satrapies with their mints at Susa and Ecbatana. At all three mints he issued the common Alexander coinage for several years.[1]

Between *c.* 305 and *c.* 300 a major change in the coinage was effected with the removal of the central mint from Babylon to the new eastern capital, Seleucia on the Tigris. At Babylon only the local coinages, gold double darics and lion staters (above, p. 48), continued for some years, the lion staters perhaps down to the end of Seleucus' reign. But the international Alexander coinage from Babylon, which was by far the most prolific, came to an end. It was replaced by new issues of tetradrachms (**132**) with fresh and distinctive types from Seleucia, now in the name of Seleucus, who assumed the royal title in 305–4. The obverse shows a laureate head of Zeus which recalls the representation on Philip II's silver coins, while the reverse is occupied by an Athena fighting with shield and javelin from a war chariot drawn by four horned elephants. In the field above appears the anchor, badge or emblem of Seleucus I, and the inscription reads *ΒΑΣΙΛΕΩΣ ΣΕΛΕΥΚΟΥ*. The tetradrachms are accompanied by a few drachms of the same type (**133**), but the rather rare gold staters (**134**) preserve the types of Alexander and change only the inscription to the name and title of Seleucus. The introduction of this new coinage was dated by Newell to *c.* 300 but it may actually have begun somewhat earlier, in 304 or 303. In favour of the latter date one might argue that the prominence of the war elephant on the reverse reflected the military power of Seleucus after his treaty with Chandragupta in 303, by which he ceded Alexander's Indian territories against a corps of 500 war elephants. In any case, the tetradrachms with the types head of Zeus/Athena in elephant chariot provided the first coinage of Seleucia on the Tigris and were continued down to the end of the reign. The types were used at Susa from *c.* 300, where the reverse chariot is generally a biga, i.e. one drawn by *two* elephants (**135**), and from a slightly later date (*c.* 295?) at a new mint established by Seleucus in Bactra, the capital of the important and rich Bactrian satrapy. From Ecbatana and Susa we also have rare and beautiful gold staters (**136**) with the types head of Apollo/Artemis standing in elephant biga.

At Susa and Ecbatana small issues of lion staters were issued around 300, undoubtedly for local use by the indigenous population. A couple of special issues from these mints of about the

---

1 The standard works are Newell 1938c (*ESM*) and 1941 (*WSM*).

same time deserve notice. At Ecbatana we find a few double darics (**137**) showing on the obverse the head of Alexander the Great in elephant's scalp, on the reverse a standing Nike. A symbol, the head of a horned horse, connects these coins with other issues from Ecbatana. Following the tradition of the darics, the coins are not inscribed. The obverse type seems to be copied from the silver of Ptolemy I of Egypt, issued from *c.* 320 to 300, and was also used on some bronze issues of this period from Seleucia on the Tigris with the name of Alexander. At Susa the lion staters were followed by an issue of elephant staters (**138**). Their obverses show the same head of Zeus as the tetradrachms, but the reverses represent a single elephant walking right, with a spearhead symbol in the field above. The weights of these coins come close to that of normal Attic tetradrachms, but their relation to the lion staters is obvious from the small diameter of the dies and the very dumpy flans. They also lack a proper inscription.

At Susa we find another very interesting series of tetradrachms (**139**) and drachms (**140**) issued by Seleucus.[2] The obverse type is a young male head in a helmet covered with the skin of a leopard and adorned with the horn and ear of a bull. The reverse shows a Nike crowning a trophy consisting of the trunk of a tree on which a cuirass, a helmet and a shield are hung. The inscription gives the name of Seleucus and the royal title. The obverse type has often been regarded as a portrait of Seleucus I, but in view of its youngish features and the divine attributes on the helmet I would prefer to see in it a representation of Alexander the Great assimilated to Dionysus, the conqueror of India and master of leopards.[3] The victory type on the reverse has been connected with the resounding victory at Ipsus over Antigonus Monophthalmus in the summer of 301, but this explanation raises the problem of why this victory should have been celebrated by special coin issues only at the comparatively small mint of Susa in the East. I would prefer a somewhat wider interpretation, referring the propaganda message conveyed by these coins in a general way to the victories of Alexander over the Orientals and to Seleucus as his rightful successor in the Iranian provinces. One might even speculate on the possibility that some specific victory celebration after Seleucus' Indian campaign provided the occasion for the first issue of this type. If this were the case, and there were no connection with Ipsus, the precise date of the coins would become uncertain, though the place of the issues in the sequence from Susa shows that here they must belong to the years before 300.

All the coinages so far mentioned had a limited circulation area. Even the large tetradrachm issues from Seleucia on the Tigris (**132**) with the head of Zeus/Athena in elephant chariot are rarely found west of the Euphrates. The explanation of this phenomenon must be that in the regions bordering on the Mediterranean the Alexander types had become the recognized international means of exchange, and the bulk of the silver coinage from Susa and Ecbatana consequently continued to take the form of Alexander-type tetradrachms (**141**). Newell believed that the name of Alexander was retained at Susa down to *c.* 301 and at Ecbatana to *c.* 293, before it gave way to the name of Seleucus.

At Ecbatana the tetradrachms were accompanied by an unusually large range of smaller

2 Newell distributed this coinage between Susa and Persepolis, but see now Houghton 1980a.

3 See also Hadley 1974b.

denominations in silver down to the hemiobol. A few drachms (**142**) and hemidrachms (**143**) show an interesting reverse type: a horseman with horned helmet and flying *chlamys* galloping to the right on a horned horse. On account of the horned helmet the rider must be the same as the one portrayed on the victory series of Susa just mentioned, and consequently Newell identified him with Seleucus. My contention, that Alexander is here represented, seems to receive some support from the horned horse on the small silver of Ecbatana. This can hardly be other than the most famous horse of its time, Alexander's Bucephalus or Ox-head. The only feasible way of representing a horse of this name on the small scale of the coins would be to supply it with horns, and legend did indeed provide Bucephalus with such a feature. If this argument is accepted, the horseman must be Alexander, the only person ever to ride that famous steed.

Even at Seleucia on the Tigris the need for a coinage of western type was felt, and from *c.* 295 several issues of Alexander gold staters and silver tetradrachms were produced, partly in the name of Alexander, partly in that of Seleucus (**144**). On some of the tetradrachms the Zeus on the reverse carries a small figure of Nike instead of the usual eagle, a feature borrowed from some issues of Antigonus from Carrhae (above, p. 61). From 292 they were supplemented by further issues of the same type in the name of Seleucus' son Antiochus, who had been appointed viceroy of the eastern satrapies in this year.[4] The rank and position of Antiochus were also acknowledged on a series of coins from the Bactra mint (**145**). They are of the head of Zeus/Athena in elephant chariot type, but give the names of both Seleucus and Antiochus. The new legend may have been introduced in order to differentiate them from the earlier issues, because at the same time the weight of the tetradrachm was reduced to a little below 14.00g in order to make them conform with the local Indian standard. They were issued between 292 and 281.

At this point we may mention an issue of a certain Sophytes.[5] His coins, mostly drachms (**148**), show on the obverse a male head in a wreathed helmet, on the reverse a cock with a caduceus as symbol and the inscription *ΣΩΦΥΤΟΥ*. As he has no title, we cannot be sure of his exact status, but the fact that his coins correspond in weight to the Seleucid issues from the Bactra mint *c.* 292–281 makes it likely that he was a dynast, located somewhere in Afghanistan, presumably in the border region between Bactria and India. Apparently he had been able to carve out a small principality for himself between the Seleucids and the Mauryan kings of northern India. He belonged, most probably, to the early third century.

Before leaving the eastern provinces of the Seleucid kingdom another independent coinage consisting of silver tetradrachms of Attic weight with accompanying drachms and smaller denominations should be discussed. A find from Persepolis (*IGCH* 1797) containing a victory issue of Seleucus from Susa and coins of several priest-kings of Persis is crucial for the dating of the last-named coinage. From their relative wear it seems that the issues of at least two of the priest-kings of Istakhr, Bagadates and Oborzos, may have been struck before 280. Two entries

4 Waggoner 1969.
5 Whitehead 1943.

in Polyaenus seem to throw light on them.[6] The first mentions the annihilation of some rebellious Persians under a King Seleucus, the second a strategem of Oborzos directed against 3,000 Greek colonists in Persis. If both episodes relate to the same events, the Seleucus mentioned can only be Seleucus I, and the most plausible reconstruction would be that Bagadates, priest-king at Istakhr, asserted his independence around 290 or 285, at a time when Seleucus himself had confided the administration of the eastern provinces to the crown prince Antiochus. Oborzos would then have continued the revolt. It is in fact remarkable that the death of Alexander was not followed by any rebellions among the native populations. That the first oriental reaction against Macedonian rule should come from Persis, the homeland of the Achaemenids, is hardly surprising. It is only difficult to understand why it came so late.

The most interesting fact regarding the coinages of Bagadates and Oborzos is the conscious and complete orientalization of their types and inscriptions.[7] The obverses show the heads of the two princes. Both have strongly oriental facial features (most pronounced for Oborzos) with a moustache and wear the satrapal headdress, the *kyrbasia*. On Oborzos' head its flaps are turned down and tied around the chin. Bagadates has two different reverse types. On the first (**146**) he is depicted seated on a throne, holding a sceptre and a flower(?); in front of him is placed a standard with tassels. The second reverse type shows the prince standing in a position of prayer or adoration in front of a fire-temple with battlements above. On the left the same standard is shown as on the first type. The oriental symbolism of both types, more especially that of the latter, is too obvious to need any explanation. The prince is represented as high-priest of the sacred Iranian fire. This type was taken over by Oborzos (**147**) and the succeeding rulers of Istakhr.

The coins are inscribed in an Aramaic often written with little care and difficult to read.[8] In addition to the names of the two princes we find the Iranian title *fratarak*, which is known from the Persian period in Egypt where it means 'governor' or 'chief'. On the coins of Bagadates the patronymic Biurat occurs. After Oborzos at least two more rulers struck coins of similar types, but they in all probability belong to the years after 280 and are discussed later (p. 119).

Until 301 Seleucus had been confined to the East. Ipsus gave him a considerable increase in territory. Northern Mesopotamia and Syria were his share of the spoils from the division of the Antigonid dominions, and but for the intervention of Ptolemy of Egypt he might have gained Coele-Syria and Phoenicia as well. In his new possessions he found the mints of Carrhae, Antigonea, Marathus and Aradus in operation. At Carrhae the Alexander coinage was continued, but now in the name of Seleucus. Aradus apparently closed its mint for the next fifty years. Marathus issued a small coinage for its new master, but only two obverse dies for tetradrachms were used. The first of them provides an interesting numismatic illustration of the troubled period around 301 when Seleucus took possession, for this single obverse die is found with different reverses in the names of Alexander, Philip III Arrhidaeus, and finally Seleucus (**149–**

6 Polyaenus 7. 39–40.
7 See Hill in *BMC, Arabic, etc.*, clx–clxviii.
8 See Naster 1968.

51). The posthumous appearance of Philip III is especially surprising. The style of the reverse die in his name suggests that it had somehow survived in the mint for about fifteen years, and was brought back into use at a moment when nobody knew for certain who was going to win the war.

The mint at Antigonea was also closed by Seleucus, who replaced its coinage by copious issues from his new foundations in northern Syria, the famous *tetrapolis* of Seleucia Pieria, Antioch on the Orontes, Apamea and Laodicea ad Mare. The direct successor to Antigonea was Seleucia, the earliest foundation, where tetradrachms of Alexander type in the name of Seleucus were produced by the same die cutters who earlier worked at Antigonea. Soon, however, Antioch became the most important mint, especially for bronzes. During the reign of Seleucus, Apamea issued only a few bronze coins with the types elephant/horned horse's head, presumably an allusion to the large military arsenal for cavalry and elephants which Seleucus established at the place. Laodicea ad Mare, on the other hand, produced a quite substantial series of tetradrachms (**152**). Here the eagle-bearing Zeus was retained in contrast to Seleucia Pieria and Antioch, where Zeus generally carries a Nike. At the two latter mints we also find some series of autonomous bronze coins issued by the people of Seleucia (**154**) and Antioch (**153**) respectively. Apparently by conceding the privilege of coining bronzes to his two major foundations in Syria, Seleucus intended to put them on a level with the old Greek cities of mainland Greece and Asia Minor, from which they also derived their other civic institutions. The experiment, however, was short-lived and did not survive the reign of Seleucus. While there were four different issues of autonomous bronzes from Seleucia, only one is known from Antioch.

In 294 Seleucus I managed to wrest the district of Cilicia from Demetrius Poliorcetes, then his father-in-law. He thereby acquired the mint at Tarsus and immediately proceeded to strike his own coins there, gold and silver of Alexander type (**155**) except for the small deviation that Zeus on the tetradrachm reverses carries Nike instead of an eagle.

When Seleucus crossed the Taurus mountains in 282 in order to settle his score with Lysimachus he may have established a small mint in Cappadocia, but the evidence relating to this establishment is not conclusive. He next marched directly on Sardis and by a stratagem secured its citadel with the treasure deposited within its walls. Sardis was the seat of a mint under Lysimachus (below, p. 81), and Seleucus at once began to use it for his own coins (**156**). In the year or so before his death (*c.* September 281) he produced tetradrachms of Alexander type, using four different obverse dies, and some bronze coins.

In early 281 the two surviving generals of Alexander, Seleucus and Lysimachus, met on the battlefield of Corupedium. Seleucus reaped the harvest of victory by incorporating Lysimachus' dominions into his own kingdom, but on his way to Macedonia to take possession of Lysimachus' European provinces he was murdered by Ptolemy Ceraunus scarcely six months after his triumph. During these six months a few bronze coins were struck at Magnesia on the Maeander and a small issue of tetradrachms was produced at Pergamum. Here the fortress with its treasures had been under the command of a certain Philetaerus, one of a group of local officials who had deserted Lysimachus at the end of his reign and asked Seleucus for help. The victory of Seleucus was celebrated at Pergamum by the issue of splendid tetradrachms (**157**) which repeated the military types of the bronzes from Apamea. The obverse presents the spirited head of a bridled horse with two horns, while the reverse shows an impressive Indian war elephant walking to the right. By these types the cavalry and elephant corps of the Seleucid king were duly commemorated for their part in his victory.

Little has been said in the preceding sections on the bronzes. Coinage in this metal was fiduciary and the coins were struck *al marco*. The weights of individual specimens in consequence vary widely, but it seems clear that each denomination was intended to represent the half of the next larger unit.[9] The coins under Seleucus I comprised five denominations, designated by Newell quadruples, doubles, units, halves and quarters. The largest denomination, the quadruple, had an average weight of 12–13g and was probably worth four chalkoi or half a silver obol. The same standards were maintained from Seleucus I to Antiochus III, with a larger piece, the octuple, appearing under Seleucus II.[10] Value marks indicating four, two and one (chalkoi) first occur on some issues of Antiochus IV (175–164), and it has been noted[11] that the averages of these bronzes with value marks, respectively 16.80g, 8.40g and 2.10g, correspond to those of the now reduced silver coins, the largest of them, the tetrachalkon or hemiobol, being the same weight as the tetradrachm, reduced at the same time from 17.00g to 16.80g. Towards the end of his reign Seleucus I tried to make the bronze coinage more uniform throughout his realm. A series of issues (**158–60**) with the types head of Medusa/butting bull appears at Seleucia on the Tigris, Susa, Ecbatana, Antioch, Sardis and Magnesia on the Maeander in four different denominations. Their first appearance at Antioch is dated after 286, and this type is the only one from Sardis and Magnesia.

9 Newell 1938c (*ESM*), 170.
10 *Ibid.* 172.
11 Schlösser 1985a. [This paragraph has been reworded to take account of Schlösser's article.]

8

MACEDONIA, ASIA MINOR AND GREECE

(a) DEMETRIUS POLIORCETES

It has been seen already (p. 61) that Antigonus Monophthalmus never issued coins in his own name but kept to Alexander issues throughout his life. It was only after the disaster of Ipsus in 301 that his son Demetrius Poliorcetes, who was left with a powerful fleet and a number of bases in the eastern Mediterranean and the Aegean, began to issue coins in his own name and soon also with new and personal types though retaining the Attic weight standard.[1]

On the coast of Phoenicia Demetrius maintained his hold on the two important cities of Sidon and Tyre. At the date of the battle of Ipsus only Tyre was minting coins, the mint at Sidon having been closed a few years earlier. At Tyre the Alexander-type coinage, silver tetradrachms (**161**) with head of Heracles/seated Zeus, was continued by Demetrius, but the name of Alexander was replaced by his own name to which a royal title was soon added. The change was apparently made in some haste, for on the first reverse die the name of Demetrius was re-engraved over Alexander's. We actually possess coins struck with this reverse die in both its stages. The tetradrachm coinage of Demetrius may have started in *c.* 298 and lasted for only a few years. In 295, or more probably 294, both Tyre and Sidon were acquired by Ptolemy I, which would have brought the coinage of Demetrius to an end.[2]

Another possession which remained with Demetrius was the island of Cyprus, acquired by the Antigonids after the sea battle with Ptolemy off Salamis in 306. At this time Salamis was the only active mint on the island, and it continued to issue an Alexander coinage for Antigonus and Demetrius down to *c.* 300. But shortly after the defeat of Ipsus Demetrius himself arrived in Cyprus, where he found his mother Stratonice, who had fled from Cilicia with all the treasure within her reach. Demetrius set out energetically to re-establish his position. He also made a significant change in his coinage. While the gold coinage at first preserved Alexander's types and name, the silver tetradrachms (**162**) now showed on the obverse a winged figure of Nike carrying a trumpet in one hand and a signal mast (*stylis*) in the other. She is alighting on the forecastle of a defeated galley, the prow ornament (the *stolos*) of which has been broken off. The type was evidently intended to remind the world of Demetrius' great sea victory of 306.

---

1 The standard work is Newell 1927.
2 Cf. Merker 1974.

In the period of general despair after Ipsus Demetrius had to recall his earlier success in order to show his unbroken spirit and proclaim his intention of continuing the fight. Cases of conscious propaganda in Greek coin types are rare, but this, together with the Porus issues of Alexander (above, pp. 52–4), presents perhaps the most obvious example. The type has been connected with one of the greatest works of art of Antiquity, the Nike of Samothrace in the Louvre, but the general opinion is now that the statue is somewhat later in date and there is no direct connection between them. This, of course, does not exclude the possibility of the coin type having served as model or inspiration for the statue. The reverse of Demetrius' new tetradrachms shows a magnificent striding Poseidon, brandishing his trident. The god of the sea was the natural patron of Demetrius, who now depended to a large extent on his fleet for his survival and who may also have wanted to assert that Poseidon had already rendered his assistance at the naval battle off Salamis. The coins are inscribed *ΔΗΜΗΤΡΙΟΥ ΒΑΣΙΛΕΩΣ*.

New types were introduced only slightly later for a single issue of gold staters (**163**). The obverse has the same type as the silver, but the reverse shows an Athena fighting to the left with shield and spear. The figure is strongly reminiscent of the contemporary Athena on the Ptolemaic silver (above, p. 64), and it may be that the choice of type was influenced by a wish to appropriate this fighting Athena, emphasize her earlier assistance at the battle of 306, and ensure her help in future fighting. The inscription is the same as that of the silver. A single issue of bronze coins (**164**) (young male head in Corinthian helmet adorned with a bull's horn/prow and *ΒΑ*) has also been attributed to Salamis. The head may be an early idealized portrait of Demetrius. The coinages came to an end in *c.* 294, when Ptolemy of Egypt succeeded in conquering the island from Demetrius.

Across the waters from Cyprus the province of Cilicia after Ipsus was allotted to Pleistarchus, the brother of Cassander, who did not strike coins in his own name. As early as 299 Demetrius was operating in Cilician waters and managed to raid the fortress of Cyinda, where he seized what was left of its famous treasure. In the same or the following year, with the approval of Seleucus who had concluded an alliance with Demetrius and married his young daughter, he was able to conquer the province. The mint at Tarsus immediately began to coin for Demetrius in gold, silver and bronze. The gold preserved the Alexander types but was inscribed with Demetrius' name and royal title. The silver (**165**) showed the types of Nike and Poseidon, while the bronze (**166**) was at first similar to the bronze issue of Salamis. A later bronze issue (**167**) used as types a head of Poseidon and a fighting Athena. The silver tetradrachms were accompanied by issues of drachms and hemidrachms showing the same type as the larger denomination. The issues were struck between *c.* 298 and 294 when Seleucus – now in alliance with Ptolemy, who took Cyprus and the Phoenician cities of Tyre and Sidon – acquired Cilicia as his share of the liquidation of Demetrius' eastern possessions.

On the west coast of Asia Minor very few places remained loyal to Demetrius, but among them were the large and important commercial centres of Ephesus and Miletus. At Miletus an Alexander coinage (**168**) in gold and silver was issued from *c.* 300 to 294, and towards the end of this period an additional, apparently quite small issue of tetradrachms was struck in the name of Demetrius with the types of Nike and Poseidon. At Ephesus the coinage of similar tetradrachms was much larger, and the Ephesian tetradrachms were accompanied by an interesting series of drachms and hemidrachms. The reverses of the smaller coins show the same striding Poseidon with trident, but on the obverses the Nike on prow gives place to the earliest portrait of Demetrius (**169**). He appears adorned with the royal diadem and bull's horns, the bull being the sacred animal of his patron deity Poseidon. In spite of the small format, some of the royal heads are excellent examples of early Hellenistic portraiture, showing a lifelike representation of marked individuality. The bull's horns indicate that Demetrius claimed divine honours for himself, or at least accepted the divinity bestowed upon him by the Greek cities, the first certain numismatic example of deification of a living ruler. Already in 307 he and his father had been the subjects of deification at Athens, and again in 292 he was praised as a god manifest in the famous *ithyphallicus* sung in his honour on his arrival in the city. In accordance with his extravagant nature, he seems to have enjoyed these honours more intensely than the other contemporary kings. At both Ephesus and Miletus the coinage of Demetrius stopped about 294, when Lysimachus was apparently able to increase his dominions in Asia Minor at the expense of his rival.

We have seen how in 295 and 294 Demetrius was deprived of all his possessions east of the Aegean Sea by the concerted efforts of Ptolemy, Seleucus and Lysimachus. From *c.* 296 Demetrius had been campaigning in Greece in order to recover Athens, which had revolted against him immediately after Ipsus, and to secure his positions in the Peloponnese, where Corinth and a few other places were still in his hands. At Corinth he issued the Alexander tetradrachms mentioned above, p. 61. At the time of the loss of his Asiatic stronghold Demetrius was prevented from taking energetic measures to defend his possessions by conditions in Macedonia, which now offered more interesting prospects. Since the death of Cassander in 297 Macedonia had been ruled by his sons. After the very brief reign of Philip, the eldest son, the power had been divided between two younger sons, Antipater and Alexander. Their quarrels between themselves led to an invitation from Alexander to Demetrius, asking his military assistance against Antipater. Demetrius invaded Macedonia and promptly murdered Alexander in order to assume the position of king of Macedon (294). His losses in Asia were more than compensated by the possession of the old and traditional kingdom of Macedon.

In Macedonia Cassander and his sons had continued the striking of Alexander coins in gold and silver at Pella and Amphipolis, at the latter mint supplemented by issues of posthumous tetradrachms of Philip II. As we have seen already (above, p. 60), Cassander had issued bronze coins in his own name, and an anonymous bronze coinage (**73**) (Macedonian shield; in centre thunderbolt or *gorgoneion*/Macedonian helmet; *BA*) may belong to his sons.[3] When Demetrius became king he immediately began to issue his own coins at both Macedonian mints. At first the gold staters (**170**) retained the Alexander types but were inscribed with the name of Demetrius, to which a royal title was soon added. But the silver tetradrachms (**171**) were struck with the types of Demetrius, Nike on prow/Poseidon, which we already know from his coinages in the east.

After a few years, in *c.* 292/1, the types of the silver were changed (**172**). The obverse now

3 [See now Liampi 1986.]

showed a portrait of Demetrius with diadem and bull's horns. The first obverse die of this new series from Pella provides us with an excellent realistic portrait of a man in middle age, obviously affected by the years of strenuous effort through which he had lived. Later dies show a younger, more idealized head of lower artistic value. The portraits from Amphipolis are generally of a rather poor style. The reverses of the new silver coins were occupied by a seated Poseidon, holding in his right hand the *aphlaston*, an ornament placed in the stern of Greek war galleys, while his left hand rests on the trident. This reverse type was used only for a very short time. The third silver coinage (**173**) of Demetrius, introduced *c.* 290, shows a similar portrait on the obverse, but on the reverse Poseidon is now depicted standing with his right foot on a piece of rock, leaning on his trident and gazing intently towards the horizon. This series is accompanied by new gold staters (**174**). On the obverse they have the head of the king, while the reverse is occupied by a Macedonian horseman wearing the characteristic broad-brimmed hat, the *kausia*, charging to the right with a spear in his hand. The inscription, as on the silver, reads *ΒΑΣΙΛΕΩΣ ΔΗΜΗΤΡΙΟΥ*. The horseman may be intended as a representation of the king himself.

From *c.* 290 Demetrius was engaged in great military preparations, striving to build a new fleet and collecting troops for a planned invasion of Asia. His dockyards at Pella, Chalcis, Piraeus and Corinth were teeming with activity. The necessary money was supplied by large issues of the gold staters and silver tetradrachms of his third coinage, not only from Pella and Amphipolis but also from Chalcis on Euboea, where a royal mint was opened in *c.* 291. The portraits of Demetrius from the last mint often have a youngish, idealized appearance. Smaller mints were located in Thebes in Boeotia and Demetrias in Thessaly, an important new foundation and harbour town intended as capital and royal residence. It may be that Corinth, in addition to the Alexander coinage, also issued a few tetradrachms of Demetrius' type.[4]

The great activity of Demetrius naturally aroused the fears of his enemies. Ptolemy, Seleucus and Lysimachus formed an alliance against him which was also joined by Pyrrhus, the young and ambitious king of the Molossians in Epirus. The allies proceeded to attack before Demetrius could finish his preparations. In 288 Macedonia was invaded from the west by Pyrrhus and from the east by Lysimachus. Demetrius had to leave his kingdom and was reduced to his Greek possessions, where Athens soon revolted against him. Pyrrhus and Lysimachus divided Macedonia between them and Pyrrhus struck some bronze coins (**175**) in Pella, the capital of his part of Macedonia. He did not strike silver in his own name, but some of the posthumous Alexanders may belong to his reign, although they have not yet been identified with certainty. In 285/4 Pyrrhus was driven out by Lysimachus, who united the whole of Macedonia to his other possessions in Thrace and Asia Minor as a powerful kingdom. In the meantime Demetrius had continued his preparations in Greece, but the pressure from his enemies and the opposition of his Greek subjects forced him to act rashly. In 287, after having concluded a separate peace with Pyrrhus, he launched an expedition into Asia Minor. This great attempt to redress the balance of power ended in disaster. After campaigning in Asia Minor for nearly two years he was hunted down by his enemies and had to surrender to Seleucus, who placed him in

4 These would be the issues ascribed by Newell 1927, 144–7, to Sicyon.

honourable captivity until his death in 283. During his campaign in Asia Minor his European possessions melted away. His son, Antigonus Gonatas, who was left in charge in Europe, had great difficulty even in maintaining his position in a few places like Corinth and Chalcis. While the other Greek mints of Demetrius ceased to issue his coins in 287, it is possible that Chalcis continued until 285, perhaps even to the date of his death.

(b) LYSIMACHUS

We have already noted the curious fact that, apart from a few small issues of tetrobols from Lysimachia to be dated *c.* 306/*c.* 301 (above, p. 61), Lysimachus had no mint and did not strike any coins before Ipsus. As a consequence of this great victory Lysimachus acquired western Asia Minor with its many important minting cities as his share of the spoil.[5] For a couple of years he continued the issue of Alexander drachms from Lysimachia in Europe as well as from his newly acquired mints in Asia Minor: Lampsacus, Abydus, Teos, Colophon and Magnesia. Colophon, Magnesia and Sardis struck a few issues of tetradrachms, while Sestus and Abydus each provided a single issue of gold staters. All these issues were still struck with the types and in the name of Alexander, but they are distinguished from earlier issues by the appearance as a symbol in the field of Lysimachus' badge, the forepart of an attacking lion. From *c.* 299/8 to 297/6 the same mints continued to issue the same denominations (**176–7**), but the legend was changed to read *ΒΑΣΙΛΕΩΣ ΛΥΣΙΜΑΧΟΥ*. Drachms of this type were also issued at Teos and Lampsacus (**180**) and at Mytilene on Lesbos. The former was apparently closed as a royal mint after these issues.

After this period of consolidation Lysimachus in 297/6 made the important change to a completely new coinage of his own. The Attic weight standard was retained, but uniform types and inscription were now used for both gold and silver. The obverses (**178–9, 181–2**) present the head of the deified Alexander with the royal diadem and the ram's horn which shows him to be the son of Zeus Ammon. Lysimachus thus refrained from following the examples of Demetrius and Ptolemy and placing his own portrait on his coins. On the reverses we find a seated Athena leaning her left arm against her shield. Her spear appears behind her, and on her outstretched right hand she carries a small Nike, who places a wreath over the first letter of the king's name. Behind Athena we see the royal title. The obverse type bears witness to his reverence for Alexander, but the reverse proclaims his part in the victory at Ipsus, his name being crowned by Nike at the command of Athena herself. The new coinage was struck simultaneously at many mints: Lysimachia and Sestus on the European side of the Hellespont; Lampsacus (**179**), Abydus and Alexandria Troas in north-western Asia Minor; Sardis in Lydia; Magnesia and Colophon in Ionia. The last-mentioned mint produced only a single issue of tetradrachms before being closed.

In 294 Lysimachus was able to liquidate Demetrius' last bases in Asia Minor. Ephesus became one of his mints, but Miletus apparently preserved a certain independence. Its issues consisted

5 The standard survey is Thompson 1968a.

of Alexander tetradrachms, a coinage politically neutral and commercially advantageous on account of its general prestige and acceptability throughout the Hellenistic world. During the period from 293 to 287 Ephesus, renamed Arsinoe in honour of Lysimachus' queen, supplied the bulk of the drachms. Alexandria Troas provided several issues of staters. The most important denomination, the silver tetradrachm, was produced in great quantities at Lampsacus, where about 60 obverse dies were used during these six years. Of the other Hellespontine mints, Lysimachia, Sestus and Abydus either ceased to strike coins or had a very limited production between 292 and 287. Mytilene was now reactivated for a few issues of tetradrachms and drachms, and Magnesia and Sardis produced moderate quantities of tetradrachms. Both cities joined Demetrius during his adventurous campaign in 287. Retaken by Lysimachus in 286, the mint at Sardis was closed whereas that of Magnesia was apparently allowed to continue.

In 289 the annexation of Bithynia gave Lysimachus control over Cius on the Propontis and Heraclea on the Black Sea coast of Asia Minor. From *c.* 288/7 both cities produced royal coins, Cius tetradrachms, Heraclea both staters and tetradrachms, in very limited quantity.

With his acquisition of eastern Macedon in 288, the great mint of Amphipolis came into Lysimachus' hands. It soon became his principal mint for tetradrachms (**178**), using over 70 obverse dies between 288 and 281. A little later, in 285, Lysimachus was able to drive Pyrrhus out of the western part of Macedon, gaining control of Pella, which became a royal mint with a considerable output of staters and tetradrachms (**181**).

Lysimachus issued several different series of bronze coins, but their chronology and their distribution among his mints have not yet been worked out. The commonest series consisted of two denominations (**183, 184**), both having on the obverse a head of Athena in Attic helmet and on the reverse an attacking lion in full figure or its forepart, the personal badge of Lysimachus.

After 287 Lysimachus opened a new royal mint at Smyrna, which produced a single issue comprising staters, tetradrachms (**182**) and drachms. About the same time there was a remarkable increase of coinage in northern Asia Minor. Lysimachia, Sestus and Abydus resumed their activity, adding their productions to those of Lampsacus and Alexandria Troas, and new mints were opened in Parium and Pergamum. Parium was a small mint, Pergamum one of moderate size. It may be that isolated coinages were also produced at Perinthus and Aenus in Thrace at the very end of Lysimachus' reign, but these issues may in fact be posthumous. The increased activity in this area, the very centre of Lysimachus' far-flung dominions, undoubtedly reflects the costly preparations during the last years of the reign for the final conflict between the two tough survivors among Alexander's generals, Seleucus and Lysimachus. In 281 a battle on the plain of Corupedium put an end to Lysimachus' life and rule, although not, as we shall see, to his coinage (below, pp. 145 ff.).

(c) LESSER DYNASTS AND CITIES OF GREECE AND ASIA MINOR

To the north of Macedonia, on the upper course of the Axius river, lived the Paeonians, ruled by their own princes. They began to strike coins before the middle of the fourth century. Within our period falls the coinage of Patraeus, *c.* 340–315 B.C.[6] His staters (**185**), struck on a local standard of *c.* 12.80–13.00g, show on the obverse a head of Apollo, on the reverse a dramatic battle scene, where a horseman spears a prostrate enemy. It should be remembered that the Paeonian contingent in Alexander's invasion army consisted of light cavalry. Instead of Apollo's laurel wreath the obverse head sometimes wears a *taenia* or diadem (**186**). An early reverse type shows the bust of a horse (**187**). This issue is particularly interesting, because the obverse die was re-used at the mint of Damastion, a mining city in the vicinity of the Paeonians with an extensive coinage that came to an end about 325/320, probably as a result of the exhaustion of the mines.[7] Patraeus also issued lower denominations in silver, drachms and tetrobols, with reverse types forepart of boar and eagle respectively (**188–9**).

The successor of Patraeus, Audoleon (*c.* 315–286), issued staters on the local standard with a facing head of Athena in crested helmet on the obverse and free horse walking to the right on the reverse (**190**). At some date after 305 he adopted the title of king and used it on a series of tetradrachms of Alexander type and weight. The occurrence of a specific Paeonian symbol, resembling an *upsilon* with curved arms, allowed Seyrig to attribute a series of ordinary Alexander tetradrachms (**191**) to the Paeonian mint under Audoleon.[8]

In Thrace the local dynast Seuthes III, ruler of the Odrysae, issued a number of bronze coins in various denominations.[9] He is best known for his continuous and apparently not unsuccessful fight against Macedonian domination, first against Alexander, later against Lysimachus. His reign extended from *c.* 330 to 300/295. His common reverse type is a horseman, while the obverse is generally a laureate head of Zeus (**192**). Sometimes the features of Zeus seem to be strongly individualized with a prominent aquiline nose. This has been taken to be a portrait of Seuthes III, and thus one of the earliest known ruler portraits, but the laurel wreath around the head invites caution. At most it could be called a representation of Zeus into which individual traits of Seuthes have been introduced. Many of the coins of Seuthes III are overstruck on Macedonian ones, especially on bronze issues of Cassander.

To the west of Macedonia lie the regions of Illyria and Epirus. In Illyria the Greek colonies of Dyrrhachium and Apollonia had a long tradition of coinage on the so-called Corcyrean standard with a stater of originally *c.* 11.6g or four Corinthian drachms. Towards 300 it had already been reduced to *c.* 10.5g. At this time a local prince, Monunius, ruler of the Dardanian Illyrians, was able to strike coins (**193**) at Dyrrhachium of the normal civic type, cow suckling

6 Cf. Gaebler 1927, 237–43.
7 Cf. May 1939, 146f., 151f., 162f.
8 Seyrig 1963, 12–14; Waggoner 1982. [Waggoner 1983 attributes eighteen more Alexander issues, earlier given to Pella, to Audoleon.]
9 Youroukova 1976, 22–4, 76–9. The other types mentioned here may belong to Seuthes IV around 200.

calf/double stellate pattern, which was also imitated at Corcyra.[10] He even adopted the title of king on his coinage. We do not know whether he had occupied the city or was simply allowed to use its minting facilities. At about the same time, *c.* 300–280, smaller coins of *c.* 2.4g with types head of Heracles/Pegasus were struck by the city of Dyrrhachium (**194**).

We have already mentioned the bronze coins of Pyrrhus struck in Pella (above p. 80). In his native Epirus he struck two bronze issues from 297, both with the head of Zeus on the obverse, while the reverse type was a thunderbolt (**196**), in a wreath of oak-leaves on the larger denomination, without wreath on the smaller. Both types were also used by the Epirote *symmachia* (**197–8**). The same die engravers were at work for both the king and the *symmachia*, so that both series were most probably produced at the same mint.[11]. The head of Zeus on the obverse shows strong Ptolemaic influence, reminding us of the fact that the young Pyrrhus had spent some time as a hostage in Egypt.

After an interval in which Apollonia, Corcyra and more especially Dyrrhachium were striking Corinthian-type *pegasi* for use in the West,[12] the important island of Corcyra reverted to its old types. About 300 the production of staters came to an end, but smaller denominations, drachms, hemidrachms, etc., were struck after that date. The Corcyrean didrachm (**195**) (forepart of cow/double stellate pattern) now weighed a little above 5g, conveniently close to the reduced Aeginetan standard which was developed in central Greece and the Peloponnese during the third century.

Until fairly recently it was a general assumption that the extension of Macedonian rule over Greece and Asia Minor meant that the city coinages in the districts under Macedonian rule came with few exceptions to an end. Head, for example, supposed that a great number of Thessalian coinages stopped in 344 with Philip's second invasion of Thessaly.[13] The coinage of Ambracia has likewise been supposed to have ended in 338 with Philip's occupation of the city. This is now recognized as an anachronistic point of view, based on what we know of conditions in later periods when the monetary prerogative of the ruling power was treated as a firm and indisputable principle.[14]

In Macedon itself we have already noted the bronze coinage of Uranopolis (above p. 60). Another city coinage of gold, silver and bronze (**199–201**) was issued by Philippi, all with head of Heracles/tripod as types. While the gold is on the Attic standard, the rare silver coins were struck on a rather light variant of Philip's silver standard. The coinage can be divided into two series, the second of which, comprising most of the gold, appears from its style as well as from hoard evidence to belong to the reign of Alexander.[15] The relevant hoards are the Drama bronze hoard (*ICGH* 404), with eleven different issues of the second series, and the large gold hoard

10 The dating of Monunius to *c.* 350 by Çeka 1972, 23–7, is quite impossible.
11 See Franke 1961, 249–64.
12 [See Kraay 1976, 127–8.]
13 Head 1911, 297.
14 [See now Martin 1985.]
15 Bellinger 1964; on the Saida hoard see Westermark 1980.

from Saida (*IGCH* 1508) buried *c.* 324/3, which contained one gold stater of Philippi in very good condition.

During the fourth century the most important mint in Thessaly was Larissa. As already mentioned, it was thought to have stopped its production in 344, but various objections can be raised against such a dating. A special issue (**202**), a drachm of the Aeginetan standard commonly used in Thessaly, shows on the obverse the head of the Thessalian hero Aleuas, the mythical forefather of the Aleuads who for centuries were the leading family of Larissa. Aleuas is represented three-quarters facing, wearing an ornamented conical helmet with cheek-pieces. His name appears in the right field together with a double axe, the symbol of the *tagos*, the pan-Thessalian leader. On the reverse we see an eagle standing on a thunderbolt with head reverted, identical with the first reverse type of Alexander the Great. In addition to the city name there appears the inscription *ΕΛΛΑ*, which has not yet received a satisfactory explanation. The types have been plausibly connected with Alexander the Great's proclamation as *tagos* of Thessaly in 336 and dated accordingly.[16]

The common drachms of Larissa (**203**) show on the obverse a facing female head copied from the famous facing head of Arethusa at Syracuse by Cimon, but here representing the local nymph Larissa. On the reverse a horse is represented in various positions. According to hoard evidence from Thessaly this coinage was produced down to *c.* 320.[17] Its end may have been caused by an order from Antipater after the end of the Lamian War, but also, and perhaps more probably, by the economic exhaustion of the district, which had experienced the severe famine of the 320s followed immediately by the ravages of this war fought mostly on Thessalian territory. Economic conditions are really a better explanation of the cessation of Thessalian silver coinage around this time, the Macedonian attitude to minting being rather one of non-interference.

At Delphi the Amphictyonic Council in 336 decided to issue a new coinage, reminting the stock of different coins in the temple treasury into staters, drachms and hemidrachms of a new type. The obverse shows a beautiful veiled head of Demeter, who had a sanctuary under Amphictyonic control at Anthela near Thermopylae. The reverses of the two large denominations (**204**) present the lord of Delphi, Apollo, seated on the sacred *omphalos*, with the inscription *ΑΜΦΙΚΤΙΟΝΩΝ*. On the reverse of the hemidrachms (**205**) appears the *omphalos* around which the serpent Python is coiled. The purpose was to finance the rebuilding of the temple, but in a uniform currency so as to avoid frequent exchange transactions. The new coins were naturally struck on the Aeginetan standard. This is one of the few cases where we have epigraphical evidence for the date as well as for the volume of the coinage.[18] The most recent discussion of the subject, by Philip Kinns, shows that the coinage, produced most probably between the autumn of 336 and the spring of 334, was struck from between 125 and 175 talents

16 Sordi 1956.

17 Bellinger 1965 (*IGCH* 168); Martin 1982.

18 Raven 1950; Kinns 1983. I am grateful to Dr Kinns for having allowed me to see his paper while still in proof.

of silver. A calculation of the die output leads to the surprising conclusion that a minimum of 23,300 specimens were struck from each obverse die, a figure that is more than twice as high as earlier suggested averages. The Amphictyonic coinage was an experiment of short duration. Probably coin production turned out to be more complicated than originally envisaged, and the Amphictyonic Council soon reverted to its customary practice of using the miscellaneous currencies that flowed into the temple treasury.

In Boeotia no coinage can be ascribed with certainty to the years immediately after 335. In that year the razing of Thebes to the ground deprived the region of its economic and political centre. After the rebuilding of Thebes by Cassander in 315 a small issue of Alexander coins may have been issued there by the Macedonian king, and Thebes was certainly a royal mint under Demetrius Poliorcetes.[19] A splendid autonomous tetradrachm (**206**) of Attic weight with head of Poseidon/Poseidon seated on throne, holding dolphin and trident was issued about 287. It is inscribed *ΒΟΙΩΤΩΝ* and celebrates the recovery of freedom from the domination of Demetrius.

During the latter half of the fourth century Athens continued its considerable output of owl tetradrachms. The best criterion for a relative chronological arrangement of these is offered by the form of the floral scroll that adorns the helmet of Athena on the obverse (**207**). The terminal element of this scroll from about 350 takes a form that resembles the Greek letter *pi*. This *pi* style lasted, on the evidence of the Thorikos hoard (*IGCH* 134), until the beginning of the third century.[20] In 294 Demetrius Poliorcetes conquered Athens. The *pi* style seems to have ended at that time, when a break occurred in the production of Athenian 'owls'. When their minting was resumed somewhat later, a new style appears.

Within the period covered by the *pi* style, two issues deserve special mention. A number of plated tetradrachms, buried in the Athenian Agora, have been explained as an emergency issue after Chaeronea in 338. They were apparently withdrawn by the authorities before having been put into circulation, since the leniency of Philip of Macedon brought the war to an end earlier than was expected.[21] The second issue consists of gold staters (**208**) and has repeatedly been connected with the tyranny of Lachares (297–294), the more so because we have written evidence of Lachares despoiling the Athenian temples of gold in order to pay his mercenaries. One of these rare coins was present in the Thorikos hoard. The dating of these coins to 297/294 becomes an important fixed point for the absolute chronology of the *pi*-style issues, to the latest phase of which they belong.

Between 294 and 287 Athens was under the control of Demetrius. Apparently no coinage was struck during these years, but with the acquisition of partial freedom in 287 – a Macedonian garrison still stayed at Piraeus – tetradrachms were minted again. The floral decoration on Athena's helmet now ends in four 'fingers' issuing from a common point at the base. This style

19 Newell 1927, 126–8.
20 Bingen 1973, 1975.
21 Walker 1982.

continues beyond 280 and lasts most probably to 262, when a new break in Athenian coinage occurred during the Macedonian occupation (261–229; below, p. 148).

During this period a regular issue of bronze coins of the chalkous denomination (one-eighth of an obol) was introduced at Athens.[22] Its beginning has been put as early as *c.* 350, but it may well have started only after Chaeronea. The earliest epigraphical evidence for the use of bronze coins dates from 329/8. In any case the introduction of a fiduciary coinage in Athens came relatively late. The first issues (**209**) show on the obverse the head of Athena in Athenian helmet, on the reverse a double-bodied owl, soon replaced by two owls confronted (**210**). The change to an Athena in Corinthian helmet on the obverse and a single owl on the reverse (**211**) has been plausibly connected with the period of Macedonian control after 322. During the same time bronzes with the types Triptolemus/pig were issued for Eleusis (**212**).[23]

At Corinth the production of *pegasi* (**213**) (staters of *c.* 8.6g with the types Pegasus/head of Athena in Corinthian helmet) continued till about 302. Ravel's fifth period comprises the years from *c.* 350 to 307.[24] The large coinage is divided into twelve series, the last four of which cover the last two decades of the fourth century. A chronological fixed point is established for series 12 with the Greek letters *ΔO* as an issue mark. The same letters appear on Ptolemaic drachms which can only have been struck during the Ptolemaic occupation from 308 to 306 or a little later, for it seems likely that this occupation lasted until 305 or even 304. This means that the end of the fifth period might be taken down by a couple of years.[25] The few disparate issues brought together by Ravel as the first series of the sixth period would then suffice for the remaining couple of years down to 302. The diversity of style and the frequent occurrence of underweight specimens suggest that Corinth in these last few years went through a period of economic distress. In 302 Demetrius Poliorcetes, on behalf of his father Antigonus and himself, re-established the Corinthian League as a political instrument against Cassander. About this time the striking of *pegasi* came to an end at Corinth itself, and an issue of Alexander-type tetradrachms was inaugurated. It is a moot point whether the change was due to direct royal intervention or came about as a natural consequence of unfortunate developments in the city's economy, although the latter explanation seems to me the more likely.

Among the Corinthian colonies in western Greece, Leucas continued its production of Corinthian-type staters until about the end of the century. It has recently been suggested that the production of *pegasi* was increased at Anactorium, Amphilocian Argos and Thyrrheum, all in Acarnania, during the years 305/295 in order to supply the market in South Italy and Sicily with its favourite trading coin.[26] Apparently there was a gap to be filled owing to the sharp decrease and eventual cessation of *pegasi* from Corinth herself after 305.

---

22 Kroll 1979.
23 Thompson 1942.
24 Ravel 1948. The dates given here are those of Jenkins 1958b, 371–4.
25 On this possibility, involving the redating of the Chiliomodi hoard (*IGCH* 85) to 304, see Mørkholm 1980b, 156.
26 Burnett 1977, 97–8 and 111.

Trihemidrachms (**214**) of the types Bellerophon on Pegasus/chimaera were also struck at Corinth down to *c.* 330 or later.[27] The smaller denominations in silver and the bronze issues, introduced *c.* 350, also continued.

During the fourth century large and important series of silver staters on the Aeginetan weight standard (*c.* 12.2g) had been issued at Sicyon, Argos and Elis. At all three places the stater coinage was affected by the Lamian War. At Argos, Sicyon and the Hera mint of Olympia it came to an end around 322, while the Zeus mint of Olympia continued on a reduced scale until the end of the third century. In the absence of modern monographs on Sicyon and Argos one cannot yet date the coins of this period (**215**) with any precision.[28] For Elis (**216**) the work of Seltman allows us a greater degree of certainty.[29] As far as I know his chronology has not been seriously challenged for the period here under consideration. For all these mints, as for the Peloponnese and central Greece in general, the future lay with the smaller denominations, especially the hemidrachms, which became the most important coin in this area from the late fourth century onwards. This development will be dealt with in the next chapter.

During the years from *c.* 330 to 280/270 the island of Crete experienced an explosion of silver coinage.[30] No fewer than 28 mints, scattered over the whole island, took part in its production, many of them striking coins for the first time. They produced staters of Aeginetan weight, which seems to have declined a little from the original *c.* 12.2g. A frequency table of staters from the material collected by Le Rider shows a concentration in the interval from 11.5g to 11.9g, a sign of a not very careful adjustment of the individual weights. The most important mints were Gortyn and Phaestus on the southern Messara plain and Knossos to the north, all in the central region of Crete. At Gortyn the staters (**217**) present on the obverse the nymph Europa seated in a tree, with or without the eagle of Zeus, while the reverse is occupied by a bull in different positions, undoubtedly referring to the disguise in which Zeus first showed himself to Europa. The obverse types at Phaestus are more varied. In addition to Heracles standing (**218**), seated (**219**) or fighting the Lernaean Hydra (**220**), we find the local hero Velchanos seated with his cock (**221**) and the winged giant Talon standing to front (**222**). The reverse type is again a bull, which sometimes appears within an olive wreath. The artistic quality of some of the obverses is remarkable, both the seated figures and the fighting Heracles.

At Knossos the obverses show female heads that have not been identified with certainty. Towards the end of the period appears a head of Hera wearing a *stephanos* (**223**), obviously copied from the staters of Argos. The reverse is adorned by the labyrinth rendered in different

27 Warren 1968.

28 Work on these two mints is being carried out by J. Warren (Mrs Cargill Thompson) and T. Hackens respectively. To the first I am obliged for advance information on the chronology of the coinage from Sicyon.

29 Seltman 1921. Seltman extended the activity of the Zeus mint till after 191, but this is now recognized as being too late.

30 These coinages were earlier dated to a much broader period, but I follow Le Rider 1966, esp. 194–8 (synopsis), whose conclusions are based mainly on an examination of the Cretan coin hoards *IGCH* 151–4.

forms. A drachm (**224**) (head of Apollo/Zeus or Minos carrying Nike and seated on the labyrinth) is provided with a monogram that also appears on a stater of the East Cretan city of Olus (**225**). This latter coin is interesting because the reverse type is a copy of the seated Zeus with eagle from the silver coinage of Alexander the Great, thus providing a chronological clue of some importance.

The artistic quality of the Cretan coins of these years is extremely varied, ranging from pure unmitigated barbarism to representations that equal the best of the period. In Chersonesus in central Crete, for instance, we find two reverse types, a seated Apollo on *omphalos* (**226**) and a fighting Heracles (**227**), that are excellent. But the second of these at least is derivative, being a close copy of a fourth-century coin type from Stymphalus in Arcadia (**228**) which had evidently gained some reputation. The coinage of Sybrita shows late fourth-century numismatic art at its very best. One stater (**229**) has a seated Dionysus on the obverse and a standing Hermes on the reverse. Another coin of the same denomination (**230**) represents Dionysus riding on a panther and, on the reverse, a Hermes leaning forwards and strapping or adjusting the sandal of his right foot. This is exactly the position of a famous statue by Lysippus and, with the Cretan coin dated around 300, it may well be considered a copy of the sculpture. A third coin (**231**), showing the heads of Dionysus and Hermes, maintains the same high artistic level.

An interesting obverse die link has been observed between the cities of Eleutherna and Hierapytna and with a third (unidentified) mint (**232–4**).[31] The two cities are far apart from each other, with numerous other city-states in between. The best explanation of the phenomenon is probably that an itinerant die engraver brought with him an obverse die, representing a rather neutral head of Zeus, and used it at various places. His obverse seems to be copied from the Arcadian Zeus, a further indication of the artistic links between Crete and the Peloponnese.

Before leaving Crete the problem of the sudden and drastic increase in coinage between *c.* 330 and 280/270 has to be discussed. Two facts are relevant. In the first place, Cretan silver tended to stay at home and is rarely found outside the island. Secondly, a very high proportion of Cretan coins of this period are overstruck on imported coins, especially in the most productive mints at Gortyn and Phaestus.[32] Many of these overstrikes used coins of Cyrene as flans, a fact convincingly explained by Le Rider as a result of Cretan mercenaries fighting under Thibron in Cyrene *c.* 332 (see above, pp. 67–8). This explanation should perhaps be extended, for it is well known that Cretan mercenaries took part in Alexander's expedition and during the wars of the Successors will still have been in great demand. Veterans returning from military campaigns abroad would have brought their hard-earned riches back to Crete, where they were converted into local coin. Apparently, after 280/270, the production of silver coins in Crete dropped rather suddenly, indicating that the golden days of mercenary adventure had passed. However, as practically no silver coins were exported from Crete, the large production of the decades around 300 should have sufficed to cover the need for coinage on the island far into the third century.

31 Mørkholm 1982b, 209; Hess-Bank Leu (7.iv.1960), 197.
32 Le Rider 1966, 133–98.

On Rhodes the Hellenistic coinage starts with an issue of splendid gold staters of Attic weight (**235**).[33] They were present in the Saida hoard (*IGCH* 1508) in excellent condition and therefore probably struck between *c.* 333/2 and 323. The types are the usual Rhodian ones, facing head of Helios/rose, and, like most Rhodian silver before 305/4, had a square incuse on the reverse. The rare contemporary tetradrachms (**236**), and a slightly later and more common issue that was perhaps intended to pay for reconstruction after a devastating flood in 316, were struck according to a reduced Chian standard of *c.* 15.2g instead of 15.6g. During the period 333–305/4 copious issues of didrachms (**237**) were struck to weights of only *c.* 6.7g/6.9g. By 305/4 the final Rhodian standard with a didrachm of *c.* 6.7g (**238**) was firmly established. The same standard was used for the smaller denominations. An abundant series of chalkoi (profile head of Rhodos/rose) was struck in the later fourth century and continued sporadically into the third.

After the famous siege of Rhodes by Demetrius Poliorcetes, which lasted for about a year (305/4) and earned the Rhodians a certain freedom of action and a close political and economic connection with Ptolemy I of Egypt, we find no more gold and no tetradrachms for many years. The didrachm of 6.7g, now with a round incuse or none at all, predominated and was issued in various series (**239**) throughout the third century and the first decade of the second. It became one of the great Hellenistic coinages with a respectable circulation in the eastern Mediterranean, although its special weight did act as a barrier against its use as a truly international means of exchange. We have to remember, however, that much Rhodian trade was conducted with Egypt, and any Rhodian coins spent there would have been melted down and re-issued as Ptolemaic silver, thus disappearing without trace.

Among the Cyclades only Tenos seems with certainty to have issued silver during our period. A rare tetradrachm (**240**) shows on the obverse the head of Zeus Ammon, on the reverse a Poseidon enthroned, holding a dolphin and trident. The position of the seated Poseidon is obviously copied from the seated Zeus of Alexander the Great. The god is represented with one foot drawn back, which provides a *terminus post quem* of *c.* 325. A date around 320 seems reasonable. Another contemporary tetradrachm of Tenos simply copies the other Alexander coinage as regards both types and weight. A remarkable fact which serves to put our coins in a category apart is the use of the Attic weight standard, for on the islands the Chian standard or one of its lighter derivatives was universally used in the later Hellenistic period.

On the island of Euboea the Macedonian victory at Chaeronea in 338 heralded a new epoch in its political and monetary history.[34] The Euboean League was dissolved and the coinage left to the initiative of the individual cities. Chalcis, the most important of the island's four cities, issued between 338 and 305 a large series of drachms (**241**) comprising eleven issues (head of the nymph Chalcis/eagle carrying serpent) plus the same number of issues of bronze coins. The bronzes (**242**) have a striking obverse type: a facing head of Hera placed on the capital of an Ionic column. While Eretria did not issue coins during this period, Carystus in the south and

33 [The text of this section has been revised by Richard Ashton, for whose help Mørkholm had already expressed his indebtedness in the original version. See also Ashton 1988a.]

34 The following account is mainly based on Picard 1979.

Histiaea in the north both minted small series of drachms, at the latter place supplemented by so-called octobols and tetrobols. The drachms of Carystus (**243**) carried the types head of Heracles/bull recumbent, while those of Histiaea (**244**) showed a head of a Maenad/bull standing before vine. The other denominations of Histiaea had the same obverse type as the drachms, but on the reverse we see the nymph Histiaea seated on the stern of a galley and holding a *stylis* that is sometimes inscribed with the name of a deity.[35]

The weight standard used in Euboea has often been called 'reduced' Attic. Frequency tables of the drachms of Chalcis, for which the material is easily available, show fluctuations between 3.4g and 3.7g, i.e. with weights moving within the limits of the original Chian and the final Rhodian standard. I think the connection of the Chalcidian weight is with this area rather than with Athens herself.

The 'octobols' and 'tetrobols' of Histiaea are also assumed to be struck on the Attic standard. However, they might as well be regarded as drachms and hemidrachms of Aeginetan weight, already slightly reduced. In view of Histiaea's close ties with Thessaly, a district accustomed to the Aeginetan standard, this view has much to recommend it. It would have been an obvious advantage if these denominations could be made to fit into two different weight systems.

In 304, with the conquest of Euboea by Demetrius Poliorcetes, the Euboean League was revived, and the League coinage of drachms and bronzes replaced the issues of the cities.[36] The coinage of drachms (**245**) (head of the nymph Euboea/head and neck of bull) consisted of six issues with weights concentrated around 3.6g to 3.9g, or slightly heavier than the preceding Chalcidian drachms. A technical innovation is the use of dies adjusted in a vertical upright position. This is probably the earliest example of the use of adjusted dies in Greece itself. The fashion is of eastern origin and must have come to Greece from the Levant. These League issues were minted at Chalcis, as argued by Picard, rather than at Eretria, as assumed by Wallace and earlier scholars. According to Picard they lasted until *c.* 290, but as far as I can see nothing prevents us from lowering this date to *c.* 285, when Demetrius Poliorcetes finally disappeared from the political scene. The dissolution of the League and the new return to civic issues will then have been the work of Antigonus Gonatas during the first years of his reign in Greece, when his position was very uncertain and he may well have been susceptible to the adoption of administrative measures that favoured the cities. It is curious that the drachms of Chalcis, in spite of their slightly lighter weight, enjoyed a wider circulation outside Euboea than the silver of the League. Hoards and single finds show that Chalcidian drachms were accepted in central Greece as well as in the Peloponnese. I mentioned in an earlier chapter (p. 61) two issues of Alexander tetradrachms at Chalcis (**246–7**) and dated them *c.* 304–300. A slightly later chronology has been proposed by Picard,[37] who regards them as civic and not royal issues and puts them *c.* 310 (or *c.* 300)–*c.* 290. As the two differ in various points of style, a third possibility that is quite attractive would be to date the first issue *c.* 304–300 and place the second around 290.

35 On the early Histiaean coinage see Newell 1921a and Noe 1958.
36 Wallace 1956.
37 Picard 1979, with my review in *Gnomon* 52 (1980), 451–6.

One of the professed aims of the Panhellenic expedition against Persia under Alexander was the liberation of the Greeks in western Asia Minor. A natural consequence of this propaganda must have been that the old Greek cities in this region were allowed to continue their local coinages to the extent that the civic authorities found it expedient and profitable to do so.

Among the many cities a few can be selected for which recent scholarship has established a plausible chronology,[38] though in many cases the coinages of the fourth century cannot be readily divided into pre- and post-liberation issues.

The city of Erythrae in central Ionia had issued tetradrachms (**248**) and drachms of reduced Chian weight (*c.* 15.1g–14.8g) during the decade 350–340. The types were head of young Heracles/club and bow in case with ethnic and magistrate's name. About 325/315 the same types were used for a new coinage of tetradrachms and drachms. Here the Heracles head on the obverse clearly reveals stylistic influence from the Heracles head of Alexander's coinage. The weight was now further reduced to about 14.9g/14.4g for the tetradrachms and *c.* 3.7g/3.6g for the drachms. Although six different magistrates signed the tetradrachms, only one obverse die was used, which must have had an extraordinarily long lifetime. Around 310/297 two series of Attic-weight drachms (**249**) were produced, to be followed in 297/294 by issues of silver drachms and hemidrachms of reduced Rhodian weight (*c.* 2.8g and 1.4g) together with gold third-staters or tetrobols of Attic weight. It has been suggested that this was an emergency coinage of the troubled years when Lysimachus and Demetrius fought for the control of the Ionian coast. The silver coins might also be called hemidrachms and quarter-drachms of the Persian standard. One of the gold issues (**250**) shows an unusual reverse type: a goddess with *kalathos* standing facing, holding a spear and an uncertain globular object. This is probably an old Anatolian deity who was often equated with Artemis by the Greeks.

Several bronze denominations (**251**) were struck between 325 and 295, the largest being the obol, with weight ranging between 15g and 8.5g. Many of these were countermarked after the cessation of the issue, some with two different countermarks. A rare dichalkon issue may show a portrait of Demetrius Poliorcetes on the obverse. It is dated *c.* 306–304 by Kinns, which if correct would make it one of the earliest portraits of a living ruler in Hellenistic coinage.

A second series of bronzes was issued between 295 and 280 in three different denominations. All were countermarked, either in 280 or during the Galatian troubles *c.* 277–275. Here as elsewhere the countermarking of bronzes by the issuing city itself was a device to increase the profits from minting and therefore often used in times of financial difficulty.

At Teos and Colophon the issue of coinage in our period is more restricted. The largest silver denomination at both mints consists of drachms (**252**) weighing *c.* 3.0g (reduced Rhodian?) introduced *c.* 310. The mint of Teos also struck a gold tetrobol of Attic weight (running griffon/chelys with three strings), which is probably contemporary with the Erythrean gold issues of *c.* 297–294. Various denominations of bronze coins (**253–4**) were also issued, most plentifully at Colophon.[39]

---

38 The following account of the coinages of Erythrae, Teos and Colophon is based on an unpublished dissertation of Philip Kinns, which he kindly placed at my disposal.

39 For Colophon see Milne 1941, but its chronology has been superseded by that of Kinns.

Both Teos and Colophon are commonly regarded as Alexander mints, producing especially drachms (above, p. 50). The identification of these mints seems very plausible to me. This implies a situation with Alexander drachms and civic issues in silver and bronze being issued concurrently at the same place, but personally I feel no hesitation over accepting this possibility.

The flourishing city of Ephesus issued an abundant coinage throughout the fourth century.[40] The principal denomination was the tetradrachm (**255**) of reduced Chian weight, *c.* 15.6g, with the bee on the obverse and the forepart of a stag, head reverted, placed before a palm-tree on the reverse. The number of magistrates signing this coinage is very large, and it has been dated from *c.* 387 to 301. As usual it is impossible, without a proper die study, to say which part of the coinage was struck after the advent of Alexander. The tetradrachms were accompanied by drachms and smaller denominations in silver as well as by various bronze issues.

Between 301 and 281 Ephesus was in the possession of Demetrius Poliorcetes and subsequently of Lysimachus. Its mint was used by both kings (**256–8**) (above, pp. 78–9, 81–2). During the latter's reign the city was enlarged by synoecism with Colophon and Lebedus and renamed Arsinoea in honour of Lysimachus' wife, the Egyptian princess Arsinoe II. Some silver and bronze issues were produced with the new name of the city. The reverse types were traditional to Ephesus, but on the obverses the veiled head of Arsinoe appears. The coins are of special importance because they can be securely dated to the years between 289/8 and 280 (or 281, according to Le Rider), when Ephesus returned to her old name and came under Seleucid domination.

Another Lysimachus refoundation in Asia Minor was Smyrna. In addition to a royal issue, bronze coins were minted, showing that the name of the city had been changed to Eurydicea in honour of a daughter of Lysimachus.

On Samos an issue of reduced Rhodian didrachms was struck between *c.* 310 and 300, weighing *c.* 6.3g/6.5g, together with a few smaller denominations.[41] The common Samian types, mask of lion/forepart of an ox, were used (**259–60**) except for the smallest denomination, the rare trihemiobol (**261**), which showed head of Hera/prow.

Miletus was one of the drachm mints of Alexander, but there is a gap in the production of Alexander coins between *c.* 319/18 and 300. Part of this interval [*c.* 310–300] may have been filled by civic issues, primarily didrachms (**262**) of reduced Rhodian weight (head of Apollo/lion walking, head reverted, above star) similar in fabric to the Samian didrachms but some of them bronze (**263**).[42] After *c.* 300 Demetrius used the mint for Alexander gold staters, plus tetradrachms, and more especially drachms, to which he added a tetradrachm of his own first type.[43] After *c.* 294 the city of Miletus, escaping the domination of Lysimachus which, as far as

40 [Le Rider 1973a dates them 386–336/334. There seem to be no silver coins between 334 and 301.] For a good survey of the coinage of Ephesus see Stefan Karwiese in *PW* Suppl. XII (1970), 297ff.

41 Barron 1966, 124–40.

42 [See now Deppert-Lippitz 1984 and Kinns 1986.]

43 Newell 1927, 59–63.

we can see, did not extend south of the Maeander river, at least not permanently, started a production of Alexander tetradrachms (**264**). Now, however, the monogram of the city was added, indicating that we are here dealing with a civic issue. This is one of the earliest of this category which became so popular in the third and early second centuries and to which we shall return in the next chapter.

Another early example of a civic Alexander issue (**265**) is provided at Mylasa in Caria. Here a modest issue of drachms and tetradrachms was struck between *c.* 300 and *c.* 280, probably in the later years of this period.[44] To the time shortly after 300 belongs a unique gold stater from the same mint, struck with the types and in the name of Philip II.

During the Classical period the Propontis area and the adjacent districts of Asia Minor were distinguished numismatically by their issues of old-fashioned electrum (Cyzicus, Mytilene and Phocaea) and gold (Lampsacus). These coinages came to an end in the first year of the Hellenistic period, at Lampsacus already in *c.* 329 with the establishment of an Alexander mint, at the three electrum mints *c.* 326/5.[45] The coinages in electrum and gold were used especially in the important trade with the north coast of the Black Sea, and the demand for gold in these regions did not disappear. Replacements for the obsolete coinages had consequently to be found. This situation explains the large gold issues from the Alexander mints at Lampsacus and Abydus (see above p. 50), and also supplied the incentive for a couple of cities to strike gold staters on the Attic standard, made popular by Philip and Alexander. Between *c.* 334 and 323 a single issue was struck at Pergamum, while Cius produced six issues signed by different magistrates.[46] The types are local: at Cius (**266**) head of Apollo/prow of galley, at Pergamum (**268**) head of Heracles (copied from the Alexander coinage)/statue of fighting Athena standing to front. The Pergamene issue is anepigraphic according to the age-old tradition for gold and electrum coinages in Asia Minor, but the attribution is secured by the occurrence of small silver coins with the same types and inscribed *ΠΕΡΓΑ*. The staters from Cius are inscribed only with magistrates' names, but again the ascription is certain owing to the existence of somewhat earlier silver coins with similar types and the city name inscribed. The short duration of these issues shows that they were quickly ousted by the enormous production of royal gold in the same region.

The influence of the new gold standard was also felt among the trading partners of the Greeks. About the middle of the fourth century Panticapaeum had minted gold staters on a local standard of a little above 9g with the types head of Pan/standing griffin. An issue of about 320, however, in a more 'Scythian' style (**269**) contained a small group of coins, all from the same obverse die, that was struck on the Attic standard.[47]

The gold coins of Cius just mentioned were accompanied by a silver coinage of Persian hemidrachms and quarter drachms weighing *c.* 2.50g and 1.25g (**267**). Hemidrachms were

---

44 Thompson 1981b, 207–8, 215–16 ('second sequence').
45 Bodenstedt 1976, 19; 1981, 46–7.
46 The issues of both Pergamum and Cius were represented in the Saida hoard of *c.* 324/3. See Westermark 1980, 30–2.
47 Regling 1931, 36.

minted in large quantities between *c*. 340 and 300 at the important cities of Byzantium (**270**) and Chalcedon (**271**) on the Bosphorus.[48] The co-operation or alliance of the two cities is shown by their use of the same obverse type: a standing bull. The reverse is an old-fashioned incuse in a kind of windmill pattern. The issues are distinguished by the initials of the two cities as well as by the addition of a dolphin below the bull at Byzantium, while at Chalcedon the animal is standing on an ear of corn. During the same period, *c*. 340–300, hemidrachms of Persian weight were also issued in the Thracian Chersonese (**272**) and at Parium in Mysia (**273**).

The only city in this region to mint larger denominations in silver was Cyzicus. After the end of its electrum coinage it continued to issue silver staters of the types head of Kore Soteira/Apollo seated on *omphalos* (**274**). They were dated *c*. 300–280 by von Fritze, but belong more probably to the last decades of the fourth century.[49] The weights are irregular, vacillating between *c*. 13.4g and 10.8g, i.e. between the newly introduced Rhodian and the Persian standards.

During his expedition against Persia Alexander never entered the northern provinces of Asia Minor, the districts along the coast of the Black Sea. These regions consequently preserved their independence longer than other parts of Asia Minor, and this circumstance provided the basis for a separate development there, culminating in the establishment of a number of minor principalities and kingdoms.

Of the Greek cities along the southern shore of the Black Sea Heraclea in Bithynia was undoubtedly the most important. From 337 to 305 it was under the rule of a tyrant, Dionysius, who struck silver coins in his own name. They are staters (**275**) on a local standard of 9.5g/9.6g, sometimes assumed to be 'reduced Persian', but this is extremely doubtful. The types are head of Dionysius/Heracles erecting trophy. After 305, when Dionysius' able widow Amastris acted as guardian for her sons, the types were changed to head of Dionysus/standing Heracles, and the coins (**276**) were now issued in the name of the city. In 302 Amastris married Lysimachus, who thus provided himself with a valuable base for his final fight with Antigonus Monophthalmus. The types changed again to head of Heracles (copied from the Alexander coinage) and a seated Dionysus. Owing to the influence of Lysimachus the new silver was issued both as staters on the local standard (**277**) and as Attic-weight tetradrachms (**278**), unless the latter coinage belongs to the period immediately after the death of Lysimachus. The formal independence of Heraclea, however, was demonstrated by the continued use of the city name on the coinage. Only in 288/7, after the death of Amastris and the removal of her sons, did Lysimachus use the mint at Hereaclea for his own coinage (see above p. 82).

About 300 Amastris founded a city in Paphlagonia and gave it her name. The first coinage of the new foundation (**279**), which was created by a synoecism of several minor cities, showed a head of Mithras in Persian headdress on the obverse, while a seated female deity carrying a

48 Le Rider 1963, esp. 50–6. His chronology has been rejected by Schönert-Geiss 1970, 38–9, but see in reply Le Rider 1971b, 143–53.
49 Fritze 1914, 46–51 (Group v), but see Le Rider 1963, 54–5.

Nike, the Persian goddess Anaitis, or the Tyche of the town Amastris, was placed on the reverse. The inscription *ΑΜΑΣΤΡΙΟΣ ΒΑΣΙΛΙΣΣΗΣ* bears witness to the self-confidence of Amastris, the first queen to sign a Hellenistic coinage, while the choice of types proudly proclaimed her Persian extraction and descent from the royal house of the Achaemenids. These staters were struck on the same local standard as at Heraclea. After the death of the queen the coinage was continued to *c.* 280, the only difference being that it now carried the name of the city (**280**).

In the same area the rich city of Sinope in Paphlagonia was next in importance to Heraclea. Its main coinage consisted of drachms of Aeginetan weight (*c.* 6.0g) with the types head of the local nymph Sinope/eagle standing on dolphin. Issues of this type covered most of the fourth and part of the third centuries. At some date in the second half of the fourth century an *aphlaston* was placed before the head of the nymphs (**281**). One of the issues of this type was inscribed in Aramaic with the name of Ariarathes, Persian satrap of Great Cappadocia, who maintained himself in his satrapy until he was captured and executed by Perdiccas in 322. Ariarathes, however, struck his coins (**282**) as Persian shekels (*c.* 5.6g).[50]

The same Ariarathes also struck silver at Gaziura in Pontus. His Persian shekels (**283**) of this mint were copied from the issues of Mazaeus in Cilicia.[51] On the obverse is represented a seated Ba'al with the inscription *Ba'al-Gazur* in Aramaic letters. The reverse shows an animal combat, a griffin attacking and bringing down a stag. Ariarathes' name appears again in Aramaic. After his defeat by the Macedonians his descendants continued the fight with success, so that Ariarathes became the founder of the royal dynasty of Cappadocia that was firmly established during the third century.

50 Robinson 1920, 11–12.

51 Simonetta 1975b, 91–5. His conclusion, that the same die engravers were working for both Mazaeus and Ariarathes, is hardly probable. It is undoubtedly a simple case of type imitation.

PART III

THE BALANCE OF POWER: EASTERN HELLENISM, *c.* 280–188

From *c.* 280 to the end of the third century an uneasy balance of power existed in the eastern Mediterranean world. This was not based on any conviction or theory, but on a political situation which had resulted in a practical balance between the three great kingdoms of Egypt, Syria and Macedon. Down to about 223 the strongly centralized kingdom of Egypt with its strict economic organization was the most aggressive of the three 'superpowers': confronting Syria in Phoenicia and along the southern and western shores of Asia Minor; disputing with Macedon the hegemony of the Aegean islands and the Greek mainland. Each of the three great powers strove to extend its zone of influence at the expense of the others, but if one power became too dominant, the other two were generally willing to combine their efforts against the aggressor and thus restore the balance.

At the beginning of the period Macedon was devastated by barbarian invasions from the north, suffering almost irreparable losses of manpower. The greatest danger came from the Gaulish tribes which later crossed into Asia Minor, where they created further problems for the Seleucids and the Greek cities of Asia Minor. As the century progressed the centrifugal tendencies within the far-flung Seleucid empire became more and more apparent, both on its eastern frontier, where new states were created by the Parthians and by the Greeks in Bactria, and in Asia Minor, where several principalities in the northern part of the peninsula (Pergamum, Bithynia, Pontus, Cappadocia) developed into independent kingdoms. These factors go far to explain Egyptian pre-eminence during the first sixty years of the period.

The balance of power allowed the smaller states a certain room for political manoeuvre between the 'big three'. This possibility was used by Rhodes and other city-states like Cyzicus and Byzantium. In Greece itself the Achaean and Aetolian Leagues grew into states of some importance in opposition to Macedon.

Towards 220 the picture changed. The young, energetic rulers of Syria and Macedon, Antiochus III and Philip V, assumed the initiative, while Ptolemaic Egypt relapsed into a state of inertia under Ptolemy IV. Towards the end of the century the balance of power seemed threatened by this development. The rule after 205 in Egypt of a minor, Ptolemy V, sharpened the appetite of Antiochus and Philip to a point where the whole system of balance seemed to some of the lesser Greek states to be jeopardized. Pergamum and Rhodes, as well as several other city-states, became alarmed and took the momentous step of asking the Romans to intervene. The Fifth Syrian War between Egypt and Syria (202–200), the Second Macedonian War (*c.* 200–197), and the war with Antiochus (191–188) which ended with the peace of Apamea marked the dissolution of the political system of the Hellenistic golden age. In the future the steady encroachment of Rome became the only political question of real importance, although the pretence of Greek political liberty was for some time upheld.

Map 2. Ptolemaic mints

Ptolemaic mints are underlined. Some had only a brief existence, notably *Tarsus* under Ptolemy III and several of those opened under Ptolemy IV in Phoenicia and Palestine during the Fifth Syrian War (202–200). Ptolemy I minted also at *Corinth* during his Greek campaigns, and Ptolemy III at *Aenus* (Thrace) and *Ephesus* (Ionia). This map does not include *Cyrene* or *Euhesperides*, further to the west along the North African coast (see back endpapers).

9

THE PTOLEMIES, *c.* 283–200

We have seen already that Ptolemy II, at the beginning of his reign, continued the issues of his father, retaining even his father's portrait. For the common denominations, the gold pentadrachms and silver tetradrachms on the local Ptolemaic standard, it is impossible to say exactly when Ptolemy I's coins were succeeded by those of his son.[1] The early years of Ptolemy II saw an extension of the coinage to three Phoenician cities, Tyre, Sidon and Ptolemais, which produced quite substantial coinages, although the output of the mint of Alexandria was still far larger than these. The issues of the Phoenician mints were distinguished by the initials of the various cities, at Tyre generally in connection with the club of Heracles, and at Tyre the practice of dating the tetradrachms by regnal years was introduced in the king's regnal year 20 (=266/5).

At some date, at Alexandria, a shield was added as a symbol in the field on issues in all three metals (**284**). The shield is of Celtic type and seems to have been the personal emblem of Ptolemy II,[2] though its Celtic connotations are far from clear. A substantial series is further differentiated by the monogram . Many of these coins have a Greek letter placed between the eagle's legs (**285**). The letters have been interpreted as years of the reign of Ptolemy II, but this would spread a quite homogeneous coinage over a period of twenty years and they should more probably be regarded as some kind of issue numbering, with the entire series produced over a period of between five and ten years. The series has sometimes been ascribed to Cyprus, but as the bronze coins with this monogram have been found frequently in Egypt, they may quite well be from Alexandria.[3]

At Cyrene the governorship had since *c.* 300 been entrusted to Magas, the stepson of Ptolemy I. In *c.* 277, a few years after the accession of Ptolemy II in Egypt, Magas declared himself independent and ruled in Cyrene until *c.* 250.[4] Some silver and bronze coins may be ascribed to his period of rule. A unique tetradrachm in Paris is of the conventional Ptolemaic types, but the symbol of a *silphium* plant on the reverse indicates its origin. Two didrachm issues of Ptolemaic weight are also known. The first (**286**) shows the same types and legend as the

1 The basic work of Svoronos 1904–8 is quite arbitrary on the point, but no better suggestions have been made. The notes that follow are as a rule limited to works modifying or correcting Svoronos.
2 For various proposed explanations of the shield see Voegtli 1973; Ritter 1975; and Salzmann 1980.
3 Le Rider 1969b. [The series is discussed in Davesne and Le Rider 1989, 275–7.]
4 For the dates of Magas see Mørkholm 1980b, 145–7. The Ptolemaic issues of Cyrenaica are discussed by Robinson in *BMC, Cyrenaica*, cxl-cxlii.

tetradrachm just mentioned, but the style is provincial. The other issue (**287**) shows on the obverse the head of Magas' mother, Berenice I, while the reverse has a club within a wreath and the inscription *ΒΑΣΙΛΙΣΣΗΣ ΒΕΡΕΝΙΚΗΣ*. On both issues a monogram consisting of the first letters of Magas' name is frequently found. The weights are also rather irregular and the metal often appears of inferior quality. In addition, Magas issued several series of bronze coins, the most notable of which (**288**) is an issue with the head of Ptolemy I on the obverse and a head of Libya with her characteristic corkscrew curls on the reverse. The latter type became very popular and appears frequently on subsequent Ptolemaic bronze issues from Cyrene. Most of the coins were struck at the mint of the city of Cyrene, but a few may derive from other Greek cities in Cyrenaica such as Apollonia or Euhesperides.

After the death of Magas in *c.* 250 an interesting constitutional change occurred at Cyrene. Two philosophers from Megalopolis, Demophanes and Ecdemus, organized a federation, a *koinon*, which struck coins in silver and bronze. The types are copied from the old autonomous issues: head of Ammon/*silphium* plant, and the legend reads simply *ΚΟΙΝΟΝ*. The silver (**289**) is struck in the form of didrachms of *c.* 7.60g, a reduced Chian standard. The bronze coins (**290**) are often overstruck on the previous Ptolemy/Libya bronzes. The experiment did not last long and Cyrenaica soon reverted to Ptolemaic sovereignty.

At some undetermined date, 261/60 or earlier, the inscription of the silver coins from Alexandria (**291**) and various Phoenician mints was changed from *ΠΤΟΛΕΜΑΙΟΥ ΒΑΣΙΛΕΩΣ* to *ΠΤΟΛΕΜΑΙΟΥ ΣΩΤΗΡΟΣ*, thus emphasizing the reverence of Ptolemy II for his father, whose cult name was Soter. Apparently the issue of gold coins was discontinued for several years, and there are no pentadrachms with the new legend. The date of the change can be established from the Phoenician issues with regnal years. At Tyre (**292**) the Soter title was introduced in year 25 of Ptolemy II (261/60). Simultaneously the regnal years and the new legend appear on coins from Sidon (**293**) and Ptolemais, and at the same time new mints were opened at Joppa and Gaza. The five Phoenician mints struck this coinage practically continuously throughout the reign of Ptolemy II and down to year 6 of Ptolemy III (242/1), when the production of silver tetradrachms was stopped for quite a long period. During the twenty years from 261/60 to 242/1 the portrait lost many of the individual features of Ptolemy I and became a somewhat anonymous royal head. The end of the coinage coincides with the end of the Third Syrian War or War of Laodice between Ptolemy III and Seleucus II of Syria, which particularly affected the border province of Phoenicia.

The date 261/60 for the introduction of the Soter coinage in Phoenicia is presumably a *terminus ante quem* for its appearance in Alexandria, but the great central mint may have adopted the new title one or two years earlier. Whether this is the case or not, the issue of Soter coins at Alexandria was of rather short duration, while in Phoenicia it continued for twenty years. Few issues from Alexandria are actually known, and the mint soon saw a reconstruction of the whole coinage system. In honour of his deceased sister-wife Arsinoe II Philadelphus (died 270, or ?268), Ptolemy II inaugurated a copious series of silver decadrachms (**294**) weighing *c.* 35.50g, to be followed *c.* 261/60 by issues of gold octodrachms (**295**) of *c.* 27.80g and of silver tetradrachms regularly struck from the same obverse dies as the gold. The obverse type is a fine, although somewhat rigid head of the dead queen wearing the diadem below a crown or *stephane* and partly covered by a veil. A ram's horn encircles her ear, and behind the portrait we see a sceptre, the lotus-formed finial of which appears above the top of the head. The reverse is adorned by the double cornucopiae, filled with fruit and cakes and with the royal diadem tied around it on decadrachms and octodrachms, while the silver tetradrachms (**296**) show the Ptolemaic eagle. The inscription reads *ΑΡΣΙΝΟΗΣ ΦΙΛΑΔΕΛΦΟΥ*. The extensive series just mentioned was accompanied by a few tetradrachms with a head of Ptolemy I on the obverse and the usual eagle reverse, inscribed with the name of Ptolemy.

The Arsinoe coins are, with a few exceptions, provided with a numeral on the obverse. The decadrachms offer a nearly complete series of numbers – only four are missing – running from *Α* to *Ω* (= 1–24) and then from *ΑΑ* to *ΩΩ* (= 25–48), concluding with two issues marked by the monograms [monogram] and [monogram]. We are thus dealing with a series of numbers from 1 to 50. According to Svoronos, the numbers represent years of an era of Arsinoe, counting from her death in 270 and running to the end of the reign of Ptolemy III in 221. This neat, well-fitting scheme has been accepted by most scholars, and the explanation has been thought to achieve additional confirmation from the existence of a series of Roman didrachms with exactly the same system of numbering, running from 1 to 49. The friendly relations and exchange of ambassadors between Ptolemy II and Rome in 273 can be adduced as providing the likely circumstances for the Romans' borrowing of the Egyptian dating system. Unfortunately further research in the Roman series and the discovery of several die links between coins with quite different numbers have proved beyond doubt that the Roman numbers cannot represent yearly dates.[5] With that in mind it is easy to recognize that the style of the decadrachms is so uniform that they can hardly have been struck over half a century. About thirty years seem *a priori* more likely and, as in other instances, we must regretfully recognize that an apparently securely dated series is once more floating in time. The numerals do not indicate years and must be regarded rather as issue numbers of short but uncertain duration.[6]

While the silver decadrachms, with very few gaps, show the complete series of numbers from 1 to 50, the gold octodrachms stop much earlier. Only the numbers up to 14, again with a few gaps, are represented. A careful stylistic analysis by Mrs Troxell has shown that the two series are not parallel, but that the gold started later and then ended at about the same time as the decadrachms, around 240. Another series of gold octodrachms and tetradrachms, glorifying the dynasty as such rather than Arsinoe alone, may have been introduced at the same time as the Arsinoe gold or probably a little earlier in the 260s. The obverse of these issues (**297–8**) shows the jugate heads of Ptolemy II and Arsinoe facing right and behind the heads the shield symbol, while the reverse is occupied by the heads of Ptolemy I and his queen, Berenice. By these types dynastic continuity was expressed and demonstrated to all who handled the coins. The inscription

5 Küthmann 1958, 95–6; Burnett 1977, 119.

6 The account of the Arsinoe coinage derives from a paper by Troxell (1983), which the author kindly allowed me to see before publication. The material is there divided on stylistic criteria into four groups – the first consists of decadrachms only – and dated between 270 or later and 242/1. The dated issues from Phoenician mints allow Mrs Troxell to date the transition from Group 2 to Group 3 to the year 253/2, but other dates are approximate.

reads *ΘΕΩΝ ΑΔΕΛΦΩΝ*, the cult name of Ptolemy II and his sister-wife. The two words are first placed together on the obverse, but soon they were divided between the two faces of the coins, *ΑΔΕΛΦΩΝ* on the obverse, *ΘΕΩΝ* on the reverse, perhaps now referring to Ptolemy I and Berenice, though this would not be accepted by all scholars. A few gold didrachms and drachms with the same types were also struck.[7]

The gold octodrachm was called a *mnaeion* because it originally equalled a *mna* or 100 silver drachms (ratio 1:12.5), and consequently the gold tetradrachm was called a *pentekontadrachmon* or 'piece of 50 (silver) drachms'.[8] The last designation can only apply to the *Theoi Adelphoi* series, because gold tetradrachms were not struck with Arsinoe types. The names of the gold pieces giving their value in silver demonstrate that silver was the basis of the accounting system, as we also know from countless papyri. However, the ratio of 1:12.5 implied by the names was not real. In the first place, the coins were struck too light: instead of the full weight of an octodrachm, *c.*28.40g, the coins weigh about 27.80g, which gives a ratio of *c.* 1:12.8. Moreover, we know from the papyri that the gold coins commanded a premium or *agio* of *c.* 10% or more when exchanged against silver, so that the actual relationship between the two metals moved around 1:13 and upwards.

As to the introduction of the new gold coinage, the dated coins of the Phoenician cities (Tyre: **299**) show that here gold octodrachms of the Arsinoe type were struck from year 25 of Ptolemy II (=261/60) and then, intermittently, to 242/1, year 6 of Ptolemy III, when the gold issues came to an end together with the silver. Another *terminus ante* is provided by a famous letter from the Zenon archive. Here an official of the mint in Alexandria complained to Apollonius, *dioiketes* or Minister of Finance to Ptolemy, about various difficulties encountered in connection with a mint operation that consisted in the restriking of foreign and old gold coins for a new coinage which was to enjoy a monopoly as a means of exchange with Egypt.[9] The old Egyptian gold coins are specifically mentioned in the text. They are the *trichrysa* of Ptolemy I and of the early years of Ptolemy II, and it seems evident that the new gold coinage must be the octodrachm coinage of Arsinoe type and the gold of the *Theoi Adelphoi*. Moreover, the difficulties and confusion at the mint are best explained on the assumption that the order to restrike and exchange into the new coinage was fairly recent. The letter of Apollonius is fortunately dated to year 28 of Ptolemy II (=258/7).

Arsinoe octodrachms were also struck at Salamis, Citium and Paphos simultaneously with the Phoenician and Alexandrian issues.[10] Both the Arsinoe and the *Theoi Adelphoi* octodrachms were struck at intervals during the succeeding reigns, the Arsinoe type being by far the more popular, even down into the second century. During this time the portrait of the queen changed perceptibly. Sometimes, as we shall see, the face even borrowed the features of one or another of the later queens.

---

7 Troxell 1983.

8 *Pap. Cairo Zenon* 59022. Undated, but from internal evidence most probably to be assigned to years 28 or 29 of Ptolemy II, 258/7 or 257/6. Cf. Pestman 1981, 544.

9 *Pap. Cairo Zenon* 59021. Cf. Schubart 1922.

10 Troxell 1983, 62–4.

During the first part of the reign of Ptolemy II his bronze coinage also followed the system of his father, but with the most important denomination (**300**) (laureate head of Zeus/eagle with open wings on thunderbolt) weighing slightly less, 14.00–18.00g. These coins were current in the 260s, as we know from various finds in Attica which can be connected with the Ptolemaic support to Athens during the Chremonidean War (268/7–262/1).[11] But at some date, perhaps coinciding with the introduction of the Arsinoe gold in *c.* 261/60, a series with eight different

Table 2. *Bronze denominations of Ptolemy II*

Types	Diameter (mm)	Weights (g)	Probable theoretical weight (g)
A Head of Ammon/eagle, wings open (**301**)	48	76–105	*c.* 92
B Head of Ammon/2 eagles, wings closed (**302**)	42	62–78	*c.* 68
C Head of Ammon/eagle, wings open (**303**)	36	41–50	*c.* 46
D Head of Zeus/eagle, wings closed (**304**)	30	17–25	*c.* 22
E Head of Alexander/eagle, wings open	24	9–15	*c.* 11
F Head of Alexander/eagle, wings open (**305**)	20	5–8	*c.* 6.8
G Head of Ammon/eagle, wings open (**306**)	18	4–6	*c.* 5.2
H Head of Ammon/eagle, wings open	16	2–4	*c.* 3.4

denominations was introduced. Their types and weights are shown in Table 2, the legend being always *ΠΤΟΛΕΜΑΙΟΥ ΒΑΣΙΛΕΩΣ*.

The individual weights vary a great deal, but the concentration of weights within the individual denominations, when calculated from frequency tables, shows that it is possible to regard them as belonging to a coherent system graduated 1 : $1\frac{1}{2}$: 2 : 3 : 6 : 12 : 18 : 24. The smaller denominations (from D downwards) seem to have been issued on a slightly lighter standard, presumably to compensate for the greater amount of work involved in producing many small coins instead of a few larger ones. The highest denomination corresponds closely to the native Egyptian weight unit, the *deben*, and it seems clear that from the beginning the intention of the new bronze coinage was to replace silver as a medium of exchange in the Egyptian countryside

11 McCredie 1966, 9–10, 30–1, 47–8 (Svoronos Class *Z*, Series *B*).

outside Alexandria and the few Greek cities. Although the coinage was certainly fiduciary, i.e. there was no direct relationship between the metal content and the nominal value assigned to the coins by the government, the new coinage was made attractive to prospective users by the exceptionally heavy denominations produced in large numbers. When the Arsinoe decadrachms in silver ceased to be struck, probably around 210, Egyptian coinage was virtually restricted to the large gold coins, meant for trade and for the Greek cities, and the heavy bronze lumps circulating predominantly in the *chora*. Gold was obtained from the mines in Nubia, while Cyprus was the source of copper. Nearly all silver, on the other hand, had to be imported from regions outside direct Ptolemaic control.

During the reign of Ptolemy III Euergetes (246–222), the coinages of his father were continued down to *c.* 242/1 in Phoenicia (**315**; above, p. 204) and presumably also in Egypt. To the following period belong some remarkable issues (**307**) in the name of the queen, Berenice II, the daughter of Magas of Cyrene. The obverses show a beautiful bust of the queen, wearing the royal diadem and a veil which covers the back of the head. The reverses show a single cornucopiae with the royal diadem tied around it. The inscription reads *ΒΕΡΕΝΙΚΗΣ ΒΑΣΙΛΙΣΣΗΣ*, and symbols such as two stars or the two conical caps (*pilei*) of the Dioscuri appear frequently. The most interesting aspect of these issues is their range of denominations and their weights. We meet with gold decadrachms, pentadrachms, two-and-a-half drachm pieces, drachms, hemidrachms and quarter-drachms and silver dodecadrachms (12 drachms), pentadrachms and two-and-a-half drachm pieces, all struck on the Attic weight standard, which had not been used in Egypt since *c.* 310. The coins are not particularly rare and various monograms or letters serve to differentiate successive issues. The use of the Attic standard at this date at the mint of Alexandria has not yet received a satisfactory explanation. A remarkable issue recently discovered is a gold double octodrachm (weight 55.5g) of Arsinoe types (**308**). The symbols *pilei* and stars show that it was minted during the reign of Ptolemy III.[12]

The system of heavy bronze coins introduced by Ptolemy II in Egypt may have survived into the following reign. Soon, however, Ptolemy III issued a substantial series of bronze coins of normal types but with a cornucopiae as a symbol in the reverse field or carried by the eagle on its shoulder. The heaviest denomination weighs *c.* 68g, corresponding to denomination B of Ptolemy II. There are now ten different denominations as listed in Table 3 and having, unless otherwise stated, a cornucopiae as symbol in the field.

If we again give the heaviest denomination the value of 24 units as in the preceding series of Philadelphus, we get a system with the following steps: $\frac{1}{2}:1:1\frac{1}{2}:2:4:6:8:12:16:24$. This arrangement derives some confirmation from the fact that in both systems the denomination with the head of Zeus as an obverse type (D in the preceding table, E in this one) has the identical value of 6 units. What seems to have happened was that some time during the reign of Euergetes the weight of the bronze coins were reduced by 25% and several new denominations were introduced. The new system must have functioned well into the reign of Ptolemy IV

12 Bank Leu 20 (25.iv.1978), 174. Cf. Troxell 1983, 64.

Table 3. *Bronze denominations of Ptolemy III*

	Types	Diameter (mm)	Weights (g)	Probable theoretical weight (g)
A	Head of Ammon/eagle, wings closed	43–5	59–78	*c.* 68
Bi	Head of Ammon/eagle, head reverted, cornucopiae at shoulder	40	39–53	*c.* 46
Bii	Head of Ammon/eagle, head reverted, wings opened, no cornucopiae	40	38–53	*c.* 46
C	Head of Ammon/eagle, wings closed (**309**)	35	28–38	*c.* 35
D	Head of Ammon/eagle, wings closed	30	19–25	*c.* 22
E	Head of Zeus/eagle, wings open	27	10–16	*c.* 15
Fi	Head of Ammon/eagle, wings closed	25	9–13	*c.* 11
Fii	Head of Alexander/eagle, head reverted, cornucopiae at shoulder	25	8–12	*c.* 10–11
G	Head of Ammon/eagle, wings closed, cornucopiae at shoulder	20	4.5–6	*c.* 5.5
H	Head of Alexander/eagle, wings closed	17	3–5	*c.* 4.2
I	Head of Ammon/eagle, wings closed	16	2–3	*c.* 2.7
J	Head of Alexander/eagle, wings closed	13	1–2	*c.* 1.4

Philopator, for two issues of these bronze coins have control markings which also appear on gold and silver ascribed to this king.

The existence of two variants of denominations B and F is also best explained as a chronological sequence of the respective issues, indicating that they covered a fairly extensive period of time. Various heavy bronze issues were attributed by Svoronos to the Phoenician cities under Philadelphus, but as they seem to follow the second system of weights rather than the first, they are better dated to the reign of Euergetes. To the same reign belong some smaller bronze coins, with the head and name of Queen Berenice II on the obverse, which may have been struck in various Phoenician cities.

Another series of bronze coins (Svoronos 997–1100) was most probably struck at Alexandria for circulation in Greece, where they have been found especially in the Peloponnese.[13] They

13 Varoucha-Christodoulopoulou 1941, 677; Hackens 1968, 82–3.

show on the obverse the bust of Ptolemy III with laurel wreath, on the reverse the Ptolemaic eagle with a cornucopiae as symbol in the field (**310**). They were struck in three denominations of *c.* 17g, *c.* 8.5g, and *c.* 5.7g. Both their obverse type and their weights distinguish them from the normal Egyptian coinages of the same period.

The same is true of another bronze series (**311**) of five denominations ranging from *c.* 1.6g to *c.* 17.4g. Their obverse type is the usual head of Ammon, but on the reverse we find a facing female statue, placed on a base, wearing a high *polos* on her head. The statue has with some plausibility been identified with that of the famous Paphian Aphrodite. Consequently the coins have been attributed to Cyprus, where they are quite frequently found.

Ptolemy III also issued various series of silver tetradrachms of ordinary types in the Egyptian possessions in Asia Minor and Europe which he had partly inherited from his father, partly acquired himself. Most of them probably belong to the first part of his reign and both forms of the legend (*ΠΤΟΛΕΜΑΙΟΥ ΒΑΣΙΛΕΩΣ* and *ΠΤΟΛΕΜΑΙΟΥ ΣΩΤΗΡΟΣ*) occur. The certain mints are Tarsus in Cilicia (**312**), Ephesus in Ionia, and Aenus in Thrace, but several more seem to be involved, although we cannot identify them. On some of the issues the royal head is definitely a portrait of Ptolemy III, but in other cases it is quite nondescript. At Ephesus an issue of gold octodrachms for Berenice II (**313**) shows a very beautiful but quite uncharacteristic head of the queen. Apparently the die cutter had never seen her real likeness and created a portrait out of his own imagination.[14]

Towards the end of his reign, from *c.* 230, Ptolemy III resumed the striking of silver and issued a copious series of tetradrachms at Alexandria (**314**). They bear a cornucopiae in the field and their style is quite different from that of the earlier silver coins, indicating an extensive chronological gap. The head has now lost most of the individual characteristics of Ptolemy I and has become an anonymous representation, although the inscription, *ΠΤΟΛΕΜΑΙΟΥ ΣΩΤΗΡΟΣ*, shows that Ptolemy I was still intended. To the same period I would also attribute a few issues in gold and silver of Berenice II, but now of Ptolemaic weight. A few gold octodrachms of the Arsinoe type may also be mentioned here, since the head of the brother-loving queen has assumed the features of Berenice II. Or perhaps it is the other way round, with Berenice II represented as Arsinoe Philadelphus in order to share in her popularity.

From the last years of the reign we have an issue of gold octodrachms of Arsinoe type and silver tetradrachms of Soter type from the five Phoenician mints. They were all issued under the joint authority of one magistrate, whose monogram appears on all issues. The few coins from Gaza and Joppa are dated to year 23 of Ptolemy III (= 225/4), and the issues of Ptolemais, Sidon and Tyre (**315**), although undated, must belong to the same time.[15]

Under Ptolemy IV Philopator (222–205), new coin types were adopted at Alexandria for both gold and silver. An extensive series of gold octodrachms was struck posthumously for Ptolemy III (**316**). On the obverse they have a portrait of the dead king, remarkable for the divine symbols with which it is equipped. In addition to the radiate crown of Helios, the sun,

14 Troxell 1983, 64–6.
15 Mørkholm 1980a. For the gold see Troxell 1983, 66–7.

and the *aegis* of Zeus, the king carries over his shoulder the trident of Poseidon, lord of the sea. The middle prong of the trident ends in a lotus finial, known from the sceptre of Arsinoe. The concentration of such symbols is perhaps intended to show the deceased king as the master of the three elements, heaven, earth and sea. A few dies show the king as quite young, but the normal type shows him in middle age. The reverse is adorned with the cornucopiae, tied with the diadem and surmounted by the rays of the sun. The inscription is *ΠΤΟΛΕΜΑΙΟΥ ΒΑΣΙΛΕΩΣ*. The commonest issue from Alexandria is marked by the initials *ΔΙ* and comprises also a few gold tetradrachms and drachms.

The same initials, *ΔΙ*, appear on a new silver series (**317**) inaugurated by Ptolemy IV. The obverse type is the jugate heads of Sarapis and Isis, the two great Hellenistic gods of Egypt. The eagle on the reverse bears the cornucopiae at its shoulder and turns its head backwards. A substantial issue of bronze coins of the second system (**318**) also carries the initials *ΔΙ* and seems to belong to the reign of Philopator. Under the same ruler, apparently in 210, a change in accounting was introduced, the silver drachm being replaced by the copper drachm as the unit of account at the ratio of 1:120.[16] Book-keeping was as usual slow to adapt itself to realities. Since *c.* 240, at the latest, the production of silver coins in Egypt had been quite insufficient and the heavy bronze coins had taken the place of silver in internal circulation. Only after a delay of some thirty years was book-keeping adapted to the new situation.

The first years of Ptolemy V (205–180) saw a resurgence of coinages in Phoenicia, undoubtedly a result of the menacing attitude of Antiochus III of Syria and the ensuing Fifth Syrian War from 202 to 200, which deprived Egypt of her Syrian and Phoenician territory for ever. As part of the frantic effort to stave off the Syrian invasion, coins were issued in a great number of localities. Ascalon (?), Joppa (**319**), Dora (**320**), Tyre, Sidon, Berytus, Byblus, Tripolis and Damascus (?) are probable or certain mints. Several other series belong to the same general area and were struck during the same years but cannot be localized with greater precision.[17] Many of the mints had never struck coins before, and some of the issues betray by their style and weight variations the hands of unskilled and incompetent people, working at great speed during a time of pressure. Some of the issues used conventional types: gold octodrachms of *Theoi Adelphoi* type as well as silver tetradrachms of the Soter type and of the Sarapis and Isis type introduced by Ptolemy IV. A gold issue with a posthumous portrait of Ptolemy III, of which only a single specimen is known, was produced at Sidon, and there are several interesting new types related to Ptolemy V and to his parents Ptolemy IV and Arsinoe III.

The accession of Ptolemy V, who was only five or six years old in 205, was shrouded in violence and intrigue. Arsinoe, the natural guardian of her son, had been murdered by a court camarilla at the death of his father, and his succession had been delayed for some time. As rumours of the sinister happenings spread in Alexandria, the leading clique at the court tried to dispel suspicions by a show of devotion to the royal house, but its members were lynched by

16 Reekmans 1948, 1949.

17 The coinages of Joppa, Dora and an uncertain mint are discussed by Mørkholm 1981. For a survey see Mørkholm 1983a.

the people of Alexandria at the instigation of their rivals for power. To the year 204/3 and to the mint of Alexandria I would ascribe the issue of three different gold octodrachms of the following types:

1	(Svoronos no. 1139) (**321**)	*Obv.* Diademed bust of Ptolemy IV *Rev.* Eagle standing r. on thunderbolt; in field, monogram; *ΠΤΟΛΕΜΑΙΟΥ ΦΙΛΟΠΑΤΟΡΟΣ*
2	(Svoronos no. 1159) (**322**)	*Obv.* Bust of Arsinoe III wearing diadem and *stephane*; behind her, sceptre. *Rev.* Cornucopiae with diadem tied around it; *ΦΙΛΟ-ΠΑΤΟΡΟΣ ΑΡΣΙΝΟΗΣ.*
3	(Svoronos no. 1254) (**323**)	*Obv.* Bust of Ptolemy V wearing diadem and radiate crown; at shoulder, spear. *Rev.* Cornucopiae with diadem surmounted by radiate crown; in field, two stars; *ΠΤΟΛΕΜΑΙΟΥ ΒΑΣΙΛΕΩΣ.*

These coin types with their emphasis on the dynasty were eagerly copied at the Phoenician mints, but a portrait of Ptolemy V without the radiate crown (**324**) was generally preferred. In this province there was a tendency to unite the control over several mints in the hands of one official, as we have already seen under Ptolemy III. Thus a man with the initials *ΣΩ*, often in monogram, signed issues from Tyre, Sidon (**325**) and Ptolemais, plus a bronze series of uncertain localization (**326**) dated to years 3 and 4 of the new reign (203/2 and 202/1).[18] Another magistrate put his initials *NI* on coins from Tyre, Berytus and Tripolis. He also signed the largest series of the whole group. It has no indication of mint and has usually been attributed to Alexandria, but a travelling mint in Phoenicia, following the Ptolemaic army during the Fifth Syrian War, is a more likely source. Certain letters on this series have been regarded as yearly dates running up to year 12 (= 194/3), but a study of die linkages has proved this impossible. Single letters in any case alternate with monograms, and both undoubtedly refer to subordinate mint officials. The series consists of silver tetradrachms with heads of Ptolemy IV and V, linked by the use of identical reverse dies, and gold octodrachms of Arsinoe and Ptolemy V. In some cases the gold coins with portrait of Ptolemy V were struck from the same dies as the silver tetradrachms. An interesting detail is that an ear of corn often appears attached to the diadem of Ptolemy V (**324**), perhaps suggesting that he was a new Triptolemos bringing abundance of crops to his subjects.[19]

Another interesting series consists of *Theoi Adelphoi* octodrachms in gold (**327**), ordinary Soter tetradrachms in silver (**328**) and another issue of tetradrachms with the diademed bust of Ptolemy V on the obverse (**329**). The reverse type is unusual, a winged thunderbolt with two stars in the field, one on either side. The inscription reads *ΠΤΟΛΕΜΑΙΟΥ ΕΠΙΦΑΝΟΥΣ*, the first appearance of an honorary epithet used during a king's lifetime except for the *Theoi Adelphoi* series. According to our written sources, the name Epiphanes was first used from 199/8,

18 Svoronos nos. 1177–81, 1184–7, 1190–1, 1193–4. These coins are generally attributed to Ptolemy IV.
19 Mørkholm 1979c.

but coins which are certainly Phoenician show its use before the summer of 199. The issues of this series are united by the appearance of the monogram  and the symbol of a spearhead in very conspicuous positions on all the coins. The exact occasion for this special issue escapes us, but the style of the Soter tetradrachms is very close to that of similar coins from Tyre.

At this time the useful habit of dating the coins clearly by prefixing the sign **L** (demotic for 'year') to a regnal year makes its appearance in Phoenicia (**319**). The latest date on coins of Ptolemy V is year 6 (=200/199) on an issue from Joppa. In the preceding year the fate of the province had been decided by the victory of Antiochus III at Panium. The Ptolemies lost this important province for ever and their coinage there came to an abrupt end, except for an enigmatic series which will be discussed below (p. 144). A coin find from Syria, buried during the Fifth Syrian War, shows that the mint of Alexandria had already before 200 started the production of a new series of tetradrachms without any monogram or other distinguishing mark (Svoronos no. 1231).[20]

20 *CH* 7 (1985), 22, no. 90.

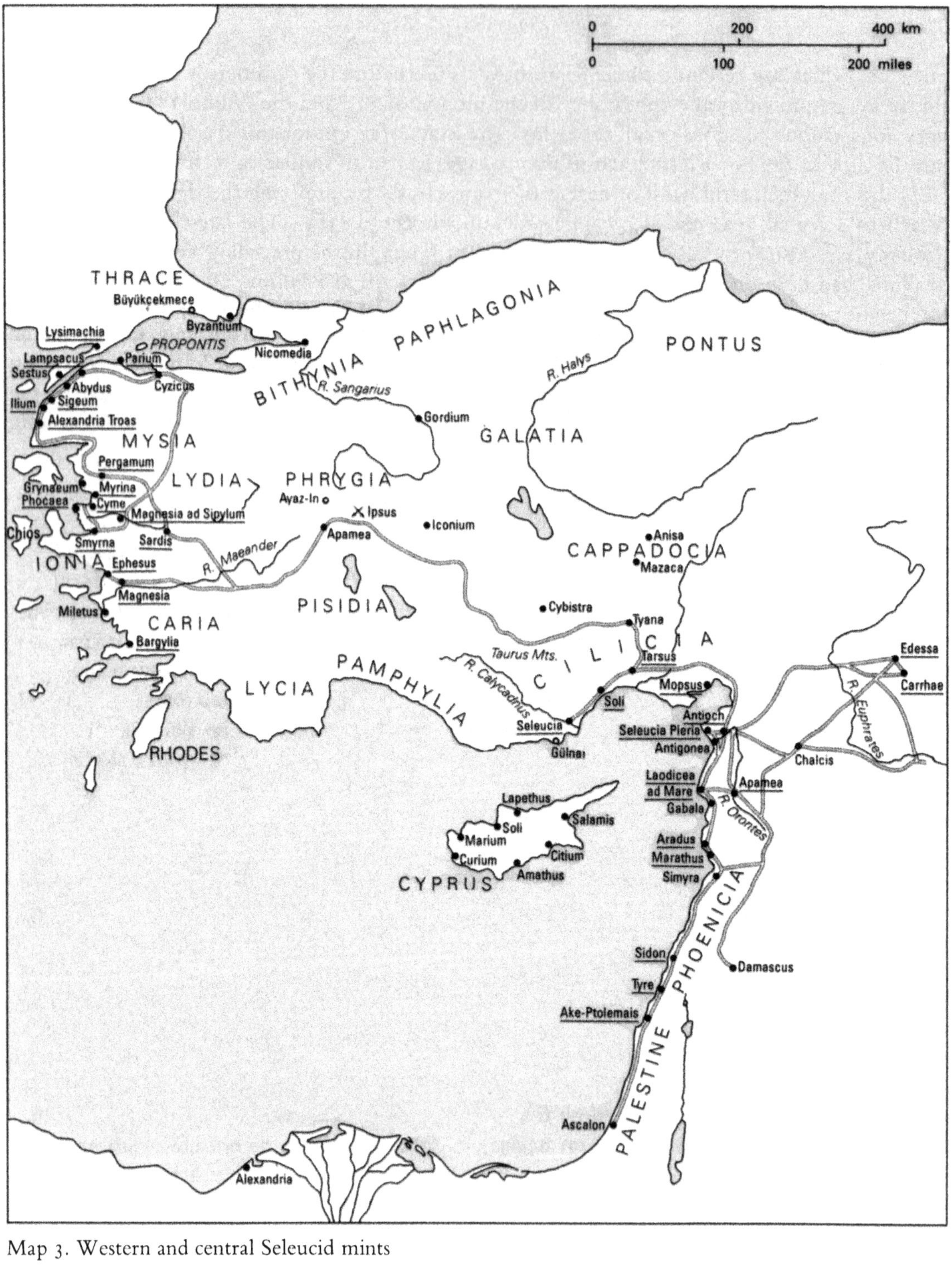

Map 3. Western and central Seleucid mints

Seleucid mints are underlined. Main highways and desert tracks are marked with double lines

10

THE SELEUCIDS

(a) THE CENTRAL REGION, 281–187

The central region of the Seleucid empire comprised down to *c.* 200 northern Syria and Cilicia. The Syrian territory was divided between the capital Antioch and its sister foundations, Seleucia Pieria, Apamea and Laodicea ad Mare, which together formed the Syrian Tetrapolis. In Cilicia the administrative centre was at Tarsus, the ancient seat of the government in that province.[1]

The first silver issues of Antiochus I (281–261) from Antioch retained the old Alexander types (*WSM* 931–2), but they were soon replaced by tetradrachms of a new type (**330**). The obverse shows a realistic portrait of Antiochus I, while the reverse is occupied by the patron god of the dynasty, Apollo represented seated on the sacred *omphalos* and holding an arrow in his right hand, while the left hand rests on his bow. This type became a coat of arms for the dynasty and was used far down into the second century for the coinages in noble metals as well as for some bronze issues.

Antiochus II (261–246) placed his own youthful and idealized portrait on his tetradrachms (**331**), while Seleucus II (246–226) preferred his own personal coin types. His portrait on the obverse of his gold and silver is even more idealized (**332**), and for the reverse types he broke with the tradition of his predecessors by introducing a standing Apollo, leaning against a tripod on the tetradrachms (**333**) but against a bow on the gold staters and silver drachms. On the last denomination (**334**) the royal portrait was often replaced by a beautiful head of Athena in Attic helmet.

The accession of Seleucus II was not uncontested, and it appears that initially there was a kind of interregnum. To the years 246–244 Newell ascribed an issue of tetradrachms and bronzes inscribed *ΣΩΤΗΡΟΣ ΑΝΤΙΟΧΟΥ* and bearing a portrait of Antiochus I (**335**). More recently a gold octodrachm of this issue (**336**) has made its appearance, the first known example of this heavy denomination in Seleucid numismatics.[2] Its obverse die was one also used for the contemporary silver tetradrachms. Newell ascribed the Soter issue to Apamea, but the coin

1 This and the Seleucid parts of the following sections are again based on Newell's *WSM* and *ESM*, to which a general reference is here given.
2 Cox 1966, 52.5, but with incorrect attribution to Seleucus III.

finds from Antioch suggest that it may well derive from the capital.[3] Under Seleucus II the gold coinage of Antioch was relatively abundant, presumably a consequence of the loss of the Bactra mint, which had supplied most of the gold coinage during the preceding reigns (below, p. 119).

Seleucus III (226–223) returned to the traditional Seleucid Apollo type. A single issue (*WSM* 1028) shows a variant (**337**): Apollo on the reverse is seated but rests his left elbow against a tripod. This issue may belong to Apamea. A gold octodrachm (**338**), again from an obverse die known for the silver, has recently appeared in a hoard from Gordium.[4] Antiochus III (223–187) also adhered to the traditional types. Two issues of gold octodrachms (**339**) (*WSM* 1074 and 1097) seem to belong to the last decade of the third century. His tetradrachms from Antioch are abundant and allow us to follow his portraits from smooth youthfulness to rugged old age (**340**).[5]

While Seleucia Pieria disappeared as a mint after a few bronze issues for Antiochus I – it was occupied by the Ptolemies from *c.* 246 to 219 – Apamea had a continuous production of tetradrachms down towards the middle of the reign of Antiochus III. A couple of bronze issues from this mint are of special interest. A unit (**341**) (*WSM* 1167–8) shows a bearded and draped bust of Seleucus II on the obverse, while the reverse represents a flying Pegasus, both very unusual types. Another special issue is remarkable by its denomination. It is an octuple (**342**), weighing *c.* 20g/24g and showing the normal clean-shaven portrait of the king on the obverse, a horseman with spear (who may be the king himself) galloping left on the reverse. It is perhaps relevant that Apamea was the great military arsenal of the Seleucids and also the home garrison of their cavalry.

At the mint of the seaport of Laodicea tetradrachms and drachms of Alexander type and inscribed in the name of Seleucus I were produced down to the reign of Antiochus III. Only then do 'normal' tetradrachms (**343**) with the royal portrait and the seated Apollo make their appearance.[6]

The important mint of Tarsus continued under Antiochus I. He first struck a single issue with Alexander types (*WSM* 1294), then changed to his normal types with his own portrait and the seated Apollo (**344**). Antiochus II also issued tetradrachms of similar types. During the Third Syrian War (246–241) the Cilician coast and Tarsus were occupied by Egyptian forces. Ptolemy III used the mint at Tarsus for a series of tetradrachms of Ptolemaic weight and types but signed by the same magistrates who had been active under Antiochus II. The portrait on these coins seems to be a fairly good likeness of Ptolemy III.

Seleucus II, however, soon recovered Tarsus, although some of the coastal cities remained in Ptolemaic possession for nearly fifty years. He soon resumed Seleucid coin production there,

---

3 Waage 1952, 6–7, nos. 53 and 59. Cf. also Houghton 1983, 29.

4 Cox 1966, 52–3. There is a second specimen in the Houghton collection (no. 58).

5 Boehringer 1972, 73–98, has developed a new chronology for the issues of Antiochus III, in general lowering Newell's dates for the earlier series.

6 *WSM* nos. 1328–9 (Tarsus) have been transferred to Laodicea by Mørkholm 1965b, 147–8.

but it now becomes very difficult to distinguish the issues of Tarsus from those of Sardis (below, p. 123) and the problem of attribution has not yet been satisfactorily solved.

We are on more certain ground with the silver issues of Seleucus III and Antiochus III. The latter series (**345**) was ascribed by Newell to Tyre in Phoenicia, but its transfer to Tarsus seems certain and has been generally accepted.[7] The same two kings may have issued a few coins at Seleucia on the Calycadnus, although the attribution depends on the slender evidence of a symbol, a head or forepart of a horse, that also appears on the later autonomous bronze coinage of the city. After 197 a subsidiary mint was established at Soli, recently recovered from the Ptolemies. Here Antiochus III issued a series of tetradrachms and a single drachm which earlier were ascribed to Phoenicia (**346**).[8]

Between the Seleucid and Ptolemaic frontier in Phoenicia lay the buffer state of Aradus, consisting of the island of Aradus itself and its extensive possessions on the mainland, its *peraia*. Seleucid coins had not been struck on its territory since the days of Seleucus I, and its era of liberty dated from 259/8. It is consequently surprising to find an issue of tetradrachms (**347**) under Seleucus III.[9] The reverse type is that of Seleucus II, the standing Apollo leaning against a tripod, but the Phoenician date in the exergue follows the Aradian era, indicating that the coins were struck in 225/4. The mint is indicated as Simyra, a small place in the southern part of the *peraia*. Apparently Seleucus III had persuaded the Aradians to let him set up a mint at Simyra as part of his preparations for an attack on Ptolemaic Egypt. This is a good illustration of the need for a free city to accommodate its policy to the actual power situation at any given moment.

In the preceding section only sporadic mention has been made of the bronze coinage which was issued in large quantities from most of the mints. The common denominations were half, unit and double, weighing *c.* 1.5–2.5g, 3.5–4.6g, and 6–8g respectively (**349–53**).[10] Under Antiochus III quadruples (**348**) weighing *c.* 12–15g were issued at Antioch and Apamea. The octuples from Apamea mentioned earlier remain an exception in this part of the Seleucid empire. The types of the bronzes were very diverse. At Tarsus there seems to have been a predilection for Athena and the Dioscuri (**352**), and after Antiochus III's eastern expedition elephants appear very frequently as a reverse type at Antioch (**353**)

As a result of the Fifth Syrian War, which probably ended in 200, Antiochus III acquired Phoenicia and its hinterland from the Ptolemies. No silver was struck in the new province until the following reign, but the city of Tyre issued some bronze coins with local reverse types. Some of them carry dates of the Seleucid era, corresponding to 198/7–189/8.

7 Mørkholm 1964a, 53–8. For confirmation see Seyrig 1973, 19. He shows that the series continued under Seleucus II and Seleucus III, who cannot possibly have struck coins at Tyre.

8 Mørkholm 1964a, 58–62.

9 Seyrig 1971, 7–11. See also Seyrig 1973, 17 and 20.

10 I follow the first system outlined by Newell 1938c (*ESM*), 270–3, which I much prefer to his alternative solution sketched on 273–4.

(b) THE EASTERN SATRAPIES AND THE SUCCESSOR STATES IN THE EAST, 281–c. 187

At Carrhae in Mesopotamia the mint of Seleucus I continued under Antiochus I. Gold and silver (**354A-B**) were struck in small quantities but with interesting types: the head of the deified Seleucus I adorned with bull's horn occupies the obverse, while the reverse shows a horned horse's head. Most of the coins are in the name of Seleucus, but common monograms connect them to bronze issues of Antiochus I and thus date them to his reign.

No coins of the following Seleucid kings have been ascribed to Carrhae, and already under Antiochus I the mint may have been moved to neighbouring Edessa, where a bronze coinage of rather better quality was issued. Soon, however, both these western Mesopotamian cities were replaced by Nisibis further to the east. A few bronze issues of Antiochus II and Seleucus II (**355**) show on the obverse the busts of the Dioscuri, one in profile and one three-quarters facing, a very unusual and striking type that was also used at Seleucia on the Tigris (*WSM* 18, no. 207 A–C). Under Seleucus II a prolific issue of silver tetradrachms with his common types was inaugurated. Some of them (**356**) show a portrait of the king wearing a short beard. The issue of silver continued at Nisibis under Seleucus III and Antiochus III, culminating under the latter with substantial issues of tetradrachms, which have been related to his eastern *anabasis* of 212–205. Some types (**357–9**) have on the reverse an elephant, representing the famous elephant corps of the Seleucid army, instead of the seated Apollo. Specimens appear in mint condition in hoards from Asia Minor buried *c.* 190, which affects both their chronology and their place of minting. If they are to be connected with the war against Rome, their date must be lowered by more than a decade, and an attribution to a (temporary?) mint in Asia Minor becomes an attractive alternative.[11] Houghton, however, prefers to give all elephant issues to Nisibis.[12]

The capital of the eastern provinces and their most important mint was Seleucia on the Tigris. The Alexander-type coins in the name of Antiochus I are now recognized as belonging to his period as viceroy in the East from 292 to 281 (above, p. 73). At the beginning of his sole reign a new type of tetradrachm (**360**) was introduced. The reverse shows the Seleucid Apollo, while the obverse presents the portrait of the king, first as a mature man, later with obvious signs of advancing age. Probably owing to the popularity of Antiochus in the East, this type of coin with the aged portrait was continued under Antiochus II, with the result that the point of transition from one reign to the next must be arbitrarily fixed. Seleucus II used his own types with the standing Apollo on the reverse, while the seated Apollo reappeared on the tetradrachms of Seleucus III and Antiochus III. Gold coinages are rare at this mint. Single issues of staters were struck by Antiochus II and Antiochus III.

At the beginning of the reign of Antiochus III the usurper Molon, who assumed the royal title in 222, struck a series of bronze coins at Seleucia (**361**), the types being head of Zeus and standing Apollo Citharoedus.[13] The bronzes of Seleucia generally showed a predilection for

11 Seyrig 1973, 45–6.
12 [Houghton 1986.]
13 [Fischer 1988. A silver tetradrachm appeared in an Emporium (Hamburg) sale in 1987.]

Map 4. Eastern Seleucid mints.

Seleucid mints are underlined. Main highways and desert tracks are marked with double lines

three-quarters facing obverse types, especially representing a laureate bust of Apollo (**362**). The common denominations were double, unit and half with a few quadruples interspersed. Despite the occurrence of large numbers in the finds from Susa,[14] careful examination of such technical details as the form of the edge of the flan and the die position has allowed Le Rider to transfer a number of bronze coins to Seleucia from Susa, where they had been placed by Newell.

Like Laodicea in Syria, Susa continued to strike Alexander-type tetradrachms with the name of Seleucus down to the reign of Seleucus III. Under Seleucus II a few issues of his own types appear, but it is only with Antiochus III that Susa conformed to the normal pattern of other Seleucid mints. The tetradrachms of Antiochus II from Susa are numerous, a fact presumably to be related to the eastern campaigns of the king.[15] Other denominations in silver are non-existent, and coinages in gold and bronze are scarce at this mint. However, the first bronze coinage of Antiochus III (**363**) presents an interesting obverse type: the diademed head of the young king adorned with bull's horns as a sign of deification. The reverse shows a seated Athena copied from the well-known type of Lysimachus.

In contrast to the relative uniformity of Susa, the great mint at Ecbatana showed a great diversity so far as denominations are concerned. Gold staters were issued under Seleucus I in some quantity with both seated and standing Apollo on the reverses. The tetradrachms were issued by all kings with their normal types, but under Antiochus II tetradrachms with elephant reverses, traditionally attributed to Ecbatana, were more probably minted at Nisibis.[16] Among the smaller denominations in silver the drachm appears most frequently, with issues becoming increasingly prolific during the reign of Antiochus III (**364**). But silver down to the obol was minted at intervals (**365–6**). Similarly the range of bronze denominations is more varied than at most other mints. Under Antiochus III the octuple of *c.* 25g/29g becomes a regular feature (**367**), and even the rare triple denomination makes an appearance more than once. A bronze issue of Seleucus II (**368**) shows the king with a pointed beard, and a single bronze issue of Molon interrupts the series of genuine Seleucids. The last, very comprehensive bronze issue of Antiochus III (**369**) shows a marked preference for horses and elephants as reverse types.

A small and somewhat enigmatic mint was located by Newell at Hecatompylus in Hyrcania or Artacoana in the district of Aria, in both cases on the highway that linked distant Bactria with Ecbatana and Seleucia. Hecatompylus seems to me to have the better claim of the two cities. Whatever the location, the coinage of this mint belongs to the three kings Antiochus I, Antiochus II and Seleucus II (**370**) and consisted exclusively of silver tetradrachms and drachms of the types normal to these kings. Under the last two kings the style deteriorates, and the end of production may well have come quite early in the reign of Seleucus II.

At Bactra the first issues of gold and silver by Antiochus I (**371–3**) showed the head of the king and, on the reverse, the head of a bridled and horned horse. The weight is now Attic, the local weight of the last years of Seleucus I (see above, p. 73) remaining an isolated episode. Later

14 Le Rider 1965a, 9–32.
15 The tetradrachms *WSM* 1198–1201 have been moved from Apamea to Susa by Le Rider 1965a, 25.
16 [Houghton 1986. Mørkholm's original text gave the traditional mint attribution.]

in the reign Antiochus I used his traditional types. Antiochus II may have started by using his father's portrait, but soon replaced it by his own. The Bactra coinage of both kings is remarkable for its unusually high proportion of gold staters, probably to be explained by an influx of gold from central Asia or perhaps even from distant Siberia.

During the reign of Antiochus II a most intriguing development took place at Bactra. A silver tetradrachm in the name of Antiochus II shows a new portrait and the reverse type of a striding Zeus wielding the thunderbolt.[17] Both types are those of Diodotus I (**374–5**) to whom we shall return later.

In chapter 7 we discussed the first independent coinage of Persis under Bagadates and Oborzos, dating it to the decade or so before 280 (above, pp. 73–4). After this date the coinage was continued by the priest-kings of Istakhr.[18] The types were practically identical with those of Oborzos: head of the prince to right in Persian headdress tied below the chin/the priest-king in adoration in front of fire-temple. Two of the series carry the names of Artaxerxes (**376**) and Autophradates (**377**). The latter ruler introduced some variations. On all his coins the winged half-figure of Ahura-Mazda is shown hovering above the temple, further stressing the strong Iranian sentiment expressed by these coins. Some of the coins show the ruler crowned by a Nike, a Greek convention but presumably used here *against* the Graeco-Macedonian ruling class.

In addition to the series of Artaxerxes and Autophradates there exist anepigraphic coins of the same type and a few issues inscribed with uncertain names, so that there may be a total of three or four rulers to be placed after 280. This will bring the end of the coinage down to *c.* 250. The next issues from Persis belong to the second century and must be viewed in the context of the second Parthian expansion around the middle of the century. From the literary sources we know of a Seleucid governor of Persis at the beginning of the reign of Antiochus III, which means that at some date between *c.* 250 and 223 the satrapy of Persis returned to Seleucid sovereignty.

With this exception the Seleucids did not have much success in maintaining their power in the eastern parts of their empire. A Seleucid governor of Parthia named Andragoras was defeated by the Parthians around 240 according to Justin.[19] Gold staters and silver tetradrachms inscribed *ΑΝΔΡΑΓΟΡΟΥ* without any title have been attributed to this Andragoras, implying that shortly before the Parthian attack he had made himself independent of his Seleucid overlord. This would presumably be Seleucus II at the very beginning of his reign when he was occupied by the Third Syrian War. During this war Ptolemy III, at least according to his own propaganda, conquered large parts of the Upper Satrapies, which may have created a political situation that encouraged or perhaps even enforced Andragoras' defection.

This reconstruction of events, however, is based on the assumption that the coins of Andragoras are genuine, and here I must confess to serious doubts, an attitude shared by a number of

17 For some forgeries in this series see Jenkins 1965.
18 Hill in *BMC, Mesopotamia, etc.*, clxviii–clxx.
19 Justin 41.4, 7. For a discussion of the coinage see Hill in *BMC, Mesopotamia, etc.*, cxlviii–cxlix.

earlier scholars. The types, bearded head of deity/Nike and armed warrior in quadriga for the gold (**378**), turreted head of Tyche/standing Athena holding owl for the silver (**379**), are odd for the time and place. Many details are clumsy in execution: the hair and beard of the deity, the legs of the horses, Tyche's hair and the way in which the lance of Athena is left floating in the air. The coins all derive from the Oxus treasure (*IGCH* 1822), but this find passed through Rawalpindi where numerous forgeries are known to have been added. The awkward details of the coins mentioned above might, of course, be the result of their being produced by inexperienced craftsmen working in an isolated place. But on balance it seems rash to build a reconstruction of historical events on the shaky evidence of a few coins which may be modern forgeries, and for the moment the question must be left in this rather unsatisfactory state of uncertainty.

About 250 the nomadic Parni, a tribe of the Dacae, began a movement southwards along the eastern shore of the Caspian Sea. From their lands north of the Ochus they moved into the valley of this river, the district of Astavene, where their chieftain Arsaces was proclaimed king, most probably in spring 247, the epochal date of the Parthian era. During the following years they spread to the south and east, overrunning the Seleucid provinces of Hyrcania and Parthia where they defeated Andragoras, the Seleucid governor of Parthia. In this way the communication lines to the eastern Iranian satrapies were cut, and the Seleucid mint on the highway to Bactra, whether it was located at Hecatompylus or at Artacoana, stopped production about 240 or shortly afterwards. In spite of the great danger, Seleucus II could not deal with the matter immediately, his attention being diverted to the west and kept there by the rebellion of his brother Antiochus Hierax in Asia Minor. The resulting civil war lasted more than a decade, and not until 228/27 was Seleucus able to lead an army eastwards. Nothing permanent came of this expedition.

According to some scholars the Parthians, as they were now called from their central province, began to issue coins almost immediately after the conquest.[20] However, the issues in question, ascribed to the shadowy figures of Arsaces I (*c.* 238) and Arsaces II/Tiridates I (?–*c.* 211), belong in my opinion to the reign of Mithridates I and so to the second century B.C.

At about the same time as these events the satrapy of Bactria was also lost to the Seleucids. We have seen already that the last issues of Antiochus II from Bactra were provided with new types.[21] Soon his name disappeared to be replaced by that of Diodotus, former Seleucid governor of Bactria, who thus revealed himself as the person behind the new portrait. But we are here confronted with a problem that returns again and again in discussions of the Bactrian and Indo-Greek coinages: the question of homonymous rulers. Two different portraits already existed on the coins that were still being issued in the name of Antiochus II, an older (**375**) and a much younger one (**374**), and two portraits continue to run in parallel on the coinage signed 'of King

20 Abgarians and Sellwood 1971; Sellwood 1980, 20–7, types 1–6.

21 A great wealth of material for these eastern regions, lavishly illustrated, is collected in Mitchiner 1975, but the text must be used with caution. The most confident assertions often turn out to be mere assumptions, some of a very idiosyncratic kind, more especially with regard to metrology and the location of mints.

Diodotus' (**380**). It seems necessary to assume the existence of two Diodoti, father and son, and explain numismatic material on the assumption that the younger Diodotus II was co-regent with his father from the very beginning of Bactrian independence in *c.* 250. Diodotus II survived his father and would have been sole ruler for a few years. In addition to the gold and silver coinage the Diodoti issued a few bronze coins with types of Hermes/Athena (**381**) and Zeus/Artemis (**382**). Their flans are of typical oriental fabric: thick and dumpy with strongly bevelled edges.

About 230 the rule of Bactria was assumed by Euthydemus I, who had removed Diodotus II by force. He was king at the time of Antiochus III's eastern anabasis and withstood the Seleucid king during a two-year siege of Bactra in 208–206. He may have reigned until *c.* 200. The development of his coin portrait indicates in any case a long reign.[22] The reverse type of his gold and silver is a seated Heracles, resting after his labours, a typical Hellenistic motif and symbolizing the eternal human fight for physical and moral survival. On the earlier issues he rests his club on a separate pile of rocks, obviously placed for this purpose but in a rather awkward fashion. Later the representation shows him supporting the club against his thigh or knee, a much more satisfactory composition.

The earliest portraits show a youthful, idealized head (**383**) that soon gives way to a more rugged, middle-aged man (**384**). It is, however, with his aged portrait that the die engravers in Bactria showed their remarkable skill, an impressive rendering of the old ruler affected by many years of toil and effort that have left obvious marks on the face. The corners of the mouth are drawn down, and a deep furrow running from the nose downwards enhances the impression of fatigue and worry. Nevertheless the glance of the eye is calm and confident, showing a man old and battered but far from beaten. It is a wonderful study in human psychology.

Euthydemus struck two denominations in gold. His staters (**385**) are of a rather common style with a youthful head, but a unique octodrachm (**386**) is a masterpiece of numismatic art.[23] The portrait is that of the aged king and stands out in a very high relief that gives it an extraordinary sculptural quality. The seated Heracles on the reverse is more harmonious and better proportioned than most other representations, and great care has been bestowed on the details, as for instance the lion's skin with which Heracles has covered the rock before sitting down. All in all, it is one of the most successful creations of Hellenistic numismatics. One can hardly doubt that this remarkable coin must have been issued on some very special occasion, but unfortunately we have no clue to any specific event which it may have celebrated. The end of the war with Antiochus III, which resulted in a negotiated agreement, would have been a suitable occasion, but that is no more than speculation. We can only say from the portrait that the coin must belong to the later years of Euthydemus' reign.

The silver of Euthydemus is quite common, especially his tetradrachms, although drachms and smaller denominations were also produced. A distribution among different mints has been suggested, but in the absence of a proper die study this remains hypothetical. The only certain

22 Bivar 1951, 22–9.
23 Le Rider 1969a, 26.

mint is Bactra, and all Euthydemus' coins may well have been struck there. A sign of the popularity and wide use of his tetradrachms is that they were extensively imitated in Sogdiana and among the tribes living to the north of the Jaxartes. The copies show various degrees of barbarism, and some of them carry the names of various nomadic chieftains in Aramaic.[24] They are generally much underweight and often their metal is so debased that this is apparent to the naked eye. Euthydemus also struck bronze coins (**387**) with the types head of Heracles/prancing horse in various denominations, the heaviest and most common being the double or dichalkon of *c.* 7–8g.

(c) WESTERN SELEUCID MINTS

To the west of the Taurus mountains the Seleucids ruled over a large part of Asia Minor. The capital in this part of their kingdom was Sardis, where the most important mint was also located. The coinage of Antiochus I from the mint starts with a silver tetradrachm of unusual types: diademed and horned head of Seleucus I/head of horned horse (**388**), types that we have met otherwise only at Carrhae (**354–5**). After an issue of Alexander-type tetradrachms Antiochus I returned to the horned head of his predecessor, but now with a seated Apollo on the reverse (**389**). A new detail is that Apollo is holding a bow and not the usual arrow in his extended right hand. These later portraits of Seleucus I are quite realistic, showing an aged and wrinkled face. Soon, however, Antiochus I turned to using his own portrait and the normal Apollo with arrow on his tetradrachms. These types continued for some time under Antiochus II (**390**), until the portrait of the new ruler was substituted on the obverse.

During the reign of Antiochus I bronzes were issued at Sardis with the types facing Athena/Nike standing (**391**). The same devices appear on contemporary issues from the two Magnesias, at Mt Sipylus and on the Maeander. Under Antiochus II a very extensive bronze coinage (head of Apollo/tripod above anchor) was produced at Sardis (**392**). This issue enjoyed a wide circulation throughout western Asia Minor and was also exported to the European side of the Straits and the Propontis. Specimens of this type were overstruck in large numbers at Lysimachia, and they appear not infrequently in present-day Bulgaria, often with countermarks of the city of Cabyle.[25] Their presence in this part of the world has been plausibly related to Antiochus II's Thracian expedition about 250.

Seleucid coins were produced at many other mints in western Asia Minor under Antiochus I and II. A new reverse type, a seated Heracles leaning against his club, was used by one or both of the kings for their tetradrachms from Magnesia ad Sipylum (?) (**393**), Phocaea, Aegae, Cyme and Myrina, i.e. in a restricted area in northern Ionia and Aeolis. The type is reminiscent of that latter used by Euthydemus in Bactria but they are not identical, and the idea of using a resting Heracles as a coin type may well have occurred quite independently at different places.

---

24 Mitchiner 1975, IV. 287–94. His so-called 'prototype' issues struck on the Persian weight standard are too heavy for this standard and are quite simply the earliest of the barbarous imitations.

25 Münsterberg 1915 (overstriking at Lysimachia); Youroukova 1982 (finds in Bulgaria).

The common Seleucid silver types appear at Magnesia on the Maeander, where the seated Apollo carries a bow,[26] and at Smyrna. At the latter mint Antiochus II issued an interesting gold stater (*WSM* no. 1497). The obverse shows his portrait, but the reverse presents a standing Athena carrying Nike. We do not know the specific occasion for this remarkable issue, but it may have been related to the successes of Antiochus II in Asia Minor during the Second Syrian War, notably the liberation of Miletus and the capture of Ephesus. At Ephesus a single issue of bronze coins was struck for him, but with local types.

Ordinary Seleucid silver was also struck at Phocaea and Aegae in addition to the Heracles tetradrachms,[27] and similar coins emanated from the mints of Ilium, Alexandria Troas, Abydus and Lampsacus as well as from Lysimachia in Thrace (**394**). In the last of these Antiochus II used the portrait of his father as an obverse type. Under the same king an interesting phenomenon has been observed. Tetradrachms which according to their symbols must have been struck at Abydus, Ilium and Alexandria Troas (*WSM* nos. 1555, 1560, 1563–4) share a common obverse die. The most likely explanation is that the die was transferred from one mint to another.[28] Alexandria Troas was the last station, because here a wing was added to the royal diadem, and to judge from the illustrations the die may have started its career at Abydus.

While the portrait of Antiochus I is always easy to recognize, and in some cases, as for instance at Sardis (**390**) (*WSM* nos. 1385–8), is of an artistic quality that led Newell to compare these obverses with the best Bactrian portraits, the representations of Antiochus II are more difficult to identify. In addition to idealized and youthful portraits of excellent quality from Sardis (**395**) and Magnesia on the Maeander, we find at several mints a middle-aged head with broad, sometimes nearly puffy features, often of slight artistic value. This mediocre western style was continued by Antiochus Hierax, with the result that the coins of the two kings are sometimes hard to separate from each other.

At the beginning of the reign of Seleucus II (*c.* 246–*c.* 242/1), his silver coins were issued at Sardis (but we have already seen that there are difficulties over distinguishing between Tarsus and Sardis at this period) and at Ilium. Magnesia on the Maeander produced a few bronze coins. Although a few more mints may have been active, their coins now being listed as 'uncertain western', this production is very restricted when compared to that of his predecessor. The probable explanation is that the Third Syrian War (246–241) kept Seleucus busy in the central region and prevented him from taking an active interest in the west. And no sooner was the Third Syrian War brought to an end than Antiochus Hierax, brother of Seleucus II, made himself independent in the west and inflicted a humiliating defeat upon Seleucus in 240 or 239. The ensuing 'fratricidal' war lasted until 226, when Antiochus Hierax was finally defeated, not by Seleucus II but by Attalus I of Pergamum. During this period the mints of the western provinces of Asia Minor were closed to Seleucus II.

---

26 Seyrig 1963, 31–3, transfers the coins of Antiochus II given by Newell to Ephesus (*WSM* nos. 1486–8) to Magnesia on the Maeander.

27 For a new coin of this type at Phocaea see Troxell 1977, 24, no. 12.

28 Mørkholm 1982b, 212.

Antiochus Hierax produced numerous coins of his own, but he is undoubtedly, as far as his portrait is concerned, the most elusive of all Seleucid kings. To cite a few passages from Newell (*WSM*, pp. 392–3) 'Hierax evidently possessed certain features characteristic of his father, Antiochus II, others of his brother, Seleucus II, while the general effect frequently bears a deceptive similarity to the early portraits of his cousin, Antiochus III ... The various die-cutters seem indeed to have experienced unusual difficulties in catching the likeness of Hierax ... The result is that they have given to the portraits a Proteus-like quality which proves rather disconcerting when we attempt to select any one likeness as being that of this man.' When we add that Hierax is assumed to have often used posthumous portraits of both Antiochus I and Antiochus II, the possibilities for iconographic confusion become legion. I have the clear impression that despite the heroic efforts of Newell the coinages have not yet been completely disentangled.

The silver coinage attributed by Newell to Sardis under Antiochus Hierax belongs in my opinion to another mint, most probably Tarsus, and was struck by Antiochus III at the beginning of his reign. I have substituted another series, composed partially of specimens which Newell labelled 'uncertain mints', partially of recently discovered coins, to which an issue ascribed by Newell to Tarsus has been added.[29] The last issue comprises the portrait bust that in my opinion gives the best likeness of Hierax. With this rearrangement of the material, the numismatic evidence for any activity of Hierax to the east of the Taurus mountains disappears. An issue of small bronze units from Sardis, however, can be attributed to him.

Together with the last issue of Hierax a tetradrachm issue of Seleucus II (**396**), distinguished by a very impressive portrait with long beard, must be moved from Tarsus to Sardis. This provides evidence that the capital of the western Seleucid provinces was in the possession of Seleucus II for a short period between 228 and 226 before being finally lost to Attalus I of Pergamum. It is worthy of note that these coins of Seleucus II combine an excellent portrait with very feeble reverses, where both the standing figure of Apollo and the lettering are far below normal standard. This phenomenon of acceptable obverses coupled with reverses of bad style or vice versa becomes even more pronounced at this mint under Antiochus III.

Sardis apart, the coining activity of Antiochus Hierax was concentrated in the region of the Hellespont, where Alexandria Troas became his main mint with a considerable output of silver tetradrachms (**397**), comprising at least seventeen obverse dies. A special feature at this mint, already introduced under Antiochus II, is the wing that is invariably attached to the royal diadem. The fashion spread, and the wing appears sporadically at Ilium and Lampsacus.

A few tetradrachms, all from one obverse die, may have been struck at Scepsis, and a larger series from eight obverse dies has been transferred from Sigeum and some uncertain Hellespontine mints to Ilium.[30] Further issues are identified by their symbols (eagle and forepart of Pegasus respectively) as coming from Abydus and Lampsacus, situated only about 20km apart on the Asiatic coast of the Hellespont. Apart from the civic symbols, the two series are

29 Mørkholm 1969a (Antiochus Hierax and Seleucus II).
30 Bellinger 1961, 18–19.

closely related by style, a moneyer's monogram and the symbol of a long torch. Obviously, the same die engravers and mint officials were active at both places. Moreover, two out of six obverse dies of the Abydus series were also used at Lampsacus. This close relationship led Newell and later scholars to assume either that the Abydus mint was at some date transferred to Lampsacus, or that the whole Abydus series was actually struck at the larger mint of Lampsacus, which used at least ten obverse dies of its own.[31] In spite of the strong indications here presented I am not so sure of a centralized production in one mint. Considering the geographical position of the two cities – close neighbours and with easy communication between them both by sea and land – I still find it possible and reasonable to regard their mints as separate establishments although closely co-operating with each other.

Further tetradrachm issues of Hierax, earlier attributed to Magnesia ad Sipylum, have been convincingly ascribed to the important city of Parium on the Hellespont (**398**), whose coinage during the third century has been the object of a careful study by Seyrig.[32] The last mint of Hierax in this area is Lysimachia on the European side of the strait. To the one issue ascribed by Newell to this place (**399**) it has recently been proposed to add all the coins, except one, which Newell gave to the same mint under Antiochus III, thus increasing the number of obverse dies used from one to three.[33]

It is worthy of note that no royal bronze coins accompany this quite substantial silver coinage of Hierax in the Hellespontine area. Probably the cities continued their civic issues of bronzes. For Ilium, indeed, we know that this was the case. However this may be, the considerable quantity of his silver coins, comprising in all some fifty obverse dies, shows beyond any doubt that Antiochus Hierax' economic and political power base was in this area. Indeed, to judge from its coinage, Alexandria Troas may actually be regarded as his capital.

At the beginning of the short reign of Seleucus III (226–223) western Asia Minor was completely lost to the Seleucids, all their territories in this part of the world having been occupied by Attalus I of Pergamum. The young king set out from Antioch in 223 in order to rectify the situation, but on his expedition he was killed somewhere in Phrygia. A numismatic memorial of this ill-fated Seleucid has survived in the form of a tetradrachm issue (**400**) signed by two magistrates known from Antioch but with an obverse of a typical Asia Minor style.[34] The most remarkable feature about this obverse is that it also occurs with a reverse in the name of Antiochus III (**401**) and signed by one of the magistrates from the issue of Seleucus III. The explanation must be that this is a military issue, struck in the Seleucid camp in Phrygia. After the death of Seleucus III the soldiers invited Achaeus, who belonged to a collateral branch of the Seleucid dynasty, to assume the crown, but with remarkable loyalty he preserved the throne for the younger brother of the murdered king, Antiochus III. When it was found necessary to

31 Houghton 1978. The number of obverse dies is taken from his note 1.

32 Seyrig 1958a.

33 Boehringer 1972, 161 and no. 29. The question now seems decided in favour of Hierax by the appearance of a couple of these coins in the Meydanicikkale (Gülnar) hoard, buried *c.* 240/230 (Davesne 1981, 369; [Davesne and Le Rider 1989]).

34 Mørkholm 1969a, 12–20 (Seleucus III to Antiochus III).

issue coins in the camp the portrait of the new king was presumably still unknown, and it was decided to retain the obverse die originally made for Seleucus III.

At the head of the royal Syrian army Achaeus was soon able to recover the Seleucid provinces and force Attalus I back to his original small principality around Pergamum. At Sardis the re-establishment of Seleucid power occasioned an issue of tetradrachms for Antiochus III (**402**). However, the portrait of the new young king being still unknown, the die cutter produced a representation that has no obvious resemblance to the well-known youthful portrait of Antiochus III. The monogram of the first issue is identical with the one appearing on the two coins from Phrygia just discussed. The attribution to Sardis rests on a certain similarity between our portrait and the portraits of Antiochus Hierax and Achaeus from Sardis. The coins can be dated between 222 and 220.

The loyalty of Achaeus towards the legitimate king, clearly demonstrated in 223, soon wore thin, and in 220 he assumed the title of king and declared his independence. The motives behind his action are unknown. It may be that Achaeus was carried away by his success against Attalus, and Egyptian machinations may be suspected behind the sudden change. This, however, is a matter for speculation.

At Sardis Achaeus issued gold staters and silver tetradrachms (**403**). The obverses show a fine portrait bust of the usurper with a short beard, while the fighting Athena on the reverses expresses the desire of the king to be shown as a victor who has acquired a legitimate right to his possessions by his successes as a military leader. Both obverse and reverse types are of high artistic quality, as one might expect from the obvious propaganda value attached to the coins. Achaeus also issued bronze coins (**404–5**), mostly doubles and units with head of Apollo on the obverse. On the reverse a standing eagle with a palm branch over its shoulder or a wreath in its claws may reveal Ptolemaic influence. The coins are often countermarked with a horse's head. This was done at Sardis and may have been intended to increase their nominal value during the siege of the city by Antiochus III. Sardis seems to have been the only mint of Achaeus although he ruled over most of the former Seleucid territories in Asia Minor.

In 215 Antiochus III took the lower city of Sardis, and in 213 the citadel was forced to surrender. From then on Sardis remained the capital of the Seleucid provinces in western Asia Minor until 190. A number of tetradrachms have been ascribed to this period. Their most remarkable feature is the tremendous variety of style, which ranges from the acceptable to the outright barbarous. This applies especially to the reverses, where a sloppy rendering of the seated Apollo is often combined with insecure lettering (**406**). But even the obverse portrait is sometimes quite barbarous and hardly recognizable as a likeness of Antiochus III. If it were not for several die links, indeed, some of these coins would most naturally have been relegated to the category of barbarous imitations. Their weights, however, seem to be quite good.

In addition to Sardis, Bargylia in Caria and Lysimachia on the Thracian Chersonese produced a few tetradrachm issues for Antiochus III. The former mint may have functioned briefly during Antiochus III's visit to western Asia Minor in 204 and 203 or later in 196. On this occasion the king stayed at Lysimachia and at least one issue was struck for him there.

Early in this chapter it was suggested that many of the coins ascribed to Nisibis under Antiochus III were actually struck to the west of the Taurus mountains as part of the military preparations for Antiochus' fatal war with the Romans. A number of the tetradrachms assigned to uncertain western mints by Newell may also have the same explanation. Their attribution to specific mints is impossible at the moment, and some of them are of such low artistic quality that it is difficult to accept them as official Seleucid coins. However, strange things may happen with style in periods of haste and pressure. In any case, the picture we get is one of feverish activity in the coin production of western Asia Minor on the eve of the final battle with Rome, with some issues produced at temporary mints in Seleucid camps for strictly military purposes. Mercenaries from the mountainous districts of Asia Minor would presumably be less susceptible to the style of the coinage with which they were paid, and this, together with the general need for haste in a critical situation, may go some way to explain the surprising hideousness of some of these issues.

11

ASIA MINOR, MACEDONIA AND GREECE

(a) THE LESSER KINGDOMS OF ASIA MINOR, *c.* 281–188

We have seen in the preceding chapter how the history of the western Seleucid provinces was entwined with that of Pergamum. After the death of Seleucus I, Philetaerus cautiously tried to feel his way through a complicated political situation fraught with danger. It is consequently not surprising that his first coinage consisted of tetradrachms with the name and types of Alexander the Great, a coinage that combined the advantages of being both popular and inoffensive.[1]

Between about 279 and 274 the mint of Pergamum issued tetradrachms of Alexander type but in the name of Seleucus I (**407**). A similar posthumous coinage appeared at a couple of Seleucid mints (Laodicea ad Mare, Susa), but in the case of Pergamum its explanation is probably different. It is tempting to regard it as a subtle political move of Philetaerus, allowing him to acknowledge Seleucid suzerainty while at the same time avoiding any demonstration of loyalty to the actual king, Antiochus I. The coinage implied that Philetaerus regarded Seleucus I as his benefactor and saviour from the tyranny of Lysimachus, but that his debt of gratitude was not automatically extended to the Seleucid dynasty as such.

This attitude becomes even more apparent with his subsequent coinage. From *c.* 274 new types were introduced for the silver (**408**). The obverse now carries a forceful although slightly idealized portrait of Seleucus I, while the seated Athena of Lysimachus has inspired the reverse. There are some differences in details. On Philetaerus' issue Athena supports her shield, placed in front of her, with her extended right hand, resting her left elbow against the throne. However, the most important aspect of the new coinage is that it was issued in the name of Philetaerus. An important political step was taken by this open declaration of independence from Seleucid rule.

With the succession of Eumenes I in 263 a war broke out with Antiochus I, which resulted in the preservation and strengthening of Pergamene independence. At this juncture a further change was made in the coinage (**409**), the obverse being now adorned with a portrait of the

1 For this and the following coinages see Newell 1936b and Newell 1941 (*WSM*), 316–18. There is a recent survey by Mørkholm 1984a.

founder of the dynasty.[2] Philetaerus is shown with a tubular taenia or diadem round his hair. The big solid head fills most of the flan. The cheek is large and flat. The heavy chin and the small deep-set eye convey an impression of stubborn energy and dogged perseverance, qualities that were essential to maintain Pergamene autonomy through one of the most turbulent periods of Greek history. All in all, the artist has succeeded in combining the fundamental lack of classical beauty of the former officer with such an expression of strength and determination as to make this portrait one of the best in the numismatic art of the early Hellenistic period.

Still under Eumenes I a minor modification was made. Philetaerus' diadem was entwined with a laurel wreath, creating an unusual composite ornament. With the accession of Attalus I in 241 the reverse underwent certain changes (**410**). First the shield was moved to the left side of Athena, to the position known from the type of Lysimachus. Shortly afterwards the inscription *ΦΙΛΕΤΑΙΡΟΥ* was transferred from the right to the left field, and the seated Athena was given a wreath in her extended right hand with which to crown the initial of the name, again an approach to the Lysimachean prototype. At about the same time the composite crown of Philetaerus was replaced by an ordinary laurel wreath. This became the standard type of the Pergamene silver coinage for the next sixty or sixty-five years, although the composite diadem reappears at intervals.

In or shortly after 240, as a result of his first victory over the Galatians, Attalus I assumed the royal title, but this important change in the official position of Pergamum and its ruler had no consequences for the coinage. The Philetaerus silver continued completely unaffected to the end of Attalus' reign in 197 and during the first years of that of his successor, Eumenes II. At some date, however, the issue of Philetaerus tetradrachms was supplemented by a series of posthumous Alexanders (**411**).[3] The occurrence on both of the same monograms and symbols shows that the two series were struck concurrently for quite a long time, and evidence from hoards suggests that it happened at the turn of the third/second century, presumably about *c.* 210/190. The two series were both struck on the Attic weight standard, and the issue of posthumous Alexanders might well seem superfluous. The explanation is to be found in the political situation of the time. Pergamum's involvement as the ally and friend of Rome in the First and Second Macedonian Wars, as well as in the war with Antiochus of Syria, made extraordinary demands on Pergamene finances. The hiring of mercenaries was particularly expensive, and these troops showed a predilection for being paid in Alexander coins as the most popular and acceptable currency of the time. Thus the demand of the mercenaries is probably the reason behind the introduction of a posthumous Alexander coinage at this particular moment.

Two classes of bronze coin were struck at Pergamum: royal issues in the name of Philetaerus (**412**) and municipal ones in the name of the city (**413**). It seems likely that the Philetaerus bronzes belong mostly to the third century and the city issues to the second, but there was undoubtedly some overlapping. Sometimes the royal bronzes can be correlated to the silver by

2 Westermark 1960.

3 Kleiner 1971, 96–104, 114–25. His chronology is modified by Boehringer 1972, 41–4, whose dating is here followed.

the occurrence of the same monograms and symbols, but generally they cannot be distributed among the various reigns. The most prominent deities on the Philetaerus bronzes are Athena, Apollo and Asclepius, whose sanctuary in Pergamum became one of the most famous healing centres in the Greek world.

The first Bithynian king to strike coins was Nicomedes I (*c.* 280–*c.* 250). He is best known in history for having brought the Gauls from Europe to Asia in 277 in order to enlist them against his brother and Antiochus I. This short-sighted decision was the beginning of the Galatian terror that haunted the Greeks of western Asia Minor for more than a century.

About 260 – Eusebius gives the date as 264 – Nicomedes provided his kingdom with a new capital, Nicomedia on the Propontis, where he proceeded to strike coins. His silver coins, tetradrachms (**414**) and drachms (**415**) of Attic weight, show on the obverse the realistic portrait of an aged king with large and rugged facial features. The reverse of the tetradrachms shows Bendis, the Thracian Artemis, seated on a rock. Her function as a goddess of war is indicated by the two spears in her right hand and by the shield that is leaning against the rock. The drachm reverses present Ares in exactly the same position.

Nicomedes I struck a few bronze coins, and his successor Ziaelas (*c.* 250–*c.* 230) also produced bronzes of which only a few specimens have survived (**416**). The types are portrait of the king/trophy.

With the reign of Prusias I (*c.* 230–182) the Bithynian kingdom was provided with a more regular coinage in both silver and bronze. His tetradrachms show on the obverse two different portraits: a younger head of square proportions with whiskers or a short beard, leaving the chin free. The second portrait (**417**) gives a more mature expression without any signs of age. The beard is slightly longer. In contrast to many other ruler portraits of the third century the strength and will-power of the ruler is not emphasized, and we are faced with a fine and delicate representation, apparently somewhat idealized. Hoard evidence shows that the second portrait was in use about 210/200 and continued to the end of the reign.[4] The reverse type is a standing figure of Zeus, crowning the name of the king with a wreath. This becomes the standard reverse for all later Bithynian kings. Presumably Zeus Stratius is represented. A statue of this deity, the work of a Bithynian sculptor Doedalses who belongs around the middle of the third century, was placed in the great temple of Zeus at Nicomedia.

In most published catalogues no attempt is made to distinguish the bronzes of Prusias I from those of Prusias II. However, some specimens (**418**) with the reverse type of a trophy recall the bronze issues of Ziaelas and should therefore be ascribed to Prusias I. And for stylistic reasons an issue of large and heavy bronze coins (**419**), weighing about 36g, should be dated to the same reign. The obverse type of this interesting series is a head of Hermes wearing the *petasos*. The reverse shows the same god in the form of an archaistic statue in frontal view, placed on a round base. The right hand is lifted towards his head, the left holds a caduceus.

---

4 Newell 1937, 44; Boehringer 1972, 51.

Like Bithynia, the kingdom of Pontus used an era beginning in 297/6. The origins are rather obscure, but the first coinage may with some probability be ascribed to Mithridates II, whose reign is usually assumed to have lasted from *c.* 255 to *c.* 220. The only coins ascribed to him are gold staters of Alexander type (**420**) but with the legend *ΜΙΘΡΑΔΑΤΟΥ ΒΑΣΙΛΕΩΣ*.

Towards the end of his reign Mithridates III (*c.* 220–185) issued a quite substantial series of silver tetradrachms (**421**) and drachms. The reverse type is a seated Zeus holding an eagle, copied from the widespread Alexander type. In the field the dynastic badge of the royal dynasty, a star and a crescent, makes its first appearance, to remain on the Pontic coinage in gold and silver until its end.

The great interest of this coinage, however, resides in the royal portrait. The Pontic kings were proud of their Iranian descent, and although they soon married into the Seleucid dynasty their attachment to their oriental roots remained strong. This gave a series of excellent Greek die engravers a unique opportunity to create a gallery of semi-barbarian royal portraits that has no real parallel in Hellenistic portraiture. The first of these excellent likenesses is that of Mithridates III, probably created about 200. His head or bust is rendered with extreme realism, emphasizing his oriental features that are so different from Greek idealization or Macedonian heaviness. The Pontic portraits are equal to the best Bactrian portraits as far as realism is concerned, and seem to me to surpass them in psychological insight. The meeting of Greek artists with oriental models has created a unique and exceptional portrait art that stands quite isolated and outside the main development of portraiture in the Hellenistic age.

Between the kingdom of Pontus and the Seleucid district of Cilicia, the former Persian satrapy of Cappadocia also developed into a kingdom during the third century. The descendants of Ariarathes I (d. 322; above, p. 96) fought tenaciously and with success to create an independent principality. His grandson Ariaramnes, who reigned around the middle of the third century, was the first Cappadocian prince to strike coins.[5] Only bronzes are known, the first group signed with his name in monogram, the second with the name written in full. Ariaramnes did not claim the royal title. The coin types are, on the obverse the head of the dynast in the Persian *kyrbasia*, on the reverse a grazing horse (**422**) or a horseman galloping to the right with a spear in his hand (**423**). Some of the issues are inscribed with the name of Tyana, the important Cappadocian city from which a main road ran through the Cicilian Gates of the Taurus mountains and down into the fertile plain of Seleucia in Cilicia. It is important to realize that the Cappadocians already around the middle of the third century controlled the most important land route between the central Seleucid region and the Seleucid districts in western Asia Minor. This led to an alliance between the Seleucids and the Cappadocian ruling house, sealed by a dynastic marriage between the son of Ariaramnes and a Seleucid princess.

Ariarathes III (*c.* 230–*c.* 220) continued to issue bronze coins. His portrait on the obverses is covered by a pointed *kyrbasia* tied below the chin. His coins fall into two classes, one bearing

5 The latest survey of Cappadocian coinage is that of Simonetta 1977. Its many disputable attributions impose caution in its use; see the review, with many corrections, by Mørkholm in *NC*[7] 19 (1979), 242–6.

his name alone, the other with the royal title added to the name. The promotion of the Cappadocian principality to a kingdom thus occurred during his reign. The common reverse types are again a free horse or a galloping horseman (**424**). However, an interesting new reverse type is added: a half-figure of a goddess in strictly frontal view (**425**), sometimes with a sphinx on either side. This must be the Semitic goddess Astarte, introduced into Cappadocia at an early date by the Assyrians. In addition to Tyana, the city of Cybistra on the road between Tyana and Iconium also functioned as a mint,[6] while bronzes with the Astarte reverse were struck in Morima (**426**) and Anisa, both situated in the interior of Cappadocia.[7]

The long reign of Ariarathes IV (*c.* 220–163) is conveniently divided into two parts by the peace of Apamea in 188. During the first half, which is the only one that here concerns us, the king was the ally of Antiochus III of Syria. In this period he issued a few bronze coins in two denominations (**427–8**). The obverses show his head turned towards the left in a pointed *kyrbasia* with the flaps hanging loose. The reverse types consist of a seated Athena carrying Nike and an archer running toward the right and shooting. The seated Athena must be the great Cappadocian goddess Ma, identified by the Greeks with Athena Nicephorus, by the Romans with Bellona. No mint-place is indicated.

In comparison with Pontus, not to mention Bithynia, the coinage of Cappadocia in the third century is not very impressive, and to judge by the coins Hellenistic culture was much slower in penetrating this remote and inaccessible part of Asia Minor.

(b) THE KINGDOM OF MACEDON, *c.* 281–196

Before Seleucus I could reap the fruits of his victory over Lysimachus at Corupedium and take possession of Macedon he was himself killed. The murderer, Ptolemy Ceraunus, the exiled son of Ptolemy I, ascended the throne of Macedon, but after only about a year's reign he met his own death on the battlefield against the Celtic invaders. This was the beginning of several years of anarchy. One ephemeral king succeeded another, to be replaced by an elected *strategos* for a couple of years. The land suffered terribly from the depredations of the barbarian invaders, while its most important resource, its manpower, decreased in an alarming way. It was only with the return to Macedon in 276 of Antigonus Gonatas, son of Demetrius Poliorcetes, that some stability was achieved. However, Pyrrhus of Epirus, returned from his western adventures, was still a menace, invading western Macedonia in 274 and 273. Only after his death in 272 could Antigonus Gonatas regard his position in Macedon as reasonably safe. His reign lasted until 239.

During the years of confusion and the first years of Gonatas' reign posthumous Alexander gold staters and silver tetradrachms were issued in Macedon. A recent survey of these ascribes most of them to Amphipolis, where at least 87 obverse dies were used for the tetradrachms,

6 Yarkin 1981.

7 Regling 1935. On the location of Anisa (= Kanish), 18km to the north-east of Eusebeia-Mazaka, and the Hellenization of Cappadocia, see Robert 1963, 457–523.

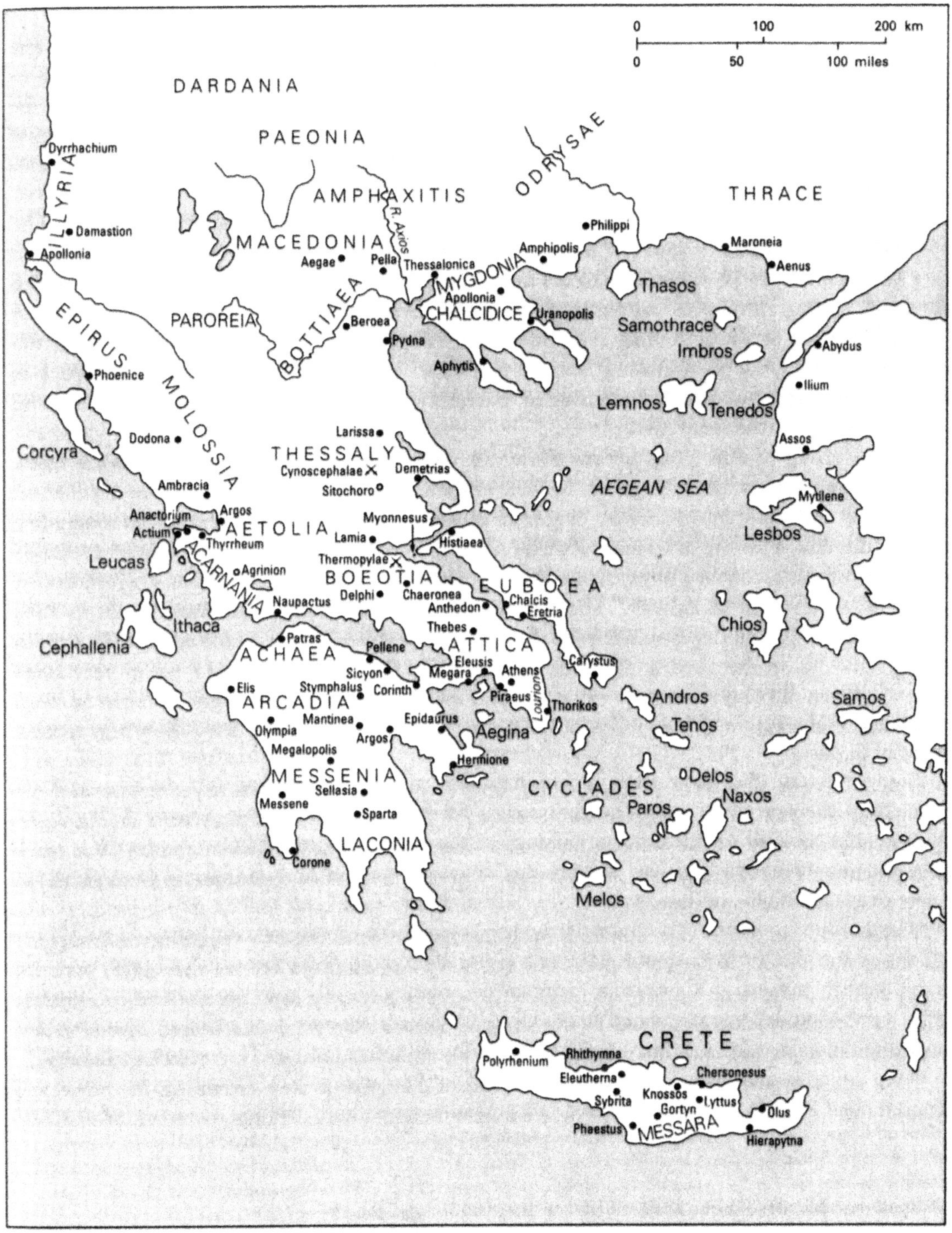

Map. 5. Macedonia and Greece

while a couple of issues, struck from only fourteen obverse dies, are assigned to Pella.[8] The largest issue from Amphipolis (**429**) is distinguished by a helmet symbol and must belong to the reign of Gonatas. At Pella the last posthumous Alexander tetradrachms share an obverse die with a small group of coins which retain the Alexander types but were struck in the name of King Antigonus. Similarly, a few gold staters of Alexander type but with the name of Antigonus are known. They too were presumably struck in Pella.

From about 270 Antigonus Gonatas issued a new type of silver tetradrachm (**430**). The obverse is occupied by the head of Pan with a *pedum* at his shoulder placed as the central emblem on a Macedonian shield, a reference to the help of the god when he caused a panic terror among the Gauls during Antigonus' battle with them near Lysimachia in 277. The reverse shows an Athena fighting to the left with a thunderbolt. The helmet symbol is continued from the posthumous Alexanders, indicating that the main part of the Pan tetradrachms were struck at the same mint, Amphipolis. A small issue of drachms (**431**) with the types head of Zeus/fighting Athena belongs to the same mint.

A small group of Pan tetradrachms shows the Athena on the reverse fighting to the right. They also differ from the main group in their elegant style as well as in their use of another set of symbols and monograms. Their origin at another mint thus seems certain, although one obverse die link with the left-facing Athena series is known. Pella has recently been proposed as the seat of this secondary mint, an attribution more plausible than the earlier suggestion that the coins were struck at Athens.[9] The transfer of one obverse die from Amphipolis to Pella seems more likely than its moving from Amphipolis to Athens. One of the coins with Athena facing right has on the obverse the inscription *ΒΑΣΙΛΕΩΣ ΑΝΤΙΓΟΝΟΥ* cut in very small letters between the two concentric circles around the head of Pan. This might be taken to mean that King Antigonus was here represented as Pan, but the head of the deity shows no specific portrait features.

Eighty obverse dies have been recorded for the main series of Pan tetradrachms and ten (including the one die-linking the two series) for the small issue with Athena facing right. Presumably the bulk of the coinage belongs to the 260s, when the Chremonidean War made heavy demands on the finances of Macedon, whereas the last two decades of Gonatas' reign were relatively quiet and peaceful.

The distribution of the Macedonian bronze coinages between the two kings named Antigonus (Gonatas and Doson) is far from clear. It is generally agreed that a bronze issue (**432**) with the types head of Athena in Corinthian helmet/Pan erecting trophy must be ascribed to Gonatas. This very copious issue circulated in the parts of Greece that were attached to Macedon and was often incorporated into the local circulation by countermarking, for instance in Euboea.[10]

Two other bronze issues (**433–4**), with head of Heracles/jockey crowning his horse and Macedonian shield with monogram/Macedonian helmet, may belong to either of the two

8 Mathisen 1981. See also the brief remarks of Boehringer 1972, 99–100.

9 Merker 1960, 47–9. I prefer to follow the reconstruction of Mathisen 1981.

10 Picard 1979, 180–1.

Antigoni. Similar types occur under both Demetrius II (239–229) and Philip V (from 220).

Antigonus Gonatas was succeeded in 239 by his son Demetrius II. The latter issued no silver coinage in his own name, but it may well be that some posthumous Alexanders, now lurking among the unattributed issues, were struck in Macedon during his reign. An issue of bronzes is known (**435**): Macedonian shield with Demetrius' monogram in centre/Macedonian helmet, *ΒΑ ΣΙ*.

To Antigonus III Doson (229–221) we may ascribe a coinage of silver tetradrachms (**436**). On the obverse there is a quite impressive head of Poseidon, and on the reverse Apollo seated comfortably, looking at a bow in his right hand, on a prow on which the title and name of the king are inscribed.[11] The series falls into two sections, a main group which may come from Amphipolis and a smaller group with a trident symbol (**437**) that has been ascribed to Corinth after 223 but may also derive from Pella. The naval symbolism of this coinage is unusual in Macedon and may be related to Macedonian activities at sea. Antigonus Doson's Carian expedition and the mysterious naval battle of Andros, which has been attributed to [dates as far apart as 245 and] *c.* 227, are both events that could have been celebrated by the coinage. The difficulty of attributing any bronze coins to Doson has already been noted.

Shortly after his accession in 220 Philip V issued his first series of silver tetradrachms (**438**), the types being a diademed head of the king right with short beard/Athena fighting to left with thunderbolt. It has been regarded as a special issue commemorating Philip's accession, but was more probably connected with the Social War of 220–217, when the Macedonian king and his allies confronted the Aetolians. At all events it was a modest issue, comprising only three obverse dies.[12]

A second issue of tetradrachms, accompanied by a few gold staters (**440**), belongs to the period of the first and second war between Macedon and Rome, i.e. to the years *c.* 214–197. The silver (**439**) was struck from nineteen obverse dies. The obverse type shows the head of the hero Perseus, his special sword, the *harpa*, at his shoulder, as the central device of a Macedonian shield. He is wearing a Phrygian helmet with a griffin's head and a cock's comb in place of the crest and a wing attached to the lower part. The reverse is occupied by a club; type, inscription and monograms are surrounded by a wreath of oak leaves. The gold presents the same types, but without the encircling wreath on the reverse.

The silver series just described was for a long time attributed to Andriscus, the Macedonian usurper of 149/8, who was assumed to have reigned in Macedon as Philip VI. The basis for this ascription was thought to be the existence of coins from a couple of recut dies. Recently two independent studies have shown this theory to be untenable and have restored the coinage under discussion to Philip V.[13] An interesting question is raised by the introduction of the Perseus head

11 Merker 1960; Boehringer 1972, 99–100. [See further Hammond and Walbank 1988, 594–5, 599, who follow the view of the American scholar C. T. H. R. Ehrhardt in an unpublished dissertation and date the battle of Andros to 245, attributing the coins in consequence to Antigonus Gonatas.]

12 Boehringer 1972, 104–7. [The chronology of Philip V's coinage has since been discussed at length by Hammond in Hammond and Walbank 1988, 460–8.]

13 MacKay 1968b; Boehringer 1972, 107–10, 116–18.

as an obverse type and its relationship to the contemporary head of Roma on the earliest denarii, for this has the same peculiar and elaborate form of helmet. The symbolism of the hero Perseus, for whom Philip's son and heir to the throne, born *c.* 212, was named, is connected with the fact that he was regarded by a popular etymology as the eponymous ancestor of the Persians. Thus from being a common ancestor to the Macedonian royal house and the former ruling people of the Persian empire, he became a symbol of the Macedonian king's aspirations towards world domination, an idea that since 217 had occupied Philip's mind.[14] As long as the difficult chronological question of the priority of Philip's second silver issue or of the Roman denarius remains open, further discussion of the apparent propaganda dialogue between the two powers during the First Macedonian War can hardly lead to any sensible conclusions.

The bronze issues of Philip V are more numerous and varied than those of his predecessors. No less than fourteen different issues have been ascribed to the period before 197.[15] Many of the types are known from the earlier kings: head of Heracles, jockey on horse (**441**), a fighting Athena (**442**), etc. A new variant as obverse type (**443**) is the head of Zeus, wearing a wreath of oak leaves. This must be a representation of the famous Zeus of Dodona in Epirus, showing Philip's interest in his western neighbour and in the Adriatic Sea, an interest that was obvious during his early operations in the first war with Rome. The hero Perseus appears on a number of denominations in exactly the same way as on the second silver series of Philip, with which they must be contemporary. An issue with head of Poseidon/prow shows that Philip also had naval ambitions (**444**).

After the defeat at Cynoscephalae in 197 an epoch in Macedonian history came to an end. The coinage was interrupted for several years and when it was taken up again after nearly a decade a new and different coinage system was introduced (below, p. 163). But the first phase of Philip's coinage here discussed does show some new developments. With his first silver series an undisguised portrait of the living ruler appears on Macedonian coins for the first time since the reign of Demetrius Poliorcetes. His choice of types for both silver and bronze bears witness to a more conscious use of coinage as a means of propaganda, for while earlier kings had been content with celebrating victories already won, Philip used the coin types as a vehicle for propagating his ideas of the future, the political development as he wanted it and planned it to be.

A pendant to the defeat of Macedon in 197 was the issue, naturally not in Macedon but somewhere in Greece, of a commemorative series of gold staters (**445**) struck for Flamininus, the victorious Roman general. His bearded portrait appears on the obverse, whereas the reverse carries a standing Nike with wreath and palm branch copied from the well-known type of Alexander the Great. But here the goddess of victory places the wreath over the name of the Roman general, inscribed in Latin: T. QVINCTI. The portrait is an excellent representation of the sophisticated Roman aristocrat, who professed his philhellenism on all occasions and

14 Boehringer 1972, 118–24; Stöckli 1975, 84–6, but his low chronology for both Macedonian and Roman issues is unacceptable.

15 Mamroth 1935, 219–33, nos. 1–13. To these should be added his no. 26; see Boehringer 1972, 117.

succeeded in making at least some Greeks believe in his sincerity. The mint and date of these rare coins are both uncertain. They may have been struck at Corinth immediately after the famous declaration of Greek freedom in 196. But another possible mint is Chalcis, where Flamininus after the war received quite extraordinary honours as the saviour and benefactor of the city.

(c) POSTHUMOUS ALEXANDERS AND LYSIMACHI AND RELATED COINAGES

We have seen how the coinage of Alexander the Great was continued after his death by all the Successors except Ptolemy I, and in Macedon right down to 294. In the years preceding 280 a new development has been noted, the occurrence of Alexander coins as civic issues in Miletus, Mylasa and, possibly, Chalcis on Euboea (above, pp. 93–4, 91).

In the following decade the silver coinage of Macedonia consisted exclusively of Alexander coins (above, pp. 132, 134), and around the year 200 tetradrachms of Alexander type were issued by the Pergamene king for a specific purpose (above, p. 128). In this section I propose to discuss the production of gold and silver coins of the types introduced by Alexander the Great and Lysimachus by a large number of city-states and minor principalities throughout the Greek world. The importance of these issues has never been fully realized, because they have always been classified together with the lifetime issues of the two kings.[16] Our understanding of the coin production and economic significance of many cities has been severely distorted as a result of scholars ignoring the gold and large silver coins that formed the international medium of exchange. This is the case with the Berlin *Corpus* volume devoted to Byzantium.[17] The commercial position and economic importance of the city during the Hellenistic period have been completely falsified by the exclusion of the enormous series of gold staters and silver tetradrachms of Lysimachus types produced there for nearly 200 years.

In the Peloponnese the third century saw several issues of Alexander tetradrachms.[18] In the decade 270–260 two series were produced, probably at Argos (**446**) and at Megalopolis (**447**) from ten and four obverse dies respectively. They have been plausibly connected with the establishment of pro-Macedonian tyrants in the two cities by Antigonus Gonatas. Their issue may also be related to the Chremonidean War (268–262/1), which opposed Sparta (and Athens) to Macedon and her allies. Later in the century modest issues were produced at various places: Sicyon (**448**), Argos and Corinth (**449**) in the north, Megalopolis and Messene (**450**) further south. Two unique coins may be ascribed to Hermione in the Argolid and Pellene in Achaea. Most of these coins belong to the last quarter of the third century. Megalopolis was completely destroyed by Cleomenes of Sparta in 223, and its small issue, using four obverse dies, most probably dates from the time immediately preceding the destruction. Some of the Sicyonian

16 See Seyrig 1958a, 603–4. A useful account of the occurrence of posthumous Alexanders in hoards from Asia Minor is provided by Boehringer 1972, 190–9.
17 Schönert-Geiss 1970. See Le Rider 1971b, 152.
18 Troxell 1971, 51–81. The issues of Argos and Megalopolis are listed by Noe 1962, 37–41.

coins seem to be contemporary with these, but most of the other issues are better ascribed to the period of the Social War, 220–217. The latest issues from Sicyon and Argos, and the few coins from Messene (all from one obverse die), may be even later. As they occur only in hoards from Asia Minor, their striking has been connected with Achaean help to Rome in the war with Antiochus III, which would date them *c.* 192/190.

From the above it appears that all these issues of Peloponnesian Alexanders may, without forcing the evidence unduly, be ascribed to periods of war and unrest. Moreover, it seems probable that all the strikings of the late third to early second century were produced by member states of the Achaean League as part of the League's contributions to the various wars. We know from literary evidence that both Antigonus Doson, during the war with Cleomenes, and Philip V, during the Social War, obtained subsidies from the League to pay their armies. These posthumous Alexanders would have been eminently suitable for that purpose as well as for paying the Achaean auxiliary forces which followed the Romans to Asia Minor in 190.

Another region with considerable issues of posthumous Alexanders was the western shore of the Black Sea, along the coast of present-day Bulgaria and Rumania. Mesembria, Odessus, Callatis, Tomis and Istrus all issued gold staters in large quantities at some mints during the years from *c.* 280 to 230. Callatis was the most productive mint. The weight of these north Pontic issues is slightly reduced, to *c.* 8.45g/8.50g. Most of these issues are represented in the Anadol hoard buried *c.* 225 (*IGCH* 866).[19] Silver tetradrachms were also issued at all these mints except Tomis and Istrus. A small series of tetradrachms that definitely belongs to the same region may tentatively be ascribed to Dionysopolis.

The inland city of Cabyle in Thrace was also a mint for posthumous Alexander tetradrachms (**451**).[20] One of these shares an obverse die with a tetradrachm signed by the Celtic king Cavarus, who is known from literary sources to have reigned around 220, when he intervened in the war between Byzantium and Rhodes concerning the freedom of traffic through the Bosphorus. He is mentioned again in 213 or 212 when his reign probably came to an end. This provides an important chronological point of reference for the whole series.

In the mints of the Black Sea region it was customary to include the title of 'king' in the inscription, in contrast to most of the other posthumous Alexanders, which are simply signed *ΑΛΕΞΑΝΔΡΟΥ*.

On the southern shore of the Black Sea the cities of Sinope and Heraclea Pontica issued an Alexander coinage during the third century, Sinope many gold staters (**454**) and relatively few silver tetradrachms (**453**),[21] Heraclea only tetradrachms (**452**).

About 225 the Alexander coinage of Sinope was replaced by an issue of autonomous tetradrachms of Attic weight (**455**). The obverse bears an uncertain head to the right, while the

19 Seyrig 1969, 36–45; Poenaru Bordea 1979.
20 Gerassimov 1958.
21 Newell 1918b.

reverse shows Apollo with lyre, seated on an *omphalos*. Another series is generally placed somewhat earlier in the third century, but in my opinion its style points to a later date, around the turn of the century or perhaps in the first decade of the second century. It consists of a rare tetradrachm and several didrachms of rather irregular weights (*c.* 5.3–8.3g) that often fall far below the Attic standard. The Tyche on the obverse of these coins is facing left; the reverse of the tetradrachms (**456**) shows a standing archaistic figure of Apollo carrying a laurel branch, the didrachms (**457**) a seated Poseidon. All the specimens of the second series (and some of the first) are countermarked in a very special fashion. Normally the countermark was applied to one side of the coin only, but the Sinopean marks were made by a small pair of dies that left an 'obverse' countermark in high relief and 'reverse' impression in the negative. The reverse mark carries an inscription which shows that the countermarking was done by the city itself, presumably in order to revalidate or increase the nominal value of the coins in question. The precise occasion for the application of these countermarks escapes our knowledge. In 220 Sinope was threatened by the Pontic king Mithridates II or III, but was saved by Rhodian intervention. In 183, however, the city had fallen to Pharnaces I, the son and successor of Mithridates III. Between these dates the history of Sinope is a blank, but it is a reasonable assumption that the countermarking is related to the long struggle with the kingdom. The irregular weights of the second series also point to a period of stress and economic difficulty.

In the district around the Propontis and the straits leading from the Black Sea to the Mediterranean, civic Alexander tetradrachms were struck at Parium on two different occasions. The first issue belongs to the years shortly after 280, while the second (**458**) is dated to the 220s after the defeat of Antiochus Hierax by Attalus I.[22] At Lampsacus Alexander tetradrachms (**459**) were struck between *c.* 280 and *c.* 250. A single issue of gold staters (**460**) from the same mint has been dated to the 220s.[23] Another mint in the same region was Alexandria Troas. Its Alexander tetradrachms also fall into two groups, one dated just after 280, the second (**461**) belonging to the 220s. The latter group shows by its monograms a connection with the last issues of Antiochus Hierax from the same mint. A gold stater of Alexander type has been ascribed to the same period, but here the monogram connection is with the first coins of Antiochus Hierax, implying that the Alexander coin may rather have been struck about 245–240.[24] We know so little of the history of this period that the possibility of a short period of independence for Alexandria Troas around this time cannot be excluded.

A series of Alexander tetradrachms with a long torch as a prominent symbol (**462**) has been attributed to Cyzicus, but the ascription cannot be regarded as certain. From their style these coins seem to date from about the middle of the third century.

During the third century western Asia Minor teemed with cities issuing posthumous Alexanders. We have already dealt with the issues from the royal mint at Pergamum (above, p. 128). In the

22 Seyrig 1958a, 603–24.
23 Baldwin 1924, 67–72; Seyrig 1969, 39.
24 Bellinger 1961, 82, 91–3; 1969, 36–8; Bauslaugh 1979, 19–20.

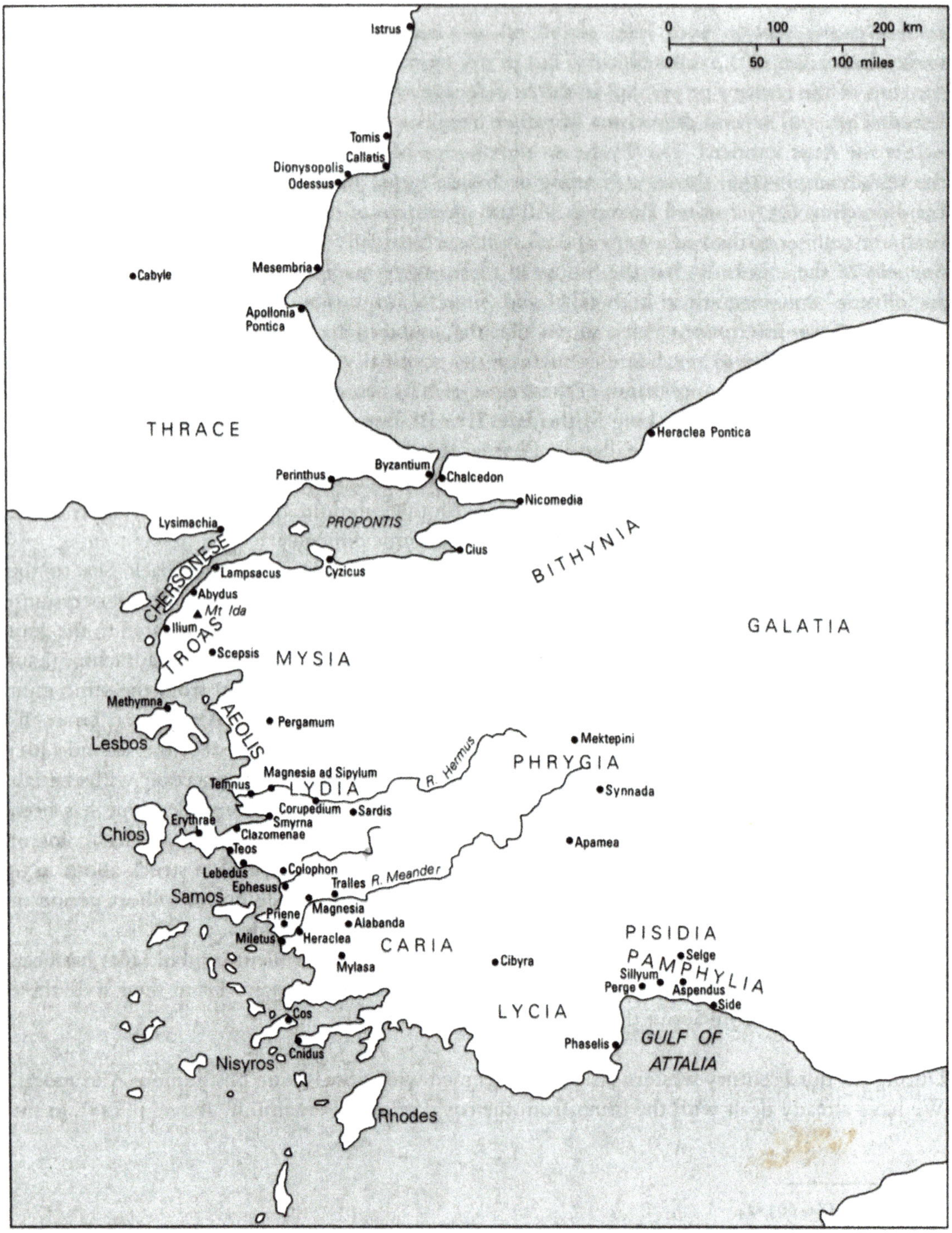

Map 6. Western Asia Minor

same area we find Alexander tetradrachms from Assus, Mytilene and Methymna on Lesbos, Cyme, Myrina and Temnus. Further south, in Ionia, the list comprises the cities of Phocaea, Smyrna, Clazomenae, Erythrae, Chios, Teos, Colophon, Ephesus, Magnesia on the Maeander, Priene, Samos and Miletus. To these should be added inland Sardis and, in Caria, Mylasa, Cos, Cnidus, possibly Nisyros, and Rhodes. Some of the coinages are small and apparently produced within a limited period, while other mints had a more extensive production in quantity as well as in time.

Only a few of these issues have been the object of proper die studies, and many problems, especially regarding their dating, are still awaiting solutions. That we are able to produce a list of mints such as the one above is mostly owing to the existence of a number of large and important hoards buried between *c.* 235 and about 190/89, the last group in connection with the war between Rome and Antiochus III and Cn. Manlius Vulso's Galatian expedition. They provide us with a representative cross-section of the issues just mentioned and allow some conclusions regarding their relative chronology.[25] In addition we have a few fixed points for the absolute chronology, and working from these a careful analysis of local and regional styles may throw some light on the chronological position of other issues. The best example of this last procedure is offered by the issues from Sardis. Here an autonomous tetradrachm of Attic weight (head of Heracles/Zeus Lydius standing with eagle and sceptre: **463**), is stylistically connected with a small group of posthumous Alexander tetradrachms (**464**) and a single drachm (**465**). From the position of Sardis as a royal Seleucid mint it appears that these coins can only have been struck in the short interval between 226 and 220 when Sardis was lost to the Seleucids. Now it appears that specimens of very similar style are found at Priene, Miletus (which share a common obverse die) and sometimes at Mylasa. We are thus confronted with a regional style which is dated to the 220s by the coins from Sardis.[26]

One of the few issues of posthumous Alexanders that has been carefully studied is the series from the island of Chios, easily recognizable by the marks of the city, a seated sphinx on nearly all tetradrachms and a bunch of grapes on the drachms.[27] A modest issue of tetradrachms (**466**) dates from the decade 280–270. By style and by a common monogram it is connected with a small issue from Erythrae, comprising a tetradrachm and a couple of drachms. The use of a common control mark points to some form of co-operation between these two neighbouring cities, but exactly what form this co-operation took is impossible to tell. A more extensive series of drachms from Chios (**467**) has been ascribed to the same period but may be somewhat later, perhaps rather from 260–250.[28]

---

25 The place of honour goes to the Mektepini hoard published by Olcay and Seyrig 1965. Other important hoards include Ayaz-In (Seyrig 1973, no. 8), the Sardis pot hoard (*IGCH* 1318), two hoards from Gordium (*IGCH* 1405–6), and a hoard from central Asia Minor (*IGCH* 1411; Boehringer 1972, 172–9).

26 Seyrig 1963, 35–8.

27 Bauslaugh 1979.

28 This lowering of the date for the drachms of Chios is suggested by Kinns in his unpublished dissertation on the coinage of Erythrae. It implies lowering the dates of a couple of hoards or treating Chian drachms in these as intrusions.

The second series of Chian tetradrachms (**468**), covering the period *c.* 270–*c.* 220, was quite extensive, as no less than 25 obverse dies have been recorded. The series also included a few drachms and two gold staters (**469**) that may have been struck for commercial reasons, perhaps for trade with the Black Sea area. A third series of tetradrachms (**470**), struck from 14 obverse dies, has been dated *c.* 202–*c.* 190 and related to the wars of these years against Philip V and Antiochus III, in which Chios is known to have been involved.

The same period of unrest and upheaval produced similar effects in the coin production of many other cities in Asia Minor, among them Erythrae and Rhodes. According to hoard evidence the issues of Erythrae may have begun somewhat earlier, around *c.* 220. The Rhodian series (**471**) comprised 37 obverse dies, providing a good illustration of the economic strength of this island as compared to a state of secondary importance like Chios.[29] At Rhodes the practice of letting some magistrates sign the issues for which they were responsible with their full names was introduced in this period (**472**), undoubtedly copied from the civic issues where this fashion had been common for centuries. Other cities followed the Rhodian example, for instance Clazomenae, and the custom of placing magistrates' names in full on posthumous Alexanders was adopted by most cities after 190/89. At Samos a small issue of Alexander tetradrachms (**473**), struck from only five obverse dies, has been dated between *c.* 205 and *c.* 189.[30]

We have already seen that Miletus was one of the first cities to issue civic Alexanders (above pp. 93–4). After 280 the difficult economic situation created by the Galatian raids and the rivalry between the Seleucids and the Ptolemies may have stopped the production of both autonomous coins and posthumous Alexanders.[31] However, in about the middle of the third century economic conditions improved, and an apparently continuous production of posthumous Alexanders was inaugurated in about 225, lasting until *c.* 190/89 or perhaps even a little longer (**474**). The production rate may have increased towards the end of the period.

Mylasa was a much smaller mint than Miletus, but also an early producer of civic Alexanders (above, p. 94). A further series of Alexander tetradrachms and drachms, most of them marked with a *bipennis* symbol, was struck between 280 and 250.[32]

Except for a single gold stater of the types of Philip II from the early part of the third century, Alabanda in Caria did not issue any coinage of Macedonian types during our period. However, at this point her autonomous silver coinage of Attic weight may conveniently be mentioned.[33] In deference to the Seleucids, the city changed her name from Alabanda to Antiochia of the Chrysaoreis, probably already by the middle of the third century. Antiochus III was regarded as the protector and benefactor of the city and allowed it to produce a silver coinage with civic types: on the obverse a head of Apollo, on the reverse a Pegasus. Tetradrachms (**475**) and

29 Kleiner 1971, 105–25.
30 Barron 1966, 148–9, 223.
31 This is the conclusion of Dr B. Deppert-Lippitz, who kindly made her unpublished manuscript on the Hellenistic coinage of Miletus available to me. [See now Deppert-Lippitz 1984.]
32 Thompson 1981b.
33 Boehringer 1972, 9–11, 186–90. [Waggoner 1989.]

drachms (**476**) are known, signed by sixteen different magistrates, either with monograms or with their full signatures. The tetradrachms alone belong to twelve or thirteen different magistrates. So few obverse dies were used for the production of all these variants that the magistrates cannot be regarded as annually elected; either they functioned for part of a year only or several of them were working simultaneously on a collegiate basis. The idea that they were performing a liturgy cannot be rejected, and the dating of the whole series to the years *c.* 197/*c.* 190–188 seems plausible. After the defeat of Antiochus III the city reverted to her old name of Alabanda.

From the Pamphylian area (including the east coast of Lycia facing the gulf of Attalia) we possess a very extensive coinage of posthumous Alexander tetradrachms from several mints. The issues of Sillyum (**477**) were modest, but the cities of Aspendus (**478**), Perge (**479**) and Phaselis (**480**) produced tetradrachms in such quantities as to seem quite incommensurate with the economic significance of these places. Most of the coinage was exported to other districts of Asia Minor and, especially, to the Seleucid kingdom, where they occur in a considerable number of hoards from the first forty years of the second century. By 175 they had come to constitute by far the largest part of the foreign coinage imported into Syria, where they were frequently countermarked. With them circulated autonomous tetradrachms of Side. This Pamphylian city produced only a single issue of posthumous Alexanders and then changed to tetradrachms (**481**) of the same Attic weight but with civic types: head of Athena in Corinthian helmet/Nike.

At Perge a series of autonomous tetradrachms (**482**) and smaller denominations (head of Artemis/Artemis standing with wreath and long sceptre; at her side, deer) was issued before the Alexanders, *c.* 255 to *c.* 240. Their inscription, *ΑΡΤΕΜΙΔΟΣ ΠΕΡΓΑΙΑΣ*, provides the earliest example of an issue in the name of a deity, perhaps struck in connection with a religious festival in her honour. The coinage seems to be dated between year 1 and year 13, indicating a coinage connected with an annual celebration rather than with a trieteric or penteteric festival as one might have expected.

The most important feature of the Pamphylian Alexanders is their dates. They all carry a series of numerals. From Sillyum only a few are known (3–6 and 11), but at Phaselis and Perge the sequence runs from 1 to 33, at Aspendus from 1 to 31, in all three cases with a few breaks. The problem consists in establishing the era or eras used on these coinages. On account of the obvious parallels between the issues it seems *a priori* most likely that they were all dated according to the same provincial Pamphylian era. Seyrig argued convincingly from the hoard provenances, and from general historical considerations, that the coins are best placed between 221/20 and 189/8. The more recent attempt of Boehringer to assume three different eras for the coinages of Phaselis, Aspendus and Perge has been disproved by the discovery of an obverse die link between the issues of Aspendus and Perge. An attempt to return to the old dating of an era beginning in 190/89 or 189/8 breaks down when confronted with hoard evidence from Syria, where the mixed hoards available can of course be dated by the royal Seleucid coins included.[34]

34 The most important discussion of the Pamphylian issues is that of Seyrig 1963, 38–63. For the chronological

Another dated series of posthumous Alexanders, all with the symbol palm-tree, was produced at Aradus. This important city on the Phoenician coast had acquired its autonomy as early as in 259/8, the first year of its civic era. After an undated issue of *c.* 250 to *c.* 245, Aradus followed the excellent practice of dating its tetradrachms (**483**) from year 17 (243/2) to year 45 (215/14) with Phoenician numerals. The series shows considerable gaps in the sequence, however. A new series, now with Greek numerals (**484**), was issued from year 58 (= 202/1) to year 69 (= 191/90), and only one year, 67, is here missing. Between the two series there is a gap of twelve years. Most of this interval was occupied, in my opinion, by a series of pseudo-Ptolemaic tetradrachms (**485**), comprising one undated issue and others carrying dates in Greek numerals between 48 and 55 on the Aradian era, or 212/11 and 205/4. This pseudo-Ptolemaic coinage continued, with some intervals, far into the second century, circulating almost exclusively in Phoenicia and Palestine in spite of the fact that since 200 this region was under Seleucid government. The relative chronology obtained from a number of hoards as well as their circulation pattern make it virtually certain that these coins were actually produced at Aradus.[35]

The implications for the history of this city are most important. In the first place it shows the city-state acting with a remarkable degree of freedom in a sphere related to foreign policy, a most exceptional phenomenon in the relationship between cities and kings in the early Hellenistic period. Secondly, it shows that Aradus during these years consciously directed its economy towards the Ptolemies, separating itself from the area using Attic-weight coins to which Seleucid Syria belonged. This could hardly have been done without the tacit approval of the Egyptian government, which would see a political advantage in incorporating such an important buffer state in its own economic system. But as soon as the Fifth Syrian War broke out Aradus returned to the production of Attic-weight Alexanders, a wise decision in the light of the outcome of that war.

The years 30 to 35 of the Aradian era (= 230/29 to 225/4) saw a production of Alexander tetradrachms at several mints on the Aradian mainland: Gabala, Carne, Marathus and Simyra.[36] At Marathus we also find an autonomous tetradrachm issued in year 33 (= 227/6) with head of Tyche/Marathus seated on a pile of shields holding *aphlaston*. The last issue especially seems to indicate that Aradus in this period was loosening her grip on her mainland possessions and had to concede the cities there an independent status.

Outside the Graeco-Macedonian world Alexander's coinage was also copied. Recent finds from the Persian Gulf area have disclosed the existence of several series of Alexander imitations from that region.[37] One series (**486**), where the Zeus on the reverse is identified with Shamash, the Arabian sun-god, by an inscription in Arabic, has been ascribed to the important trading centre

problems see Boehringer 1972, 52–58; Fischer 1976, 51–8 (requiring an impossible lowering of the burial dates of a great number of hoards); and Mørkholm 1978c. [For Side see Leschhorn in Francke *et al.* 1988, 23–44.]

35 Seyrig 1951; 1964, 9–50. On the pseudo-Ptolemaic issues see Mørkholm 1976.

36 Cox 1966, 37, no. 24.

37 Mørkholm 1960b, 1972, 1979a. A different chronology has been proposed by Robin 1974.

of Gerrha on the Arabian coast near Bahrein. The series fall into several different issues that seem to date from *c.* 240 to *c.* 210, the lower limit being established by the occurrence of the latest coins from Gerrha in a number of hoards deposited around 200.

More barbarous imitations (**487**) were issued by two kings, Abyal and Harithat, who reigned at Hagar, a principality not exactly located but which may have included Bahrein and part of the mainland opposite the island. They belong to the time around 230 and seem to have been copied from the issues of Aradus. The seated god on the reverse carries a rhyton formed as the forepart of a horse instead of the usual eagle. Another series comprising both tetradrachms and drachms (**488–9**) was issued by a certain Abyatha around 210. The coinage must have originated from the same general area, the Arabian coast along the Persian Gulf, but a more exact location is impossible at present. All these issues bear witness to the popularity of the posthumous Alexanders and their widespread use thoughout the Hellenistic world.

In some regions posthumous gold and silver coins of the Lysimachus type were just as popular as the posthumous Alexanders. Their production seems to have started immediately after the death of Lysimachus. In some cases, for instance with the first issues of Perinthus and Aenus, it is uncertain whether we are dealing with late lifetime issues or early posthumous ones. An issue of Lysimachus tetradrachms from Aenus (**490**) is signed by a certain Scostocus, a Scythian or Thracian dynast who must have made himself master of the Greek city in the troubled decade after the death of Lysimachus. Other cities that continued to strike Lysimachus coins after his death include Lysimachia, Cius, Parium and Mytilene. An obverse die from Mytilene was used for a rare issue of Lysimachus tetradrachms at Clazomenae, a locality that had not functioned as a mint for Lysimachus during his lifetime.[38]

The most important producer of posthumous Lysimachi was undoubtedly Byzantium (**491**) which must be discussed in association with its neighbour on the Asiatic side of the Bosphorus, Chalcedon.[39] The developments at these two allied cities run parallel well down into the second century. Their first issues of Lysimachus coins date from the 270s. A few of the earliest silver coins of Chalcedon (tetradrachms and drachms) are signed by the city (**492**), while the contemporary gold staters carry the name and title of Lysimachus. Another independent city that took up the striking of posthumous Lysimachus coins was Cyzicus (**493**). Together these cities formed the nucleus of the so-called Northern League that opposed the attempts of Antiochus I to establish Seleucid domination over this area.

About 250 the city of Byzantium received a considerable number of Ptolemaic tetradrachms. For some reason unknown to us it was decided to let them enter into circulation, in spite of their different weight standard. Consequently, they were countermarked with the initials of the city ΠΥ (**494**) – Π is an old Corinthian form of B – within which was placed the initial or monogram of a magistrate. As no less than eight different magistrates were employed in this

38 Seyrig 1958a, 617–18; Thompson 1968a, 176 (Mytilene and Clazomenae), 182 (Perinthus and Aenus). On Scostocus see Youroukova 1976, 26–9.

39 The following sections are mainly based on Seyrig 1968.

operation, it seems likely that the Ptolemaic coins arrived over a certain number of years rather than as one payment. Whether they represented a subsidy paid by Ptolemy II or came by normal trade we cannot tell.

The production of the Lysimachus coinage continued at Byzantium and Chalcedon down to *c.* 235 when it was suddenly interrupted by issues of autonomous silver coins, with obverse head of Demeter and reverse a seated Poseidon at Byzantium (**495**), a seated Apollo at Chalcedon (**496–7**). The denominations of these issues are also peculiar: drachms of Persian weight (*c.* 5.5g) accompany tetradrachms of a local standard, weighing *c.* 13.90g. We know of at least ten different issues from Byzantium and six from Chalcedon, signed by different magistrates, at Byzantium the *hieromnemon*, the yearly eponym of the city. Their occurrence in the Büyükçekmece hoard allows us to date these issues to the period *c.* 235–*c.* 220.[40]

The hoard from Büyükçekmece contained, in addition to the autonomous issues just mentioned, a variety of Attic-weight coins: lifetime and posthumous issues of Alexander the Great and Lysimachus (including a few specimens from Byzantium and Chalcedon), coins of Demetrius Poliorcetes, and royal issues from Pergamum, as well as a series of Seleucid tetradrachms ending with Antiochus Hierax (241–228/7). The remarkable thing about these Attic-weight coins is that they are all, without any exception, countermarked with the small official marks of the cities of Byzantium and Chalcedon.

The fact that all the Attic-weight coins in the hoard from Büyükçekmece were countermarked, while the autonomous issues of the two cities were not, led Seyrig to a careful examination and reconstruction of this intriguing interlude in the monetary history of Byzantium and Chalcedon. Apparently financial difficulties, presumably caused by the heavy subsidies paid to the Galatian chieftains of the hinterland of Byzantium, compelled the two cities at the entrance to the Black Sea to explore all possibilities of increasing their revenue. One expedient was to establish a monetary monopoly by introducing a local coinage of special weight and forcing the merchants to use only this currency within their territory. Attic-weight coinages of different origin, including earlier issues of Byzantium and Chalcedon themselves, were called in to be melted down and used as bullion for the lighter autonomous coins. As the mints were unable to produce the new coinage in sufficient quantity for the needs of the merchants, recourse was had to countermaking. Instead of exchanging their Attic-weight coins for the new local coins, merchants might get them validated by the authorities against the payment of a fee corresponding to the fee on the exchange, and the validation was confirmed by the application of a countermark. In this way the two cities obtained the customary income provided by a monetary monopoly and, at the same time, ensured a sufficient supply of money for circulation. To this convincing explanation I should like only to add that the circulation together of countermarked coins, Attic-weight coins and the new coins of local weight, as revealed by the Büyükçekmece hoard, seems to indicate that the new tetradrachms were regarded as equal in value to the pieces of Attic weight. If this was the case the new coinage was overvalued by

40 Thompson 1954.

c. 19%, a handsome profit for the two cities which they would enjoy either from the exchange of Attic-weight coins or from the countermarking.

Towards 200 Byzantium and Chalcedon reverted to the use of posthumous Lysimachus coins of Attic weight. The production of local coinage remained an isolated episode. Various reasons may be adduced for the abandonment of a lucrative source of revenue. The financial situation of the two cities may have become less strained owing to some temporary weakness of the Galatians. Foreign merchants would undoubtedly have objected strongly to this as to any other forms of tolls or taxes. It may even be that this financial measure was found by the city authorities to result in a reduction of the volume of trade and therefore not to be quite as profitable in the long run as was first expected. However this may be, the return to normal monetary conditions in Byzantium and Chalcedon most probably formed part of the settlement in 220, when Rhodes succeeded in negotiating a peace with the two cities by which freedom of trade through the Bosphorus was secured for all Greek states.

About 215 the Lysimachus gold staters from Byzantium began to show a trident in the exergue, and from *c.* 205 both gold and silver openly proclaimed their mint by placing the letter ΠΥ (later replaced by *BY*) on the throne of Athena on the reverse (**498–9**). Simultaneously Chalcedon signed its issue with a *K*, and often an ear of corn appeared as a symbol in the exergue. A further change occurred in *c.* 195, when the tetradrachms of Byzantium also added a trident in the exergue (**499**). At the same time the ear of grain became a constant feature on the issues from Chalcedon, and these are now signed *ΚΑΛ* or *ΚΑΛΧΑ* (**500**). At both mints the production of posthumous Lysimachi continued well beyond 180.

With a reasonable chronological arrangement of the extensive series of posthumous Lysimachi from Byzantium it becomes possible to date a number of other issues which were obviously influenced by Byzantine prototypes. Some rare issues with a shield and a sword as symbols have been attributed to Leucon II, king of the Cimmerian Bosphorus (Crimea) about 240 or 230. The identification rests on the fact that a shield and sword of the same characteristic types were used on the bronze coins of this king.[41] These issues from the northern coast of the Black Sea are important because they show the direction of the trade of Byzantium, demonstrating her unquestioned position as the transit station for the commerce between the Black Sea and the Aegean.

From the Mektepini hoard (*IGCH* 1410) and other deposits buried about 190 we know that the production of posthumous Lysimachi, mostly tetradrachms, was resumed at a number of mints from *c.* 220. This applies to Heraclea Pontica, Cyzicus, Lysimachia, Lampsacus, Abydus, Ilium and Tenedos, all cities situated at or near the waterway into the Black Sea.[42] Within the period *c.* 205/*c.* 190 the island of Rhodes issued a gold stater of Lysimachus types, copied from the contemporary issues of Byzantium (below, p. 157).

While the posthumous Alexander coinage represents a truly international currency, circulating

---

41 Seyrig 1963, 7–11.
42 Seyrig 1958a, 623–4 with fig. 4.

freely wherever the Attic weight standard was accepted, the production of posthumous Lysimachus coins was more geographically restricted. With few exceptions the mints are concentrated in the Black Sea area and its approaches. Some cities, as for instance Parium and Lampsacus, produced both Alexanders and Lysimachi during the third century, although not simultaneously. It seems reasonable to regard the production of Lysimachi as catering to a special demand for this type of coinage from the trade partners of the Greeks in southern Russia and on the Crimea. This tendency was strengthened by the very large coin production of Byzantium, which clearly greatly influenced the other neighbouring cities. The posthumous Lysimachi thus became a regional coinage of the first importance.

Another matter of importance connected with these posthumous coinages is that they present us, in a very clear form, with the varying motives behind the issue of coins. The Alexander issues of the Peloponnesian mints, and of Pergamum and Rhodes, can plausibly be connected with financial exigencies of armaments and military undertakings. By contrast, the large series from Byzantium and the heavy issues of the Pamphylian cities during a quite restricted period must be ascribed primarily to commercial considerations, perhaps in the latter case combined with a profit motive. And the many small issues from mints in Asia Minor after the death of Antiochus Hierax in 226 may reflect civic pride in a newly won autonomy and a desire to demonstrate it to the Greek world.

(d) LEAGUES AND CITIES IN GREECE AND ASIA MINOR, *c.* 280–190

We have already seen (above p. 86) that there was a probable break in the production of Athenian silver coinage between *c.* 294 and 287. After 287 the production of tetradrachms was resumed, now in the 'four-finger' style, so called because the floral scroll on Athena's helmet terminates in a figure with four strokes starting from a common base (**501**). It was this coinage that financed the Chremonidean War, when Athens and Sparta, heavily subsidized by Ptolemy II of Egypt, tried to eliminate or reduce the Macedonian influence in Greece. With the Macedonian victory and conquest of Athens in 261 both her silver and bronze coinage seem to have come to a stop, although the bronze may have continued for another decade.[43]

The Macedonian occupation of Athens lasted until 229/8, when the city bought its freedom from a Macedonian garrison commander. Economic conditions apparently precluded an immediate resumption of silver coinage. First about 220 a few issues of drachms were struck, appearing in a very fresh condition in a hoard from Corinth (*IGCH* 187) buried about 215.[44] These drachms are distinguished from earlier Athenian issues by their style, the scroll on Athena's helmet now taking a resemblance to an *aphlaston*, as well as by the addition of some symbol on the reverse (facing head, prow, trident, etc.). About ten issues are known. These drachms were accompanied by a few tetradrachms (**502**), which have been known for a long time, but the number of variants has been much increased by a hoard from Sitochoro/Larissa (*IGCH* 237;

43 Kroll 1979, 139–54.
44 Noe 1962, 24–6.

buried *c.* 167),[45] so that we now know eleven different tetradrachm issues with symbols or monograms or both. It seems possible to arrange them in a chronological sequence, mostly according to technical details such as the diameter of the flan, which tends to increase. Stylistic elements also show some development in the general direction of the New Style coinage which succeeded it.[46] Our group of drachms and tetradrachms with symbols or monograms may well have lasted for about thirty years or more, but the question of their chronology, especially the end phase, is intricately connected with the much discussed problem of the date of the introduction of the New Style coinage which I have examined elsewhere.[47]

Sparta, the second opponent of Macedon in the Chremonidean War, was very late in issuing coins. According to the Lycurgan constitution the possession and use of coinage was forbidden within Sparta's frontiers. The first to break with these old-fashioned rules was King Areus, who in 267 to 265, during the Chremonidean War, struck a small series of Attic-weight tetradrachms (**503**), using the common types of Alexander the Great but inscribing the coins *ΒΑΣΙΛΕΟΣ ΑΡΕΟΣ*.[48] The coinage may well have been struck outside Spartan territory during one of the king's military expeditions. Only three specimens are known, struck from three different obverse dies.

The first coinage of Sparta itself consisted of obols of reduced Aeginetan weight (head of bearded Heracles/club, on either side star: **504**). They have been dated *c.* 265 and connected with Areus but may belong to the decade 260–250 and represent an attempt to bring Sparta into line, economically, with the other states in the Peloponnese. It is remarkable for the time that they should be anepigraphic.

A second issue of tetradrachms (diademed head of ruler/archaistic cult statue of Artemis Orthia, *ΛΑ*: **505**) has been plausibly attributed to the time of Cleomenes III's military expeditions in the Peloponnese between 227 and 222. This late attempt at extending Spartan influence came to an end with her disastrous defeat by Antigonus Doson at Sellasia in 222. The obverse type, undoubtedly representing Cleomenes, shows the influence of Hellenistic monarchical ideas even in conservative Sparta. The inscription, however, does not reveal the name of the king but consists of the initials of the Lacedaemonian state.

During the 220s Cleomenes III had been handsomely subsidized by Ptolemy III. This is reflected in the Lacedaemonian bronze coinage of the decade. Two different denominations (**506–7**) were provided with Ptolemaic types: eagle on thunderbolt/winged thunderbolt. They must also have come to an end in 222. Two other issues carry local types related to Heracles and the Dioscuri.

The next Lacedaemonian coinage, struck from *c.* 219 to 196, consists of triobols or hemidrachms weighing *c.* 2.40g (**508**). The types are head of Heracles/amphora with *pileus* of Dioscurus on either side. Such hemidrachms of reduced Aeginetan weight were to become the

45 [See now Price 1989.]
46 Nicolet-Pierre 1982.
47 Mørkholm 1984b.
48 Troxell 1971, 70–80. For this and the following sections see also Grunauer von Hoerschelmann 1978.

most popular denomination in the Peloponnese and in central Greece in the late third and the second centuries.

A third group of Attic-weight tetradrachms has been ascribed to Nabis, tyrant of Sparta from 207 to 192. It consists of three different but interrelated main types:

(a) Head of Athena in Corinthian helmet/Heracles seated on rock leaning on his club; *ΛΑ* (**509**).
(b) Same types, but reverse inscribed *Λ Α ΝΑΒΙΟΣ* (**510**).
(c) Laureate head of Nabis right/Heracles seated as before: *ΒΑΣΙΛΕΟΣ ΝΑΒΙΟΣ* (*sic*) (**511**).

While (b) and (c) are known only from one specimen of each variety, group (a), comprising fifteen coins struck from nine obverse dies, can be further subdivided by the appearance of various symbols. The attribution to Nabis is, of course, evident for groups (b) and (c), and the unique coin with the portrait of Nabis and the royal title (in the Laconian dialect) can with some plausibility be dated to 196, when he received Roman recognition. This is the only example of a typical Hellenistic royal coinage produced at Sparta.

For group (a) the dating depends on the burial date of a hoard from Sparta (*IGCH* 181) which contained all the different variants of this group. It was originally dated *c.* 220, and it may prove difficult to bring it as far down as *c.* 196. The seated Heracles on (b) and (c) is also of a style different from the preceding representations, Heracles appearing more vigorous and muscular and seated in a more active upright position. This stylistic difference is perhaps an argument for allowing a certain interval between group (a) and the following issues. Group (a) may belong to the time of Lycurgus and Machanidas, *c.* 219–207, especially to the years between 211 and 207 when Sparta became involved in the first war between Macedon and Rome. The Sparta hoard might then have been buried *c.* 207, when Philopoemen plundered and ravaged in Laconia after his victory over Machanidas at Mantinea. Type (b) would then belong to the period 207–196. Three different issues of bronze coins are ascribed to the last years of Nabis' reign, *c.* 196–192.

Apart from Sparta, the only city-state in the Peloponnese to issue autonomous tetradrachms of Attic weight was Messene (**512**). The types were head of Demeter/standing figure of Zeus Ithomatas brandishing thunderbolt. Owing to lack of hoard evidence they can only be dated by their style to the period *c.* 280–250, and the specific occasion of their issue cannot be determined.

To the north of the Corinthian Gulf the district of Aetolia, as the political and military centre of the Aetolian League, assumed an important position during the third century, extending her political influence over most of central Greece. Her struggle against Macedon and the Gaulish invaders had given her control of Delphi and she also intervened in Peloponnesian affairs, where she was in competition with the Achaean League. She was late in striking coins, her first issue of Attic-weight gold staters and silver tetradrachms dating to about 220, the beginning of the Social War between Philip V of Macedon and his allies.[49]

The obverse types for both gold staters (**513**) and silver (**514**) are taken directly from the coinage of Alexander: heads of Athena and Heracles respectively. The reverses show a figure of Aetolia, seated on a pile of Macedonian and Gaulish shields, presumably copied from a statue erected by the Aetolians at Delphi. On the gold she carries a Nike on her right hand, on the silver she holds a sword in scabbard. The latter representation is the more original of the two. Gold drachms or hemistaters (**515**) were also issued. The reverse shows the same type as the staters, the obverse a head of Heracles in both bearded and unbearded forms. A unique tetradrachm carries a bust of Artemis on the obverse.

In addition to their Attic-weight coinage the Aetolians also issued silver staters (didrachms), drachms and hemidrachms of the Corcyrean or reduced Aeginetan standard weighing *c*. 10.5g/10g, 5.2g/5g and 2.6g/2.5g. The types are for the stater (**516**): youthful male head with wreath and diadem/naked warrior (Aetolus) standing left with one foot on rock, leaning against spear. The head on the obverse has sometimes been identified with Antiochus who was elected *strategos* of the Aetolian League in 192 in preparation for the war against Rome. The head, however, is rather impersonal in its characterization and the resemblance too vague to carry conviction. The drachms (**517**) show a head of Artemis on the obverse, Aetolia seated on the reverse, whereas the hemidrachms (**518**) present the head of Aetolia wearing *kausia* and, on the reverse, the running Calydonian boar. All these issues were started in the period *c*. 220 to 189, the time of Aetolia's wars with Macedon and, subsequently, with Rome. That the military demands of this period should have caused an extraordinary economic effort is not surprising. Coin output seems to have been especially heavy during the last fatal struggle with Rome, when according to the latest survey at least 58 obverse dies for triobols were used. Some of these, however, may date from the period after the war, when a heavy indemnity had to be paid to Rome. Several series of bronze coins were issued in Aetolia during the same period. The most interesting (**519**) bears as types a laureate head of Apollo and, on the reverse, a spearhead and the jaw-bone of a boar. The issue cannot be dated with certainty, but the same types were used by several states with close political connections to the Aetolian League.

To the west of Aetolia the Acarnanian League also issued coins on the same standards. Rare gold coins (stater, hemistater, quarter-stater) of Attic weight are known, whereas the silver (staters and drachms) followed the Corcyrean standard (**520–1**). The types are head of the river god Achelous in the usual form of a man-headed bull and, on the reverse, the Actian Apollo seated, holding bow. The introduction of these coins has generally been dated *c*. 250 for insufficient stylistic reasons, based on a comparison of the seated Apollo with the seated Apollo on a prow of tetradrachms of the Macedonian king Antigonus.[50] He was earlier identified with Gonatas (276–239), but is now commonly assumed to be Doson, who reigned from 229 to 221 (above, p. 135). The stylistic parallels thus belong to the 220s. Moreover, the territory of

49 Scheu 1960, 37–52 (wrong chronology); Noe 1962, 30–1; Laix 1973.
50 See Schwabacher 1951. For the history of the Acarnanian League cf. Larsen 1968, 264–73.

Acarnania was divided between Aetolia and Epirus between *c.* 250 and 231. This division must have meant the temporary dissolution of the League, and, consequently, no league coinage can have been issued during the period of subjection.

In 231 the part of Acarnania held by the Epirotes regained its independence, and the League was apparently reconstituted. From that date a league coinage of the Acarnanians would have become feasible, but the choice of the Apollo of Actium as the reverse type may perhaps indicate a later date for its actual beginning. About 216 the League assumed responsibility for the temple of Actian Apollo and his festival, which had until then been under the control of the city of Anactorium. It seems reasonable to assume that this creation of a federal religious capital would have been reflected in the choice of the coin type, in which case the initial series of Acarnanian coins would be dated to the years of the First Macedonian War, *c.* 214–205. Another possibility would be to relate the first Acarnanian coinage to the Social War (220–217) in which Acarnania was deeply involved. At this time the Acarnanian capital was situated at Leucas, where the coins were most probably struck.

The coinage of the Epirote *symmachia*, which existed alongside the tribal kingdom of the Molossians, has been referred to already (p. 84). The bronze coins of the *symmachia* were issued down to 234/4 or 232, when the kingdom was abolished and a republican league replaced the *symmachia*. The new Epirote League proceeded to strike silver staters and drachms on the Corcyrean standard.[51] The staters (**522**) show on the obverse the jugate heads of Zeus and Dione, on the reverse a charging bull. The more abundant drachms (**523**) carry the types head of Zeus/eagle. Obverse and reverse of both denominations are encircled by a wreath of oak leaves, the oak being the sacred tree of the main deity of Epirus, Zeus of Dodona. This special feature was later imitated by Philip V in Macedon and, through Macedonian coinage, came to influence the so-called wreath coinages which became fashionable in many Greek cities during the first half of the second century.

Other denominations (one-third and one-sixth staters) are also known, but they most probably belong to the years shortly before 168. Several series of bronze coins (**524**) were also issued by the League. If the volume of coinage is taken to provide any indication of economic conditions, the relative abundance of Epirote coinage between *c.* 230 and 167 and the introduction of a continuous silver coinage point to increased prosperity and to closer commercial integration between Epirus and neighbouring districts during this period.

On the island of Corcyra the issues of drachms and hemidrachms on the Corcyrean standard (above p. 84) continue far down into the third century. At some date, commonly assumed to have been around 229 but perhaps somewhat later, new types were introduced for the drachms: head of Dionysus/Pegasus (**525**). At about the same time new denominations make their appearance: drachms weighing about 3.3g–3.4g and hemidrachms of half this weight. The types on the drachms are bust of Dione/Pegasus within wreath (**526**), on the hemidrachms Pegasus/head of Aphrodite or head of Apollo/Pegasus.

The Corcyrean colonies of Dyrrhachium and Apollonia along the Adriatic coast were

51 Franke 1961, 134–217.

apparently the places where this new standard was created. For their drachms and hemidrachms they retained the old types borrowed from Corcyra: cow suckling calf/stellate pattern for the drachms (**527–8**), forepart of cow/stellate pattern for the hemidrachms (**529**). On the obverses a name in the nominative case indicates a monetary magistrate, whereas a name in the genitive on the reverses most probably denotes an annual eponymous *prytanis*. The two series are thus absolutely parallel, but the output at Dyrrhachium was more comprehensive than that of Apollonia, providing us with about 130 names of eponymous officials out of a total of nearly 200. An analysis of several large and fairly well-dated hoards leads to the conclusion that the coinage must have started *c*. 250–240 at both cities.[52]

In handbooks and catalogues these large and important coinages are commonly called victoriates and half-victoriates, because their weight is identical with that of the Roman victoriate, *c*. 3.4g or three Roman scruples. Earlier it was often assumed that the Illyrian cities actually took over the Roman coin standard, but the dating of the introduction of the Roman victoriate to *c*. 213 or later has deprived this theory of its foundation.[53] There is really no need to explain the change of standard in Illyria by the direct Roman influence in the area from about 229. An explanation is more likely to be found in the context of Greek monetary conditions around 250–240.

Actually, the new standard represented an excellent middle position between the Rhodian and the Corcyrean weight systems. It may be regarded as a drachm on the Rhodian system, the main denomination at Rhodes at this time being the didrachm of *c*. 6.8g. At the same time we know from later coinages of Epirus and Acarnania that it could also function as a third or a sixth of the Corcyrean stater of *c*. 10g. I feel no doubt that these simple connections with two of the most important regional standards in the Greek world provided the main motivation for the introduction of the so-called victoriates in Dyrrhachium and Apollonia about 250–240. An additional advantage would derive from the fact that the standard might also facilitate exchanges with the Greek cities in South Italy. After the war between Pyrrhus and Rome, Tarentum and other cities produced reduced didrachms of *c*. 6.6g, and this standard was adopted about 240 by Rome for its issues of ROMA-didrachms and quadrigati. The Illyrian drachms could be regarded as halves of these Italian coinages. It should be remembered that commercial and political relations between the states on both sides of the Adriatic became more intense at this period. The first contacts between Apollonia and Rome in fact date from *c*. 266, when an embassy from the Illyrian city visited Rome. Roman intervention against Illyrian pirates in the Adriatic in 229 also presupposes a period of intensive commercial activity across the Strait of Otranto since at least the middle of the century.

Returning from the Adriatic coast to central Greece and the Peloponnese we find that drachms

52 Cf. Giovannini 1978, 103–13. It goes without saying that calculations of this kind can give only approximate results. My chronology differs slightly from that of Giovannini because I date the burial of the key hoard from Bakerr (*IGCH* 559) to 168/7, while Giovannini prefers a date around 150.

53 See Thomsen 1961, II. 320–91.

of Corcyrean or reduced Aeginetan standard were issued in Boeotia (facing head of Persephone/standing Poseidon: **530**) and at Elis (eagle with hare/winged thunderbolt: **531**). While the Boeotian drachms can be dated only loosely to around the middle of the third century, the Elean coinage belongs to the years *c.* 230–190, a period of strong Aetolian influence in the district.[54] A frequency table of the Boeotian drachms shows a peak at 5.00g/5.09g, while the corresponding peak for the somewhat later drachms of Elis occurs at *c.* 4.80g.

However, in the Peloponnese the reduced hemidrachm became the most common denomination of the third and second centuries. In the late fourth century a mass production of this denomination had already taken place at Argos and Sicyon. In the third century it was adopted by the most important political power in the peninsula, the Achaean League.[55] The types of the League hemidrachms are head of Zeus/monogram ΑΧ within laurel wreath. The earliest coins (**532**) are anepigraphic or inscribed with a single letter on the reverse. The later coinages (**533–4**) are differentiated by symbols or abbreviated ethnics indicating the place of minting and by initials or monograms of local officials. The production was not continuous but concentrated in certain periods, often reflecting the League's involvement in military affairs. The first group among the later coinages has been ascribed to the years *c.* 195–188 (the Syrian and Aetolian Wars) and was struck at seven mints at least: Corinth, Argos, Sicyon, Patras, Elis, Messene and Corone. The output varied greatly from mint to mint.

A famous passage in Polybius where he compares the Peloponnese to a city-state 'using the same laws and weights and measures and coins' might be used as an argument for maintaining that the Achaean League coinage was the only one struck at this time.[56] This, however, would be a wrong deduction, as several member states issued their own coinage during their period of membership. What was common to these silver coinages was the use of the same reduced Aeginetan weight standard and the same denomination, the hemidrachm. A very extensive series with the monogram of the Arcadian League was issued at Megalopolis. The obverse shows a head of Zeus Lycaeus and the reverse Pan seated on a rock, holding a *lagobolon* in his left arm. The first group of these coins (**535**), weighing about 2.8g, belong to the third century and may have been struck before Megalopolis entered the Achaean League in 235. The next groups (**536–7**), distinguished by the placing of an eagle on the knee of Pan, show a reduced weight of about 2.40g/2.30g and definitely belong to the second century, the first issues being dated to *c.* 195–182.[57]

Local hemidrachms were also issued at Epidaurus and Hermione in the Argolid. These coinages are commonly assigned to the fourth century, but the weights seem to indicate that some at least of them may well belong to the second half of the third. However, the material at our disposal is too small to warrant any definite conclusions, and the meagre hoard evidence has not yet been analysed in sufficient detail.

---

54 Schwabacher 1939.

55 Earlier studies of the Achaean League coinage have been largely superseded by the publication of the Agrinion hoard (*IGCH* 271) by Thompson (1968b).

56 Polybius II. 37.10–11.

57 Dengate 1967. For the dating of the earliest hemidrachms of Megalopolis see Warren 1969.

We have seen already (p. 89) that the issue of silver coins in Crete dropped dramatically after *c.* 270. At the mint of Gortyn a single emission of drachms of Rhodian weight was struck *c.* 260 (Europa in tree/standing bull: **538**). About 250 the first Gortynian bronze coinage was produced (**539**). The types are Europa in tree on the obverse (identical with the silver) and Europa seated on a bull on the reverse. The series was probably initiated about 250 and was issued for several decades. Shortly afterwards a second, larger denomination was introduced (**540**) with a head of Artemis/standing bull, similar to the silver reverse type.[58]

To the period about 250 belongs an interesting inscription from Gortyn that in a graphic way illustrates the dearth of silver at Crete in this period.[59] The use of the bronze coins of the city is forced upon the population and it is expressly forbidden to use the silver obols formerly in circulation, a heavy fine being imposed on persons not complying with the new regulations. It is tempting to relate the decree to the first bronze coinage of Gortyn just described. It also offers a clear testimony to the popular distrust of a fiduciary coinage that apparently was not backed by a sufficient issue of silver.

The next Gortynian issues in precious metals were struck in connection with the city's alliance with Knossos in 221, the prelude to the so-called Lyttian War. They consisted of staters in gold of Attic-weight, with types head of Zeus/bull standing (**541**), and a series of drachms and hemidrachms of reduced Aeginetan weight. The obverse type was the same as for the gold, but on the reverse the drachms show Europa seated on a bull (**542**), the hemidrachms a charging bull (**543**). Bronze coins in several denominations with the same types as the silver drachms accompany these issues.

At Knossos there is no silver that can be assigned to this period with any certainty. A bronze issue (Europa seated on bull/labyrinth: **544**) may commemorate the alliance with Gortyn, as her characteristic type is used for the obverse.

When Knossos and Gortyn had defeated Lyttus in 220, the city of Polyrhenium, allied with Lyttus, appealed to Philip V of Macedon and the Achaeans for help and was saved by their intervention. An issue of silver tetradrachms has been connected with this event. The obverse shows a head of Apollo with bow and arrow at his shoulder, the reverse a seated Artemis Dictynna carrying Nike (**545**). The head on the obverse is whiskered and shows very individualized facial features, indicating that a portrait of a living person is intended. It has been identified, quite plausibly, with Philip V. The main objection to this is that the certain portraits of Philip on Macedonian coins always give him a full, close-cut beard, but the conventional representations of Apollo may have exerted their influence on the coin. A bearded Apollo is unheard-of, as far as I know, and even prominent whiskers are unusual for this deity, but it seems nonetheless probable that the coin of Polyrhenium presents us with Philip V in the guise of Apollo. The coin is commonly regarded as a tetradrachm of Attic weight. Apart from a few barbarous copies, however, we know it only from a single specimen of 15.51g, and since this is well preserved such a weight must be adjudged too low for an Attic tetradrachm in this

58 Le Rider 1966, 151–2; Jackson 1971.
59 *Inscriptiones Creticae* IV, no. 162.

period. There are obvious dangers in drawing any conclusion from the weight of a single coin, but I personally believe that we are dealing with a tetradrachm of Chian weight, a standard used in some of the Cyclades during the third century.

Towards the end of the century bronzes were issued at a Cretan city called Arsinoea: head of Athena/two dolphins, *ΑΡΣΙ* (**546**). From the find distribution and from the fact that the same types were used at Rhithymna on the north coast of Crete, Arsinoea has convincingly been identified with that city.[60] It most probably received its new dynastic name under Ptolemy IV (222–205) in honour of his sister-wife Arsinoe III.

Several issues of Rhodian-type drachms, weighing between 2.0g and 2.5g and dating *c.* 200, are found mainly or exclusively in Crete.[61] Some may have been struck by local cities, but most are generally assumed to have been struck by Rhodian commanders in the 'Cretan War' against Cretan piracy in the last years of the century. A larger denomination (**547**) has the usual facing head of Helios on the obverse replaced by a facing Medusa or Gorgo, an evident pun on the magistrate's name which appears on the reverse. The denomination is uncertain. Ashton sees in it a didrachm of the same weight standard as the drachms, but Mørkholm regarded it as a Rhodian trihemidrachm (=9 obols) of *c.* 4.80g, or in practice substantially less. A treaty of *c.* 200 between Rhodes and the Cretan city of Hierapytna concerning mercenaries stipulated that the daily payment of a soldier should be 9 Rhodian obols.

However this may be, didrachms (*c.* 6.70g) were issued on the island of Rhodes in large quantities throughout the third century and the first decade of the second.[62] The usual types are head of Helios facing/rose, though others also exist. A small series of didrachms (**548**) of *c.* 290/*c.* 280 shows a head of Helios in profile, perhaps representing the Colossus, which was erected at about that time. From about 265 magistrates' names were added to the reverse, and from *c.* 250 the head of Helios became radiate (**239**). Drachms, hemidrachms (**549**) and diobols (**550**) were issued sporadically during the same period. A single issue of gold staters of normal type but Attic-weight can be dated *c.* 250/*c.* 225, contemporaneously with one of Philip-type gold staters. About 225 the production of tetradrachms (**551**) was resumed at the reduced weight of *c.* 13.4g. The first issues may have been struck in connection with the reconstruction work after the great earthquake of *c.* 227, an event that provided the Hellenistic kings and other states with an opportunity of showing themselves benefactors of the important merchants' republic. A second group may have been struck after a less well-known earthquake in 199/8. Several special bronze issues seem to have been struck to commemorate Egyptian help on the first occasion. Of the two denominations the larger one (**552**) carries the types head of Zeus/rose. The smaller one (**553–4**) has on the obverse a veiled female head but on the reverse either a prow to the right or the usual rose. The head of Zeus may derive from the usual Egyptian type,

60 Le Rider 1968a.

61 [This paragraph has been largely rewritten by Richard Ashton in the light of Ashton 1987b, but cf. also Hackens 1970.] For the treaty between Rhodes and Hierapytna, see Schmitt 1969, no. 551. 314–20.

62 [Cf. Leschhorn 1986. This section has been substantially revised by Ashton, on whose advice over dating Mørkholm had relied in his original text, and in the light of Ashton 1986, 1988a.]

whereas the female head is perhaps a representation of Berenice II, the queen of Ptolemy III, one of the main benefactors of the Rhodians. Bronzes of smaller module (head of Rhodos/rose: **555**) were issued sporadically during the third century, and two further series, likewise chalkoi (rose/rose or profile rayed Helios/rose) were struck in the late third and early second centuries.

We have already seen that towards 200 the Rhodians, in addition to their normal coinage, issued Lysimachus staters in gold and Alexander tetradrachms is silver (above, pp. 147 and 142). The Lysimachus stater is copied from a contemporary coin of Byzantium and is signed by a magistrate, Aristobulus, who is also known from the Alexander tetradrachms and the autonomous coins of the island. At about the same time, between *c.* 205 and 188, the production of drachms (**556**) considerably increased but their weight was reduced to *c.* 2.5g/2.8g. It is strange that only the drachms were reduced, for the tetradrachms and didrachms maintained the Rhodian standard unchanged. These light drachms may have been reserved for export, as they are rarely found on the island of Rhodes itself or in her possessions on the mainland.

The island of Cos, which was under direct political influence from Rhodes, issued didrachms of Rhodian weight during most of the third century. The types were beardless head of Heracles/crab (**557**).

Already prior to 300 the Cyclades had been organized in a League of the Islanders under the protection of Antigonus Monophthalmus and his son Demetrius. After *c.* 290 Ptolemy I of Egypt assumed the patronage of this confederation, and towards the end of the third century the leadership passed to Rhodes. It is to this last stage that I would ascribe the coinage of some of the islands. Melos and Paros struck some quite rare tetradrachms, whereas rather commoner didrachms were issued by Paros and Naxos. The coins of Paros and Naxos were struck on the full Chian standard, with tetradrachms weighing up to *c.* 15.60g and didrachms around 7.70g/7.80g. One might have expected the lighter Rhodian weight to have been used. The Melian tetradrachms carry the types head of Athena in Corinthian helmet/Apollo seated to right, playing lyre (**558**). They are too few and too worn to give any certain indication of their weight standard. The heaviest specimen weighs 14.77g, and thus a reduced Chian standard may be intended. At Paros a young head of Dionysus appears on the obverse and a seated Demeter holding corn ears on the reverse of the tetradrachms (**559**). A rarer reverse type is the most illustrious son of the island, the poet Archilochus seated on a stool and holding a lyre. This is one of the earliest numismatic examples of the Hellenistic reverence for the early Greek poets and sages. The didrachms from Paros show a head of Kore/standing goat (**560**). The common type of Naxian didrachms (**561**) presents an archaizing bearded head of Dionysus and, on the reverse, a *krater* and *thyrsos*, types most appropriate for an island famous for its wine. A single issue (**562**) has on the reverse a standing naked Zeus, holding thunderbolt and eagle, in a typical archaizing style.

At Carystus on the southern end of Euboea an interesting series of didrachms was produced. The first issue shows the types of Philip II of Macedon: head of Apollo/Nike in biga towards right (**563**). On later issues (**564**) the head of Apollo was replaced by a portrait head with a diadem entwined in a laurel wreath and, on the reverse, Nike driving a biga towards left and holding a palm branch instead of the usual whip. The weight, *c.* 7.00g/7.19g, shows the coins to be Ptolemaic didrachms. They have been dated *c.* 235–200 by Wallace,[63] and the portrait has been thought to belong to an otherwise unknown tyrant of Carystus from this period. Picard, on the other hand, dates the coins to *c.* 250 and has, tentatively but plausibly, revived an old identification of the portrait as that of Alexander, son of Craterus and nephew of Antigonus Gonatas. Alexander made himself independent of his uncle and ruled most of the Macedonian possessions in Greece, including Euboea, from 253/2 to his death in 245. This short span of time fits in well with the fact that the whole series was struck from only eight obverse dies.

From *c.* 270 to 250 there seems to be a gap in the coinage of both Chalcis and Eretria on Euboea. During the short reign of Alexander, son of Craterus, a few bronze emissions of the Euboean League were produced. It was only after 245 that Chalcis resumed its coinage. A single but apparently quite small issue of silver drachms is accompanied by twelve issues of bronze coins in two different denominations. The types are unchanged from the preceding period (above, p. 90). The last issue belongs to the first years of the second century, the whole group coming to an end towards 196.

At Histiaea, on the northern tip of Euboea, the striking of so-called tetrobols (**565**) continued throughout the third century with a marked increase towards its end. The types were unchanged: head of Maenad/nymph Histiaea seated on stern, holding stylis. The series continued throughout the second century, but in the absence of a detailed analysis it is often impossible to distinguish between early and late issues.

On the west coast of Asia Minor a number of cities issued local coins in silver and bronze in addition to the posthumous Alexanders of Attic weight.[64] The question of weight standards and denominations is unusually intricate. From the period around 250–200 we have issues of a little below 5.00g from Ephesus (head of Artemis and forepart of stag/palm-tree: **566**). At Priene (**567**) a series weighing *c.* 4.00g–4.09g (head of Athena/trident) and a Milesian coinage (**568**) (head of Apollo left/lion with head reverted looking at star) of *c.* 5.00g/5.20g must be regarded as the same denomination. The island of Samos (**569**) produced a somewhat lighter series weighing 4.55g/4.65g (lion's mask facing/forepart of ox to right). At several mints smaller denominations were also struck.

The weight system of these coinages has caused much discussion. The old notion, that it is derived from the cistophoric or the Rhodian plinthophoric standard, can be safely discarded because these weight systems were first introduced in the second century. To Le Rider they are octobols of a reduced Attic-weight, but as the normal Attic octobol weighs *c.* 5.60g the reduction would be considerable. Since the Attic octobol was practically identical in weight with the Persian *siglos*, however, the coins might with equal right be regarded as reduced sigloi. Barron has suggested that the Samian pieces are octobols of the Ptolemaic standard (*c.* 4.70g/4.75g),

63 Wallace 1968; Picard 1979, 151–2. My section on Euboean coinages is essentially based on Picard's work.
64 For Ephesus, Priene and Miletus see Le Rider 1973a. For Samos cf. Barron 1966, 141–54. [For Miletus see also Deppert-Lippitz 1984 and Kinns 1986.]

which is satisfactorily close to the actual weights. But there were also Rhodian trihemidrachms of 4.80g (above, p. 156), and under these circumstances the choice seems difficult. Personally I am in favour of relating the weights to the Rhodian and Ptolemaic systems. The confusion in terminology does in fact suggest that these coins were from the beginning designed to fit into several different weight systems, which would greatly have increased their usefulness.

Towards the end of the third century the cities in Ionia again produced silver coinages. Ephesus struck Rhodian didrachms weighing *c.* 6.60g [and Miletus Persian drachms and hemidrachms of *c.* 5.00g and *c.* 2.40g]. The types are head of Artemis/forepart of stag at Ephesus (**570**), head of Apollo left/lion left, head reverted, looking at star at Miletus (**571**). At Priene (**572**) a series with the same types as the preceding one (**567**) weigh *c.* 6.90g, 3.60g and 1.70g. These coins must be regarded as didrachms, drachms and hemidrachms on the Ptolemaic standard. Between *c.* 210 and 190 we find in Samos (**573–4**) a coinage of local types (lion's mask facing/forepart of ox right and head of Hera/prow) in two denominations weighing *c.* 2.8g/2.9g and 1.45g respectively. They may be called tetrobols and diobols of Attic weight (Barron) or half- and quarter-sigloi on the Persian standard.

On the Carian coast the city of Cnidus had a substantial production of silver and bronze coins during the third century.[65] A small silver coin (**575**) with the types head of Aphrodite/ox's head facing and weighing *c.* 1.30g was struck between *c.* 300 and 225. A very large series (**576**) weighing between 2.40g and 2.60g was produced by at least 32 magistrates during the latter half of the third century. The types are bust of Artemis/tripod. To the years *c.* 210/185 belongs a series comprising a unique coin of 11.44g, most probably a tetradrachm, and not uncommon pieces weighing *c.* 5.30g (**577**). The obverse type head of Helios or Apollo facing shows Rhodian influence, whereas the reverse presents the old Cnidian type, forepart of lion right.

Again the weight system of the last two issues is debatable, but in view of the geographical proximity of Cnidus to Rhodes it seems plausible to regard them as light-weight drachms and didrachms of the peculiar reduced standard used at Rhodes between *c.* 205 and 188 (above, p. 156) rather than as reduced Attic- or Persian-weight coins.

Another area along the south coast of Asia Minor clearly maintained the Persian standard of the third century. A find from southern Turkey (*IGCH* 1430) revealed the existence of a quite extensive coinage of double sigloi or staters (**578**), weighing *c.* 10.20g/10.40g, from Phaselis in eastern Lycia. The types are prow of galley/stern of galley, and the excellent style of the coins dates them to the first half of the third century. No fewer than 25 magistrates are known, but the condition of the coins in the hoard and the occurrence of numerous obverse die links indicate that colleges of officials must have been working simultaneously within a relatively short period of time.

Other places where the Persian standard survived were nearby Aspendus in Pamphylia and Selge in Pisidia. A group of Aspendian double sigloi of acceptable style belongs to the years just after 280, while coarser variants, with regard to both style and fabric, may have been produced down to the middle of the third century or even later. For both groups the types are

65 The Cnidian material was collected by J. H. Nordbø in an unpublished thesis for the M.A. degree at the University of Oslo 1972.

the same: two wrestlers/slinger (**579–80**), introduced early in the fourth century. The name of the city on all these issues is still inscribed in the Pamphylian dialect. Apparently Aspendus (**580**) was slower than her neighbours, for instance Perge and Selge, in adopting the Hellenistic *koine*. Selge used the same types as Aspendus, but on an issue (**581**) that is most probably contemporary with the better Aspendian pieces, i.e., of 280–260, the slinger on the reverse is replaced by a fighting Heracles who may have been copied from a slightly earlier representation on the coinage of Phaestus on Crete. On later issues the slinger reappeared. At both Aspendus and Selge the third-century slingers pose in an artificial attitude, moving on tip-toe like dancers, and on the last issues the wrestlers become remarkably short and stocky. The reverses of the coins are also completely flat, not slightly concave as in most Greek coinages.[66]

The survey of the autonomous Greek coinages in this and the preceding section leaves the impression that the production of coins in precious metals by the cities was generally pursued on a very reduced scale in the period from *c.* 280 to *c.* 240. There were exceptions to this rule, e.g. at Rhodes and Byzantium, but taken as a whole this period represents the floodtide of the royal coinages, while those of the free Greek states were at a low ebb. The domination of the kingdoms in the currency system is thus just as evident as it is in the sphere of international policy. Only about 240/230 does the balance seem to change slowly in favour of the cities and, more especially, of the leagues which are now beginning to play a more important role in the international concert of powers.

66 See Seyrig 1963, 43–4.

EPILOGUE

A. THE END OF MACEDONIAN COINAGE

After Philip V's defeat at Cynoscephalae in 197 (above, p. 136) no royal coinage seems to have been struck in Macedon for about a decade. In 188 or 187 the king, disappointed in his hopes of receiving some reward for his subsequent loyalty to Rome, embarked on a new policy of confrontation. Among the measures taken to strengthen his kingdom Philip re-opened old mines and prospected for new ones with some success. In a conference with Roman ambassadors he revealed his temper by his famous boast, that 'the sun of all his days had not yet set', which might be and actually was regarded as a threat by the Romans and their Greek allies.[1]

About the same time, in 188 or 187, a new silver coinage was introduced, comprising tetradrachms, didrachms, drachms and hemidrachms. On the obverse of the tetradrachms (**582**) Philip placed his own portrait with the helmet and the special weapon of Perseus, the *harpa*, as the central emblem of a Macedonian shield, whereas the smaller denominations (**583**) carried a normal portrait with diadem. The reverse type common to all denominations was the club of Heracles placed horizontally within an oak wreath bound to the left. The silver coins were each signed by three officials, one a semi-permanent director of the mint and two frequently changing subordinates. The nine different issues were probably annual, giving the two known directors respectively five and four years under Philip. All the coins seem to be from the mint of Amphipolis. The last director, using the monogram ⫯ , continued under Perseus.[2]

Several different issues of bronze accompany the silver series, but of the fifteen issues only a few can be mentioned here. One of the earliest (**584**), produced already in 187, shows on the obverse a youthful head of Heracles, while two recumbent goats occupy the reverse. The style of the head of Heracles is very close to the one on a series of posthumous Alexanders, to which we shall return below. More traditional is another issue with a Macedonian shield decorated in the centre with a star of six sickle-shaped lines on the obverse and a club on the reverse (**585**). From the end of Philip's reign come two issues with interesting types: radiate head of Helios/winged thunderbolt within oak wreath (**586**). The head of Helios is new as a Macedonian coin type and is undoubtedly inspired by the Rhodian coins that circulated in great numbers in Macedonia. This series is the heaviest of Philip's bronzes, weighing *c.* 12–15g. Artemis

1 Livy 39.24.2: ...*metalla etiam et vetera intermissa recoluit et nova multis locis instituit....* Livy 39.26.9: *elatus deinde ira adiecit* (*sc. Philippus*) *nondum omnium dierum solem occidisse.*

2 Mamroth 1930, 277–90; Boehringer 1972, 102–4.

Tauropolos makes her first appearance here, but later becomes a very common type, while the standing eagle anticipates the well-known coin type of King Perseus. The last issue to deserve special mention carries the types bearded head of Heracles/*harpa* within oak wreath (**587**). Some specimens of this type are struck on serrated flans, a fashion that was more common in Seleucid Syria and may have originated there. The bronzes of Philip show no differentiated mint marks and the great majority will have been struck at his mint in Amphipolis. Within some emissions stylistic differences may indicate that more than one mint was engaged in their production.[3]

The silver coins of Perseus (tetradrachms (**588–9**), didrachms and drachms (**590**)) all show the diademed head of the king on the obverse, whereas an eagle standing on a thunderbolt, all within oak wreath, occupies the reverse of the tetradrachms. The didrachms carry the *harpa* of Perseus and the drachms the club of Heracles as reverse types, in each case encircled by a wreath of oak leaves. The first and best portraits of Perseus carry the name of the mint director Zoilus, inscribed in full below the head of the king (**588**). This has caused some scholars to assume that Zoilus, in addition to the administrative duties which he continued from Philip's reign, was also suddenly active as die engraver, a most unusual and unlikely combination of functions. The later portraits differ considerably in artistic quality. At some moment the post of mint director was transferred to a new man who signed with the monogram [monogram]. All silver seems to have been struck at Amphipolis.

During the last years of his reign Perseus, engaged in the final struggle with Rome, reduced the weight standard of his tetradrachms. Whereas the last series of tetradrachms of Philip V and their continuation under Perseus show a peak on the frequency table at 16.80g/17.00g, his last tetradrachms weighed between 15.30g and 15.60g, a reduction of *c.* 1.5g or about 8 to 10%. There can hardly be any doubt that this was primarily an emergency measure undertaken in order to stretch the supply of bullion for the duration of the war with Rome. It is possible that deeper economic considerations also played a part, for there may have been a desire to assimilate the Macedonian silver coinage more closely to one of the lighter weight standards used in Greece.[4]

The most common bronze coinage of Perseus was struck in two denominations. It shows on the obverse the hero Perseus in winged helmet, on the reverse an eagle standing on a plough or on a thunderbolt (**591**).

Under Philip V and Perseus an important innovation took place in the coinage system.[5] A number of districts and cities were allowed to strike their own coins, mostly small denominations in silver and bronzes. At Amphipolis Attic 'tetrobols' and 'diobols' with the types Macedonian shield with club as central device/helmet (**592**) were produced under Philip, the inscription being *MAKE* or *MAKEΔONΩN*. During the reign of Perseus two new types of 'tetrobols' were introduced: Macedonian shield with star of sickle-shaped lines/stern of galley (**593**) and head of Maenad/stern of galley (**594**). The Maenad type was copied from Histiaea on Euboea,

3 Mamroth 1935.
4 Mamroth 1928; Franke 1957; Boehringer 1972, 100–2.
5 Gaebler 1926a, 111–16; 1926b.

and the weight of both issues is reduced to *c.* 2.1g/2.3g, corresponding to the Histiaean tetrobols. Many bronze coins accompanied the silver. One of the types (head of Poseidon/club in oak wreath: **595**) is struck on serrated flans similar to those used by Philip V. The dating is secure because we find the same monogram combinations as on the royal coinage, showing that the same officials were in charge of both the royal issues and the autonomous ones.

Other issues were struck at Thessalonica for Amphaxitis, the region on both sides of the lower course of the Axius river. Even a coinage of tetradrachms was produced here: Macedonian shield with star of sickle-shaped lines in the centre/club within oak wreath, *ΜΑΚΕΔΟΝΩΝ ΑΜΦΑΞΙΩΝ*. It is signed by Zoilus, and several bronze issues carry the district name in full or a characteristic monogram. The types are partly the same as on the royal bronzes, partly new, as for example head of Apollo/tripod (**596**) or head of young Dionysus/goat standing to right, which from the monogram combinations seem to belong to the reign of Perseus.

In the district of Bottiaea the capital was Pella. Here silver 'pentobols', a few 'tetrobols' and '2½ obols' were struck. The types are Macedonian shield with star of sickle-shaped lines as central device/stern of galley, *ΒΟΤΤΕΑΤΩΝ* (**597**). A convincing stylistic similarity between the head of Heracles on some bronzes of Philip V and on an issue of posthumous Alexanders has revealed that the latter coins, all marked with the Greek letter *Β*, were struck at Pella for the district of Bottiaea.[6] They date most probably from the first years after Philip's reform of 187. The district also issued several bronze coinages. One obverse type is especially interesting, the head of Athena Parthenos in elaborate helmet, imitated directly from the Athenian New Style silver coinage. The reverse shows a grazing ox, with *ΒΟΤΤΕΑΤΩΝ* (**598**).

A few other districts such as Paeonia and Paroreia seem to have participated in the issue of regional bronze coins after 187. In addition the district capitals of Amphipolis, Thessalonica and Pella issued autonomous city coinages, and the same was done by a few cities such as Aphytis in Chalcidice and Apollonia in Mygdonia. The chronology is supported by a couple of overstrikes: Paroreia over Demetrius II of Macedon and Apollonia over Paroreia.

The right to strike coins in silver and bronze bestowed on the districts and cities represents an important concession of the king and must mark a radical change in the relationship between the Macedonian people and its ruler. Philip was apparently attempting to boost the morale of his subjects and attach them to the crown by establishing a partnership in the economic sphere. The bronze coinages more especially would have provided the issuing authorities with a handsome profit.

In Macedon the Attic weight standard had been used exclusively for both gold and silver coinage since the days of Alexander the Great. The new silver denominations of the districts are therefore generally regarded as struck on a reduced Attic standard. But such denominations as 5-obol and 2½-obol pieces are most unusual, and if we look more closely at the weights of the district silver we discover that the so-called tetrobols and diobols correspond to Aeginetan hemidrachms and quarter-drachms of the reduced standard used in central Greece and in the Peloponnese at the end of the third and in the first half of the second century. Of the 'tetrobols'

6 Seyrig 1963, 14–16.

there are two varieties, one weighing *c.* 2.40g/2.60g, the other 2.10g/2.30g, exactly the same as the Histiaean 'tetrobols' that circulated in Macedon in quantity. On the other hand 'pentobols' and '2½-obols' are equal to light Rhodian drachms and hemidrachms, and their weights were in all probability determined by this correspondence. Rhodian coinage is frequently found in coin hoards from the Greek mainland and Macedonia. In addition to 'ideological' considerations, therefore, Philip by leaving part of the silver coinage to the districts created a new range of denominations within the Macedonian currency system particularly suited to compete with or replace some of the most common foreign coins circulating in Macedonia.

After the Roman victory at Pydna in 168 a settlement was finally imposed on Macedon by the end of 167. Macedonia was divided into four districts, with regulations against inter-regional commerce and intermarriage. To weaken the country further the operation of the important mines was forbidden until 158, a measure that must soon have led to a reduced coin production.

To the interval between Pydna and the final arrangement belong some bronze issues of the Roman quaestors Gaius Publilius and Lucius Fulcinius (**599**). Both used a head of Roma as an obverse type, presumably at Amphipolis. In addition Publilius continued the regional issues of Amphaxitis and Bottiaea. At the latter place the types head of Athena Parthenos/grazing ox were retained (**600**). An anonymous bronze issue (**601**) with the types of mask of Silenus facing/*D*(ecreto) *ΜΑΚΕΔΟΝΩΝ* within ivy wreath may belong to the immediately following period. Some specimens are overstruck on coins of Publilius and Fulcinius.[7]

Immediately after the final settlement the first district from its capital Amphipolis issued a magnificent coinage of silver tetradrachms (**602**).[8] The obverse type is a head of Dodonaean Zeus with an oak wreath, a representation of the highest artistic quality. The reverse carries a spirited scene: Artemis Tauropolos holding a long torch in each hand and seated on the back of a running bull. The inscription is *ΜΑΚΕΔΟΝΩΝ ΠΡΩΤΗΣ*, and two monograms identify the mint officials concerned with the production. It is unusual for a Macedonian silver coinage of this period *not* to show a wreath on the reverse, encircling both type and inscription. After the substantial reduction of Perseus' last silver coinage, Macedonia with this issue reverts to a normal Attic standard.

This splendid coinage is followed by a gap of nearly a decade, resulting presumably from lack of bullion. When in 158 the mines were re-opened tetradrachms in quantity were struck for the first Macedonian district at Amphipolis (**603**), together with a few pieces for the second district at Thessalonica, the types being Macedonian shield with bust of Artemis Tauropolos at centre, and on the reverse, the club of Heracles placed horizontally within an oak wreath. The third district (around Pella) issued no coins at all, and the fourth district, comprising the mountainous regions of Upper Macedonia, struck only very rare bronze coins. The tetradrachms of the first district are very common. They were exported in large numbers into present-day Bulgaria and Rumania, where they were frequently imitated. It is difficult to draw an exact

7 MacKay 1968a.
8 Boehringer 1972, 32–3. [Price 1989, 237–8.]

line between originals and imitations, but as they were minted in Macedonia for a relatively short period, *c.* 158–150, it is plausible to regard a fair proportion of the coins from the Balkans as local imitations. The Attic standard is maintained, the majority of the coins falling between 16.60g and 16.99g on the frequency table.

After having disposed of Andriscus, to whom no coinage can be ascribed (above, p. 135), the Romans in 148 sanctioned a new Macedonian issue of tetradrachms (**604**). The types are the head of Artemis in the centre of a Macedonian shield/club placed horizontally within oak wreath. There are two variants, both inscribed *MAKEΔONΩN*, but the first issue has in addition the Latin inscription LEG (for *legatio* or *legati*) and a symbol consisting of a hand holding or extending a leafy branch. The symbol has been taken as a pun or canting badge on the name of the Roman praetor P. Juventius Thalia (*θαλλός* = branch) who was defeated and killed by Andriscus in early 148. Recent research, however, has shown that the coins most probably belong to the period after the defeat of Andriscus, and that the Latin inscription and the symbol refer to the peace and order established in Macedonia by a Roman commission after two years of revolt and turmoil.[9]

The style of these coins, especially the head of Artemis, is much superior to that on the preceding issues of the first Macedonian district. Only seven obverse dies were used and they carry no mint identification, but they were presumably struck at Amphipolis. In the following period no silver coinage was struck in Macedonia, but bronze coins were issued at Pella, Thessalonica and Amphipolis down to the reign of Augustus.

The last Macedonian silver issue of the Hellenistic period is a prolific coinage struck in the name of the Roman *quaestor* Aesillas (**605**). The series consists of tetradrachms and a few rare drachms. The types are: head of Alexander the Great with flowing hair and the horn of Zeus Ammon/club placed vertically between money-chest and *quaestor*'s stool; all within laurel wreath. The name of the Roman magistrate is inscribed in Latin on the reverse, while the Greek legend *MAKEΔONΩN* appears on the obverse. Most of the coins bear privy marks (B, B̶, *Θ*, S·I· which were formerly interpreted as indicating mints, or in the case of S·I· standing for the value 16 (IS), i.e. 16 sestertii or 4 denarii. Die linkages between the marks make it more likely that they are simply control marks within a single mint, though the *Θ*, which is overwhelmingly the most abundant mark, may in fact stand for Thessalonica.[10] On a few coins a *praetor* CAE = Caesar has been identified as the provincial governor under whom Aesillas served, and SVVRA as a *legatus pro quaestore* named Sura who took over Aesillas' function at some uncertain date. Of the three persons involved Aesillas is completely unknown other than from his coins, a Caesar appears as governor of Macedonia in an inscription which unfortunately cannot be dated with any precision, and a Brettius Sura is mentioned by Plutarch and Appian as a *legatus*

9 MacKay 1968b. [But see Burnett 1985; the coins could be later in date, like the Aesillas ones.]

10 [Mørkholm's original text repeated the customary identification of *B* and *Θ* as the mint marks of Pella (in Bottiaea) and Thessalonica respectively, and of S·I· as a mark of value. The text has been altered in the light of Fisher 1985 and Burnett 1985. See also Bauslaugh 1987.]

of C. Sentius, governor of Macedonia, operating in Greece and Macedonia against the Pontic force of Mithridates VI in 88. On the basis of this slender evidence Caesar has been identified with L. Julius Caesar, *cos.* in 90 and *praetor* some year earlier. His governorship in Macedonia would then most probably fall in 94, with Aesillas serving first under him and later under his successor C. Sentius *c.* 94–88 to be replaced by Sura in 88.

Recently this reconstruction has been challenged and the three Roman magistrates have been moved to the 60s of the first century, despite this implying the rejection of our one small item of non-numismatic evidence, the connection between Sura and Macedonia in 88. The reason for such drastic action is the need to accommodate an overstrike of an Aesillas tetradrachm on an Athenian New Style silver coin which is generally thought to belong somewhere in the 70s. The vexed question of the Athenian New Style chronology I have discussed in detail elsewhere.[11] I have there suggested that the enormous output of coins probably indicates that the type was struck not only between 94 and 88 but revived at intervals during the following decades, making it possible for the overstrike to be explained by one of these revivals of 'posthumous' Aesillas coins. We could thus date the overstrike to the 60s without discarding the evidence for placing Aesillas and his associates in the years 94–88. [There are, however, good numismatic reasons for being sceptical of the 'immobilization' theory, as the coins clearly form a compact group, while CAE is not a normal abbreviation for *Caesar* and could stand for some otherwise unrecorded official. Burnett, in describing a hoard of mixed Roman denarii and Aesillas tetradrachms, and another hoard of coins of Athens, Thasos and Macedonia (including Aesillas), suggests the early 70s as the most likely date for the coins.]

Just outside the Macedonian frontier, along the southern coast of Thrace, three mints issued Attic-weight tetradrachms. The most comprehensive series derives from the island of Thasos, where the types are head of young Dionysus/standing Heracles, *ΗΡΑΚΛΕΟΥΣ ΣΩΤΗΡΟΣ ΘΑΣΙΩΝ* (**606**). Struck from *c.* 180 onwards, this series was exported in large quantities to inland Thrace and Dacia, where it was also extensively imitated during the second and first centuries. Some of the imitations show the inscription *ΘΡΑΚΩΝ* instead of *ΘΑΣΙΩΝ*. A parallel and very large coinage[12] was issued at Maroneia (**607**). The obverse type is identical with that of Thasos, but the reverse carries a standing Dionysus who on three sides is surrounded by the inscription *ΔΙΟΝΥΣΟΥ ΣΩΤΗΡΟΣ ΜΑΡΩΝΙΤΩΝ*. These coins followed the Thasian pieces into Thrace and further north, where they are often found mixed with tetradrachms of the first Macedonian district. Finally there are small issues from Samothrace of tetradrachms, didrachms and bronze coins with the types head of Athena to left in Corinthian helmet/seated Cybele (**608**). They were earlier dated to the third century, but both style and fabric suggest a dating to the second century, where they fit in with other city issues struck on the characteristic spread flans of this period. The presence of one of the rare tetradrachms in the Babylon hoard (*IGCH* 1774) confirms this dating.

11 Mørkholm 1984b.
12 [Corpus by Schönert-Geiss 1987.]

B. LATER HELLENISTIC COINAGE

The last two centuries of Hellenistic coinage evolved in the shadow of Rome. The successive victories of Rome over Macedon at Cynoscephalae in 197 and Antiochus III at Magnesia in 190 marked only two of the stages in an advance that ended with her complete domination of the eastern Mediterranean and the incorporation of its surrounding lands in what we think of as the Roman empire. Other events and dates are familiar: the battle of Pydna in 168 and the ensuing partition of Macedon; the war with Andriscus of 149/8 and the effective annexation of Macedon in 146; the destruction of Corinth in the same year; the bequest of Pergamum to Rome in 133; the three Mithridatic Wars (88–84, 83–81 and 74–63) ending with the annexation of most of Asia Minor and Syria; the battle of Actium (31) and the acquisition of Egypt by Octavian in 30. How far this extension of Roman power was the result of a consistent expansionist policy and not a series of reactions to political crises as they occurred, and, if it was the result of a fixed policy, whether this was deliberately annexationist or arose simply from a determination not to risk the continued existence of any power that might threaten Rome, are questions on which diverse views have been held. Mørkholm himself believed that Rome wished to dominate, and only secondarily to annex. He was impressed by the continuity of Roman foreign policy despite the troubled domestic history of the city, and he believed that while an annexationist spirit was occasionally dominant, and the personal ambitions of members of the aristocracy were evident from time to time, the desire to eliminate possible rivals played a larger and more effective role.

However that may be, Roman monetary policy was a much more cautious one.[1] The 'freedom of Greece' proclaimed by Flamininus in 196 implied a continuation if not an encouragement of the assertion of the minting rights which the cities had always enjoyed, and although some of Rome's actions carried with them direct consequences for the coinage – the break-up of Macedon, the destruction of Corinth – the coinages of most of the cities and other governments were allowed to carry on unchanged. This effectively meant a continuation of coinages of silver and bronze, since gold, which for some reason seems to have been in short supply, was being less and less frequently struck even in Egypt. Hoard evidence shows that prior to Augustus little attempt was made to extend the Roman denarius into the eastern Mediterranean area, and even after the Republic had been replaced by the Empire the bulk of the small change in the East

1 Crawford 1985, 116ff.

continued to be of local manufacture, so that 'Hellenistic' coinage was succeeded by what numismatists are accustomed to describe as 'Greek Imperial' (or 'Roman Provincial') coins in contrast to 'Roman Imperial' ones.

How Roman territorial advance could result in change is apparent in the coinage of Macedon discussed in the preceding section. By the second half of the second century this coinage was no longer available to its normal users in Hellas and the Islands, and its place had largely been taken by the tetradrachms of what numismatists have baptized the 'New Style' coinage of Athens. These are distinguished from the 'owls' of the Classical period in their general appearance, being struck on the broad, thin flans customary at the period instead of on thick, dumpy ones; in their style, which is no longer deliberately archaic but woefully and quite unattractively 'modern'; and finally in their details. The naturalistically designed head of Athena on the obverse closely copies the fifth-century Athena Parthenos of Pheidias with its elaborately decorated and triple-crested Attic helmet, and the owl on the reverse is shown perched on a recumbent amphora and hedged in by a clutter of letters, syllables or symbols, the whole design being surrounded by the olive wreath that gave the coins their contemporary name of *stephanophoroi* ('wreath-bearers'). The coins were of traditional Attic tetradrachm weight, about 17g, and of good silver. The letters and symbols in the field are the marks of an elaborate control system, the names being those of the persons responsible for each issue and perhaps recording the sources of the metal, the letter on the amphora actually defining the month when each coin was struck (**609–11**).

Margaret Thompson's meticulous die study of the huge coinage,[2] a masterpiece of numismatic scholarship, determined the order of issue of the various marks, for obverse dies were sometimes carried over from one month or even from one year to the next, but the absolute chronology has been much debated. Thompson's own dating (196/5 to 88/7) was immediately questioned by D.M. Lewis, who argued for 164/3 to *c.* 50,[3] and scholars quickly divided into two schools, for evidence favouring a 'high' chronology seemed incompatible with other evidence pointing equally decisively towards a 'low' one. Mørkholm himself argued[4] for *c.* 185/*c.* 180–*c.* 45/*c.* 40, but while the terminal date is generally agreed the initial one is still subject to discussion, with the evidence of hoards suggesting a date as late as the 160s.[5] An early specimen (*SNG Berry* 742) links an obverse close to the type with the *aphlaston* scroll with a reverse exhibiting some features of the new: the owl perched on an amphora, the initials of the city distributed on both sides of the bird, and the whole enclosed in an olive wreath. The coinage itself saw several interruptions or partial interruptions, and one exceptionally large issue, coinciding with a marked change in style and attributable to 145/4, was evidently intended to compensate for the sharp decline in the coinage of the Greek Leagues after the end of the Achaean War in 146. The occurrence of

2 Thompson 1961.
3 Lewis 1962.
4 Mørkholm 1984b.
5 Price 1989, 238.

New Style coins in hoards over a wide area is evidence both of the renewed economic prosperity of Athens and of the role they played in the commerce of Greece and the Islands, though unlike the older owls they did not circulate beyond the confines of the Greek world and the policy of Pergamum, and of the Seleucids and Ptolemies, resulted in their exclusion from Asia Minor, Syria and Egypt. An important element in their success was the Athenian recovery of Delos in 166, for Delos, created a free port by Rome as an anti-Rhodian measure, was a centre of international trade, especially in that of the unhappy slaves whom the incessant warfare of the period threw on the market.

Athenian tetradrachms were naturally not the only coins to be struck in Greece and the Islands. City coinages continued save in the luckless Corinth, half of whose territory was bestowed on Sicyon in 146 and half retained by Rome. There was also less of the *symmachikon argyron*, the coinages of the Aetolian and Achaean Leagues[6] which in the preceding decades had been increased in output to make good the shortages in Attic-weight silver coins resulting from the cessation of minting in Macedonia. The conspicuous wreath surrounding type and inscription of the reverses of Philip V's and Perseus' later coins and the New Style tetradrachms was copied at some other mints, notably at Chalcis and Eretria in Euboea, at Chalcis surrounding a figure of Hera standing in a quadriga with the inscription *ΧΑΛΚΙΔΕΩΝ*, at Eretria a bull standing to the right accompanied by the names of city and magistrate (**612**). A few in both cities are signed by their engravers, a feature more familiar in Sicily than in Hellas. The coins were identified by Robert[7] with the *taurophori* of some Delian second-century inscriptions, and their first issues are shown by the Anthedon hoard (*IGCH* 223) to be contemporary with the earliest New Style coins of Athens. Silver octobols (**613**) and bronzes were also struck at the two places. These Euboean coinages were in any case only two of the many still being struck in Hellas and the Islands.

In Asia Minor the counterparts of the Athenian New Style tetradrachms were the cistophori of Pergamum. Politically, prior to 133, this kingdom dominated western Asia Minor. It was the main local power to profit by the downfall of Antiochus III, and its kings were long-time allies of Rome. Eumenes II (197–158), it is true, had his difficulties with the city, which churlishly denied him entry when he tried to visit it in 167, but his resounding defeat of the Gauls led him to be recognized as the champion of the Greeks in Asia; Polybius describes him as the greatest royal benefactor of the Greek cities in his day. It was fitting that he should be the only one of Philetaerus' successors to strike a tetradrachm with his own portrait (**614**) – only two specimens are known – and not that of the founder of the dynasty.[8] But this was exceptional, as was his

6 Thompson 1968b.
7 Robert 1951, 146, 156–9. But Boehringer 1972, 32–7, prefers the Artemis Tauropolis coinage of the first Macedonian district of *c.* 168/7 (above, p. 166), and is followed by Price 1989, 237–8.
8 Westermark 1981; Bauslaugh 1982; Nicolet-Pierre 1989.

minting of another rare tetradrachm (**615**) – three specimens known[9] – combining a Victory on a prow with Athena Nikephoros brandishing a Gorgon shield, and so without a portrait at all. It was perhaps struck for the Nikephoria celebrations in 181.[10] Otherwise coins with the head of Philetaerus continued to be struck during the first years of Eumenes' reign, probably down to the 180s, though some scholars[11] believe they continued much longer. The coinage that effectively succeeded these was not the rare and short-lived portrait tetradrachm but the lighter cistophorus which, 'with its writhing serpents and over-elaborate ornamentation', was bluntly described by Robinson as 'perhaps the ugliest coin in the Greek series'.

The coins in question obtained their name ('chest-bearers') from their obverse type, a circular wicker basket (*cista mystica*) used in Dionysiac rituals, with a snake either emerging from its half-open lid or coiled round it. The reverses show two coiled serpents and an ornamented bow-case, and there are symbols, monograms or letters in the field identifying the mint, e.g. a monogram of *ΠΕΡ* for Pergamum (**616**), the letters *ΕΦΕ* for Ephesus (**617**). The coins are otherwise anonymous: only one issue, struck at four dependent cities but not at Pergamum itself, bears regnal dates (*Α–Δ*) and a shortened form of the name of a king, *ΒΑ ΕΥ* (*basileus Eumenes*), i.e. the Aristonicus who challenged his half-brother Attalus III's legacy to Rome in 133 and held out till 130 under the name of Eumenes (III).[12] The tetradrachms were accompanied by didrachms and drachms of varying designs, e.g. a bunch of grapes, or Heracles' club or lion skin in a wreath. The types are easily explained: Dionysus, from whom the Attalids claimed descent, was highly honoured at Pergamum, and the legendary founder of the city was Heracles' son Telephus. The cistophori were substantially lighter (*c.* 12.6g) than the old Pergamene tetradrachms of Attic weight (*c.* 17.0g), but were apparently overvalued and made to pass at the traditional value of these coins. This would explain why, as hoard evidence shows, they rarely circulated outside the kingdom, and why other coins equally did not circulate within its frontiers.

The problem of their date and organization was for long a matter of dispute, with some scholars starting them *c.* 200 or earlier, since they are referred to by Livy in the context of the Syrian campaigns of the late 190s, and others placing them after 133 since they bear no royal name. Kleiner and Noe, to whom we owe the fundamental study of the series,[13] favoured some date after 167, with Livy's references – or those of his sources – anachronistic in character, while Mørkholm preferred *c.* 175.[14] More recently it has been argued[15] that Livy's references have been too easily dismissed and that the coinage was introduced at Pergamum in the late 190s,

---

9 Two from the Larissa 1968 hoard (Price 1989) and one from the Ma'ar'et en Nu'man hoard from Syria (Price 1985a, 24, no. 98).
10 Le Rider 1973b, 68–71. So also Mørkholm 1979d, but cf. Price 1989, nos 239–40.
11 E.g. Nicolet-Pierre 1989, 209 (to the 150s).
12 Robinson 1954; Kampmann 1978.
13 Kleiner and Noe 1977.
14 Mørkholm 1979d, 47–50. Cf. also Leschhorn in Franke *et al.* 1988, 40.
15 Allen 1983, 112. Price 1989 likewise prefers *c.* 188, but Nicolet-Pierre 1989, 211–12, argues for a much later date (*c.* 159).

overlapping with the last issues of Philetaerus coins, but was extended to the various dependent cities only after the Roman settlement of 188. The series in its typical form lasted to 130, though from 133 to 130 as coins of a usurper, but was continued thereafter by a number of cities, sometimes with dates (e.g. at Ephesus), and eventually by the Romans, who continued to mint the denomination, though intermittently and with different types, down to the reign of Hadrian or possibly even to that of Severus. It was formerly thought that the uniformity in weight and type of the early cistophori must have resulted from a series of monetary conventions between the ten cities whose initials appear on them, but these cities were all situated in the kingdom of Pergamum and it is now accepted that they were fully 'Pergamene' and struck by the authority of the state. Die-linking shows that while some cities (e.g. Ephesus) had their own mints, Pergamum minted not only in its own name but in those of Sardis, Phrygian Apamea and Synnada, and Tralles minted for Laodicea as well as for itself. The fractional coinage was all minted at Tralles.

Cistophori were no more the only coins of Asia Minor than the New Style tetradrachms were of mainland Greece. Over a dozen independent city coinages were still being issued in western Asia Minor, from Cyzicus (**618**) and Lampsacus on the Propontis southwards by way of Cyme (**619**), Myrina (**620**), Smyrna, Colophon, Magnesia on the Maeander, Miletus and Cibyra to Rhodes and Cos. Particularly important were the tetradrachms with wreathed reverses produced in many of these places from the early 160s onwards, the wreath surrounding a representation of Apollo or some other locally venerated divinity and having a magistrate's monogram in the field.[16] The coins were produced partly for commercial reasons – several of the cities had important ceramic industries – but religious factors must often have played a role; Myrina in particular was only a few miles from the famous sanctuary and oracle of Apollo at Grynaeum. For several of the coinages, notably those of Aeolian Cyme, its neighbour Myrina, and Magnesia on the Maeander, detailed die studies are now available.[17] Further to the south, the political and economic strength of Rhodes, and the role this city played in the struggle with the pirates, made its coinage one of particular importance. The third century saw the appearance of drachms and hemidrachms with the reverse type framed in a shallow incuse square, so that the coins were termed *plinthophoroi* (from *plinthos*, a brick). The weight of the early drachms (*c.* 3.0g) may have reflected or been the precursor of the new cistophoric weight standard. Although the pre-plinthophoric drachms were probably no longer struck in Rhodes itself after the early 180s, they circulated very widely and were extensively imitated on the Carian mainland from the 180s onwards, and in northern and central Greece just before the Third Macedonian War, possibly in part by or on behalf of Perseus for the payment of his mercenaries.[18] But more striking than any of these coinages were those of the kingdoms of Bithynia, Pontus and Cappadocia north and east of that of Pergamum.

16 Mørkholm 1980c.
17 Jones 1979 (Magnesia); Oakley 1982 (Cyme); Sacks 1985 (Myrina).
18 Cf. Ashton 1988d (Lycia), 1987b (Crete), 1988b (mainland Greece), 1988c (Samothrace), 1989; Leschhorn 1985 (Syria).

The coinages of these three kingdoms,[19] like that of Pergamum, were essentially of silver and bronze, though drachms played a much more prominent role – Pergamum had none – and their tetradrachms did not undergo the same weight reduction as did those of Pergamum. There are a few cases of minting in gold, a fact of some relevance to the claim that Rome subsequently denied her client kings the right to mint in this metal.[20] The pattern of the silver coins was already set in the third century, the obverse type being as a matter of course an effigy of the reigning monarch. The reverse types are normally a seated or standing figure of Zeus or some other divinity, with royal names and titles and monograms, and sometimes, to the gratification of the numismatist, dates by the local era, in the field(**621**). The Bithynian series ended in 74, when Nicomedes III had followed the example of Attalus III of Pergamum and bequeathed his kingdom to Rome. Those of Pontus and Cappadocia continued into the first century A.D., when at various dates these kingdoms, which had long since sunk to client status, were annexed by Rome.[21] Those of Pontus were in any case sharply reduced in importance after 64, when Pompey, as part of his re-organization of Asia and Syria, broke up the old kingdom, annexing its western half to what was now the Roman province of Bithynia and leaving only a rump to continue in the east.

The third-century coinage of Bithynia[22] has been discussed already (p. 130), and Mørkholm has commented on the fine portraits of Nicomedes I (*c.* 280–*c.* 250) (**414–15**) and Prusias I (*c.* 230–182) (**417**). The main subsequent innovation was the dating of the silver coins by the Bithynian era, starting with year 150 (= 148/7 B.C.) and continuing to the end of the kingdom (**621**). The coins generally bear a magistrate's monogram as well. Mørkholm has pointed out that the distribution between the two kings named Prusias of the many copper coins with an inscription reduced to *ΒΑΣ ΠΡ* and types other than a portrait is not always as difficult as earlier scholars supposed. The only known gold coin is a stater (8.5g) of Nicomedes II with a galloping horseman as reverse type.

The early coinage of the relatively backward Cappadocia (**422–6**), with only two cities – Mazaca (the later Caesarea) and Tyana – of any consequence, has already been described (pp. 131–2). Apart from some late fourth-century drachms of Ariarathes I (d. 322) it consisted, down to halfway through the long reign of Ariarathes IV (*c.* 220–163), of small bronze coins only. Towards the end of his reign Ariarathes IV began to mint silver in the form of tetradrachms with reverse type a figure of Athena, originally seated but on later coins usually standing. The coins of subsequent rulers were usually drachms (**622**), rarely tetradrachms. Reinach's study of the coinage, which for long held the field, was superseded in 1961 by one of Simonetta, based on a much greater mass of material and in turn displaced by a more substantial one by the same

19 Reinach 1888 provides the only detailed guide to the written sources, but on the numismatic side it requires considerable updating. On the many chronological problems see Glew 1987, and, on relations with Rome, Braund 1984.

20 Braund 1984, 123–8.

21 Cf. Sands 1908; Badian 1968, 1983; also Glew 1987 for an updating of the literature.

22 Waddington *et al.* 1908 (*Recueil* I.2). Glew 1987 ranges more widely than the title suggests, and he is preparing a corpus of the royal coinage.

scholar fifteen years later.[23] Simonetta's views on a number of points were promptly challenged by Mørkholm, and over the next two decades were the subject of an increasingly acrimonious debate between the two scholars.[24] The main point at issue was whether the numerals in the field were or were not regnal dates, as had always been assumed but which was contradicted by incongruous die links, e.g. by a coin of Ariarathes IV of 'year' 5 being linked with one of 'year' 33. It also involved denying Ariarathes IV a silver coinage in his early years and a number of reattributions in the later series, Mørkholm arguing, for example, that some coins commonly ascribed to Ariarathes V (163–130) more likely belonged to Ariarathes IX, the eight-year-old son of Mithridates VI of Pontus whom his father set up as king of Cappadocia in 99.

The most remarkable portraits are those of the kings of Pontus,[25] whose realm also included much of the Caucasus and the Crimea. Mørkholm has commented (p. 28) on the brutal realism of that of Pharnaces I (*c.* 185–*c.* 170) (**623**), but this ruler's effigy had no monopoly of realism. It had been preceded by an equally striking one of Mithridates III (*c.* 220–*c.* 185) and was succeeded by that of his brother Mithridates IV (*c.* 170–*c.* 150), who indeed closely resembled him and who struck one series of tetradrachms (**624**) showing the jugate busts of himself and his queen Laodice, who in Ptolemaic fashion may also have been his sister. The coins are mainly tetradrachms of the Attic standard and usually dated by the local era, though during the period of greatest expansion new 'eras of freedom', i.e. of conquest, were devised. The most interesting coins in the series are those of the long reign of Mithridates VI the Great (*c.* 120–63), whose clean-shaven and clearly idealized portrait (**625**) is in marked contrast to the short beards and sideburns of his predecessors. His conquests made it possible for him to mint at Pergamum and other cities outside the traditional frontiers of the kingdom, and like Nicomedes II of Bithynia he minted also in gold.

East and south-east of this group of kingdoms in Asia Minor lay Greater Armenia and its dependencies, both then Armenian, Sophene and Commagene. Greater Armenia lay in the mountainous region around Lake Van and the sources of the Euphrates and Araxes. Sophene was the region south of this, in northern Mesopotamia between the Tigris and the Euphrates. Commagene lay west of Sophene and south-east of Cappadocia in what was then Syria but is now Turkey, its chief city being Samosata on the Euphrates at the point where the river emerges from the mountains into the Mesopotamian plain.

The discovery of inscriptions containing royal lists has transformed the traditional picture of early Armenian history, for classical authors failed to distinguish between rulers of Sophene, which initially included Commagene, and those of Greater Armenia.[26] It is now clear that many of the coins customarily attributed to the latter were in fact struck by kings of Sophene who

23 Reinach 1888; Simonetta 1961, 1977. There is a new work on Pontus, not yet published, by F. Callataÿ.
24 Mørkholm 1962, 1964b, 1968, 1969b; Simonetta 1964, 1973, 1975a, b; also Glew 1987.
25 On the coinage of Pontus see Kleiner 1955 and Pfeiler 1968.
26 Bedoukian 1968, 1978.

had become independent in the early third century. The bulk of these, which started under the king Samos (*c*. 260) who gave his name to Samosata, consist of copper chalkoi, about 15mm in diameter and weighing *c*. 3g, with double chalkoi as well. Their obverses show the royal portrait wearing some kind of headdress and their reverses such types as a horseman, the king in a chariot, or an eagle, accompanied by the king's name and title in Greek. Coins are known of most of Samos' successors down to the annexation of Sophene by Tigranes.

Commagene, which separated from Sophene under a certain Ptolemy *c*. 163 and which during much of its existence was a client state of Rome, had a more distinguished numismatic history.[27] No coins are known of Ptolemy himself, but his successor Samos (*c*. 140–*c*. 130) minted tetradrachms having as obverse type the king's head, either radiate and diademed or wearing a pointed headdress, and as reverse type a Nike or a *thyrsos* between two cornucopiae. The inscription, in Greek, gives his name and titles. His successors continued to mint down to Antiochus IV (A.D. 38–72), after whose death Commagene again became the Roman province it had been between A.D. 17 and 28.

Finally, in Armenia proper, there is no certain coinage before Tigranes II (95–56) unless, as Bedoukian believes, the bronze coins normally attributed to him are really of his predecessor Tigranes I (123–96). Tigranes II earned his epithet 'the Great' by a series of astonishing military and political successes which included the conquest and annexation of Sophene and Commagene, the expulsion of the king of Cappadocia, and the eventual occupation of Syria and Palestine, making him for a brief moment master of a state stretching from the Caspian to the Mediterranean and justifying his assumption of the old title of 'King of Kings'. He struck coins of greater interest, but these were minted at Antioch and Damascus, and perhaps elsewhere, during his occupation of Syria (83–69) and belong to the Seleucid tradition.[28] They consist of handsome tetradrachms (**626**) and copper coins having on the obverse his portrait wearing a decorated Armenian tiara with ear-flaps. The reverse has an altogether original design, the seated Tyche of Antioch, with the river god Orontes at her feet, which we know from Pausanias to have been a representation of a famous statue by the sculptor Eutychides of Sicyon, a pupil of Lysippus. The tetradrachm is one that has attracted the attention of forgers,[29] and there are even specimens struck in gold. Tigranes was eventually twice defeated by Lucullus, but at great cost to Rome. He was finally compelled by Pompey to come to terms and had to abandon most of his conquests, but the 85-year-old monarch was allowed to retain his throne and Armenia its independence, so that it became a convenient buffer state between the Roman and Parthian empires.

Armenia, Sophene and Commagene, like the four kingdoms of Asia Minor proper, had once formed part of the Seleucid dominions, if in the case of Armenia the link had been a tenuous one. After Magnesia (190) the Seleucids were virtually excluded from Asia Minor, retaining

---

27 Tasyürek 1975; Sullivan 1973. On the background, Sullivan 1977.
28 Macdonald 1902; Foss 1986. On his career see F. Geyer in *PW* Zweite Reihe 6A (1937), 970–8.
29 Kinns 1985, 61–2.

only Cilicia in the extreme south-east, but beyond that they remained the greatest power in the Middle East, still controlling Syria and Palestine, Mesopotamia, and much territory beyond the Tigris, where indeed Antiochus III met his death in 187.

In the mid century many of their lands were lost, though Seleucid decline was not an uninterrupted process. Antiochus III's younger son Antiochus IV (175–164), who came to the throne after the murder of his brother Seleucus IV and assumed the grandiose title of *Theos Epiphanes* ('God Manifest'), was an extraordinary character whose title was parodied by contemporaries as *Epimenes*, 'the mad', but whose coinage (**627–30**) reflects something of his policy in founding or refounding cities and campaigning in the East, and in general trying to rebuild the power of the state. In the decades that followed his death the Seleucid kingdom lapsed into virtual anarchy, with the realm divided between contesting claimants who vied with each other for foreign support, whether Pergamene, Egyptian or Roman. Mithridates I of Parthia was able to profit by the disorder, occupying Media *c.* 150 and Babylon *c.* 141. There were repeated efforts at recovery under Demetrius II Nicator (145–140, 129–126/5) (**634**) and Antiochus VII (138–129) (**633**), but neither permanently re-occupied the lost provinces. Demetrius II was captured by treachery in 140 and held captive for ten years, while Antiochus VII, after initial successes, was defeated and killed at Ecbatana in 129. In the later 120s the dominant figure was Cleopatra Thea, a daughter of Ptolemy VI and widow first of the usurper Alexander Balas (150–145) and subsequently of a restored Demetrius II (second reign 129–126/5). She put to death her eldest son Seleucus V (126/5) after a few months reign – she may have killed Demetrius II also – and became regent for his younger brother Antiochus VIII (126/5–96) until her own murder at his hands in 120. In 114/13 Antiochus VIII had to divide Syria, all that now remained of the Seleucid inheritance, with his brother Antiochus IX, and anarchy continued through a bewildering succession of contesting and usually short-lived rulers, doing their best to hold their own against Parthia, Armenia, Egypt, or local rebels, till eventually Pompey disposed of the last members of the dynasty and organized Syria as a Roman province in 64/3.

Seleucid coinage of the second and first centuries[30] differs most obviously from that of the kingdoms of Asia Minor in its greater variety – variety of types, denominations and standards. Since the number of rulers was so large there was bound to be much diversity in the portraits, and even if these are not amongst the masterpieces of numismatic art they show a high degree of individualization: the radiate head of the young Antiochus VI in the guise of Apollo (**631**), the Byronic locks of the usurper Tryphon, the beak-like nose of Antiochus VIII (**636**) which earned him the nickname of *Grypus* ('hook-nosed'), the bearded solemnity of Demetrius II (**634**). Attributions are complicated by the fact that mint officials seem to have been allowed considerable latitude in the choice of titles, at least for denominations below the tetradrachm, and there are occasionally other problems, such as separating the coins of Demetrius II's two reigns. Jugate busts occurred from time to time, notably under Cleopatra Thea (**635**), who is

30 General survey, with good bibliography, in Mørkholm 1984c. See also the many publications of Arthur Houghton listed in the bibliography.

shown with Alexander Balas or Antiochus VIII, though her most distinctive portraits are those showing her alone.

Seleucid reverse types were mainly drawn from the usual Olympian repertory, the favourite being a seated Apollo but also from Antiochus IV onwards including a seated Zeus – this was probably a chryselephantine statue at Daphne – and a seated or standing Athena or Nike. A finely designed eagle with a palm branch is frequent on the coins from Phoenician mints, its Egyptian inspiration being obvious, and Tigranes, as already noted, introduced a representation of the seated Tyche of the city on his coins of Antioch. A favourite minor type was an inverted anchor that reputedly reproduced the design of the signet ring of Seleucus I and was eventually to be borrowed by the rulers of a number of the successor states, by Mithridates I of Parthia, Kamnaskires I of Elymais, and Hyspaosines of Characene in the east, by Alexander Jannaeus at Jerusalem in the west. Local types, in contrast to dynastic ones, occur sometimes on the silver – e.g. the 'monument of Sandan' at Tarsus – but are mainly characteristic of the bronze, and the latter sometimes have the curious innovation of serrated edges (**632**).

The coinage was mainly one of silver, with gold minted only rarely and usually for special occasions that can sometimes be identified: those of Antiochus IV presumably in anticipation of his first Egyptian campaign of 167, when according to Polybius he presented a gold stater to every inhabitant of Naucratis, and those of Alexander II in an emergency to pay his troops with some of the gold coming from the figure of Nike on a statue of Zeus set up by Antiochus IV. Such occasional gold issues might even be struck by tetradrachm dies instead of having special ones engraved for the purpose. The silver consisted mainly of tetradrachms, initially of good Attic standard except in Phoenicia but with the weight declining over the years from over 17g in Antiochus IV's early years to *c.* 16g by the time of Philip and Tigranes. The Phoenician mints adhered to the Ptolemaic standard, with a tetradrachm of *c.* 14.3g. The standard copper coins were chalkoi of 2.5g/5g having a token value of an eighth of an obol, but multiples of up to four chalkoi were regularly struck at some mints and there were occasional issues of even heavier coins.

The great extent of the Seleucid empire meant in any case that its coins were struck at many more mints than in the kingdoms of Asia Minor. The eastern provinces, it is true, had normally only a single mint each – Nisibis in Mesopotamia, Seleucia on the Tigris (by far the largest) in Babylonia, Susa in Susiana, and Ecbatana in Media – but there was sometimes further minting in the north-east[31] and Antiochus IV set up a mint at Antioch on the Erythrean Sea, the chief outlet for Indian trade at the head of the Persian Gulf.[32] All of these save Nisibis were lost to the Parthians in the mid second century, and the issues of Nisibis were in any case sporadic. The western mints were much more numerous and lasted longer, in some cases down to the end of the dynasty. By far the most important was Antioch, but there was occasional minting elsewhere in Syria, notably at Seleucia Pieria. In Cilicia the chief mint was Tarsus, the capital of the province, but from time to time there was subsidiary minting at Seleucia on the

31 Bernard 1985; Houghton and Moore 1988.
32 Mørkholm 1970.

Calycadnus, Mallus and Mopsus.[33] The chief mint in Phoenicia was Tyre, where dated tetradrachms were struck from 150/49 down to 126/5, when the city became autonomous. A feature of the period, indeed, is the existence of the so-called municipal coinages introduced by Antiochus IV in 169/8. The obverse type of these is the royal portrait sometimes wearing a radiate crown, and a legend consisting of or including the name of the city as the issuing authority. Nineteen mints were initially involved, the four of the Tetrapolis in Syria Seleucis, seven in Phoenicia and Palestine, five in Cilicia, and two on the route eastwards to Nisibis, culminating in Nisibis itself. The number of such mints subsequently varied, and some of them, notably Aradus in northern Phoenicia, minted silver tetradrachms as well as bronze. The coins are usually dated by a local era.

That the Seleucid dominions eventually contracted to Syria was due in the main to the rise of Parthia. We have seen (p. 120) how the Parthians under Arsaces I and Arsaces II (? = Tiridates I) had in the 230s and 220s extended their power into Hyrcania and a huge area of eastern Iran. They suffered a temporary setback as a result of Antiochus III's eastern campaign of 209, when they lost Media and Hyrcania, but new territorial acquisitions at Seleucid expense were made in the next century under Phraates I (*c.* 176–*c.* 171). It was Phraates' brother Mithridates I (*c.* 171–138/7), however, who was the true architect of Parthian greatness, conquering Media and Babylonia in the west, Elymais (Susiana) and Persis in the south, and extensive areas of former Bactrian territory in the east. The earliest Parthian coins were minted at Hecatompylus in Hyrcania, a still unidentified site which, if it had not the hundred gates implied in its name, was at least a major road centre somewhere south-east of the Caspian, and at Ecbatana (Hamadan) in Media. From Mithridates onwards up to a dozen mints were sometimes active, both former Seleucid ones like Susa and Seleucia and new ones like Rhagae (Tehran) south of the Caspian and Nisa (Ashkabad) and Margiana (Merv) further east. Mint attributions depend sometimes on style but often on the presence of mint initials or monograms such as *M* for Margiana and a monogram of *ΑΓΠ* for AGPatana (Ecbatana).

Parthian coins[34] consist predominantly of silver drachms and various denominations of bronze chalkoi, with tetradrachms struck only at Seleucia and no gold struck at all. The predominant obverse type is the profile bust of the ruler, initially beardless but normally wearing a beard which is often long and carefully dressed, giving the kings an impressive dignity unsurpassed since the great Assyrian sculptures of the ninth century B.C. The reverse is normally a seated figure, initially a royal figure in Scythian costume with his hand extended holding out a bow; although this type lasted to the end of the dynasty, it could be varied with a seated or standing figure of a city Tyche or some Olympian divinity. The obverse bust and the figure holding a bow almost invariably face different ways, with the bust turned to the left instead of the right, in contrast to that of most other coinages of the time. The explanation may be that the two faces of the coin were intended to be taken together, with the seated figure of the founder of

33 Houghton 1989b.
34 Bibliography in Sellwood 1980, 309–17.

the dynasty on one face handing a symbol of authority to the living ruler shown on the other. Since all kings are simply styled Arsaces the attribution of particular coins has to be based partly on portraiture, partly on the varying titles in the inscriptions, and partly on changing style. Some coins are dated, but in most such cases only by regnal years; some series carry indications of month as well as year.

The earliest Parthian coins show the king beardless and wearing a pointed *bashlik* with ear-flaps and the archer seated on a backless throne, with bust and seated figure sometimes looking in the same direction as if what was to become a regular convention was not yet understood by the die sinker. The coins are usually attributed to Arsaces I and Arsaces II, in the second half of the third century, leaving a gap for the reigns of the next rulers, but Mørkholm believed them to be in fact early issues of Mithridates I, so that Parthian coinage would have started half a century later than is usually supposed (above, p. 120). The coins attributable to Mithridates I would thus show him first beardless and wearing a *bashlik* (**637**), subsequently bearded and diademed, and his conquests were reflected in the expansion of his titles, most notably in the adoption of 'Philhellene' on the tetradrachms with a standing Heracles struck at Seleucia on the Tigris. Parthian coinage is perhaps at its most impressive under the long-lived and successful Mithridates II (123/2–88/7) (**638**), who restored the kingdom's fortunes, for under his immediate predecessors it lost Babylonia first (in 130) to Antiochus VII and subsequently to the king of Characene, while much of the north-east had been overrun by the nomad Sacas. Mithridates II recovered the lost provinces and extended Parthian rule as far as the oasis of Merv and the steppe country east of the Caspian, thus enabling him to exchange embassies with distant China. It is consequently not surprising that he was the first Parthian king to be shown wearing a domed and decorated headdress, or that he added the ancient title of 'King of Kings' to such more familiar ones as 'Just', 'Beneficent', and 'Philhellene'. Parthian chalkoi and their multiples have as obverse type the head of the ruler and such varied reverses as a horse or elephant, a bow-case, a thunderbolt, or a bull's head.

East of Parthia, but with no very stable frontier between them, lay Bactria.[35] The origins of Bactrian coinage (**374–5, 380–7**) under the two Diodoti, and the coins of Euthydemus I (*c*. 230–*c*. 200), have already been described (pp. 120–1). Euthydemus' long reign, with a rich and varied coinage in both gold and silver, established the tradition of fine portraiture and vigorous reverse types that were to be characteristic of this eastern outpost of Hellenic culture. His son and successor Demetrius I (*c*. 200–*c*. 190) took advantage of the decline of the native Mauryan kingdom to extend his dominions across the Hindu Kush and become master of the Punjab, so that some of his coins show him wearing the elephant-scalp helmet of Alexander the Great in whose footsteps he had trod. After Demetrius' death the Bactrian kingdom broke up, with separate lines of rulers north and south of the Hindu Kush (see p. 196), the most notable kings

35 Excellent guide to the literature in the wide-ranging study of Bivar 1965, 69 n. 2 (with map of (presumed) mints on p. 108). Bivar's article (1970) on the sequence of Menander's drachmae is particularly valuable.

of the mid century being Eucratides I (*c.* 170–*c.* 145) in Bactria proper and Menander I (*c.* 155–*c.* 130) in southern Afghanistan and the Punjab.

These early kings have only a tenuous existence in such surviving written records as the histories of Justin and his source Trogus, the geography of Strabo, *The Periplus of the Erythrean Sea,* and occasionally Indian sources. Demetrius survived, through Justin and Boccaccio, to figure in Chaucer's Knight's Tale as the 'grete Emetreus king of Inde', and Menander appears in a famous Buddhist text as 'Milinda' debating with the sage Nagasena the merits of the Buddhist faith. His coins, however, despite their Kharoshthi script, are purely Greek, with a strong preference for Athena Alkidemos of Pella as their regular type.

Demetrius II's conquests in the Punjab meant that what was initially a purely Greek coinage merged gradually into an Indo-Greek one, struck at Alexandria Kapisa south of the Hindu Kush or at Pushkalāvati or Taxila, with Greek inscriptions and royal titles doubled in Brahmi or Kharoshthi script (**641**), the Attic weight standard supplemented and eventually replaced by an Indian one,[36] and even a square shape adopted for copper coins on the model of the earlier native ones of Taxila and Mathura. The Indian element naturally became more and more dominant after the Greeks in Bactria were squeezed out of their northern strongholds by the pressure of the Parthians and other nomadic tribes from Central Asia. But the order of succession of the heirs of Demetrius and Menander, and the areas they governed, has to be based almost entirely on hoard evidence, which can show which kings were virtually contemporary with each other or, by elimination, which had not yet come to the throne and, in the case of hoards from Afghanistan and the Punjab, can provide some indication of where they actually reigned.

The inscriptions on some coins afford the scholar a welcome aid in their record of royal relationships, but Tarn's elaborate reconstruction of Bactrian and Indo-Bactrian history on the basis of coin evidence, and even that of the numismatically more experienced Narain, have to be regarded with scepticism.[37] This is the more unfortunate since Bactrian coinage includes many of the greatest masterpieces of numismatic portraiture: Antimachus (*c.* 185–*c.* 170) wearing the flat-topped Macedonian *kausia*; Eucratides I wearing a helmet and showing the Dioscuri as reverse type (**639**); the extraordinary spear-thrusting portraits of Eucratides (**640**) and of Archebius (*c.* 120) in the guise of Zeus, shown partly from behind so as the better to display the goatskin *aegis* appropriate to his divinity. The Qunduz hoard[38] included five double decadrachms of Amyntas, and of Eucratides we have a unique gold 20-stater piece in the Bibliothèque Nationale, 56mm in diameter and weighing 168g, these being respectively the largest silver and the largest gold coins known from Antiquity. Six bilingual drachms of Agathocles (*c.* 190–*c.* 180 B.C.) which were included with 677 Indian punch-marked coins in a hoard that came to light in 1970 during the French excavations at Ai Khanum in northern Afghanistan,[39] were in

36 MacDowall 1984. The Attic standard remained for a time in use by mints south of the Hindu Kush, presumably for military payments.
37 Tarn 1951; Narain 1955, 1957.
38 Curiel and Fussmann 1965.
39 Audouin and Bernard 1973 (the punch-marked coins), 1974 (Agathocles); Bernard 1975.

their way of comparable importance, for they depicted purely Indian deities and showed that it was Agathocles and not Dionysius I or II who inaugurated the bilingual coinages. Many other coins, not all of them Bactrian, have also come to light at Ai Khanum.[40]

In addition to Parthia and Bactria, three other smaller kingdoms clustered around the Persian Gulf were carved out of the debris of the Seleucid empire. Elymais, the region also known as Susiana, with the great city of Susa on the Choaspes as its capital, was situated at the head of the Gulf east of the Tigris, and was by far the most important of the three. Characene, which took its name from its capital Spasinou Charax ('walled city of Hyspaosines') in the lower Tigris valley, was usually little more than an accessory of Elymais. Persis lay east of the Gulf but extended northwards as far as Aspadana, half-way to the Caspian. Its old Achaemenid capital of Persepolis had by now been replaced by neighbouring Istakhr, where its priest-kings tended the sacred fire of Zoroaster.

Elymais[41] became independent of Seleucid rule some time in the early second century under a dynasty whose kings, with the exception of the probably Parthian Orodes and Phraates, and of Okkonapsis and Tigraios of whom a few coins are known,[42] all bore the name of Kamnaskires. Its coins (**642**) were tetradrachms and drachms imitated from Seleucid types, with lengthy legends and lists of titles surrounding the seated Apollo or Zeus on the reverse. An exceptional issue of Kamnaskires IV (*c.* 82) has on the obverse the jugate busts of Kamnaskires and his queen Anzaze, the bearded bust of the king of a singularly nineteenth-century aspect that has served as an open invitation to forgery. Later coins have heads on both sides, and in due course silver disappears and is replaced by a coinage of copper.

The first king of Characene was Hyspaosines, an eparch appointed by Antiochus IV who took advantage of the confusion following this ruler's death to make himself independent, assuming the royal title some time before 141. For a time he even occupied Babylon, where cuneiform tablets show him to have been recognized as king in 128, but he was quickly expelled by Mithridates I of Parthia and for a time lost even his own capital. The typical coins of Characene[43] are crude but handsome tetradrachms (**643**) and drachms modelled on those of the Seleucids, with a bearded and diademed bust of the king on the obverse and a clumsily designed seated Heracles with the name of the king, at first in Greek and subsequently in Aramaic, on the reverse. Most of its known coins are of the first and second centuries A.D. and of progressively inferior alloy, the last tetradrachms being effectively of copper, and there is even, most unusually, a coinage in lead. This is known mainly from the Susa excavations and its monetary character does not seem open to doubt.

Finally, in the same area, there was the coinage of Persis.[44] Its origins under Bagadates and

40 Petitot-Biehler 1975; Bernard and Guillaume 1980; Le Rider 1987. Cf. also Rtveladze 1984.
41 The standard work is now Le Rider 1965a, superseding Allotte 1902.
42 Le Rider 1978.
43 Le Rider 1959 and 1965a, 33–43, 181–7; Nicolet-Pierre 1978. On the history of Characene, including a good survey of the coinage, Nodelman 1960.
44 Allotte 1902.

Oborzos (**146–7**) in the decade 290/280 and its continuation in the following decades have already been described (pp. 73–4, 119); Seleucid authority in the region was re-established soon after 250 and the first phase of Persian coinage came to an end. The country recovered something approaching independence in the mid second century, after Parthian expansion had deprived the Seleucids of Mesopotamia and Susiana, and coinage was restarted, but with types now Parthian in character, a seated figure replacing the earlier fire-altar and standing sovereign on the reverse.

In the Mediterranean region, south-eastern Asia Minor (Cilicia) and the coastlands of Phoenicia and Palestine, having changed hands often between Syria and Egypt, in the second century saw the introduction, or more often the revival, of city coinages (**644–5**) alongside royal ones.[45] These coinages were struck on a mixture of standards – Attic or 'reduced Attic', Aradian or 'reduced Aradian', Ptolemaic (Phoenician)[46] – and were almost exclusively of silver or bronze, many of them being dated by either the Seleucid era or by the appropriate local one. Tyre exceptionally struck a gold octodrachm in 103 under Ptolemaic influence. The second era of the autonomous coinage of Tyre began in 126, with a minting grant from Demetrius II, and that of Sidon in 111. It was the coinage of these cities that provided much of that of Palestine in the time of Christ. Tyrian shekels (**645**) especially are common in Palestinian hoards, and, despite their pagan types, their use was specifically prescribed for the payment of Temple dues. At Jerusalem itself the early silver coinage already mentioned (p. 70) was followed, after a long interval, by a fully Jewish coinage. A formal grant of minting rights by Antiochus VII to the Hasmonean kings is recorded in the Book of Maccabees, and it was formerly thought that the earliest coins were anonymous shekels and half-shekels minted by the high-priest Simon Maccabeus (145–135) and having for types a cup and a branch with three buds. These are now attributed, however, to the First Jewish Revolt against Rome in A.D. 66–70,[47] and the earliest issues were small coins of bronze (**647–8**), not silver, though whether they began under John I Hyrcanus (135–104) or under Alexander Jannaeus (103–76) is uncertain. Those traditionally attributed to John I, having on one side a Hebrew inscription surrounded by a laurel wreath and on the other two cornucopiae, may really be ones of John II (69, 63–57), and those with the name Yehuda ones of Judas II Aristobolus (67–63) and not Judas I (104/3), which would leave the earliest coinage that of Alexander.[48] There is indeed some reason to believe that Jerusalem may still have been a Seleucid mint as late as the twentieth year of Antiochus VIII (102).

Finally there was the coinage of Egypt, which remained in the pattern already set in the third century but with steadily declining resources and few innovations in design. The loss of the

45 Cf. Bloesch 1979, 1982, and Mørkholm 1987.
46 Mørkholm 1967, 1982a; Houghton and Bendall 1988.
47 See Kadman 1960, 42–71, for a full account of the controversy and evidence.
48 Meshorer 1967, 41–5, 46–9; Meshorer 1974; *contra*, Barag and Qedar 1980. On Alexander's coinage, Meshorer 1982; McLean 1981.

Phoenician mints was compensated by the increased output of those of Cyprus, which struck a long series of tetradrachms, of steadily increasing baseness, bearing city names with Ptolemaic regnal dating. Gold was rarely struck after Ptolemy V Epiphanes (205–180), and silver almost never in Egypt itself, where the currency became effectively one of bronze. Portraits are also rare after Euergetes I, though there are some handsome ones of Ptolemy VI Philometor (180–145), and of Euergetes II and Auletes. Those of Cleopatra VII (51–30) are naturally interesting because of her role in history and literature, but, if they can be relied on, they show that her charm must have depended on her personality, not on her beauty. Historically the most notable are those on base silver tetradrachms which show Mark Antony as well, but these are from Antioch or some Phoenician mint[49] – Phoenicia formed part of the territory granted to her by Antony in 36 – and not from Egypt itself. The only ones from Alexandria, on large bronze coins (**646**) of the usual types but exceptionally bearing a mark of value ($M = 40$, $\Pi = 80$, i.e. 80 bronze drachms or one-sixth of the current silver drachm of 480 bronze ones, a rate attested by papyri), are presumably those most faithful to her actual appearance, and the sharp features of these show her as scarcely attractive in appearance.

49 So Buttrey 1954, who first explained her description as *Neotera* on the coins, but the traditional attribution to Antioch is supported by hoard evidence and preferred by many scholars (Houghton and Bendall 1988, 82–3).

APPENDICES

LISTS OF RULERS

All dates are B.C.

KINGS OF MACEDON

The dates are those of Hammond and Walbank 1988.

(a) The Temenid Dynasty

PHILIP II	359–336	
ALEXANDER III THE GREAT	336–323	
PHILIP III ARRHIDAEUS	323–317	Joint kings
ALEXANDER IV	323–309	Joint kings

Alexander IV's murder by Cassander did not become public knowledge till 306/5, so that his name continued to be used in dating formulae after 309.

(b) The House of Antipater

CASSANDER, son of Antipater	316–297	

Seized power in 317, but Philip III and Alexander IV were formally kings to 317 and 309 respectively.

PHILIP IV, son of Cassander	297 (4 months)	
ANTIPATER I (sons of Cassander)	297–294	Joint kings
ALEXANDER V (sons of Cassander)	297–294	Joint kings

(c) The Antigonid Dynasty

ANTIGONUS I MONOPHTHALMUS	306–301	

Antigonus never actually ruled in Macedon, and is only included in the list as the founder of the Antigonid dynasty. He was acknowledged 'Lord (*kurios*) of Asia' in 311 and assumed the title of *basileus* in 306.

DEMETRIUS I POLIORCETES 306–283
King in Macedon from 294 to 287.

(d) Intruders

PYRRHUS 287–285 (and 274–3)
LYSIMACHUS 287–281
Only of eastern Macedon in 287–285.
PTOLEMY CERAUNUS 281–279
MELEAGER 279 (2 months)
ANTIPATER II 279 (45 days)
Antipater was succeeded by Sosthenes 279–277, but as a successful general, not as king.

(e) The Antigonid Dynasty (restored)

ANTIGONUS II GONATAS 276–239
Son of Demetrius Poliorcetes. He acquired Macedon as a result of the battle of Lysimachia (277), but not immediately, though he dated his regnal years from his father's death in 283. Pyrrhus recovered much of Macedon in 274/3.
DEMETRIUS II 239–229
ANTIGONUS III DOSON 229–221
Antigonus III, son of a half-brother of Antigonus Gonatas, was initially no more than guardian of the latter's son and natural successor, Philip V, who was only nine or ten years old in 229. In *c.* 227 Antigonus received the royal title.
PHILIP V 221–179
PERSEUS 179–168

The dynasty ended with Perseus' capture by the Roman general Aemilius after the battle of Pydna in 168. The monarchy was abolished, Perseus was taken to Rome and put to death, and Macedonia continued as four separate republics.

THE SELEUCIDS (Syria and the East)

Seleucus dated his reign, and the Seleucid era was reckoned, from his recovery of Babylon in 312, but he was king only from 305.
SELEUCUS I (Nicator) 312–281
ANTIOCHUS I (Soter) 281–261
With Seleucus I from *c.* 290
ANTIOCHUS II (Theos) 261–246
With Antiochus I from *c.* 266

SELEUCUS II (Callinicus, Pogon)	246–226/5
Antiochus Hierax, younger brother of Seleucus II, first co-regent, later (241–226) usurper in Asia Minor	
SELEUCUS III (Soter, Ceraunus)	226/5–223
ANTIOCHUS III (the Great)	223–187
ACHAEUS, grandson of another Achaeus, brother of Antiochus I, usurper in western Asia Minor 220–213	
MOLON, not a Seleucid, usurper in Mesopotamia	222–221
SELEUCUS IV (Philopator)	187–175
ANTIOCHUS IV (Epiphanes)	175–164
ANTIOCHUS V (Eupator)	164–162
DEMETRIUS I (Soter)	162–150
ALEXANDER I BALAS	150–145
DEMETRIUS II (Nicator)	145–140
Captured in 140 by Mithridates I of Parthia and held prisoner till 129	
ANTIOCHUS VI (Epiphanes)	145–142/1 (or 139/8 ?)
TRYPHON, not a Seleucid, pretender	142/1–140
ANTIOCHUS VII (Sidetes)	138–129
DEMETRIUS II, restored	129–126/5
ALEXANDER II (Zebina)	128–123
Set up by Ptolemy VIII as rival to Demetrius	
SELEUCUS V	126/5
Under the regency of his mother Cleopatra Thea	126
ANTIOCHUS VIII (Grypus)	126/5–96
With his mother Cleopatra Thea	126/5–123
ANTIOCHUS IX (Philopator, Cyzicenus)	114/13–95
In association with his half-brother Antiochus VIII, who was mainly in control 108–96	
SELEUCUS VI	95
ANTIOCHUS X (Eusebes, Philopator)	95
DEMETRIUS III (Philopator, Soter)	95–88 (in Damascus)
ANTIOCHUS XI (Epiphanes, Philadelphus) } twins	95 } in Cilicia
PHILIP I } twins	95–84/3 } in Cilicia
ANTIOCHUS XII Dionysus	87–84 (at Damascus)
PHILIP II	84–83
TIGRANES the Great (not a Seleucid)	83–69
TIGRANES II as king of Armenia	97–56
ANTIOCHUS XIII (Asiaticus)	69–68
PHILIP II, restored	68–65
ANTIOCHUS XIII, restored	65–64/3

The dynasty ended with Antiochus XIII, by whose time the kingdom had contracted to

Syria and who was only one of a group of Seleucid princelings who had been fighting for several years between themselves with the support of rival Arab sheiks. The details are very uncertain: the earlier literature was superseded by Bellinger 1949a, to which add Downey 1961, 136–42. Antiochus XIII was deposed by Pompey in 64/3 and Syria became a Roman province.

THE LAGIDS (PTOLEMIES) OF EGYPT

The most authoritative chronology is that in Skeat 1954, but important modifications on some points are proposed in Samuel 1962. Skeat's work was compiled to facilitate the dating of papyri, so that Bouché-Leclercq 1903–7 remains essential for relationships and personalities. Since Ptolemaic queens play a prominent role in the coinage, the names of the most important are included in the list below. The brother–sister marriages which became normal in the dynasty date from Arsinoe II, who was married first to Lysimachus, then to her half-brother Ptolemy Ceraunus, and finally to her full brother Ptolemy II after he had repudiated his first wife, another Arsinoe (I) of unknown parentage. The nickname Philadelphus ('loving a brother/sister') was first applied to Arsinoe and only subsequently to her husband.

PTOLEMY I (Soter) 305/4–283/2

Governor of Egypt from 323, effectively 'king' from 309 (murder of Alexander IV), and assumed the title of king early in 304 but back-dated his reign from 7 November 305, the start of the Egyptian year 305/4. He handed over power to Ptolemy II in March/April 285 (or ? January 284: Samuel) but remained nominally sovereign till his death in 282. He married (1) Artakama, (2) Eurydice, a daughter of Antipater, and (3) his former mistress BERENICE I (d.279).

Ptolemy Ceraunus. Eldest son of Ptolemy I by Eurydice, but excluded from the succession when she was set aside in favour of Berenice. King in Macedon 281–279.

PTOLEMY II (Philadelphus) 285–246

Married (1) Arsinoe I and (2) his sister ARSINOE II, who is usually assumed to have died in 270, though Grzybek 1989 argues that she was still alive in 268.

Magas, not a Lagid but a son of Berenice I by a first marriage and so half-brother to Ptolemy II. Appointed governor of Cyrene *c.* 300 and subsequently ruling (*c.* 277–*c.* 250) with the (usurped) title of King.

PTOLEMY III (Euergetes) 246–222 (December: see Pestman 1967)

Son of Ptolemy II by Arsinoe I. Married BERENICE II (murdered 221/20) daughter of Magas of Cyrene, resulting in the recovery of Cyrene by Egypt.

PTOLEMY IV (Philopator) 222–205 (late November)

Married his sister ARSINOE III (murdered 205)

PTOLEMY V (Epiphanes) 205–180 (after May)

Married CLEOPATRA I (d.176)

PTOLEMY VI (Philometor) 180–145

With PTOLEMY VIII (Euergetes II, Physcon) (his brother) and CLEOPATRA II (his sister) 170–164

PTOLEMY VIII, alone, his colleagues having been deposed 164–163
PTOLEMY VI AND CLEOPATRA II, again 163–145
PTOLEMY VII (Neos Philopator, son of Ptolemy VI) 145
PTOLEMY VIII restored 145–116 (June)
CLEOPATRA II, CLEOPATRA III (dau. of Ptolemy VI), and her son PTOLEMY IX (Soter II, Lathyrus) 116 (brief joint rule)
CLEOPATRA III and PTOLEMY IX 116–107
CLEOPATRA III and (another son) PTOLEMY X ALEXANDER I 107–101 (late)
Ptolemy X had ruled earlier in Cyprus
PTOLEMY X ALEXANDER I and CLEOPATRA BERENICE 101–88
PTOLEMY IX, restored 88–81 (or 80: Samuel)
CLEOPATRA BERENICE, with PTOLEMY X and (later) her son PTOLEMY XI ALEXANDER II 80
PTOLEMY XII (Neos Dionysus, Auletes, son of Ptolemy IX) 80–58
BERENICE IV (dau. of PTOLEMY XII), at first with (her mother?) CLEOPATRA TRYPHAENA 58–56
BERENICE IV with ARCHELAUS 56–55
Archelaus was not a Lagid but a high-priest of Comana married to Berenice IV as part of the effort to exclude Ptolemy XII.
PTOLEMY XII, restored 55–51
CLEOPATRA VII (Philopator, dau. of Ptolemy XII) 51–30
At various times with her brother PTOLEMY XIII (51–47?), with another brother PTOLEMY XIV (47–44?), and finally in association with her son Caesarion, PTOLEMY XV (nominally 41–30?), but the chronology is obscure; see Skeat 1954, Pestman 1967, and Heinen 1966, App. 3.

Alexandria fell to Octavian on 3 August 30 and Cleopatra committed suicide on the 12th or 13th, but Octavian, the future Augustus (from 27 B.C.), dated his reign from the 31st so that it would coincide with the beginning of the Egyptian year.

THE ATTALIDS OF PERGAMUM

The standard works on Pergamum under the Attalids are Cardinali 1906, Hansen 1971 and Allen 1983. The dynasty took its name from Philetaerus' father Attalus. Philetaerus, a eunuch owing to an accident in childhood, was placed in charge of the fortress of Pergamum and an immense treasure by Lysimachus just before the battle of Ipsus (301). His dates are commonly reckoned from 283, when he repudiated the authority of Lysimachus and allied himself with Seleucus I, but neither he nor Eumenes I, his nephew, adopted son and successor, bore the title of king. This was assumed sometime between 241 and 236 by Attalus I, who made Pergamum the most important state in Asia Minor.

PHILETAERUS 283–263
EUMENES I 263–241

ATTALUS I	241–197
EUMENES II	197–158
ATTALUS II	158–138
ATTALUS III	138–133
ARISTONICUS (Eumenes III)	133–130

Attalus III, dying childless, bequeathed the kingdom to Rome. His (illegitimate) half-brother Aristonicus, coins of whom are known in the name of Eumenes (III), contested the will and held out till 130, when he was captured, taken to Rome, and subsequently put to death. Some rebels continued to hold out till 126.

KINGS OF BITHYNIA

The Bithynian royal era started in the year 297/6 (not 298/7), when a local Thracian chieftain Zipoetes, having successfully resisted Lysimachus' attempts to subjugate the region, assumed the title of king. The importance of the kingdom dates from *c.* 260, when Zipoetes' successor Nicomedes I, the first to place his name on his coins, founded Nicomedia on a gulf of the Propontis and called it after himself. The dates of the earlier kings are conjectural.

ZIPOETES	297/6–*c.* 280
NICOMEDES I	*c.* 280–*c.* 250
ZIAELAS	*c.* 250–*c.* 230
PRUSIAS I	*c.* 230–182
PRUSIAS II	182–149
NICOMEDES II	149–127
NICOMEDES III	127–94
NICOMEDES IV	94–74

Nicomedes IV, who had been earlier dethroned by Mithridates of Pontus and restored by the Roman Senate, followed the example of Attalus III half a century earlier and bequeathed his kingdom to Rome.

KINGS OF PONTUS

The kings of Pontus, the eastern neighbour of Bithynia on the Black Sea coast, were, as their names imply, of Persian origin, being traditionally descended from a line of Persian governors of Cius. Diodorus Siculus' account of their early history is now regarded as largely myth, but the ruling family seems to have established itself in the region of Sinope and Amisus in the first two decades of the third century. It was probably shortly after Lysimachus' death (281) that Mithridates proclaimed himself king, though the beginning of the royal era was subsequently equated with that of Bithynia (297/6). The dates of the early kings are only approximate, and the numbering of those named Mithridates is confused, since the older books count a fourth-century ancestor as Mithridates I. The earliest coins are of Mithridates II.

MITHRIDATES I	*c.* 280–*c.* 266
ARIOBARZANES	*c.* 266–*c.* 255
MITHRIDATES II	*c.* 255–*c.* 220
MITHRIDATES III	*c.* 220–*c.* 185
PHARNACES I	*c.* 185–*c.* 170
MITHRIDATES IV (Philopator)	*c.* 170–*c.* 150
MITHRIDATES V (Euergetes)	*c.* 150–120
MITHRIDATES VI (Eupator), 'the Great'	*c.* 120–63

Mithridates VI was Rome's chief adversary in Asia Minor, and after his defeat and suicide the kingdom was broken up by Pompey. The western part was annexed by Rome and added to the province of Bithynia. The remainder carried on under separate rulers (see Sullivan 1980) till finally annexed under Nero in A.D. 64.

KINGS OF CAPPADOCIA

The name of Cappadocia was given to the whole region of east-central Asia Minor between Pontus (which was once considered part of it) to the north and the Taurus mountains to the south. It was ruled by an Iranian dynasty which traced its origins back to Ariarathes I, a contemporary of Alexander the Great, though the succession is not always clear and most dates apart from that of the death of Ariarathes I, known only because he had the misfortune to be crucified in company with most other members of his family by Perdiccas, are approximate. It was Ariarathes III who first assumed the royal title, and a continuous coinage does not begin till the last decade of the reign of Ariarathes IV (after *c.* 175). The dates below are taken, with minor modifications, from Simonetta 1977, though for the evidence regarding them one has to go back to Reinach 1888.

House of Ariarathes

ARIARATHES I	*c.* 350–322
Macedonian rule	322–*c.* 301
ARIARATHES II	*c.* 301–*c.* 280
ARIARAMNES	*c.* 280–*c.* 230
ARIARATHES III	*c.* 230–*c.* 220
ARIARATHES IV (Eusebes)	*c.* 220–163
ARIARATHES V (Philopator)	163–130
OROPHERNES, usurper	159–157
ARIARATHES VI (Epiphanes)	130–116
ARIARATHES VII (Philometor)	116–101

ARIARATHES VIII, first reign	101–99
ARIARATHES IX	99–87 (intermittently)
Son of Mithridates VI of Pontus; frequently deposed and reinstated	
ARIARATHES VIII	restored *c.* 90–86

House of Ariobarzanes

ARIOBARZANES I (Philoromaios)	95–63 (intermittently)
ARIOBARZANES II (Philopator)	63–52
ARIOBARZANES III (Eusebes)	52–42
ARIARATHES X	43–36
ARCHELAUS	36–14 A.D.

On the death of Archelaus, the last native king, who had been appointed by Antony and apparently was not of the house of Ariobarzanes, Cappadocia was annexed by Tiberius and became a Roman province.

THE ARSACIDS OF PARTHIA

Parthia was the ancient name of what is today the province of Khurasan, effectively all north-eastern Iran. The ruling dynasty was descended from Arshak (Arsaces), the Persian name of a nomad chieftain, expelled from his homeland east of the Caspian by the Bactrian king Diodotus, who invaded Parthia and killed its satrap Andragoras, already in revolt against the Seleucids. Arsaces was believed to have assumed the royal title in 247, when the Arsacid royal era begins, but our sources disagree over the date of the Parthian 'succession' (cf. Will 1979, I.287–8; *CAH* VII.i (1984), 213–20), and much of the early history of the kingdom, known to us mainly from what survives of Arrian's *Parthica*, is fabulous. The transformation of the large but relatively unimportant Parthian kingdom into the Parthian 'empire' was the work of Mithridates I (*c.* 170–*c.* 138), who expanded his dominions in the east at the expense of Bactria and conquered Media and Babylonia from the Seleucids.

The date at which Parthian coining began is debated: the coins customarily allotted to Arsaces I and Arsaces II are ascribed by Mørkholm (following Newell 1938a) to Mithridates I, an attribution based on their occurrence in large numbers in hoards mixed with coins of the Seleucid ruler Alexander Balas. Sellwood, however, prefers the traditional scheme (cf. Sellwood 1980).

The chronology is at several points very uncertain. The list below is based on those in Debevoise 1938, 270, and Colledge 1967, 179, but scholars disagree on the dates and even the names of the immediate successors to Arsaces I (cf. Wolski 1959, 1962, whose reconstruction, eliminating Arrian's Tiridates and a supposed Artabanus I, is here followed). There is also much uncertainty concerning the successors of Mithridates II between *c.* 90 and *c.* 55; for varying reconstructions see Le Rider 1965a, 394ff.; Sellwood 1962; Dobbins 1975; and Simonetta and Sellwood 1978; but other articles of Sellwood and Simonetta are concerned with the problem.

ARSACES I	217–*c.* 211
ARSACES II	*c.* 211–*c.* 191
PRIAPATIUS	*c.* 191–*c.* 176
PHRAATES I	*c.* 176–*c.* 171
MITHRIDATES I	*c.* 171–138/7
PHRAATES II	138/7–*c.* 128
ARTABANUS I	*c.* 128–124/3
HIMERUS, usurper in Media and Babylonia	124/3–123/2
MITHRIDATES II	123/2–88/7
GOTARZES I, usurper in Babylonia	*c.* 91–87/86
ORODES I	*c.* 90–80/79
SINATRUCES	76/5–70/69
PHRAATES III	70/69–58/7
MITHRIDATES III	58/7–55
ORODES II	*c.* 57–38/7
PACORUS I, son of Orodes II, minted in his own name	*c.* 51–38
PHRAATES IV	38/7–2

The Arsacid dynasty continued down to the 220s A.D., when it was overthrown by the Sassanian Ardashir I.

BACTRIAN AND INDO-GREEK KINGS

Bactria, corresponding roughly to Afghanistan north of the Hindu Kush, was the easternmost province of the Seleucid realm. Its satrap Diodotus I established his independence in the middle of the third century and struck coins in his own name, though it is not clear whether there were two Diodoti or only one. In the early second century the kingdom expanded into southern Afghanistan and north-western India but subsequently broke up under rival rulers, especially south of the Hindu Kush in the regions of southern Afghanistan known to the Greeks as the Parapamisadae (around Kabul) and Arachosia (around Kandahar) and in Gandhara (north-eastern Punjab and Kashmir). These sometimes coalesced but were more often fragmented into sub-kingdoms, and while coins provide the names of rulers, and hoards and overstrikes allow us to group these together and establish their rough chronological order, we remain ignorant of their precise dates and are often uncertain as to exactly where they ruled.

Bactria proper remained under Greek rulers down to *c.* 130 B.C., when it was taken by the people called in Chinese sources the Yüeh-chih, who with other nomad tribes (Scythians/Sacas) gradually established themselves in northern India also. The last Greek ruler in the Parapamisadae was Hermaeus (to *c.* 70 B.C.), but further south the Indo-Greeks carried on until about A.D. 20, when Strato II, ruler of a petty state around Sagala (Sialkot), close to the modern Lahore in the western Punjab, succumbed to the Scythian Rajuvala, satrap of Mathura on the Ganges. The list of rulers and dates below is based essentially on the work of Dr Osmund Bopearachchi, only partially published at the time of writing. It supersedes the earlier reconstructions of Tarn 1951, Narain 1957 and 1968, and Lahiri 1965, but *circa* must be assumed to apply to all dates save those of a few mid-second-century kings whose names appear in Babylonian or other sources.

Overlapping dates resulted sometimes from father/son associations but are more often those of rival rulers.

Diodotus I/II	250–230
Euthydemus I	230–200
Demetrius I	200–190

Bactria		*Parapamisadae*		*India*	
Euthydemus II	190–185	Pantaleon	190–185	Agathocles	190–180
Antimachus I	185–170			Apollodotus I	190–160
Demetrius II	175–165			Antimachus II	160–155
Eucratides I	170–145			Menander Soter	155–130
Eucratides II	145–140	Plato	145–140		
Heliocles I	145–130			*Gandhara*	
		Zoilus I	130–120	Agathocleia	130–125
		Lysias	120–110	Strato I	125–110
		Antalcidas	115–95	Heliocles II	110–100
		Polyxenus	100–95	Demetrius III	100–97

Philoxenus 105–95

Diomedes	95–90	Amyntas	95–90	Epander	95–90
Peucolaos	92–90	Theophilus	92–90	Thrason	92?
Menander II	90–85	Artemiodorus	88–85	Nicias	90–80
Hermaeus	90–70	Archebius	90–80		
		Maues (Indo-Scythian)	85–75		
		Apollodotus II	80–65	Telephus	75–70
		Dionysius II	65–55	Hippostratus	65–55
		Zoilus II	55–35		
		Apollophanes	32–25		
		Strato II	25 B.C.–A.D. 20		

CHRONOLOGICAL TABLE 336–187

All dates are B.C. They have often to be given in the form of successive years, for public events, unlike private documents dated precisely by day and month, are usually recorded only as having occurred in a particular year of a local era, or in the term of office of a named magistrate, and these will not have corresponded to a single year in the Julian calendar. More elusive still are events dated to a particular Olympiad and so only to some point within a period of four years.

336	Philip II murdered at Aegae (summer). Alexander III (the Great) becomes king of Macedon (to 323).
334	Alexander crosses into Asia Minor (spring), leaving Antipater as regent in Macedon.
333	Alexander enters Cilicia (August) and defeats Darius III at Issus (Nov.).
332	Alexander occupies Coele-Syria and Phoenicia and captures Tyre (July) after a seven-month siege.
332/1	Alexander winters in Egypt, founds Alexandria, and visits the oracle of Zeus Ammon at the oasis of Siwah.
331	Alexander defeats Darius at Gaugamela (1 Oct.) and occupies Babylon and Susa (Nov.)
330	Alexander occupies Persepolis, capturing the Persian royal treasure (Jan.). Darius, in flight from Alexander, is murdered by Bessus, satrap of Bactria.
330/29	Alexander's conquest of Bactria and Sogdiana.
327–325	Alexander's Indian expedition.
323	Death of Alexander at Babylon (10 June preferable to 13). He is succeeded by his half-brother, the feeble-minded Arrhidaeus, who assumes the name of Philip III (323–317) and who is subsequently associated with Alexander's posthumous son Alexander IV (323–309), offspring of his Persian wife Roxana. Antipater remains regent of Macedon, Perdiccas and Craterus share control of the royal household, and Ptolemy becomes governor of Egypt, Lysimachus of Thrace, and Antigonus of Phrygia and most of Asia Minor.
321	Perdiccas, a member of the Macedonian royal house and suspected of having designs on the crown, is murdered in Egypt after attacking Ptolemy. A new partition at Triparadeisus (autumn) leaves Antipater regent and guardian of the kings, Antigonus' realm extended to cover all Asia Minor, and Seleucus satrap of Babylon. Alexander's body, on its way to Macedon, is kidnapped

by Ptolemy and buried at Memphis, later at Alexandria.

319 Antipater dies and is succeeded as regent by Polyperchon in close association with Alexander's mother Olympias. Revolt of Antipater's son Cassander, who had expected to succeed his father as regent.

317 Philip III and his wife murdered by Olympias (Sept.) so as to leave Alexander IV sole monarch.

316 Cassander seizes power in Macedon, murders Olympias (spring), and takes custody of Alexander IV, Polyperchon being reduced to a few districts in the Peloponnese. Antigonus' defeat of Eumenes leaves him master of Asia.

315 Coalition of Cassander, Lysimachus and Ptolemy to check Antigonus. War breaks out and continues to 311.

313 Cyrene revolts against Ptolemy, who in 312 accepts its virtual autonomy under Ophellas (to 308).

312 Ptolemy defeats Antigonus' son Demetrius Poliorcetes at Gaza and occupies Phoenicia and Palestine. Seleucus recovers Babylon and subsequently the other eastern satrapies, which he rules to 281. Seleucid era begins (1 Oct.).

311 Antigonus makes peace in return for recognition of his own rule over 'Asia', though he fails to drive Seleucus out of Babylon and the East.

309 Cassander murders Alexander IV and becomes effectively king of Macedon (to 297), but war with Ptolemy over the possession of Greece ensues (to 306).

308 Ptolemy campaigns in Greece against Cassander and occupies Corinth. Ophellas of Cyrene murdered after an unsuccessful attack on Carthage and Ptolemy recovers Cyrenaica (to *c.* 305).

306 Demetrius Poliorcetes defeats Ptolemy's fleet off Salamis in Cyprus and deprives Ptolemy of Cyprus. Antigonus (306–301) and Demetrius (306–285/4) both assume the royal title.

305/4 Ptolemy, Seleucus, Cassander and Lysimachus all assume the royal title in imitation of Antigonus. Desultory war with Antigonus continues (to 301). Cyrene revolts against Ptolemy and becomes autonomous (305–*c.* 300). Demetrius fails to capture Rhodes after a year's siege.

303 Seleucus abandons his Indian claims in return for a promise of war elephants from Chandragupta.

301 Antigonus defeated and killed at the battle of Ipsus, thus ending any possibility of returning to the unity of Alexander's empire. Seleucus acquires north Mesopotamia and Syria, Ptolemy Coele-Syria and Phoenicia, and Lysimachus Asia Minor. Pleistarchus, a brother of Cassander, is given Cilicia.

300 Ptolemy recovers Cyrene and appoints his step-son Magas governor (see under 277).

299 Demetrius conquers Cilicia from Pleistarchus.

297 Cassander dies (May) and is succeeded as king of Macedon by his son Philip IV (May–Sept.), who in turn is succeeded by his younger brothers Antipater and Alexander V (both 297–294).

296	Demetrius campaigns in Greece to re-establish his hegemony over the cities.
294	Alexander V of Macedon is murdered by Demetrius, whose help he had invoked against his brother Antipater. The latter takes refuge with Lysimachus, and Demetrius becomes king of Macedon (to 288). Ptolemy recovers Cyprus from Demetrius, who also loses Cilicia to Seleucus and western Asia Minor to Lysimachus.
c. 290	Seleucus associates Antiochus I as co-ruler. Growing importance of the Aetolian League, which by the mid century comes to dominate most of central Greece from the Adriatic to the Aegean.
288	Ptolemy acquires Tyre and Sidon, which he holds to 286.
287	Demetrius expelled from Macedon by Lysimachus and Pyrrhus of Epirus, who divide the country between them, Pyrrhus taking the west (to 285) and Lysimachus the east. Two-year war starts in Asia Minor between Demetrius and Lysimachus.
285/4	Lysimachus expels Pyrrhus from Macedon and adds it to his kingdom of Thrace and Asia Minor. Demetrius is forced to surrender to Seleucus and remains a prisoner till his death in 283/2. His son Antigonus Gonatas retains only a few of his father's possessions in Greece. Ptolemy I hands over power to Ptolemy II.
283/2	Death of Ptolemy I.
281	Lysimachus defeated and killed by Seleucus at the battle of Corupedium (Jan./Feb., not April) and most of Asia Minor annexed by the latter, but Seleucus is murdered by Ptolemy Ceraunus after crossing into Europe (Sept.). Ptolemy Ceraunus left king of Macedon (to 279).
c. 280	Accession of Nicomedes I of Bithynia (to *c.* 250).
280	Refounding of the Achaean League between cities of the northern Peloponnese.
280/79	Macedonia invaded by the Gauls. Ceraunus defeated, captured, and beheaded (Jan./Feb. 279). He is succeeded in turn by his brother Meleager (2 months), his nephew Antipater Etesias (45 days), and, as general, by Sosthenes (279–277).
279	Death of Berenice I, widow of Ptolemy I.
278/7	Invasion of Asia Minor by the Gauls, partly at the invitation of Nicomedes.
277	Magas, half-brother of Ptolemy II, becomes king of Cyrenaica (to *c.* 250). Victory over the Gauls near Lysimachia by Antigonus II Gonatas.
276	Antigonus Gonatas, after a year of fighting with local pretenders, becomes fully king of Macedon (to 239).
274	Outbreak of the First Syrian War between Egypt and the Seleucids (to 271). Wars between Antigonus Gonatas and Pyrrhus (to 273).
272	Pyrrhus killed at Argos by Antigonus and the Argives.
271	End of the First Syrian War.
270 (or ?268)	Death of Arsinoe II, sister-wife of Ptolemy II.

268/7	Outbreak of the Chremonidean War (to 261), in which an alliance between Athens, Sparta and other states, organized by the Athenian politician Chremonides and with the support of Ptolemy II, attempts to overturn the Macedonian position in Greece.
266	Antiochus II Theos associated king by his father.
265	Death of Areus I (309–265), the first king of Sparta to strike coined money, when defending the Isthmus against Antigonus.
263	Death of Philetaerus of Pergamum; accession of Eumenes I (to 241). Outbreak of war with Antiochus I.
261	Death of Antiochus I (1 or 2 June); Antiochus II left sole king (261–246). Chremonidean War ends with the capitulation of Athens and the consolidation of Macedonian hold on Greece.
c. 260	Foundation of Nicomedia by Nicomedes I.
260	Outbreak of the Second Syrian War (to 253).
255	Antigonus obtains control of the Cyclades after defeating Ptolemy II in a naval battle off Cos.
253	End of Second Syrian War.
251	Aratus liberates Sicyon (May), joins it to the Achaean League against Macedon, and down to his death in 213 plays a major role in Peloponnesian affairs.
c. 250	Death of Magas of Cyrene; establishment of a short-lived *koinon*, after which Cyrenaica is recovered by Egypt.
247	Arsaces I proclaimed king of Parthia; Parthian era begins.
246	Ptolemy II succeeded by Ptolemy III Euergetes (246–221). Antiochus II dies at Ephesus (summer) and is succeeded by Seleucus II Callinicus (246–226/5), but in Asia Minor by Antiochus Hierax (246–226). Outbreak of the Third Syrian (or Laodicean) War (246–241) between Ptolemy III and Seleucus II.
241	End of Third Syrian War leaves Ptolemy III in possession of much of the south coast of Asia as well as Syria.
241	Eumenes I of Pergamum succeeded by Attalus I (241–197).
240	Attalus I defeats the Gauls and shortly afterwards (before 236) assumes the royal title.
239	Demetrius II succeeds Antigonus Gonatas as king of Macedon (to 229).
238	Outbreak of the War of Demetrius (238–229) by Macedon against Aetolia and Achaea.
235	Cleomenes III becomes king of Sparta (to 222; d. 219).
229	Antigonus III Doson succeeds Demetrius II of Macedon, becoming king *c.* 227 (to 220).
229/8	Athens buys its freedom from the commander of the Macedonian garrison.
227	Cleomenes III's victories over the Achaean League allow him to establish a despotism and carry out a social revolution in Sparta, but his aggressive foreign policy eventually brings Antigonus to the Peloponnese.
226	Death of Antiochus Hierax; Seleucus II recovers Asia Minor.

226/5 Seleucus II succeeded by Seleucus III Soter (to 223).

224 Antigonus organizes the *symmachia* of Greek cities, with himself as *hegemon*, as a basis for Macedonian control of Greece.

223 Seleucus III succeeded by Antiochus III the Great (to 187). Achaeus on the latter's behalf re-establishes Seleucid power in Asia Minor against Pergamum.

222 Cleomenes III is crushed by Antigonus at the battle of Sellasia and takes refuge in Egypt. Revolt of Molon, who assumes the royal title (to 221) in Mesopotamia. Ptolemy III is succeeded (Dec.) by Ptolemy IV Philopator (to 204).

221 Outbreak of Fourth Syrian War (to 217), Antiochus III attacking and overrunning most of Coele-Syria. Antigonus III Doson succeeded (before Oct.) as king of Macedon by Philip V (to 179).

220 Achaeus assumes the royal title in Asia Minor (to 214). Outbreak of the War of the Allies (or the Social War) in the Peloponnese between Macedon and the Aetolians and their respective allies.

219 Cleomenes III of Sparta killed in a revolt at Alexandria.

217 Egyptian victory at Raphia (22 June) ends the Fourth Syrian War, and Egypt recovers Coele-Syria except for the port of Seleucia. End of the Social War (indecisively) by the peace of Naupactus, negotiated by Rhodes and Egypt. Philip V's attention turned to Rome, where Hannibal wins the battle of Lake Trasimene (June).

215 Outbreak of the First Macedonian War (215–205) between Philip V and Rome. Antiochus re-establishes Seleucid power in Asia Minor and blockades Achaeus in Sardis.

214 Antiochus captures the citadel of Sardis after a two-year siege and kills Achaeus.

213 Death of Aratus, probably of consumption.

210 Antiochus III occupied in the East, his so-called 'Anabasis' (to *c.* 204).

207 Nabis becomes guardian of King Pelops of Sparta and on his death usurps the crown (to 192), reviving many of the projects of Cleomenes III.

206 The Aetolians and their allies come to terms with Philip V.

205 Peace of Phoenice between Rome and Macedon, following on the Graeco-Macedonian peace of the previous year, ends the First Macedonian War.

205 Ptolemy IV dies (summer) and is succeeded by Ptolemy V (to 180).

202 Outbreak of Fifth Syrian War (202–200).

201 Philip V's fleet routed by the Rhodians in alliance with Attalus I in a battle off Chios.

200 Seleucid victory at Panium ends the Fifth Syrian War; Egypt loses Coele-Syria for good, though retaining Cyprus. Outbreak of the Second Macedonian War with Rome (200–196).

197 Philip V routed by Flamininus at Cynoscephalae (June).

196 Peace treaty between Rome and Philip ends the Second Macedonian War.

	Flamininus proclaims 'the Freedom of Greece' at the Isthmian Games (mid-summer).
195	Antiochus gives sanctuary to Hannibal and makes peace with Egypt.
192	Nabis blockaded in Sparta by the Achaeans and killed by the Aetolian general Alexamenes. War (192–189) breaks out between Rome and Antiochus, who had refused to limit himself to Asia Minor.
191	Antiochus defeated by the Romans and their allies at Thermopylae (April) and driven out of Greece.
190	Antiochus' fleet defeated at Myonnesus (Sept.).
189	Antiochus totally defeated by the Scipios at the battle of Magnesia ad Sipylum.
188	Roman settlement of Asia by the Peace of Apamea (Phrygia). Antiochus pays a large indemnity, loses his fleet, and effectively surrenders Asia Minor to the profit of Pergamum, Rhodes – and Rome.
187	Antiochus ignominiously killed (3 or 4 July) while pillaging a local sanctuary in Elymais.

GLOSSARY

This includes the customary appellations of the various kings but not the miscellaneous epithets (e.g. *Dikaios*, 'Just') applied to some of them in coin legends.

ACHAEMENIDS The Persian royal dynasty overthrown by Alexander the Great. It took its name from Hakhamanish (Achaemenes), king in Persis *c.* 700 B.C.

AEGIS Originally (e.g. in Homer), the shield of Zeus, casting terror on onlookers, but apparently through a false etymology the term was transferred to a short scaly cape, covering the upper part of her body and adorned with a Gorgon's head and fringed with snakes, which is frequently worn by Athena in statues and other works of art.

AGIO The profit made in exchanging one currency against another, and, by extension, any difference in value between currencies.

AMMON The Egyptian sun-god, identified by the Greeks with Zeus and characterized in Greek art by the ram's horns of the image in the sanctuary of the oasis of Siwah visited by Alexander.

AMPHORA A jar for storing wine.

ANVIL DIE (also PILE or STANDARD) The lower of the two dies between which coins were struck.

APHLASTON The ornamented stern of a war gallery.

ARAMAIC A Semitic language spoken in Syria and neighbouring regions, with an alphabet related to Hebrew. It is used in coin inscriptions from Tarsus and elsewhere.

ARCHON Chief magistrate; more generally, ruler.

BA'AL 'Lord', the name given to their chief (male) deity by many of the Semitic peoples.

BASHLIK see KYRBASIA

BIGA A chariot drawn by two horses, or occasionally by two elephants.

BIPENNIS A battle-axe.

BLANK, also FLAN or PLANCHET The disk of unstamped metal used in making a coin.

BROCKAGE Properly speaking, any coin that is mis-struck, but mainly applied to coins on which the same design is found in relief on one face and incuse on the other as a result of the preceding coin having remained on the die and made its impress on the next one struck.

BUCEPHALUS 'Bull-headed', an epithet of a breed of Thessalian horses; in particular, the horse of Alexander the Great.

BUCRANIUM 'Ox-skull', a sculptured ornament sometimes used as a privy mark.

CADUCEUS A rod entwined by two serpents, the attribute of Hermes.

CALLINICUS 'Triumphant' (appellation of Seleucus II).

CARNYX A Gallic war-trumpet.

CERAUNUS 'Thunderbolt' (appellation of Ptolemy, the son of Ptolemy I who was briefly king of Macedon, and of Seleucus III).

CHALKOUS (pl. CHALKOI) A bronze coin, properly speaking one worth an eighth of an obol but more generally applied to all coins of base metal and low value.

CHAPELET Coin blanks were often cast *en chapelet* ('string of beads'), i.e. in a series of shallow depressions in a mould which were connected with each other by narrow channels to allow the molten metal to flow from one depression to the next. The resulting projections on the edges of the blanks should have been broken off and the edges filed smooth, but sometimes traces remain on finished coins which show how the blanks were made.

CHELYS A lyre.

CHITON A tunic.

CHLAMYS A cloak.

CHORA The countryside.

CHRYSOS A gold coin, stater.

CISTA MYSTICA A sacred basket used in Dionysiac rites that became the regular type of CISTOPHORI, on which it is shown with the sacred serpent emerging from or entwined around it.

CISTOPHORUS One of a large group of silver tetradrachms of Asia Minor of the second and first centuries B.C. having a *cista mystica* as type.

CORNUCOPIA(E) A horn of plenty, filled with various fruits.

COUNTERMARK A small letter or design punched on the face of a coin, usually with the object of changing its value or, if on a foreign coin, allowing it to be accepted as legal tender.

DARIC The gold coin of the Persian empire, probably so-called from Darius I the Great (522–486).

DEBASEMENT The reduction in the precious metal content of a coin by alloying it with some baser metal.

DEBEN A native Egyptian weight (*c.* 92g).

DECADRACHM A ten-drachma coin.

DIADEM see TAENIA.

DIADOCHI 'Successors', used especially of the successors of Alexander the Great.

DIDRACHM A two-drachma coin.

DIE AXIS The relation between the position of the reverse type of the coin to that of the obverse.

DIE LINK Two or more coins are said to be die-linked when their obverses or reverses share a common die.

DIES The stamps used in coining, composed of a lower ANVIL DIE and an upper or PUNCH DIE or TRUSSEL, and engraved with the designs in negative.

DIOBOL A two-obol coin.

DISTATER A two-stater coin.

DODECADRACHM A twelve-drachma coin.

DOSON Of uncertain meaning: traditionally 'going to give', i.e. 'always promising', but see Hammond and Walbank 1988, 337 n. 4. Appellation of Antigonus IV.

DOUBLE STRIKING The blurring of the type or legend occasioned by the die or coin having slipped between successive hammer blows.

DRACHM(A) The standard silver coin, divided into six OBOLS.

ELECTRUM An alloy of gold and silver, whether natural or artificial.

EMISSION see ISSUE

EPIPHANES, for THEOS EPIPHANES 'God Manifest' (appellation of Ptolemy V and Antiochus IV).

EUERGETES 'Benefactor' (appellation of Ptolemy III and VIII).

EXERGUE The lower segment of a coin, marked off from the rest by a horizontal ('exergual') line. Most coins of the Hellenistic period have no exergue.

FIELD The central space of a coin, more especially that left blank on either side of the main design.

FINENESS The proportion of precious metal used in an alloy in relation to its total weight.

FLAN see BLANK

FRATARAK A Persian title for a provincial governor.

GONATAS Appellation of Antigonus II of uncertain meaning, perhaps 'knock-kneed', cf. Hammond and Walbank 1988, 316 n. 3.

GORGONEION The facing head of the Gorgon Medusa, slain by Perseus, with snakes for hair.

HARPA The hooked sword used by Perseus.

HEGEMON Leader or president, especially of a confederacy such as the Corinthian League.

HELMET Various types occur on coins of the period. The most widely used, the *Corinthian,* was a large bowl, made from a single piece of metal, which covered head and cheeks, with a projecting nose-guard in front; the so-called *Attic* helmet was lighter but also covered the head closely, with a neck-guard behind, hinged cheek-pieces, and a frontlet rising upwards over the forehead; the *Boeotian* helmet, preferred for cavalry because it gave full visibility, was little more than a shallow metal hat with a downward-sloping rim; the *Phrygian* or *Macedonian* helmet had a metal peak in the shape of a Phrygian cap and hinged cheek-pieces which could be tied below the chin with a leather thong.

HEMIDRACHM A half-drachm coin.

HEMIOBOL A half-obol coin.

HERM A square pillar surmounted by a human head, usually that of Hermes (whence the name), and often serving as a boundary mark.

HIERAX 'Hawk' (appellation of Antiochus, brother of Seleucus II and usurper in Asia Minor).

HOARD A group of coins lost or hidden as a group, as distinct from coins lost separately even if sometimes found together, e.g. in a drain.

HUB A technical term used in die-sinking for a hardened bronze or iron cylinder on one end of which the coin type, or a substantial part of it, is engraved in relief.

HYBRID or MULE A coin produced from two dies, usually those of successive issues, not intended to have been used together.

IMMOBILIZATION The retention of a coin design or legend long after its details (e.g. the bust or name of a ruler) have ceased to be appropriate.

INSCRIPTION see LEGEND

ISSUE or EMISSION Coins presumed to have been issued in accordance with some specific mint directive; loosely, any related group of coins.

ITHYPHALLIC ODE An ode sung in a Bacchic procession, and by extension any poem in the same metre.

KALATHOS A vase-shaped basket.

KAUSIA A Macedonian flat-topped hat.

KHAROSHTHI An Indian script and language used in bilingual inscriptions on Bactrian coins.

KOINON A commonwealth.

KRATER A large bowl.

KTISTES 'Founder', 'restorer' (of a city or state).

KYRBASIA An oriental headdress with ear-flaps known from representations of Persian satraps and other officials. Often equated with BASHLIK, the Russian term for a hood with ear-flaps worn in the Caucasus and Iran.

L A symbol used as a prefix to the regnal years on late Ptolemaic coins and derived from an Egyptian notation used in papyri to indicate that the letters following it are year numerals.

LAGOBOLON or (Lat.) PEDUM A shepherd's crook, attribute of the god Pan.

LEGEND or INSCRIPTION The letters or words on a coin.

LITRA A weight originally used for bronze in South Italy and Sicily; by extension, a silver coin having the same value.

LITURGY A responsibility, accepted as an honour, entrusted by the state to a wealthy citizen and requiring him to defray the expenses of some public task (e.g. the presentation of a play, the equipment of a trireme).

MINA or MINE (*mna, mina*) An ancient oriental weight intermediate between the talent and the shekel but varying greatly according to nature, time and place; by extension, an accounting unit of 100 silver drachmae.

MINT A place where money is coined.

MINT MARK A symbol or one or more letters placed on a coin to indicate where it was struck; see also PRIVY MARK.

MODULE The diameter of a coin after striking.

MONEYER A person responsible for minting, including all the personnel of a mint.

MONOPHTHALMUS 'One-Eyed' (appellation of Antigonus I).

MULE see HYBRID

NEW STYLE (ATHENIAN) The term used by numismatists for the second- and first-century coins of Athens, which differ from those of the Classical period in their broad, thin flans, in their 'modernized' head of Athena, and in their cluttered reverse, the customary owl being shown perched on an amphora and flanked with a symbol and an inscription in several lines, the whole surrounded by a wreath.

NICATOR 'Victorious' (appellation of Seleucus I).

NIKE The winged goddess of Victory.

OBVERSE The side of the coin which bears the more important device or inscription. Usually identical with the face of the coin struck by the lower (anvil) die.

OCTOBOL An eight-obol coin.

OCTODRACHM An eight-drachma coin.

OFFICINA A workshop, subdivision of a mint.

OMPHALOS The sacred 'navel-stone' of Apollo at Delphi which was thought to mark the centre of Earth.

OVERSTRIKE A coin for which the blank was an older coin, traces of the earlier impression being still visible.

OWLS The popular name of Athenian coins (more especially tetradrachms) which had the owl of Athena as reverse type.

PEDUM see LAGOBOLON

PEGASI Coins of Corinth, and of mints under her influence, having the horse Pegasus as reverse type.

PENTADRACHM A five-drachma coin.

PERAIA An area of country 'on the other side' of a river or narrow sea, e.g. a stretch of coastland facing an island. Cf. Latin *trans* in, e.g., Trans-Jordan.

PETASOS A hat with a wide curving brim.

PHILADELPHUS 'Brother/sister-lover' (appellation of Arsinoe II and Ptolemy II).

PHILOPATOR 'Father-lover' (appellation of Ptolemy IV).

PILEUS A conical felt cap, e.g. that worn by the Dioscuri.

PLANCHET see BLANK

PLINTHOPHORIC A word used to describe a late Rhodian weight standard and based on the shallow incuse square, thought to resemble a brick (*plinthos*), containing the reverse design of the Rhodian coins.

POGON 'Beard' (appellation of Seleucus II).

POLIORCETES 'City-Besieger' (appellation of Demetrius, son of Antigonus I).

POLOS A high headdress.

PRIVY MARK A symbol or letter(s) placed on a coin as an element of mint administration or control. Privy marks were normally used for identifying mints (MINT MARKS) or the magistrates responsible for different issues.

PRYTANIS President, e.g. of a city council.

PUNCH DIE The upper die, also called a TRUSSEL.

QUADRIGA A chariot drawn by four horses, or occasionally four elephants.

QUADRIGATUS A silver coin (*c.* 6.9g) of the Roman Republic of the end of the third century, having as reverse type Jupiter in a quadriga.

RETROGRADE An inscription that reads backwards instead of forwards, either intentionally or through the carelessness of the die sinker.

REVERSE The opposite face of a coin to the OBVERSE (*q.v.*).

SANDAN The chief local deity of Tarsus, identified with Heracles by the Greeks.

SATRAP The title of a provincial governor in the Persian empire, retained under Alexander and his successors.

SHEKEL A standard unit of silver coinage in the Near East, called in Greek a SIGLOS and comparable to the DRACHMA in Greece.

SHIELD Various types occur on coins of the period. The *Argive* shield was large and circular (*hoplon*, 'round', whence 'hoplite'); the Macedonian shield was likewise circular but much smaller; the *Boeotian* shield was oval with an oval indentation at either side; the *Gaulish* shield was oval or ellipsoid.

SIGLOS see SHEKEL

SILPHIUM An extinct aromatic plant used in medicine and found only in Cyrenaica, where a representation of it regularly appears as a coin type.

SOTER 'Saviour' (appellation of Ptolemy I, Antiochus I and Seleucus III).

SPHINX A mythical monster having a human head and the body of a lion, usually winged.

STANDARD Properly speaking, an authorized exemplar of a unit of weight, which would vary from place to place, and by extension the system of weight based on this, so that a coin can be described as being struck to, e.g., the Attic standard. The word is also sometimes used for the lower ANVIL DIE.

STATER The principal denomination of a coinage, especially of gold, but could be applied to whatever coin predominated in circulation, such as the three-drachm piece at Corinth.

STEPHANOPHORUS ('wreath-bearer') A contemporary term, known from Delian inscriptions, for the 'New Style' Athenian tetradrachms, the name deriving from the wreath surrounding the reverse type.

STEPHANOS A crown, wreath.

STOLOS The beak or other ornament on a ship's prow.

STRATEGOS A military commander, general.

STYLIS Naval standard in the form of a pole with a crossbar.

SYMMACHIA A political alliance, defensive and offensive.

SYNOECISM Originally the merging of several separate communities in a single city, but by extension any close political league between neighbouring cities.

TAENIA A ribbon or band tied round the head, esp. as a sign of victory or rulership, i.e. a DIADEM.

TAGOS The head of the Thessalian Confederacy.

TALENT A unit of 60 minae or 6,000 drachmae.

TETARTEMORION A quarter-obol coin.

TETRADRACHM A four-drachma coin.

TETRAPOLIS 'Four cities', more especially the four Seleucid foundations in northern Syria of Seleucia Pieria, Antioch on the Orontes, Apamea and Laodicea ad Mare.

TETROBOL A four-obol coin.

THEOS 'God' (appellation of Antiochus II).

THUNDERBOLT The traditional weapon of Zeus, forged by Vulcan and shown on coins as a rod, often with three or more forked points at each end and often grasped by an eagle, the 'king of birds' consecrated to Zeus.

THYRSUS An attribute of Bacchus consisting of a staff or lance wrapped with ivy.

TRICHRYSON A Ptolemaic three-stater gold coin.

TRIHEMIDRACHM A three-hemidrachm coin, i.e. a piece of $1\frac{1}{2}$ drachms.

TRIHEMIOBOL A three-hemiobol coin, i.e. a piece of $1\frac{1}{2}$ obols.

TRIPOD A bronze three-legged stand supporting a bowl which was the sacred emblem of Apollo.

TRIPTOLEMUS The legendary inventor of agriculture.

TRUSSEL or PUNCH DIE The upper die.

TYCHE The goddess of Fortune, usually identified with the goddess of a city and shown wearing a mural crown (i.e. a crown with battlements).

TYPE The main design on each face of a coin; also a class or group of coins having the same design.

VICTORIATE A silver coin (*c.* 3.4g) of the Roman Republic of the late third century, having as reverse type a Victory crowning a trophy of arms.

XOANON A primitive, crudely carved image, usually of wood.

SELECT BIBLIOGRAPHY

The following pages include all works referred to in Mørkholm's footnotes, together with standard publications whose existence he took for granted but to which he had no occasion to refer. It has been updated by the inclusion of a selection of works published since his death and, to make it more generally useful, extended to include the later Hellenistic period.

A. LIST OF ABBREVIATIONS

AEPHE	*Annuaire de l'Ecole pratique des Hautes Etudes* (IVe section)
AIIN	*Annali [del] Istituto Italiano di Numismatica*
AJA	*American Journal of Archaeology*
AJN	*American Journal of Numismatics*
AMUGS	Antike Münzen und Geschnittene Steine
ANRW	*Aufstieg und Niedergang der römischen Welt: Geschichte und Kultur Roms im Spiegel der neueren Forschung*, ed. H. Temporini and W. Haase (Berlin/New York, 1972–)
ANS	American Numismatic Society
ANSMN	*Museum Notes* (American Numismatic Society)
BAR	British Archaeological Reports
BCH	*Bulletin de correspondance héllenique*
BMC	*Catalogue of the Greek Coins in the British Museum* (with suffix denoting area; see list in Section C)
BSFN	*Bulletin de la société française de numismatique*
CAH	*Cambridge Ancient History*
CH	*Coin Hoards*
CRAI	*Comptes-Rendus des Séances. Académie des Inscriptions et Belles Lettres*
ESM	see Newell 1938c
Essays Robinson (1968)	*Essays in Greek Coinage Presented to Stanley Robinson*, ed. C.M. Kraay and G.K. Jenkins (Oxford, 1968)
Essays Thompson (1979)	*Greek Numismatics and Archaeology. Essays in Honor of Margaret Thompson*, ed. O. Mørkholm and N.M. Waggoner (Wetteren, 1979)
Festschrift Mildenberg (1984)	*Festschrift für Leo Mildenberg*, ed. A. Houghton, S. Hurter, P. Erhart Mottahedeh and J. Ayer Scott (Wetteren, 1984)
IAPN	International Association of Professional Numismatists

IGCH — *An Inventory of Greek Coin Hoards*, ed. M. Thompson, O. Mørkholm and C.M. Kraay (New York, 1973)

INC — *International Numismatic Congress* (followed by place and date, as in the next entries, listed in chronological order)

INC London (1936) — *Transactions of the International Numismatic Congress, London, 1936*, ed. J. Allan, H. Mattingly and E.S.G. Robinson (London, 1938)

INC Paris — *Congrès international de numismatique, Paris, 6–11 juillet 1953*. I: *Rapports* (Paris, 1953); II: *Actes* (Paris, 1957)

INC Rome — *Congresso internazionale di numismatica, Roma. 11–16 settembre 1961*. I: *Relazioni* (Rome, 1961); II: *Atti* (Rome, 1965)

INC Copenhagen — *A Survey of Numismatic Research 1960–1965*. I: *Ancient Numismatics*, ed. O. Mørkholm (Copenhagen, 1967)

INC New York–Washington Surv. — *A Survey of Numismatic Research 1966–1971*, I: *Ancient Numismatics*, ed. P. Naster, J.-B. Colbert de Beaulieu and J.M. Fagerlie (New York, 1973)

INC New York–Washington Proc. — *Proceedings of the 8th International Congress of Numismatics, New York–Washington, September 1973* (IAPN Special Publ. 4, Paris-Basel, 1976)

INC Berne Surv. — *A Survey of Numismatic Research 1972–1977*, ed. R. Carson, P. Berghaus and N. Lowick (Berne, 1979)

INC Berne Acts — *Actes du 9e Congrès international de numismatique, Berne, septembre 1979*. I: *Numismatique antique*, ed. T. Hackens and R. Weiller (IAPN Special Publ. 6, Louvain-la-Neuve, 1982)

INC London (1986) — *A Survey of Numismatic Research 1978–1984*, ed. M. Price, E. Besly, D. MacDowell, M. Jones and A. Oddy. I: *Ancient, Medieval and Modern Numismatics*; III: *Index* (IAPN Special Publ. 9, London, 1986)

INJ — *Israel Numismatic Journal*

Inscriptiones Creticae — *Inscriptiones Creticae*, ed. F. Halbheer. I– (Rome, 1935–)

JHS — *Journal of Hellenic Studies*

JNG — *Jahrbuch für Numismatik und Geldgeschichte*

KME (1989) — *Kraay–Mørkholm Essays. Numismatic Studies in Memory of C.M. Kraay and O. Mørkholm* (Numismatica Lovaniensia 10, Louvain-la-Neuve, 1989)

KUML — *KUML. Årbog for Jysk Arkæologisk Selskab*

NAPM (1975) — *Numismatique antique; problèmes et méthodes. Actes du colloque organisé à Nancy du 27 septembre au 2 octobre 1971* (Etudes d'archéologie classique IV = Annales de l'Est, Mém. no. 44, Nancy/Louvain, 1975)

NC — *Numismatic Chronicle*

NCirc. — *Numismatic Circular*

Nickle Papers — *Ancient Coins of the Graeco-Roman World. The Nickle Numismatic Papers*, ed. E. Heckel and R. Sullivan (Ontario, 1984)

NNÅ — *Nordisk Numismatisk Årsskrift*

NNM	Numismatic Notes and Monographs (American Numismatic Society)
NS	Numismatic Studies (American Numismatic Society)
OGIS	*Orientis graeci inscriptiones selectae*, ed. W. Dittenberger (2 vols., Leipzig, 1903)
Pap. Cairo Zenon	*Catalogue générale des antiquités égyptiennes du Musée du Caire. Zenon Papyri*, ed. C.C. Edgar (4 vols., Cairo, 1925–31)
PCG	*A Guide to the Principal Coins of the Greeks from circ. 700 B.C. to A.D. 270 based on the work of Barclay V. Head* (revised edn, London, 1959)
PW	A. Fr. von Pauly and G. Wissowa, *Realencyclopädie der Altertumswissenschaft* (Stuttgart, 1892ff.)
QT	*Quaderni ticinesi di numismatica e antichità classiche*
RBN	*Revue belge de numismatique*
Recueil	see Waddington *et al.* 1902–12
RN	*Revue numismatique*
RSN	*Revue suisse de numismatique* (= *SNR*)
SAN	*SAN. Journal of the Society for Ancient Numismatics*
SM	*Schweizer Münzblätter*
SNG	*Sylloge Nummorum Graecorum* (followed by Roman numeral for British volumes or by name of place or owner, e.g. Copenhagen or von Aulock, for non-British. See list of relevant volumes in Section C)
SNR	*Schweizerische Numismatische Rundschau* (= *RSN*)
Studia Naster (1982)	*Studia Paulo Naster oblata.* I: *Numismatica antiqua*, ed. S. Scheers (Orientalia Lovaniensia Analecta 12, Louvain, 1982)
Studies Grierson (1983)	*Studies in Numismatic Method Presented to Philip Grierson*, ed. C.N.L. Brooke, B.H.I.H. Stewart, J.G. Pollard and T.R. Volk (Cambridge, 1983)
Studies Miles (1974)	*Near Eastern Numismatics, Iconography, Epigraphy, and History. Studies in Honor of George C. Miles*, ed. D.K. Kouymjian (Beirut, 1974)
Studies Robinson (1951)	*Studies Presented to David Moore Robinson*, ed. G.E. Mylonas (2 vols., St Louis, 1951)
WSM	See Newell 1941
YCS	*Yale Classical Studies*
ZfN	*Zeitschrift für Numismatik*

B. REGIONAL BIBLIOGRAPHIES

The most complete regional bibliographies are provided by a series entitled 'Literaturüberblicke der griechischen Numismatik', initially published in *JNG* 1955ff. and continued in *Chiron* 1972ff., though the earlier of these are necessarily now out of date and not all regions are covered. Several detailed ones are included in works listed in Section D (Alföldi 1978; Bosch 1949). Current literature can be traced in the periodical *Numismatic Literature* (New York, 1949–), published by the ANS, which summarizes the contents of the works it lists, and in the 'Surveys of numismatic research' published in connexion with recent international numismatic congresses (see preceding section, s.v. *INC*).

The 'Literaturüberblicke', other than those concerned with western coinages, are as follows:

'Epirus, Makedonien', *JNG* 7 (1956), 77–138 (by P.R. Franke)
'Peloponnes', *JNG* 8 (1957), 57–120 (by H. Chantraine)
'Euboea', *JNG* 9 (1958), 19–56 (by H. Chantraine)
'Mysien, Troas, Aeolis, Lesbos', *JNG* 10 (1959/60), 91–162 (by F. Kiechle)
'Cistophoren', *JNG* 11 (1961), 159–88 (by D. Kienast)
'Ionien', *JNG* 12 (1962), 113–88 (by D. Kienast)
'Moesien, Thrakien', *JNG* 15 (1965), 75–194 (by E. Schönert-Geiss)
'Zentralgriechenland: Locris – Phocien – Boeotien', *JNG* 17 (1967), 35–93 (by H. Gesche)
'Altjudische Münzen', *JNG* 17 (1967), 159–298 (by B. Janael)
'Cypern', *JNG* 20 (1970), 161–216 (by H.R. Baldus)
'Kolchis', *Chiron* 2 (1972), 565–610 (by K. Golenko)
'Pontus und Paphlagonien (Veröffentlichungen in Russland und der Sowjetunion)', *Chiron* 3 (1973), 467–99 (by K. Golenko)
'Nordliches Schwarzmeergebiet', *Chiron* 5 (1975), 497–642 (by K. Golenko)
'Bithynien', *Chiron* 8 (1978), 607–57 (by E. Schönert-Geiss)
'Seleukiden', *Chiron* 15 (1985), 283–389 (by T. Fischer)
'Kilikien', *Chiron* 18 (1988), 91–170 (by S. Schultz)

C. PRINCIPAL PUBLISHED COLLECTIONS

Since 'Greek' coins – this term traditionally covers all ancient coins that are not 'Roman' – are customarily arranged regionally under mints, and there are few collections specifically concerned with coins of the Hellenistic period, the material is inevitably very scattered. That in published collections has to be supplemented by the contents of auction catalogues, which are usually well illustrated and in some cases, notably in catalogues published over recent decades by the firms of Münzen und Medaillen AG Basel, Bank Leu (Zurich) and Frank Sternberg (Zurich), the descriptions of rarities are accompanied by scholarly discussions of attribution and dating. Auction catalogues are too numerous to be included here. The more important ones on ancient numismatics are listed in P. Grierson, *Bibliographie numismatique* (2nd edn, Brussels, 1979), 278–89. The list in Vol. 7 of the *Dictionary Catalogue of the Library of the American Numismatic Society* (Boston, 1962; *Supplements* 1968, 1973, 1978) is much fuller, but since it is arranged under dealers and owners and not under subjects it is less easy to use.

Aberdeen	see *SNG GB* 1.2
ANS	see *SNG ANS* and *SNG Berry*
Aulock, von	see *SNG von Aulock*
Berlin	*Beschreibung der antiken Münzen* (3 vols., Berlin, 1888–94). These cover only the northern Balkans and early Macedon. Many otherwise unpublished coins in the Berlin collection are illustrated in Regling 1924
Berry	See *SNG Berry*
BMC	*Catalogue of Greek Coins in the British Museum* (London, 1873ff.; repr. Bologna, 1963ff.). The volumes containing coins of the Hellenistic period, other than western ones, are as

follows, in order of date of publication; *Thrace*, by P.V. Head and P. Gardner (1877); *Seleucid Kings of Syria*, by P. Gardner (1878); *Macedonia*, by B.V. Head (1879); *Thessaly to Aetolia*, by P. Gardner (1883); *Ptolemaic Kings of Egypt*, by R.S. Poole (1883); *Central Greece*, by B.V. Head (1884); *Crete and the Aegean Islands*, by W. Wroth (1886); *Peloponnesus*, by P. Gardner (1887); *Attica, Megaris, Aegina*, by B.V. Head (1888); *Corinth and her Colonies*, by B.V. Head (1889); *Pontus, Paphlagonia, Bithynia and Kingdom of Bosphorus*, by W. Wroth (1889); *Mysia*, by W. Wroth (1892); *Alexandria and the Nomes*, by R.S. Poole (1892); *Ionia*, by B.V. Head (1892); *Troas, Aeolis and Lesbos*, by W. Wroth (1894); *Caria and the Islands*, by B.V. Head (1897); *Lycia, Pamphylia and Pisidia*, by G.F. Hill (1897); *Galatia, Cappadocia and Syria*, by W. Wroth (1899); *Lycaonia, Isauria and Cilicia*, by G.F. Hill (1900); *Lydia*, by B.V. Head (1902); *Parthia*, by W. Wroth (1903); *Cyprus*, by G.F. Hill (1901); *Phrygia*, by B.V. Head (1906); *Phoenicia*, by G.F. Hill (1910); *Palestine*, by G.F. Hill (1914); *Arabia, Mesopotamia, Persia, etc.*, by G.F. Hill (1922); *Cyrenaica*, by E.S.G. Robinson (1927). The coins of Bactria were relegated to the first volume of the *Catalogue of Indian Coins in the British Museum: The Coins of the Greek and Scythic Kings of Bactria and India* by P. Gardner (London, 1886; repr. Chicago, 1960; New Delhi, 1971)

Boston	A. Baldwin Brett, *Museum of Fine Arts. Catalogue of Greek Coins* (Boston, 1955); see also Warren (below) and M. Comstock and C. Vermeule, *Greek Coins 1950 to 1963* (Boston, 1964)
Brussels	P. Naster, *La collection Lucien de Hirsch* (Brussels, 1959)
Cambridge, Corpus Christi College	See *SNG GB* VI
Cambridge, Fitzwilliam Museum	S.W. Grose, *Catalogue of the McClean Collection of Greek Coins in the Fitzwilliam Museum, Cambridge* (3 vols., Cambridge, 1923–9); see also *SNG GB* IV
Copenhagen	see *SNG Copenhagen*
Courtauld	G. Pollard, *A Catalogue of the Greek Coins in the Collection of Sir Stephen Courtauld at the University College of Rhodesia* (Salisbury, Rhodesia, 1970). Now Harare, Zimbabwe
Davis	H. Troxell, *The Norman Davis Collection* (New York, 1969)
Evelpidis	See *SNG Evelpidis*
Glasgow	G. Macdonald, *Catalogue of the Greek Coins in the Hunterian Collection* (3 vols., Glasgow, 1899–1905)
Gulbenkian II	G.K. Jenkins and M. Castro Hipólito, *A Catalogue of the Calouste Gulbenkian Collection of Greek Coins*. Part II: *Greece to East* (Lisbon, 1990). The first volume, by E.S.G. Robinson (Lisbon, 1971), is concerned with Western coins (Italy, Sicily, Carthage)

Harare	See Courtauld
Herat	D.W. MacDowell and M. Ibrahim, 'Pre-Islamic coins in Herat Museum', *Afghan Studies* 2 (1979), 45–51
Hirsch	See Brussels
Houghton	A. Houghton, *Coins of the Seleucid Empire from the Collection of Arthur Houghton* (Ancient Coins in North American Collections, New York, 1983)
Hunter	See Glasgow
Jameson	*Collection R. Jameson. Monnaies grecques antiques* (4 vols., Paris, 1913–32). Dispersed
Kandahar	D.W. MacDowell and M. Ibrahim, 'Pre-Islamic coins in Kandahar Museum', *Afghan Studies* 1 (1978), 67–77
Lahore	R.B. Whitehead, *Catalogue of the Coins in the Punjab Museum. 1: Indo-Greek Coins* (Oxford, 1914)
Lisbon	See Gulbenkian
Locker-Lampson	E.S.G. Robinson, *Catalogue of Ancient Greek Coins Collected by G. Locker Lampson* (London, 1923). Dispersed
Lockett	See *SNG GB* III (Lockett)
London, British Museum	See *BMC*; a selection of Greek coins is published in *PCG*
Luynes	See Paris, Bibliothèque Nationale
McClean	See Cambridge, Fitzwilliam Museum
Munich	See *SNG Munich*
Nanteuil	H. de Nanteuil, *Collection de monnaies grecques* (Paris, 1925). Still exists, but in other hands
Newnham-Davis	See *SNG GB* I
New York	See *SNG ANS* and *SNG Berry*
Oxford	See *SNG GB* V
Paris, Bibliothèque Nationale	E. Babelon, *Catalogue des monnaies grecques de la Bibliothèque Nationale. Rois de Syrie, d'Arménie et de Commagène* (Paris, 1890) E. Babelon, *Catalogue des monnaies grecques de la Bibliothèque Nationale. Les Perses Achéménides, les satrapes, et les dynastes tributaires de leur empire. Chypre et Phénicie* (Paris, 1893) J. Babelon, *Catalogue de la collection de Luynes* (4 vols., Paris, 1924–36) See also Waddington *et al.* 1902–12
Pozzi	S. Boutin, *Catalogue des monnaies grecques antiques de la collection Pozzi* (2 vols., Maastricht, 1979). A very fully illustrated catalogue (but omitting the weights of the bronze coins) of a great private collection that was prepared in 1918, left incomplete as a result of the owner's death, and published only long afterwards. It covers only European mints; for Asiatic mints and Egypt one has to use the sale catalogue, Lucien Naville, Geneva, 4.iv.1921; repr. Zurich/Amsterdam, 1966
Salisbury	See Courtauld

Salting — See *SNG GB* 1

Spencer-Churchill — See *SNG GB* 1

SNG — *Sylloge Nummorum Graecorum*. This is the general title of several series of fascicles, for the most part of identical format, whose contents are in principle limited to the illustration and summary description of the coins, without further text. Many of them, and particularly the earlier ones published, omit bronze coins as being of little consequence for die studies. They are listed here in alphabetical order of the ways in which they are commonly abbreviated

SNG Aarhus — (Danish Series B) *Aarhus University, Denmark* (1986); see also *SNG Fabricius*

SNG ANS — (American Series B) *American Numismatic Society*. Parts 1–5 (1969–88) are concerned with Western coins; 6 (1981), *Palestine–South Arabia*; 7 (1987), *Cities, Thraco-Macedonian Tribes, Paeonian Kings*

SNG Berry — (*American Series A*) *Burton Y. Berry Collection*. Part 1 (1961), *Macedonia–Attica*, by M. Thompson and R. Holloway; 2 (1962), *Megaris–Egypt*, by M. Thompson and R. Holloway. In the ANS Museum

SNG Copenhagen — (Danish series A) *The Royal Collection of Coins and Medals, Danish National Museum* (43 parts, Copenhagen, 1942–79; 39 parts repr. in 7 vols., West Milford, N.J., 1981–2). The first five fascicles (1942) cover Italy and Sicily and Parts 42–3 (1969–79) North Africa (Syrtica–Mauritania) and Spain. The others are as follows: 6–7 (1942–3), *Thrace*; 8–10 (1943), *Macedonia* (includes the coins of Alexander the Great and his Successors struck outside Macedonia); 11 (1943), *Thessaly–Illyricum*; 12 (1943), *Epirus–Acarnania*; 13 (1944), *Aetolia–Euboea*; 14 (1944), *Attica–Aegina*; 15 (1944), *Corinth*; 16 (1944), *Phliasia–Laconia*; 17 (1944), *Argolis–Aegean Islands*; 18 (1944), *Bosporus–Bithynia*; 19 (1944), *Mysia*; 20–1 (1945), *Troas–Lesbos*; 22–4 (1945), *Ionia*; 25–6 (1947), *Caria*; 27–8 (1947), *Lydia*; 29–30 (1948), *Phrygia*; 31 (1955), *Lycia–Pamphylia*; 32 (1956), *Pisidia*; 33 (1956), *Lycaonia–Cilicia*; 34 (1956), *Cyprus, Cappodocia, Uncertain Coins and Imperial Cistophori*; 35 (1959), *Syria: Seleucid Kings*; 36 (1959), *Syria: Cities*; 37 (1961), *Phoenicia*; 38 (1961), *Palestine–Characene*; 39 (1965), *Parthia–India*; 40 (1977), *Egypt: The Ptolemies*; 41 (1974), *Alexandria–Cyrenaica*. See also *SNG Fabricius*

SNG Evelpidis — (Greek series) *Athens: Collection Rena H. Evelpidis* (Louvain, 1970–). Part 1 (1970), *Italie, Sicile, Thrace*, by T. Hackens and R. Evelpidis; 2 (1975), *Macédoine, Thessalie, Illyrie, Épire, Corcyre*, by T. Hackens and R. Evelpidis

SNG Fabricius — (Danish series A + B). *The Fabricius Collection – Aarhus Uni-*

versity and Royal Collection of Coins and Medals (Copenhagen, 1987)

SNG GB — (British series) This is notionally divided into a number of 'volumes', each consisting of a number of separately published parts but each except the first (*SNG GB* I) confined to a single collection and normally referred to as such. Vol. II (*Lloyd Collection*) is confined to south Italy and Sicily and the coins are now in the BM

SNG GB I — Part 1 (1931), *Collection of Capt. E.G. Spencer-Churchill of Northwick Park* (now dispersed) and *The Salting Collection in the Victoria and Albert Museum* [*London*]; 2 (1936) *The Newnham Davis Coins in the Wilson Collection of Classical and Eastern Antiquities, Marischal College, Aberdeen*

SNG GB III — *Lockett Collection* (5 parts (unfinished), 1938–49). Now dispersed. Part 1 (1938) is purely Western. The other parts are: 2 (1939), *Sicily–Thrace*; 3 (1938), *Macedonia–Aegina*; 4 (1942), *Peloponnese–Aeolis*; 5 (1949), *Lesbos–Cyrenaica, Addenda*. The coins are lavishly illustrated in the catalogues of the sales in which the collection was dispersed (Glendining, London: 25.x.1955; 12.ii.1958; 27.v.1959; 21.ii.1961). These are in any case necessary for sections not covered in the *SNG* volumes

SNG GB IV — *Fitzwilliam Museum, Cambridge: Leake and General Collections* (in progress, 1940ff.). This complements Grose's catalogue of the McClean collection; see 'Cambridge, Fitzwilliam Museum' (above). Part 1 is Western. The others are as follows: 2 (1947; repr. 1972), *Sicily–Thrace*; 3 (1951), *Macedonia–Acarnania*; 4 (1956), *Acarnania–Phliasia*; 5 (1958), *Sicyon–Thera*; 6 (1965), *Asia Minor: Phrygia*; 7 (1967), *Asia Minor: Lycia–Cappadocia*; 8 (1971), *Syria–Nabathaea*

SNG GB V — *Ashmolean Museum, Oxford* (in progress, 1951ff.). Parts 1 and 2 are Western; Part 3 (1976), *Macedonia*

SNG GB VI — *The Lewis Collection in Corpus Christi College, Cambridge*. Part 1 (1972), *The Greek and Hellenistic Coins* (*with Britain and Parthia*), by M. Price; Part 2 (1978) consists of Greek imperial coins

SNG Munich — (German Series B) *Staatliche Münzsammlung München*. The first six parts (Berlin, 1968–80) cover Western coinages. Part 7 (1985), *Taurische Chersones, Sarmatien, Dacia, Moesia Superior, Moesia Inferior*; Part 24 (1989), *Phrygien*

SNG Sweden I — *The Collection of His Late Majesty King Gustaf VI Adolf and the Fred Forbat Collection*, by U. Westermark (Stockholm, 1974)

SNG Sweden II — *The Collection of the Royal Coin Cabinet, National Museum of Monetary History, Stockholm*. Part 1 (1976) is Western: Part 2 (1980), *Thrace–Euboea*; 3 (1990), *Attica–Aeolis*

SNG Switzerland I — *Levante–Cilicia*, by Edoardo Levante (Berne, 1986)

SNG Tübingen — *Münzsammlung der Universität Tübingen*. Part 1 (Berlin, 1981) covers Western coinages. Part 2 (1982), *Taurische Chersones–Korkyra*; 3 (1985), *Akarnanien–Bithynien*; 4 (1989), *Mysien–Ionien*

SNG von Aulock — (German Series A) *Sammlung von Aulock* (19 parts, incl. *Nachträge* and *Index*. Berlin, 1957–81; repr. West Milford, N.J., 1987). Limited to mints within the territory of modern Turkey, the collector Hans von Aulock (1895–1980) having resided in Istanbul. The parts are as follows, the author of each being von Aulock himself unless another name is given: 1–3 (1957), *Pontus, Paphlagonia, Bithynia*, by G. Kleiner; 4 (1957; 2nd edn, 1966), *Mysien*, by K. Kraft; 5 (1959), *Troas, Aeolis, Lesbos*, by K. Kraft; 6 (1960; 2nd edn, 1969), *Ionien*, by K. Kraft and H. Küthmann; 7 (1962; 2nd edn, 1969), *Karien*, by K. Kraft and D. Kienast; 8 (1963), *Lydien*; 9 (1964), *Phrygien*, by H.-W. Ritter; 10 (1964; 2nd edn, 1971), *Lykien*, by O. Mørkholm; 11 (1965), *Pamphylien*, by O. Mørkholm; 12 (1964), *Pisidien, Lykaonien, Isaurien*; 13 (1966), *Kilikien*; 14 (1967), *Galatien, Kappadokien, kaiserzeitliche Kistophoren, posthume Lysimachus- und Alexander-Tetradrachmen, Incerti*; 15 (1967), *Nachträge* I: *Pontus, Paphlagonien, Bithynien*; 16 (1967), *Nachträge* II: *Mysien, Troas, Aeolis, Lesbos*; 17 (1968), *Nachträge* III: *Ionien, Karien, Lydien*; 18 (1968), *Nachträge* IV: *Phrygien, Lykien, Pamphylien, Pisidien, Lykaonien, Isaurien, Kilikien, Galatien, Kappadokien, kaiserzeitliche Kistophoren, Incerti*; 19 (1981), *Index*, by P.R. Franke, W. Leschhorn, and A.U. Stylow

Stockholm — see *SNG Sweden*; unless otherwise stated, the references are to *SNG Sweden* II

Ward — G.F. Hill, *Descriptive Catalogue of Greek Coins belonging to John Ward* (London, 1901). Now dispersed. The collection was acquired by J.P. Morgan, presented by him to the Metropolitan Museum of Art, New York, deposited on indefinite loan for many years with the ANS, and sold by the Metropolitan Museum (Sotheby, Zürich: 4.iv.1973)

Warren — K. Regling, *Die griechischen Münzen der Sammlung Warren* (Berlin, 1906). The collection passed to the Museum of Fine Arts, Boston, and Regling's catalogue is now superseded; see Boston (above)

Weber — L. Forrer, *Descriptive Catalogue of the Collection of Greek Coins formed by Sir Hermann Weber* (13 vols. (in 4), London, 1922–9). Acquired by Spink's and now dispersed

Winterthur — H.J. Bloesch, *Griechische Münzen in Winterthur. Münzkabinett der Stadt Winterthur*. Vol. I (in 2 parts), *Spanien, Gallien, Italien*,

Sizilien, Moesien, Dakien, Sarmatien, Thrakien, Makedonien, Hellas, Inseln (Winterthur, 1988)

Woodward — E.S.G. Robinson, *Ancient Greek Coins in the Possession of W.H. Woodward* (Oxford, 1928). Dispersed; see Ars Classica Auction 15 (Lucerne), 2.ii.1930

D. SECONDARY LITERATURE

ABGARIANS AND SELLWOOD 1971 M.T. Abgarians and D.G. Sellwood, 'A hoard of early Parthian drachms', *NC*[7] 11 (1971), 103–19.

ALFÖLDI 1978 M.R. Alföldi, *Antike Numismatik.* I: *Theorie und Praxis*; II: *Bibliographie* (Munich, 1978).

ALLEN 1983 R.E. Allen, *The Attalid Kingdom. A Constitutional History* (Oxford, 1983).

ALLOTTE 1902 F.M. Allotte de la Fuÿe, 'La dynastie des Kamnaskères', *RN*[4] 6 (1902), 92–114.

1904a F.M. Allotte de la Fuÿe, 'Monnaies arsacides surfrappées', *RN*[4] 8 (1904), 174–96.

1904b F.M. Allotte de la Fuÿe, 'Nouveau classement des monnaies arsacides d'après le catalogue du British Museum', *RN*[4] 8 (1904), 317–71.

1905 F.M. Allotte de la Fuÿe, 'Monnaies arsacides de la collection Petrowicz', *RN*[4] 9 (1905), 129–69.

1931 F.M. Allotte de la Fuÿe, 'Une monnaie inédite de Phraate II', *RN*[4] 34 (1931), 1–3.

AMANDRY 1989 M. Amandry, 'Les tétradrachmes à la couronne de feuillage frappés à Lébédos (Ionie)', in *KME* (1989), 1–7.

AMANDRY AND CALLOT 1988 M. Amandry and O. Callot, 'Le trésor de Failaka 1984 (Kuwait)', *RN*[6] 30 (1988), 64–74.

ASHTON 1986 R.H.J. Ashton, 'Rhodian bronze coinage and the earthquake of 229–226 B.C.', *NC* 146 (1986), 1–18.

1987a R.H.J. Ashton, 'Pseudo-Rhodian drachms and the beginnings of the Lycian League coinage', *NC* 147 (1987), 8–25.

1987b R.H.J. Ashton, 'Rhodian-type silver coinages from Crete', *SM* 37 (1987), 29–36.

1988a R.H.J. Ashton, 'Rhodian coinage and the Colossus', *RN*[6] 30 (1988), 75–90.

1988b R.H.J. Ashton, 'A series of pseudo-Rhodian drachms from mainland Greece', *NC* 148 (1988), 21–32.

1988c R.H.J. Ashton, 'Pseudo-Rhodian drachms from Samothrace', *NC* 148 (1988), 129–34.

1988d R.H.J. Ashton, 'A pseudo-Rhodian drachm from Kaunos', *SM* 38 (1988), 67–70.

1989 R.H.J. Ashton, 'A series of Rhodian didrachms from the mid-third century B.C.', *NC* 149 (1989), 1–14.

ATHENIAN AGORA 1976 *The Athenian Agora. A Guide to the Excavations and Museum* (3rd edn, Athens, 1976).

AUDOUIN AND BERNARD 1973, 1974 R. Audouin and P. Bernard, 'Trésor de monnaies indiennes et indo-grecques d'Aï Khanoum (Afghanistan)', *RN*[6] 15 (1973), 238–89; 16 (1974), 6–41.

AULOCK 1964 H. von Aulock, 'Die Prägung des Balakros in Kilikien', *JNG* 14 (1964), 79–82.

AYMARD 1953 A. Aymard, 'Autour de l'avènement d'Antiochos IV', *Historia* 2 (1953), 49–73.

BABELON 1893 E. Babelon, *Catalogue des monnaies grecques de la Bibliothèque Nationale. Les Perses Achéménides, les satrapes, et les dynastes tributaires de leur empire. Chypre et Phénicie* (Paris, 1893).

1901–14 E. Babelon, *Traité des monnaies grecques et romaines.* I: *Theorie et doctrine* (Paris, 1901); II: *Description historique*, part 2: *Comprenant les monnaies de l'empire des perses achéménides, de l'orient sémitique et de l'Asie Mineure aux Ve et IVe siècles avant J.-C.* (Paris, 1910); part 3: *Comprenant les monnaies de la Grèce centrale et méridionale aux Ve et IVe siècles avant J.-C.* (Paris, 1914).

BADIAN 1968 E. Badian, *Roman Imperialism in the Late Republic* (Ithaca, 1968).

1983 E. Badian, *Publicans and Sinners: Private Enterprise in the Service of the Roman Republic* (2nd edn, Ithaca, 1983).

BALDUS 1964 H.R. Baldus, 'Zu den phönischen Bronzemünzen des Tryphon aus Askalon', *SM* 13–14 (1964), 145–7.

1970 H.R. Baldus, 'Der Helm des Tryphon und die seleukische Chronologie der Jahre 146–138 v. Chr.', *JNG* 20 (1970), 217–39.

1987 H.R. Baldus, 'Syria', in *The Coinage of the Roman World in the Late Republic* (B A R International Series 326, Oxford, 1987), 121–51.

BALDWIN 1924 A. Baldwin [Brett], 'The gold staters of Lampsakos', *AJN* 53, Part 3 (1924), 1–77.

BALDWIN BRETT 1938 A. Baldwin Brett, 'The aphlaston, symbol of naval victory or supremacy on Greek and Roman coins', in *INC London (1936)*, 23–32.

1945 A. Baldwin Brett, 'Seleucid coins of Ake-Ptolemais in Phoenicia', *ANSMN* 1 (1945), 17–35.

1950 A. Baldwin Brett, 'The mint of Ascalon under the Seleucids', *ANSMN* 4 (1950), 43–54.

BARAG AND QEDAR 1980 D. Barag and Sh. Qedar, 'The beginning of Hasmonean coinage', *Israel Numismatic Journal* 4 (1980), 8–21.

BARRANDON AND NICOLET-PIERRE 1989 J.N. Barrandon and H. Nicolet-Pierre, 'Analyses de monnaies royales gréco-bactriennes et indo-grecques des IIe-Ier siècles avant J.-C.', *SM* 39 (1989), 57–66.

BARRON 1966 J.P. Barron, *The Silver Coins of Samos* (London, 1966).

BAUSLAUGH 1979 R.A. Bauslaugh, 'The posthumous Alexander coinage of Chios', *ANSMN* 24 (1979), 1–45.

1982 R.A. Bauslaugh, 'The unique portrait tetradrachm of Eumenes II', *ANSMN* 27 (1982), 39–51.

1987 R.A. Bauslaugh, 'Two unpublished overstrikes: New Style Athens and Aesillas the quaestor', *ANSMN* 32 (1987), 11–21.

BEDOUKIAN 1968 P.Z. Bedoukian, 'A classification of the coins of the Artaxiad dynasty of Armenia', *ANSMN* 14 (1968), 41–66.

1970 P.Z. Bedoukian, 'A coin of Tigranes the Great of Armenia, struck in Commagene', NC^7 10 (1970), 19–22.

1974 P.Z. Bedoukian, 'Some unpublished coins of the Artaxiads of Armenia', in *Studies Miles* (1974), 27–35.

1978 P.Z. Bedoukian, *Coinage of the Artaxiads of Armenia* (Royal Numismatic Society, Special Publication 10, London, 1978).

BELLINGER 1944a A.R. Bellinger, 'The bronze standards of Antiochus III, Seleucus IV, and Antiochus IV', *Numismatic Review* 2 (1944), 5–6.

1944b A.R. Bellinger, 'Parthian drachmae of Orodes II and Phraates IV', NC^6 4 (1944), 62–4.

1945 A.R. Bellinger, 'The bronze coins of Timarchus' *ANSMN* 1 (1945), 37–44.

1948 A.R. Bellinger, 'A Seleucid mint at Elaeusa Sebaste', *ANSMN* 3 (1948), 27–30.

1949a A.R. Bellinger, 'The end of the Seleucids', *Transactions of the Connecticut Academy of Arts and Sciences* 38 (1949), 51–102.

1949b A.R. Bellinger, *The Excavations at Dura Europos. Final Report.* VI: *The Coins* (New Haven, 1949).

1961 A.R. Bellinger, *Troy. The Coins* (Princeton, 1961).

1963 A.R. Bellinger, *Essays on the Coinage of Alexander the Great* (NS 11, New York, 1963).

1964 A.R. Bellinger, 'Philippi in Macedonia', *ANSMN* 11 (1964), 29–52.

1965 A.R. Bellinger, 'The Thessaly hoard of 1938', in *INC Rome Atti* (1965), 57–60.

BÉREND 1972 D. Bérend, 'Les tétradrachmes de Rhodes de la première période. lère partie', *SNR* 51 (1972), 5–39.

BERNARD 1975 P. Bernard, 'Note sur la signification historique de la trouvaille [d'Aï Khanoum]', *RN*^{6} 17 (1975), 58–69.

1985 P. Bernard, *Fouilles d'Aï Khanoum*. IV: *Les monnaies hors trésors: questions d'histoire gréco-bactrienne* (Mém. de la délégation archéologique française en Afghanistan 28, Paris, 1985).

BERNARD AND GUILLAUME 1980 P. Bernard and O. Guillaume, 'Monnaies inédites de la Bactriane grecque à Aï Khanoum (Afghanistan)', *RN*^{6} 22 (1980), 9–32.

BEVAN 1902 E.R. Bevan, *The House of Seleucus* (2 vols., London, 1902).

BICKERMAN 1938 E. Bickerman, *Institutions des Séleucides* (Paris, 1938); see esp. 'Le monnayage séleucide' (pp. 211–38).

1968 E.J. Bickerman, *Chronology of the Ancient World* (London, 1968).

BINGEN 1973 J. Bingen, 'Le trésor monétaire Thorikos 1969', *Thorikos* VI (Brussels, 1973), 7–59.

1975 J. Bingen, 'Le trésor de tétradrachmes attiques du style P1', in *Thorikos and the Laurion in Archaic and Classical Times* (Miscellanea Graeca 1, Ghent, 1975), 161–70.

BIVAR 1950 A.D.H. Bivar, 'The death of Eucratides in medieval tradition', *Journal of the Royal Asiatic Society* (1950), 7–13.

1951 A.D.H. Bivar, 'The Bactra coinage of Euthydemus and Demetrius', *NC*^{6} 11 (1951), 22–39.

1965 A.D.H. Bivar, 'Indo-Bactrian problems', *NC*^{7} 5 (1965), 69–108.

1970 A.D.H. Bivar, 'The sequence of Menander's drachmae', *Journal of the Royal Asiatic Society* 1970, 123–36.

1984 A.D.H. Bivar, 'Maues at Taxila. Problems of his arrival route and political allegiance', *Journal of Central Asia* 7 (1984), 5–14.

BLOESCH 1979 H. Bloesch, 'Tetradrachms of Aegeae (Cilicia)', in *Essays Thompson* (1979), 1–7.

1982 H. Bloesch, 'Hellenistic coins of Aegeae (Cilicia)', *ANSMN* 27 (1982), 53–96.

BODENSTEDT 1976 F. Bodenstedt, *Phokäisches Elektron-Geld von 600–326 v. Chr.* (Mainz, 1976).

1981 F. Bodenstedt, *Die Elektronmünzen von Phokaia und Mytilene* (Tübingen, 1981).

BOEHRINGER 1972 C. Boehringer, *Zur Chronologie mittelhellenistischer Münzserien 220–160 v. Chr.* (AMUGS V, Berlin, 1972).

BOPEARACHCHI 1989 O. Bopearachchi, 'Un roi indo-grec: Télèphe. Observations sur l'iconographie de son monnayage et la date de son règne', *SM* 39 (1989), 88–94.

BOSCH 1949 E. Bosch, *Türkiyenin antik devirdeki meskûkâtina dair bibliografiya* ('Bibliography of ancient coinage from within Turkey') (Ankara, 1949).

BOUCHÉ-LECLERCQ 1903–7 A. Bouché-Leclercq, *Histoire des Lagides* (4 vols., Paris, 1903–7).

1913–14 A. Bouché-Leclercq, *Histoire des Séleucides* (2 vols., Paris, 1913–14).

BRAUND 1984 D. Braund, *Rome and the Friendly King: The Character of the Client Kingship* (London, 1984).

BREITENSTEIN 1942 N. Breitenstein, 'Studies in the coinages of the Macedonian kings', *Acta Archaeologica* 13 (1942), 242–58.

BROWN 1981 B.R. Brown, 'Styles in the Alexander portraits on the coins of Lysimachus', in *Coins, Culture and History in the Ancient World. Numismatic and Other Studies in Honor of Bluma L. Trell*, ed. L. Casson and M. Price (Detroit, 1981), 17–27.

1984 B.R. Brown, 'Art history in coins: portrait issues of Ptolemy I', in *Alessandria e il mondo ellenistico-romano. Studi in onore di Achille Adriani* (Rome, 1984), II. 405–17.

BUNGE 1974a J.G. Bunge, 'Münzen als Mittel politischer Propaganda: Antiochos IV. von Syrien', *Studia Classica* 16 (1974), 43–52.

1974b J.G. Bunge, 'Zu den ersten fünf Regierungsjahren Antiochos' IV. Epiphanes', *Historia* 23 (1974), 57–85.

1975a J.G. Bunge, 'Antiochos-Helios. Methoden und Ergebnisse der Reichspolitik Antiochos' IV. Epiphanes von Syrien im Spiegel seiner Münzen', *Historia* 24 (1975), 164–88.

1975b J.G. Bunge, 'Zu einer seltenen Münze Antiochos IV. aus Seleukeia am Tigris', *NCirc.* 83 (1975), 65–6.

BURASCHIS 1982 K. Buraschis, *Das hellenistische Makedonien und die Ägäis* (Münchener Beiträge zur Papyrusforschung und antiken Rechtsgeschichte 73, Munich, 1982).

BURNETT 1977 A. Burnett, 'The coinages of Rome and Magna Graecia in the late fourth and third centuries B.C.', *SNR* 56 (1977), 92–170.

1985 A. Burnett, 'Aesillas: two new hoards', *CH* 7 (1985), 54–67.

BURSTEIN 1984 S.M. Burstein, 'Lysimachus the *gazophylax*: a modern scholarly myth?', in *Nickle Papers* (1984), 57–68.

BUTTREY 1954 T.V. Buttrey, 'Thea Neotera on coins of Antony and Cleopatra', *ANSMN* 6 (1954), 95–109.

1982 T.V. Buttrey, 'Pharaonic imitations of Athenian tetradrachms', in *INC Berne Proc.* (1982), I. 137–40.

CAHN 1949 H. Cahn, *Frühhellenistische Münzkunst* (Basel, 1949).

CALEY 1955 E.R. Caley, *Chemical Composition of Parthian Coins* (NNM 129, New York, 1955).

CALLATAŸ 1982 F. de Callataÿ, 'La date des premiers tétradrachmes de poids attique émis par Alexandre le Grand', *RBN* 128 (1982), 5–25.

1983 F. de Callataÿ, 'Un trésor de drachmes aux types d'Alexandre le Grand conservé au Cabinet des Médailles à Bruxelles', *RBN* 129 (1983), 23–60.

1986 F. de Callataÿ, 'Les derniers rois de Bithynie: problèmes de chronologie', *RBN* 132 (1986), 5–30.

1989 F. de Callataÿ, 'A propos de certaines estampilles sur les contrefaçons modernes de monnaies grecques', *SM* 39 (1989), 84–7.

1990 F. de Callataÿ, *Histoire monétaire des guerres mithridatiques* (Numismatica Lovaniensia, Louvain-la-Neuve, 1990).

CARDINALI 1906 G. Cardinali, *Il regno di Pergamo* (Rome, 1906; repr. Rome, 1968).

CARRADICE AND PRICE 1988 I. Carradice and M. Price, *Coinage in the Greek World* (London, 1988).

ÇEKA 1972 Hasan Çeka, *Questions de numismatique illyrienne* (Tiranë, 1972).

CHAMOUX 1959 F. Chamoux, 'Hermès Parammon', *Etudes d'archéologie classique* 2 (1959), 31–9.

COLLEDGE 1967 M.A.R. Colledge, *The Parthians* (London, 1964).

COX 1950 D.H. Cox, 'The coins', in H. Goldman, *Excavations at Gözlü Kule, Tarsus* I (Princeton, 1950), 38–83.

1966 D.H. Cox, 'Gordion Hoards III, IV, V and VII' *ASNMN* 12 (1966), 19–55.

CRAWFORD 1981 M.H. Crawford, 'Hubs and dies in classical antiquity', *NC* 141 (1981), 176–7.

1985 M.H. Crawford, *Coinage and Money under the Roman Republic. Italy and the Mediterranean Economy* (London, 1985).

CUNNINGHAM 1884 A. Cunningham, *Coins of Alexander's Successors in the East* (London, 1884; repr. 1974). A reprint of articles publ. in the *NC* over the years 1868–74.

CURIEL AND FUSSMANN 1965 R. Curiel and G. Fussmann, *Le trésor monétaire de Qunduz* (Mémoires de la Délégation archéologique française en Afghanistan 20, Paris, 1965).

DAVESNE 1981 A. Davesne, 'Le trésor de Gülnar', *CRAI* 1981, 362–70.

1987 A. Davesne, 'Numismatique et archéologie: le temple de Dionysos à Téos', *RN*[6] 29 (1987), 15–20.

DAVESNE AND LE RIDER 1989 A. Davesne and G. Le Rider, *Le trésor de Meydancikkale, Cilicie Trachée, 1980* (Paris, 1989).

DAVIS AND KRAAY 1973 N.M. Davis and C.M. Kraay, *The Hellenistic Kingdoms. Portrait Coins and History* (London, 1973).

DAYET 1949 M. Dayet, 'Monnaies arsacides à bonnet satrapal', *RN*[5] 11 (1949), 9–26.

DEBEVOISE 1938 N. Debevoise, *A Political History of Parthia* (Chicago, 1938).

DENGATE 1967 J.A. Dengate, 'The triobols of Megalopolis', *ANSMN* 13 (1967), 57–110.

DEPPERT-LIPPITZ 1984 B. Deppert-Lippitz, *Die Münzprägung Milets vom vierten bis ersten Jahrhundert v. Chr.* (Typos 5, Aarau-Frankfurt am Main/Salzburg, 1984).

DIMITROV 1981 K. Dimitrov, 'The coinage of Spartocus and some problems in the political development of Thrace in the beginning of the Hellenistic age', *Études balkaniques* 1981, no. 3, 98–107.

1982 K. Dimitrov, 'Circulation de monnaies macédoniennes et monnaies des Diadoques à Seuthopolis pendant la haute époque hellénistique', in *INC Berne Actes* (1982), 227–31.

1987a K. Dimitrov, 'Observations on several hoards of gold Hellenistic coins from the Balkan peninsula', *Études balkaniques* 1987, no. 3, 103–16.

1987b K. Dimitrov, 'Studies of the numismatic material found at Seuthopolis: problems, research methods and basic conclusions', *ANSMN* 32 (1987), 1–10.

DOBBINS 1975 K.W. Dobbins, 'The successors of Mithridates II of Parthia', *NC*[7] 15 (1975), 19–45.

DOWNEY 1961 G. Downey, *A History of Antioch in Syria, from Seleucus to the Arab Conquest* (Princeton, 1961).

DOYEN 1987 J.-M. Doyen, *Les monnaies antiques de Tell Abou Danné et d'Oumm el-Marra (campagnes 1976–1985). Aspects de la circulation monétaire en Syrie du Nord sous les Séleucides* (Publ. de la Mission archéologique belge aux Tells Abou Danné et Oumm el-Marra (Syrie), Brussels, 1987).

DRAGANOV 1983 D. Draganov, 'Zu den Handelsbeziehungen der thrakischen Stadt Kabyle vom 5. bis 3. Jahrhundert v. u. Z.', *Jahrbuch für Wirtschaftsgeschichte* 2 (1983), 111–18.

1984 D. Draganov, 'Hat Alexander der Grosse Silbermünzen in Kabyle prägen lassen?', *Klio* 66 (1984), 74–84.

DRAGANOV AND POPOV 1982 D. Draganov and J. Popov, 'Bronzovoto monetosechene na grad Kabile' ('The bronze coinage of Cabyle'), *Cabyle* 1 (1982), 18–39.

DRESSEL 1922 H. Dressel, 'Ein Tetradrachmon des Arsakiden Mithradates III', *ZfN* 33 (1922), 156–77.

DÜRR 1974 N. Dürr, 'Neues aus Babylonien', *SM* 24 (1974), 34–6.

1976 N. Dürr, 'Ein "Elephantenstater" für Porus', in *INC New York–Washington Proc.* (1976), 43.

EHRHARDT 1976 C. Ehrhardt, 'A catalogue of issues of tetradrachms from Amphipolis, 318–294 B.C.', *Journal of Numismatic Fine Arts* 4 (1976), 85–9.

EMMONS 1954 B. Emmons, 'The overstruck coinage of Ptolemy I', *ANSMN* 6 (1954), 69–84.

FERGUSON 1911 W.S. Ferguson, *Hellenistic Athens* (London, 1911).

FISCHER 1971a T. Fischer, 'Die Berliner Goldmünze des Seleukiden Antiochos V.', *SM* 21 (1971), 37–9.

1971b T. Fischer, 'Basileos Kamnist(e)irou', *Chiron* I (1971), 169–75.

1972 T. Fischer, 'Zu Tryphon', *Chiron* 2 (1972), 201–13.

1975 T. Fischer, 'Johannes Hyrkanos I. auf Tetradrachmen Antiochos' VII.?', *Zeitschrift des Deutschen Palästina-Vereins* 91 (1975), 191–6.

1976 T. Fischer, 'Tetradrachmen und Kistophor', in *INC New York–Washington Proc.* (1976), 45–70.

1981 T. Fischer, 'Zur Ära der posthumen Alexander-Tetradrachmen pamphylischer Gemeinden', *Berichte der Münzen- und Medaillensammler* 21 (1981), 1457–8.

1986 T. Fischer, 'Zur Auswertung seleukidischer Münzen: Beizeichen, "Prägestätte", Prägegruppe und Zuweisung an namensgleiche Herrscher', *SNR* 65 (1986), 65–71.

1988 T. Fischer, *Molon und seine Münzen (222–220 v. Chr.)* (Kleine Hefte der Münzsammlung an der Ruhr-Universität Bochum 9, Bochum, 1988).

FISHER 1985 R.S. Fisher, 'Two notes on the Aesillas tetradrachms: mint attribution and a die control system', *ANSMN* 30 (1985), 69–88.

FORABOSCHI 1987 D. Foraboschi, 'Arsinoe seconda Filadelfo e la monetazione romana', *QT* 16 (1987), 149–59.

FOSS 1986 C. Foss, 'The coinage of Tigranes the Great: problems, suggestions and a new find', *NC* 146 (1986), 19–66.

FRANCFORT 1975 H.-P. Francfort, 'Deux nouveaux tétradrachmes commémoratifs d'Agathocle', *RN*[6] 17 (1975), 19–22.

FRANKE 1957 P.R. Franke, 'Zur Finanzpolitik des makedonischen Königs Perseus während des Krieges mit Rom 171–168 v. Chr.', *JNG* 8 (1957), 33–50.

1958 P.R. Franke, 'Zur Geschichte des Antigonos Gonatas und der Oitaioi', *Archäologischer Anzeiger* 1958, 37–62.

1961 P.R. Franke, *Die antiken Münzen von Epirus* I (Wiesbaden, 1961).

1975 P.R. Franke, 'Zur Münzprägung von Methymna', in H.-G. Buchholz, *Methymna. Archäologische Beiträge zur Topographie und Geschichte von Nordlesbos* (Mainz, 1975), 163–76.

FRANKE ET AL. 1988 P.R. Franke, W. Leschhorn, B. Müller and J. Nolle, *Side. Münzprägung, Inschriften und Geschichte einer antiken Stadt in der Türkei* (Saarbrücken, 1988).

FRITZE 1914 H. von Fritze, 'Die Silberprägung von Kyzikos: eine chronologischie Studie', *Nomisma* 9 (1914), 34–56.

FURTWÄNGLER 1982 A. Furtwängler, 'Griechische Vieltypenprägung und Münzbeamte', *SNR* 61 (1982), 5–29.

FUSSMAN 1980 G. Fussman, 'Nouvelles inscriptions Saka: ère d'Eucratide, ère d'Azés, ère Vikrama, ère de Kanishka', *Bull. de l'École française de l'Extrême-Orient* 1980, 1–43.

GAEBLER 1906, 1935 H. Gaebler, *Die antiken Münzen von Makedonia und Paionia* (2 vols. = *Die Antiken Münzen Nordgriechenlands* III. 1–2, Berlin, 1906, 1935).

1926a H. Gaebler, 'Zur Münzkunde Makedoniens, VII', *ZfN* 36 (1926), 111–41.

1926b H. Gaebler, 'Zur Münzkunde Makedoniens, VIII', *ZfN* 36 (1926), 183–99.

1927 H. Gaebler, 'Zur Münzkunde Makedoniens, IX', *ZfN* 37 (1927), 223–53.

GALLE 1984 S.A.S. Galle, 'Quelques remarques sur le début du monnayage arsacide', *RBN* 130 (1984), 208–12.

GARA 1984 A. Gara, 'Limiti strutturali dell'economia monetaria nell'Egitto tardo-tolemaico', in *Studi ellenistici* I, ed. B. Virgilio (Biblioteca di Studi Antichi 48, Pisa, 1984), 107–34.

1988 A. Gara, 'Il significato economico della politica monetaria nell'Egitto ellenistico', in *Stato, Economia, Lavoro nel Vicino Oriente antico* (Milan, 1988), 128–37.

GARLASCHELLI 1972 M. Garlaschelli, 'L'iconografia monetale dei Seleucidi', *QT* I (1972), 61–77.

GAUTHIER 1975 P. Gauthier, 'Légendes monétaires grecques', in *NAPM* (1975), 165–9.

GERASSIMOV 1958 T. Gerassimov, 'The Alexander tetradrachms of Cabyle in Thrace', in *ANS Centennial Publication* (New York, 1958), 273–7.

GERIN 1986 D. Gerin, 'Les statères de la ligue arcadienne', *SNR* 65 (1986), 13–39.

GESCHE 1974 H. Gesche, 'Nikokles von Paphos und Nikokreon von Salamis', *Chiron* 4 (1974), 103–25.

GHIRSHMAN 1974 R. Ghirshman, 'Un tétradrachme d'Andragoras de la collection de M. Foroughi', in *Studies Miles* (1974), 1–8.

GIOVANNINI 1978 A. Giovannini, *Rome et la circulation monétaire en Grèce au 2e siècle av. J.C.* (Basel, 1978).

GLEW 1987 D.G. Glew, 'The Cappadocian expedition of Nicomedes III Euergetes, king of Bithynia', *ANSMN* 32 (1987), 23–55.

GOLENKO AND KARYSZOWSKI 1972 K.V. Golenko and P.J. Karyszowski, 'The gold coinage of King Pharnaces of the Bosporus', NC^7 12 (1972), 25–38.

GRUNAUER VON HOERSCHELMANN 1978 S. Grunauer von Hoerschelmann, *Die Münzprägung der Lakedaimonier* (AMUGS VII, Berlin, 1978).

GRZYBEK 1989 E. Grzybek, *Du calendrier macédonien au calendrier ptolémaïque* (Schweizerische Beiträge zu Altertumswissenschaft 20, Basel, 1989).

HACKENS 1968 T. Hackens, 'A propos de la circulation monétaire dans le Peloponnèse au IIIe siècle av. J.-C.', *Studia Hellenistica* 16 (1968), 69–95.

1969 T. Hackens, 'La circulation monétaire dans la Béotie hellénistique: trésors de Thèbes 1935 et 1965', *BCH* 93 (1969), 701–29 (German transl. in *Methoden der antiken Numismatik* (Darmstadt, 1989), 233–73).

1970 T. Hackens, 'L'influence rhodienne en Crète aux IIIe et IIe s. av. J.-C. et le trésor de Gortyne, 1966', *RBN* 116 (1970), 37–58.

1975 T. Hackens, 'Terminologie et techniques de fabrication' in *NAPM* (1975), 3–15.

HADLEY 1974a R.A. Hadley, 'Royal propaganda of Seleucus I and Lysimachus', *JHS* 94 (1974), 50–65.

1974b R.A. Hadley, 'Seleucus, Dionysus, or Alexander?' NC^7 14 (1974), 9–13.

HAMMOND AND WALBANK 1988 N.G.L. Hammond and F.W. Walbank, *A History of Macedonia. III: 336–167 B.C.* (Oxford, 1988).

HANSEN 1971 E.V. Hansen, *The Attalids of Pergamum* (Cornell Studies in Classical Philology 36, 2nd edn, Ithaca/London, 1971).

HAVELOCK 1980 C.M. Havelock, 'The archaistic Athena Promachos in early Hellenistic coinages', *AJA* 84 (1980), 41–50.

HAWORTH 1905 H.H. Haworth, 'Some notes on coins attributed to Parthia', NC^4 5 (1905), 209–46.

HEAD 1911 B.V. Head. *Historia Numorum* (2nd edn, Oxford, 1911).

HEALY 1962 J.F. Healy, 'Alexander the Great and the last issue of electrum hektai at Mytilene', NC^7 2 (1962), 65–71.

1978 J.F. Healy, *Mining and Metallurgy in the Greek and Roman World* (London, 1978).

HEINEN 1966 H. Heinen, *Rom und Ägypten von 51 bis 47 v. Chr.* (Tübingen (diss.), 1966).

HILL 1922 G.F. Hill, 'Ancient methods of coining', NC^5 2 (1922), 1–42.

1923 G.F. Hill, 'Alexander the Great and the Persian lion-gryphon', *JHS* 43 (1923), 156–61.

1924 G.F Hill, 'The frequency-table', NC^5 4 (1924), 76–85.

1927 G.F. Hill, 'Greek coins acquired by the British Museum in 1926', NC^5 7 (1927), 193–208.

HIRMER AND KRAAY 1966 M. Hirmer and C.M. Kraay, *Greek Coins* (London, 1966). (Adapted from the German original (Munich, 1964), by Hirmer and P.R. Franke.)

HOLLEAUX 1921 M. Holleaux, *Rome, la Grèce et les monarchies hellénistiques au IIIe siècle av. J.-C.* (Bibl. des Écoles françaises d'Athènes et de Rome 124, Paris, 1921).

1938–68 M. Holleaux, *Études d'épigraphie et d'histoire grecques* (6 vols., Paris, 1938–68).

HOLLSTEIN 1989 W. Hollstein, 'Taxiles' Prägung für Alexander den Grossen', *RSN* 68 (1989), 5–17.

HOLT 1981 F. Holt, 'The Euthydemid coinage of Bactria: further hoard evidence from Ai Khanoum', *RN*[6] 23 (1981), 7–44.

1984 F. Holt, 'The so-called "pedigree" coins of the Bactrian Greeks', in *Nickle Papers* (1984), 69–91.

HOUGHTON 1978 A. Houghton, 'The Seleucid mint at Lampsacus', *ANSMN* 23 (1978), 59–68.

1979a A. Houghton, 'Timarchus as king in Babylonia', *RN*[6] 21 (1979), 213–17.

1979b A. Houghton, 'The second reign of Demetrius II at Tarsus', *ANSMN* 24 (1979), 111–16.

1980a A. Houghton, 'Notes on the early Seleucid victory coinage of Persepolis', *SNR* 59 (1980), 5–14.

1980b A. Houghton, 'Tarik Darreh (Kangavar) hoard', *ANSMN* 25 (1980), 31–44.

1982 A. Houghton, 'A tetradrachm of Seleucia Pieria at the Getty Museum', *J.P. Getty Museum Journal* 10 (1982), 153–8.

1983 A. Houghton, *Coins of the Seleucid Empire from the Collection of Arthur Houghton* (Ancient Coins in North American Collections, New York, 1983).

1984 A. Houghton, 'The Seleucid mint of Mallus and the cult figure of Athena Magarsia', in *Studies Mildenberg* (1984), 91–110.

1986 A. Houghton, 'The elephants of Nisibis', *ANSMN* 31 (1986), 107–24.

1987 A. Houghton, 'The double portrait coins of Antiochus XI and Philip I: a Seleucid mint at Beroea', *SNR* 66 (1987), 79–84.

1988 A. Houghton, 'The double portrait coins of Alexander I Balas and Cleopatra Thea', *SNR* 67 (1988), 85–93.

1989a A. Houghton, 'The royal Seleucid mint of Soli', *NC* 149 (1989), 15–32.

1989b A. Houghton, 'The royal Seleucid mint of Seleucia on the Calycadnus', in *KME* (1989), 77–98.

HOUGHTON AND BENDALL 1988 A. Houghton and S. Bendall, 'A hoard of Aegean tetradrachms and the autonomous tetradrachms of Elaeusa Sebaste', *ANSMN* 33 (1988), 71–89.

HOUGHTON AND LE RIDER 1966 A. Houghton and G. Le Rider, 'Un trésor de monnaies hellénistiques trouvé près de Suse', *RN*[6] 8 (1966), 111–27. (For a further portion of this hoard see Strauss 1971.)

1985 A. Houghton and G. Le Rider, 'Le deuxième fils d'Antiochos IV à Ptolémais', *RSN* 64 (1985), 23–85.

HOUGHTON AND MOORE 1984 A. Houghton and W. Moore, 'Some early far northeastern Seleucid mints', *ANSMN* 29 (1984), 1–9.

1988 A. Houghton and W. Moore, 'Five Seleucid notes', *ANSMN* 33 (1988), 55–69.

IMHOOF-BLUMER 1902 F. Imhoof-Blumer, *Kleinasiatische Münzen* (2 vols., Vienna, 1902).

1905 F. Imhoof-Blumer, 'Eurikleia', *Jahreshefte des österreichischen archäologischen Instituts in Wien* 8 (1905), 229–30.

JACKSON 1971 A.E. Jackson, 'The bronze coinage of Gortyn', *NC*[7] 11 (1971), 37–51.

JACOBSON 1986 D.M. Jacobson, 'The reverse of Herod's largest coin', *ANSMN* 31 (1986), 149–65.

JENKINS 1951 G.K. Jenkins, 'Notes on Seleucid coins', *NC*[6] 11 (1951), 1–21.

1955 G.K. Jenkins, 'Indo-Scythic mints', *Journal of the Numismatic Society of India* 17.2 (1955), 19–26.

1958a G.K. Jenkins, 'Hellenistic coins from Nimrud', *Iraq* 20 (1958), 158–68.

1958b G.K. Jenkins, 'A note on Corinthian coins in the West', in *ANS Centennial Publication* (1958), 367–79.

1960 G.K. Jenkins, 'An early Ptolemaic hoard from Phacous', *ANSMN* 9 (1960), 17–37.

1965 G.K. Jenkins, 'A group of Bactrian forgeries', *RN*[6] 7 (1965), 51–7.

1967 G.K. Jenkins, 'The monetary system in the early Hellenistic period with special regard to the economic policy of the Ptolemaic kings', in *The Patterns of Monetary Development in Phoenicia and Palestine in Antiquity* (International Numismatic Convention, Jerusalem 1963, Tel-Aviv/Jerusalem, 1967), 53–72.

1970 G.K. Jenkins, *The Coinage of Gela* (AMUGS 11, Berlin, 1970).

1972 G.K. Jenkins, *Ancient Greek Coins* (Fribourg, 1972; 2nd edn, London, 1990).

1987 G.K. Jenkins, 'Hellenistic gold coins of Ephesos', in *Festschrift Akurgal* (= *Anadolu* 21 (1978–80), Ankara, 1987), 183–8.

JONES 1979 N.F. Jones, 'The autonomous wreathed tetradrachms of Magnesia-on-Maeander', *ANSMN* 24 (1979), 63–109.

JUSTIN Justinus, *Epitoma historiarum Philippicarum Pompei Troqi*, ed. F. Rühl (Leipzig (Bibl. Teub.), 1886).

KADMAN 1960 L. Kadman, *The Coins of the Jewish War of 66–73 C.E.* (Corpus Nummorum Palestinensium 3, Jerusalem, 1960).

KAGAN 1984 J.H. Kagan, 'Hellenistic coinage at Scepsis after its refoundation in the third century B.C.', *ANSMN* 29 (1984), 11–28.

KAISER 1986 W.B. Kaiser, 'Alexanders Goldmünzen', *SNR* 65 (1986), 41–63.

KAMPMANN 1978 M. Kampmann, 'Aristonicos à Thyatire', *RN*[6] 20 (1978), 38–42.

KINDLER 1958 A. Kindler, *The Coinage of the Hasmonean Dynasty. The Dating and Meaning of the Ancient Jewish Coins and Symbols* (Tel Aviv, 1958)

KINNS 1983 P. Kinns, 'The Amphictionic coinage reconsidered', *NC* 143 (1983), 1–22.

1985 P. Kinns, 'Myrina and related forgeries', *ANSMN* 30 (1985), 45–68.

1986 P. Kinns, 'The coinage of Miletus', *NC* 146 (1986), 233–60.

1989 P. Kinns, 'Two studies in the silver coinage of Magnesia on the Maeander', in *KME* (1989), 137–48.

KLEINER 1955 G. Kleiner, 'Pontische Reichsmünzen', *Istanbuler Mitteilungen* 6 (1955), 1–21.

1971 F.S. Kleiner, 'The Alexander tetradrachms of Pergamum and Rhodes', *ANSMN* 17 (1971), 95–125.

1978 F.S. Kleiner, 'Hoard evidence and the late cistophori of Pergamum', *ANSMN* 23 (1978), 77–105.

1979 F.S. Kleiner, 'The late cistophori of Apamea', in *Essays Thompson* (1979), 119–30.

1980 F.S. Kleiner, 'Further reflections on the early cistophoric coinage', *ANSMN* 25 (1980), 45–52.

KLEINER AND NOE 1977 F.S. Kleiner and S.P. Noe, *The Early Cistophoric Coinage* (NS 14, New York, 1977).

KONTORINI 1979 V. Kontorini, 'L'autonomie de Ptolémais-Akko de Phénicie', *RN*[6] 21 (1979), 30–41.

KOUTSOUKOS 1984 E.A.M. Koutsoukos, 'The mass production of bronze blank castings for coining in Ptolemaic Egypt', *NCirc.* 92 (1984), 115–16.

KRAAY 1968 C.M. Kraay, *Coins of Ancient Athens* (Minerva Numismatic Handbooks 2, Newcastle-upon-Tyne, 1968).
1976 C.M. Kraay, *Archaic and Classical Greek Coins* (London, 1976).
1981 C.M. Kraay, 'Demetrius in Bactria and India', *QT* 10 (1981), 219–33.
1984 C.M. Kraay, 'Greek coinage and war', in *Nickle Papers* (1984), 3–18.
KROLL 1979 J.H. Kroll, 'A chronology of early Athenian bronze coinage, *ca.* 350–250 B.C.', in *Essays Thompson* (1979), 139–54.
KROMANN 1988 A. Kromann, 'Greek and Phoenician letters on Aradian tetradrachms', in *Studies in Ancient History and Numismatics Presented to Rudi Thomsen* (Aarhus, 1988), 104–13.
KÜTHMANN 1958 H. Küthmann, 'Zur römisch-campanischen Didrachmenprägung', *JNG* 9 (1958), 87–97.
KYRIELEIS 1975 H. Kyrieleis, *Bildnisse der Ptolemäer* (Deutsches Archäologisches Institut, Archäologische Forschungen 2, Berlin, 1975).
LACROIX 1949 L. Lacroix, *Les réproductions de statues sur les monnaies grecques* (Liège, 1949).
LAHIRI 1965 A.N. Lahiri, *Corpus of the Indo-Greek Coins* (Calcutta, 1965).
LAIX 1973 R.A. de Laix, 'The silver coinage of the Aetolian League', *California Studies in Classical Antiquity* 6 (1973), 47–75.
LARSEN 1968 J.A.O. Larsen, *Greek Federal States: Their Institutions and History* (Oxford, 1968).
LEDERER 1931 P. Lederer, 'Symbole der Aphrodite Urania', *ZfN* 41 (1931), 47–54.
LEMAIRE 1976 A. Lemaire, 'Le monnayage de Tyr et celui dit d'Akko dans la deuxième moitié du IVe siècle av. J.-C.', *RN*[6] 18 (1976), 11–24.
LE RIDER 1959 G. Le Rider, 'Monnaies de Characène', *Syria* 36 (1959), 229–53.
1963 G. Le Rider, *Deux trésors de monnaies grecques de la Propontide* (Bibl. arch. et hist. de l'Institut français d'Archéologie d'Istanbul 18, Paris, 1963).
1964 G. Le Rider, 'Monnaies de Timarque (162–160 av. J.-C.)', *BSFN* 19 (1964), 318.
1965a G. Le Rider, *Suse sous les Séleucides et les Parthes. Les trouvailles monétaires et l'histoire de la ville* (Mém. de la Mission archéol. en Iran 38, Paris, 1965).
1965b G. Le Rider, 'Un atelier monétaire séleucide dans la province de la Mer Erythrée', *RN*[6] 7 (1965), 36–43.
1966 G. Le Rider, *Monnaies crétoises, du Ve au Ier siècle av. J.-C.* (Ecole française d'Athènes, Études crétoises 15, Paris, 1966).
1967a G. Le Rider, 'Un trésor de petites monnaies de bronze trouvé à Ninève', *Irania Antiqua* 7 (1967), 4–19.
1967b G. Le Rider, 'Monnaies de Taxila et d'Arachosie: une nouvelle reine de Taxila', *Revue des études grecques* 80 (1967), 331–42.
1968a G. Le Rider, 'Les Arsinoéens de Crète', in *Essays Robinson* (1968), 229–40.
1968b G. Le Rider, 'Un groupe de monnaies crétoises à types athéniens', in *Humanisme actif. Mélanges d'art et de littérature offerts à Julien Cain* (Paris, 1968), 313–35.
1969a G. Le Rider, 'Monnaies grecques récemment acquises par le Cabinet de Paris', *RN*[6] 11 (1969), 7–27.
1969b G. Le Rider, 'Monnaies trouvées à Mirgissa', *RN*[6] 11 (1969), 28–35.
1969c G. Le Rider, 'Numismatique grecque', *AEPHE* 1968–9, 173–87.
1970 G. Le Rider, 'Numismatique grecque', *AEPHE* 1969–70, 255–71.
1971a G. Le Rider, 'Numismatique grecque', *AEPHE* 1970–1, 241–62.
1971b G. Le Rider, 'Sur le monnayage de Byzance au IVe siècle', *RN*[6] 13 (1971), 143–53.

1972a G. Le Rider, 'Tetradrachmes "au lion" et imitations d'Athènes en Babylonie', *SM* 22 (1972), 1–7.

1972b G. Le Rider, 'Les tétradrachmes pamphyliens de la fin du IIIe siècle et du début du IIe siècle avant notre ère', *RN*[6] 14 (1972), 253–9.

1973a G. Le Rider, 'Numismatique grecque', *AEPHE* 1972–3, 243–59.

1973b G. Le Rider, 'Un tétradrachme d'Athéna Niképhoros', *RN*[6] 15 (1973), 66–79.

1975 G. Le Rider, 'Contremarques et surfrappes dans l'Antiquité grecque', in *NAPM* (1975), 27–56.

1977 G. Le Rider, *Le monnayage d'argent et d'or de Philippe Ier, frappé en Macédoine de 359 à 294* (Paris, 1977).

1978 G. Le Rider, 'Deux nouveaux tétradrachmes frappés à Suse', *RN*[6] 20 (1978), 33–7.

1983a G. Le Rider, 'Un tétradrachme de Prusias I de Bithynie', in *Archéologie et religion de l'Anatolie ancienne* (Homo religiosus 10, Louvain-la-Neuve, 1983), 167–71.

1983b G. Le Rider, 'Un trésor de Bassit (1978)', *BCH* 107 (1983), 451–6.

1986 G. Le Rider, 'L'Enfant-roi Antiochos et la reine Laodice', *BCH* 110 (1986), 409–17.

1987 G. Le Rider, 'Monnaies d'Aï Khanoum', *RN*[6] 29 (1987), 236–44.

1988 G. Le Rider, 'L'atelier séleucide de Lysimachie (*WSM* 1610–1621)', *QT* 17 (1988), 195–207.

LE RIDER AND OLCAY 1988a G. Le Rider and N. Olcay, 'Un trésor de tétradrachmes d'Alexandre trouvé à Akçakale en 1958', *RN*[6] 30 (1988), 42–54.

1988b G. Le Rider and N. Olcay, 'Le trésor de Haymena', *RN*[6] 30 (1988), 55–63.

LE RIDER AND SEYRIG 1967 G. Le Rider and H. Seyrig, 'Objets de la collection Louis De Clercq donnés en 1967 au Cabinet des Médailles de la Bibliothèque Nationale par le comte et la comtesse Henri de Boisgelin', *RN*[6] 9 (1967), 7–53.

LESCHHORN 1985 W. Leschhorn, 'Zur rhodischen Münzprägung im 2. Jh. v. Chr. Ein Schatzfund rhodischer Hemidrachmen aus Syrien', *JNG* 35 (1985), 7–20.

1986 W. Leschhorn, 'Zu den rhodischen Didrachmen des 4. und 3. Jh. v. Chr. Der Schatzfund von Uşak (*Coin Hoards* 11, 78)', *JNG* 36 (1986), 67–94.

LEWIS 1962 D.M. Lewis, 'The chronology of the Athenian New Style coinage', *NC*[7] 2 (1962), 275–300.

LIAMPI 1986 K. Liampi, 'Zur Chronologie der sogenannten "anonymen" makedonischen Münzen des späten 4. Jhs. v. Chr.', *JNG* 36 (1986), 41–65.

LIPINSKI 1982 E. Lipinski, 'Egyptian Aramaic coins from the fifth and fourth centuries B.C.', in *Studia Naster* (1982), 23–33.

MACDONALD 1902 G. Macdonald, 'The coinage of Tigranes I', *NC*[4] 2 (1902), 193–201.

MACDOWALL 1978 D.W. MacDowall, 'Excavations at Kandahar 1975. Coin finds', *Afghan Studies* 1 (1978), 50–2.

1984 D.W. MacDowall, 'Der Einfluss Alexanders des Grossen auf das Münzwesen Afghanistan und Nordwest-Indiens', in *Aus dem Osten des Alexanderreiches. Festschrift zum 65. Geburtstag von Klaus Fischer*, ed. J. Ozols and V. Thewalt (Cologne, 1984), 66–73.

MACISAAC 1988 J.D. MacIsaac, 'Phliasian bronze coinage', *ANSMN* 33 (1988), 45–54.

MACKAY 1968a P.A. MacKay, 'Bronze coinage in Macedonia, 168–166 B.C.', *ANSMN* 14 (1968), 5–13.

1968b P.A. MacKay, 'Macedonian tetradrachms of 148–147 B.C.', *ANSMN* 14 (1968), 15–40.

MAGIE 1950 D. Magie, *Roman Rule in Asia Minor to the End of the Third Century after Christ* (Princeton, 1950).

MAMROTH 1928 A. Mamroth, 'Die Silbermünzen des makedonischen Königs Perseus', *ZfN* 38 (1928), 1–28.

1930 A. Mamroth, 'Die Silbermünzen des Königs Philippos V. von Makedonien', *ZfN* 40 (1930), 277–303.

1935 A. Mamroth, 'Die Bronzemünzen des Königs Philippos V. von Makedonien', *ZfN* 42 (1935), 219–57.

MARTIN 1981 T.R. Martin, 'A third-century B.C. hoard from Thessaly', *ANSMN* 26 (1981), 51–77.

1982 T.R. Martin, 'The end of Thessalian civic coinage in silver: Macedonian policy or economic reality?', in *INC Berne Proc.* (1982), 157–64.

1985 T.R. Martin, *Sovereignty and Coinage in Classical Greece* (Princeton, 1985).

MATELLI 1987 E. Matelli, 'La spedizione indiana di Seleuco I e la sua propaganda', *QT* 16 (1987), 131–48.

MATHISEN 1981 R.W. Mathisen, 'Antigonus Gonatas and the silver coinages of Macedonia *circa* 280–270 B.C.', *ANSMN* 26 (1981), 79–124.

1983 R.W. Mathisen, 'The administrative organization of the mint of Amphipolis in early Antigonid Macedonia (*c.* 280–270 B.C.)', *SAN* 14 (1983), 10–12, 14–27, 44–6.

1985 R.W. Mathisen, 'Pan heads and Poseidon heads. Two third-century Macedonian tetradrachm types', *SAN* 16 (1985), 29–35.

MATTINGLY 1979 H.B. Mattingly, 'L. Julius Caesar, Governor of Macedonia', *Chiron* 9 (1979), 147–67.

MAY 1939 J.F. May, *The Coinage of Damastion* (Oxford, 1939).

1952 J.F. May, 'The Alexander coinage of Nikokles of Paphos. With a note on some recently identified tetradrachms from the Demanhur find', *NC*[6] 12 (1952), 1–18.

MCCREDIE 1966 J.R. McCredie, *Fortified Military Camps in Attica* (*Hesperia* Supplement XI, Princeton, 1966).

MCDOWELL 1935 R.H. McDowell, *Coins from Seleucia on the Tigris* (Univ. of Michigan Studies, Humanistic Series 37, Ann Arbor, 1935).

MCGOVERN 1980 W.E. McGovern, 'Missing die probabilities, expected die production and the index figure', *ANSMN* 25 (1980), 209–23.

MCLEAN 1981 M.D. McLean, 'The initial coinage of Alexander Jannaeus', *ANSMN* 26 (1981), 153–61.

MERKER 1960 I.L. Merker, 'The silver coinage of Antigonos Gonatas and Antigonos Doson', *ANSMN* 9 (1960), 39–52.

1964 I.L. Merker, 'Notes on Abdalonymos and the dated Alexander coinage of Sidon and Ake', *ANSMN* 11 (1964), 13–20.

1974 I.L. Merker, 'Demetrios Poliorketes and Tyre', *Ancient Society* 5 (1974), 119–26.

MESHORER 1967 Y. Meshorer, *Jewish Coins of the Second Temple Period* (Tel Aviv, 1967).

1974 Y. Meshorer, 'The Beginning of the Hasmonean coinage', *Israel Exploration Journal* 24 (1974), 59–61.

1981 Y. Meshorer, 'New types of Judean silver coins', *INJ* 5 (1981), 4.

1982 Y. Meshorer, *Ancient Jewish Coinage. I: Persian Period through Hasmoneans* (Dix Hills, N.Y., 1982).

MEYER 1925 E. Meyer, *Die Grenzen der hellenistischen Staaten in Kleinasien* (Zurich, 1925).

MICHAELODOU-NICOLAOU 1989 I. Michaelodou-Nicolaou, 'Coins of King Timarchos from Nea Paphos', in *KME* (1989), 179–80.

MILDENBERG 1979 L. Mildenberg, 'Yehud: A preliminary study of the provincial coinage of Judaea', in *Essays Thompson* (1979), 183–96.
1987 L. Mildenberg, 'Numismatic evidence', *Harvard Studies in Classical Philology* 91 (1987), 381–95.
MILNE 1941 J.G. Milne, *Kolophon and its Coinage. A Study* (NNM 95, New York, 1941).
MITCHINER 1975 M. Mitchener, *Indo-Greek and Indo-Scythian Coinage* (9 vols., London, 1975–6). (Vols. I–V cover the Bactrian and Indo-Greek coins, and there is much Parthian material in Vol. VI.)
MOORE 1984 N. Moore, 'The silver coinage of Alexander from Pella', in *Nickle Papers* (1984), 41–56.
1986 W. Moore, 'The divine couple of Demetrius II, Nicator, and his coinage at Nisibis', *ANSMN* 31 (1986), 125–43.
1987 W. Moore, 'A serrated bronze issue of Demetrius I from Seleucia on the Tigris', *RN*[6] 29 (1987), 21–4.
MORGAN 1927 J. de Morgan, *Numismatique de la Perse antique* (= Vol. III. Parts 1 and 2 of E. Babelon, *Traité des monnaies grecques et romaines*; Paris, 1927, 1930).
MØRKHOLM 1957 O. Mørkholm, 'Two Seleucid coin notes', *NC*[6] 17 (1957), 6–10.
1960a O. Mørkholm, 'A posthumous issue of Antiochus IV of Syria', *NC*[6] 20 (1960), 25–30.
1960b O. Mørkholm, 'Greek coins from Failaka', *KUML* 1960, 199–207.
1962 O. Mørkholm, 'Some Cappadocian problems', *NC*[7] 2 (1962), 407–11.
1963 O. Mørkholm, *Studies in the Coinage of Antiochus IV of Syria* (Det Kgl. danske Vidensk. Selsk., Hist.-filos. Meddel. 40.iii, Copenhagen, 1963).
1964a O. Mørkholm, 'Seleucid coins from Cilicia *ca.* 220–150 B.C.', *ANSMN* 11 (1964), 53–62.
1964b O. Mørkholm, 'The accession of Antiochus IV', *ANSMN* 11 (1964), 63–76.
1964c O. Mørkholm, 'Some Cappadocian die-links', *NC*[7] 4 (1964), 21–5.
1965a O. Mørkholm, 'The municipal coinages with portrait of Antiochus IV of Syria', in *INC Rome Atti* (1965), 63–7.
1965b O. Mørkholm, 'A Greek coin hoard from Susiana', *Acta Archaeologica* 36 (1965), 127–56.
1965c O. Mørkholm, 'Le monnayage de Séleucus IV à Nisibe', *RN*[6] 7 (1965), 44–50.
1966 O. Mørkholm, 'Some western Seleucid coins', *INJ* 3 (1965–6), 8–14.
1967 O. Mørkholm, 'The monetary history of the Seleucid kings until 129 B.C.', in *The Patterns of Monetary Development in Phoenicia and Palestine in Antiquity* (International Numismatic Convention, Jerusalem 1963, Tel-Aviv/Jerusalem, 1967), 75–86.
1968 O. Mørkholm, 'The coinages of Ariarathes VIII and Ariarathes IX of Cappadocia', in *Essays Robinson* (1968), 241–58.
1969a O. Mørkholm, 'Some Seleucid coins from the mint of Sardes', *NNÅ* 1969, 5–20.
1969b O. Mørkholm, 'The classification of Cappadocian coins', *NC*[7] 9 (1969), 21–31.
1970 O. Mørkholm, 'The Seleucid mint at Antiochia on the Persian Gulf', *ANSMN* 16 (1970), 31–44.
1972 O. Mørkholm, 'A Hellenistic coin hoard from Bahrain', *KUML* 1972, 183–202.
1976 O. Mørkholm, 'The Ptolemaic "Coins of an Uncertain Era"', *NNÅ* 1975–6, 23–58.
1978a O. Mørkholm, 'The Alexander coinage of Nicocles of Paphos', *Chiron* 8 (1978), 142–7.
1978b O. Mørkholm, 'The coinages of Ariarathes VI and Ariarathes VII of Cappadocia', *SNR* 57 (1978), 145–63.
1978c O. Mørkholm, 'The era of the Pamphylian Alexanders', *ANSMN* 23 (1978), 69–75.
1979a O. Mørkholm, 'New coin finds from Failaka', *KUML* 1979, 219–36.
1979b O. Mørkholm, 'Survey of numismatic research 1972–1977. The Hellenistic period: Greece to India', in *INC Berne Surv.* (1979), 60–97.

1979c O. Mørkholm, 'The portrait coinage of Ptolemy V. The main series', in *Essays Thompson* (1979), 203–14.

1979d O. Mørkholm, 'Some reflections on the early cistophoric coinage', *ANSMN* 24 (1979), 47–62.

1980a O. Mørkholm, 'A group of Ptolemaic coins from Phoenicia and Palestine', *INJ* 4 (1980), 4–7.

1980b O. Mørkholm, 'Cyrene and Ptolemy I. Some numismatic comments', *Chiron* 10 (1980), 145–59.

1980c O. Mørkholm, 'Chronology and meaning of the wreathed coinages of the early second century B.C.', *QT* 9 (1980), 145–58.

1981 O. Mørkholm, 'Some coins of Ptolemy V from Palestine', *INJ* 5 (1981), 5–10.

1982a O. Mørkholm, 'The Attic coin standard in the Levant during the Hellenistic period', in *Studia Naster* (1982), I. 139–49.

1982b O. Mørkholm, 'The "behaviour" of dies in the Hellenistic period', in *INC Berne Proc.* (1982), I. 209–14.

1982c O. Mørkholm, 'Some reflexions on the production and use of coinage in ancient Greece', *Historia* 31 (1982), 290–305.

1983a O. Mørkholm, 'The Ptolemaic coinage in Phoenicia and the fifth war with Syria', in *Egypt and the Hellenistic World. Proceedings of the International Colloquium, Leuven 24–26 May 1982* (*Studia Hellenistica* 27, Louvain, 1983), 241–51.

1983b O. Mørkholm, 'The autonomous tetradrachms of Laodicea ad Mare', *ANSMN* 28 (1983), 89–107.

1983c O. Mørkholm, 'The life of obverse dies in the Hellenistic period', in *Studies Grierson* (1983), 11–21.

1983d O. Mørkholm, 'The last Ptolemaic silver coinage in Cyprus', *Chiron* 13 (1983), 69–79.

1984a O. Mørkholm, 'Some Pergamene coins in Copenhagen', in *Festschrift Mildenberg* (1984), 181–92.

1984b O. Mørkholm, 'The chronology of the New Style coinage of Athens', *ANSMN* 29 (1984), 29–42.

1984c O. Mørkholm, 'The monetary system in the Seleucid Empire after 187 B.C.', in *Nickle Papers* (1984), 93–113.

1984d O. Mørkholm, 'The alleged portrait of Antiochus, son and co-regent of Antiochus the Great', *NC* 144 (1984), 184–6.

1987 O. Mørkholm, 'The date of the autonomous tetradrachms of Aegeae in Cilicia', *ANSMN* 32 (1987), 57–60.

MØRKHOLM AND KROMANN 1984 O. Mørkholm and A. Kromann, 'The Ptolemaic silver coinage on Cyprus 192/1–164/3 B.C.', *Chiron* 14 (1984), 149–65.

MØRKHOLM AND SHORE 1974 O. Mørkholm and A.F. Shore, 'A coin of Artaxerxes III', *NC*^{7} 14 (1974), 1–8.

MÜLLER 1855 L. Müller, *Numismatique d'Alexandre le Grand suivie d'une appendice contenant les monnaies de Philippe II et III* (2 vols., Copenhagen, 1855; repr. Bologna, 1975).

MÜNSTERBERG 1915 R. Münsterberg, 'Grammatisches aus griechischen Münzen', *Numismatische Zeitschrift* 48 (1915), 111–15.

NARAIN 1955 A.K. Narain, *The Coin Types of the Indo-Greek Kings* (Numismatic Society of India, *Numismatic Notes and Monographs* 1, Bombay, 1955; repr. Chicago, 1968).

1957 A.K. Narain, *The Indo-Greeks* (Oxford, 1957).

1968 A.K. Narain (ed.), *Seminar Papers on the Local Coins of Northern India* c. *300 B.C. to 300 A.D.* (Varanasi, 1968).

NASTER 1950 P. Naster, 'Les monnaies séleucides attribuées à l'atelier d'Elaeusa-Sébaste', *RBN* 96 (1950), 13–16.

1968 P. Naster, 'Note d'épigraphie monétaire de Perside: *Fratakara, Frataraka* ou *Fratadara*?', *Irania antiqua* 8 (1968), 74–80.

1975 P. Naster, 'La méthode en métrologie numismatique', in *NAPM* (1975), 65–74.

NAVILLE 1951 L. Naville, *Les monnaies d'or de la Cyrénaïque* (Geneva, 1951).

NEWELL 1912 E.T. Newell, *The Reattribution of Certain Tetradrachms of Alexander the Great* (New York, 1912).

1915 E.T. Newell, 'Some Cypriote "Alexanders"', NC^4 15 (1915), 294–322.

1916 E.T. Newell, *The Dated Alexander Coinage of Sidon and Ake* (Yale Oriental Series, Researches II, New Haven, 1916).

1917 E.T. Newell, 'The Seleucid mint of Antioch', *AJN* 51 (1917), 1–151.

1918a E.T. Newell, 'Tarsos under Alexander', *AJN* 52 (1918), 69–115.

1918b E.T. Newell, 'The Alexandrine coinage of Sinope', *AJN* 52 (1918), 117–27.

1919a E.T. Newell, 'Nikokles, king of Paphos', NC^4 19 (1919), 64–5.

1919b E.T. Newell, 'Myriandros – Alexandria Kat'Isson', *AJN* 53, Part 2 (1919), 1–42.

1921a E.T. Newell, *The Octobols of Histiaea* (NNM 2, New York, 1921).

1921b E.T. Newell, *Alexander Hoards. Introduction and Kyparissia Hoard* (NNM 3, New York, 1921).

1921c E.T. Newell, *The First Seleucid Coinage of Tyre* (NNM 10, New York, 1921).

1923a E.T. Newell, *Alexander Hoards. Demanhur 1905* (NNM 19, New York, 1923).

1923b E.T. Newell, *Alexander Hoards. Andritsaena* (NNM 21, New York, 1923).

1923c E.T. Newell, *Tyrus rediviva* (New York, 1923).

1924 E.T. Newell, 'A Parthian hoard', NC^5 4 (1924), 141–80.

1925 E.T. Newell, *Mithradates of Parthia and Hyspaosines of Characene; a Numismatic Palimpsest* (NNM 26, New York, 1925).

1927 E.T. Newell, *The Coinages of Demetrius Poliorcetes* (London, 1927).

1936a E.T. Newell, *The Seleucid Coinage of Tyre* (NNM 73, New York, 1936).

1936b E.T. Newell, *The Pergamene Mint under Philetaerus* (NNM 76, New York, 1936).

1937 E.T. Newell, *Royal Greek Portrait Coins* (Racine, Wisconsin, 1937).

1938a E.T. Newell, 'The coinage of the Parthians', in *A Survey of Persian Art*, ed. A.U. Pope and P. Ackerman (Oxford, 1938), I. 475–92.

1938b E.T. Newell, *Miscellanea Numismatica: Cyrene to India* (NNM 82, New York, 1938).

1938c E.T. Newell, *The Coinage of the Eastern Seleucid Mints from Seleucus I to Antiochus III* (NS 1, New York, 1938; repr. w. additions and corrections, 1977) (= *ESM*).

1939 E.T. Newell, *Late Seleucid mints in Ake-Ptolemais* (NNM 84, New York, 1939).

1941 E.T. Newell, *The Coinages of the Western Seleucid Mints from Seleucus I to Antiochus III* (NS 4, New York, 1941; repr. with additions and corrections, 1978) (= *WSM*).

NICOLAOU AND MØRKHOLM 1976 I. Nicolaou and O. Mørkholm, *A Ptolemaic Coin Hoard* (*Paphos* I) (Nicosia, 1976).

NICOLET 1971 H. Nicolet, 'Monnaies de bronze de Cilicie (Séleucie du Kalykadnos)', RN^6 13 (1971), 26–37.

NICOLET-PIERRE 1978 H. Nicolet-Pierre, 'Thionèsis, roi de Characène (25/24–20/19 ou 19/18 av. J.-C.)', RN^6 20 (1978), 46–55.

1979 H. Nicolet-Pierre, 'Les monnaies des deux derniers satrapes d'Egypte avant la conquête d'Alexandre', in *Essays Thompson* (1979), 221–30.

1982 H. Nicolet-Pierre, 'De l'ancien au nouveau style athénien: une continuité?', in *Studia Naster* (1982), I. 105–14.

1989 H. Nicolet-Pierre, 'Monnaies de Pergame', in *KME* (1989), 203–16.

NODELMAN 1960 S.A. Nodelman, 'A preliminary history of Characene', *Berytus* 13 (1960), 83–121.

NOE 1950 S.P. Noe, *The Alexander Coinage of Sicyon* (NS 6, New York, 1950).

1958 S.P. Noe, 'A tetrobol of Histiaea', *ANSMN* 8 (1958), 55–6.

1962 S.P. Noe, 'The Corinth hoard of 1938', *ANSMN* 10 (1962), 9–41.

NORDBØ 1972 J. Nordbø, Utmyntningen fra Knidos 394 f. Kr.–ca. 200 e. Kr. (unpublished thesis, Oslo, 1972).

OAKLEY 1982 J.H. Oakley, 'The autonomous wreathed tetradrachms of Kyme, Aeolis', *ANSMN* 27 (1982), 1–37.

OECONOMIDES 1982 M. Oeconomides, 'Contribution à l'étude du monnayage d'Alexandre le Grand. A propos d'un trésor inédit du Musée numismatique d'Athènes', in *Studia Naster* (1982), 89–96.

OLCAY AND SEYRIG 1965 N. Olcay and H. Seyrig, *Le trésor de Mektepini en Phrygie* (Inst. franç. d'archéologie de Beyrouth, Bibl. archéol. et hist. 82, Trésors monétaires Séleucides 1, Paris, 1965).

PEGAN 1968 E. Pegan, 'Die frühesten Tetradrachmen Alexanders des Grossen mit dem Adler, ihre Herkunft und Entstehungszeit', *JNG* 18 (1968), 99–111.

PERL 1968 G. Perl, 'Zur Chronologie der Königreiche Bithynien, Pontos und Bosporus', in *Studien zur Geschichte und Philosophie des Altertums*, ed. J. Harmatta (Amsterdam, 1968), 299–330.

PERLMAN 1965 S. Perlman, 'The coins of Philip II and Alexander the Great and their Pan-Hellenic propaganda', NC^7 5 (1965), 57–67.

PESTMAN 1967 P.W. Pestman, *Chronologie égyptienne d'après les textes démotiques* (Leiden, 1967).

1981 P.W. Pestman, *A Guide to the Zenon Archive* (*P.L. Bat. 21*) (Papyrologica Lugduno–Batava XXI.A, Leiden, 1981).

PETITOT-BIEHLER 1975 C.-Y. Petitot-Biehler, 'Trésor de monnaies grecques et gréco-bactriennes trouvé à Aï Khanoum (Afghanistan)', RN^6 17 (1975), 23–57.

PETROWICZ 1904 A. von Petrowicz, *Arsaciden-Münzen* (Vienna, 1904; repr. Graz, 1968). (See also Allotte 1905. Petrowicz's Parthian coins were included in the Ars Classica–Naville sale 12, Lucerne, 18.x.1926.)

PFEILER 1968 H. Pfeiler, 'Die frühesten Porträts des Mithridates Eupator und die Bronzeprägungen seiner Vorgänger', *SM* 18 (1968), 75–80.

1969 H. Pfeiler, 'Eine Drachme Demetrios' I aus Soloi', *SM* 19 (1969), 42–3.

PICARD 1979 O. Picard, *Chalkis et la confédération euboienne* (Paris, 1979).

POENARU BORDEA 1979 G. Poenaru Bordea, 'Les statères ouest-pontiques de type Alexandre le Grand et Lysimaque', *RBN* 125 (1979), 37–51.

POLLAK 1970 P. Pollak, 'A Bithynian hoard of the first century B.C.', *ANSMN* 16 (1970), 45–56.

POLYAENUS Polyaenus, *Strategemeton libri viii*, ed. E. Wölfflin. (Leipzig (Bibl. Teub.), 1887).

POLYBIUS Polybius, *Historiae*, ed. L. Dindorf and T. Buttner-Wobst (5 vols., Leipzig (Bibl. Teub.), 1889–1904).

POPOVIĆ 1980 P. Popović, 'Tetradrachme Filipa II i njihove najranije imitacije iz zbirke Narodnog Muzeja u Beogradu' ('Tetradrachms of Philip II and their earliest imitations in the National Museum at Belgrade'), *Numismaticar* 3 (1980), 7–21.

PRICE 1968a M.J. Price, 'Early Greek bronze coinage', in *Essays Robinson* (1968), 90–104.
1968b M.J. Price, 'Mithridates VI Eupator, Dionysus, and the coinages of the Black Sea', NC^7 8 (1968), 1–12.
1969 M.J. Price, 'Greek coin hoards in the British Museum', NC^7 9 (1969), 1–14.
1979a M.J. Price, 'On attributing Alexanders – some cautionary tales', in *Essays Thompson* (1979), 241–50.
1979b M.J. Price, 'The coinage of Philip II', NC^7 19 (1979), 230–41.
1979c M.J. Price, 'The functions of early Greek bronze coinage', *AIIN* 25, Suppl. (1979), 351–58, with discussion on 358–65.
1982a M.J. Price, 'The "Poros" coinage of Alexander the Great: a symbol of concord and community', in *Studia Naster* (1982), 75–88.
1982b M.J. Price, 'Alexander's reform of the Macedonian regal coinage', *NC* 142 (1982), 180–90.
1983 M.J. Price, 'Thoughts on the beginnings of coinage', in *Studies Grierson* (1983), 1–10.
1985a M.J. Price, 'Greek hoards', *CH* 7 (1985), 5–37.
1985b M.J. Price, 'Thrace (1980)', *CH* 7 (1985), 42–4.
1989 M.J. Price, 'The Larissa, 1968 hoard (*IGCH* 237)', in *KME* (1989), 233–43.
PROKOPOV 1986 I. Prokopov, 'La circulation des monnaies en bronze de Philippe V et de Persée dans la Bulgarie du sud-ouest', *Numismatica* 20. 3 (1986), 5–30. (In Bulgarian, with French summary.)
RAVEL 1936, 1948 O.E. Ravel, *Les 'poulains' de Corinthe* (2 vols., Basel, 1936; London, 1948).
1938 O.E. Ravel, 'Corinthian hoard from Chiliomodi', in *INC London* (1936), 98–108.
RAVEN 1950 E.J.P. Raven, 'The Amphictionic coinage of Delphi, 336–334 B.C.', NC^6 10 (1950), 1–22.
REBUFFAT 1983 F. Rebuffat, 'Alexandre le Grand et les problèmes financiers au début de son règne', RN^6 25 (1983), 43–52.
1986 F. Rebuffat, 'Alexandre le Grand et Apollonia de Pisidie', RN^6 28 (1986), 65–71.
REEKMANS 1948 T. Reekmans, 'Monetary history and the dating of Ptolemaic papyri', *Studia Hellenistica* 5 (1948), 15–43.
1949 T. Reekmans, 'Economic and social repercussions of the Ptolemaic copper inflation', *Chronique d'Egypte* 24 (1949), 324–42.
REGLING 1906 K. Regling, 'Zum älteren römischen und italienischen Münzwesen', *Klio* 6 (1906), 489–524.
1924 K. Regling, *Die antike Münze als Kunstwerk* (Berlin, 1924).
1927 K. Regling, *Die Münzen von Priene* (Berlin, 1927).
1931 K. Regling, 'Der griechische Goldschatz von Prinkipo', *ZfN* 41 (1931), 1–46.
1935 K. Regling, 'Dynastenmünzen von Tyana, Morima und Anisa in Kappadokien', *ZfN* 42 (1935), 1–23.
REINACH 1888 T. Reinach, *Trois royaumes d'Asie Mineure: Cappadoce–Bithynie–Pont* (*Numismatique antique*) (Paris, 1888). (Reprint of articles from the *RN* 1886–8.)
RICHTER 1965 G.M.A. Richter, *The Portraits of the Greeks* (3 vols., London, 1965).
RITTER 1975 H.-W. Ritter, 'Zum Schild auf dem Münzen des Philadelphos', *SM* 25 (1975), 2–3.
ROBERT 1951 L. Robert, *Études de numismatique grecque* (Paris, 1951).
1955 L. Robert, 'Monnaie de Thibron', *Hellenica* 10 (1955), 167–71.
1963 L. Robert, *Noms indigènes dans l'Asie-Mineure gréco-romaine* 1 (Bibl. archéol. et hist. de l'Institut français d'archéologie d'Istanbul 13, Paris, 1963).
1966 L. Robert, *Monnaies antiques en Troade* (Publ. du Centre de recherches d'histoire et de philologie de la IVe section de l'École pratique des Hautes Études, Paris, 1.i, Paris/Geneva, 1966).

1973 L. Robert, 'Les monétaires et un décret hellénistique de Sestos', *RN*[6] 15 (1973), 43–53.

1977 L. Robert, 'Monnaies hellénistiques', *RN*[6] 19 (1977), 6–47.

1982 L. Robert, 'Trois ateliers monétaires d'Ionie et de Carie à l'époque impériale', in *INC Berne Actes* (1982), 309–19.

ROBIN 1974 C. Robin, 'Monnaies provenant de l'Arabie du nord-est', *Semitica* 24 (1974), 83–125.

ROBINSON 1920 E.S.G. Robinson, 'A find of coins from Sinope', *NC*[4] 20 (1920), 1–16.

1921 E.S.G. Robinson, 'Aspeisas satrap of Susiana', *NC*[5] 1 (1921), 37–8.

1954 E.S.G. Robinson, 'Cistophori in the name of King Eumenes', *NC*[6] 14 (1954), 1–8.

ROGERS 1927 E. Rogers, *The Second and Third Seleucid Coinage of Tyre* (NNM 34, New York, 1937).

ROSTOVTZEFF 1939 M.I. Rostovtzeff, 'Some remarks on the monetary and commercial policy of the Seleucids and Attalids', in *Anatolian Studies Presented to William Helburn Buckler*, ed. W.M. Calder and J. Keil (Manchester, 1939), 277–98.

1941 M. Rostovtzeff, *Social and Economic History of the Hellenistic World* (3 vols., Oxford, 1941).

ROUSSEVA 1986 B. Rousseva, 'Un trésor d'Alexandres du village "Pet Moguili" (*IGCH* 856)', *Numismatica* 20.1 (1986), 11–34. (In Bulgarian, with French summary.)

ROUSSEVA AND KOEV 1986 B. Rousseva and K. Koev, 'Trésor monétaire hellénistique de Toutrakan (*IGCH* 836)', *Numismatica* 20.4 (1986), 3–13. (In Bulgarian, with French summary.)

RTVELADZE 1984 E.V. Rtveladze, 'La circulation monétaire au nord de l'Oxus à l'époque gréco-bactrienne', *RN*[6] 26 (1984), 61–7.

SACKS 1985 K.S. Sacks, 'The wreathed coins of Aeolian Myrina', *ANSMN* 30 (1985), 1–43.

SALZMANN 1980 D. Salzmann, 'Überlegungen zum Schild auf den Münzen des Ptolemaios Philadelphos und verwandten Denkmälern', *SM* 30 (1980), 33–9.

SAMUEL 1962 A.E. Samuel, *Ptolemaic Chronology* (Münchener Beiträge zur Papyrusforschung und antiken Rechtsgeschichte 43, Munich, 1962).

SANDS 1908 P.C. Sands, *The Client Princes of the Roman Empire under the Republic* (Cambridge, 1908).

SCHEU 1960 F. Scheu, 'Coinage systems of Aetolia', *NC*[6] 20 (1960), 37–52.

SCHINDEL 1983 P.C. Schindel, 'Contribution à la numismatique d'Alexandre le Grand: localisation des ateliers frappant des hémidrachmes et suggestion pour une meilleure définition des critères d'atelier', *Cercle d'études numismatiques: Bulletin* 20 (1983), 1–5.

SCHLÖSSER 1985a E. Schlösser, 'Denominations and weights of bronze coins of Antiochus IV of Syria and their relation to the silver coinage', *SM* 35 (1985), 33–6.

1985b E. Schlösser, 'Bestimmung des Gewichtes der Tetradrachmen Alexanders des Grossen', *Geldgeschichtliche Nachrichten* 20 (1985), 160–2.

1986 E. Schlösser, 'Gewichte der attischen Tetradrachmen der Seleukiden aus der Münzstätte Antiocheia am Orontes', *SM* 36 (1986), 61–6.

SCHMITT 1957 H.H. Schmitt, *Rom und Rhodos* (Münchener Beiträge zur Papyrusforschung und antiken Rechtsgeschichte 40, Munich, 1957).

1969 H.H. Schmitt (ed.), *Die Staatsverträge des Altertums.* III: *Die Verträge der griechisch–römischen Welt von 338 bis 200 v. Chr.* (Munich, 1969).

SCHÖNERT-GEISS 1970 E. Schönert-Geiss, *Die Münzprägung von Byzantion.* I: *Autonome Zeit* (Berlin/Amsterdam, 1970).

1977 E. Schönert-Geiss, *Griechisches Münzwerk: Die Münzprägung von Bisanthe, Dikaia, Selymbria* (Berlin, 1977).

1987 E. Schönert-Geiss, *Griechisches Münzwerk: Die Münzprägung von Maroneia* (2 parts, Berlin, 1987).

SCHUBART 1922 W. Schubart, 'Die ptolemäische Reichsmünze in den auswärtigen Besitzungen unter Philadelphos', *ZfN* 33 (1922), 74–82.

SCHWABACHER 1939 W. Schwabacher, 'A hoard of drachms of Elis', *NC*[5] 19 (1939), 239–65.

1951 W. Schwabacher, 'Some unknown federal coins of the Acarnanians', in *Studies Robinson* (1951), II. 218–23.

1953 W. Schwabacher, 'Der Parthenos-Archetyp der hellenistischen Silbermünzen Athens', in *Opuscula Atheniensia* I (Lund, 1953), 104–14.

SEEGER 1972 A. Seeger, 'An unpublished drachm of Antiochos VI', *NC*[7] 12 (1972), 305.

SELLWOOD 1962 D.G. Sellwood, 'The Parthian coins of Gotarzes I, Orodes I, and Sinatruces', *NC*[7] 2 (1962), 73–89.

1963 D.G. Sellwood, 'Some experiments in Greek minting technique', *NC*[7] 3 (1963), 217–31.

1965 D.G. Sellwood, 'Wroth's unknown Parthian king', *NC*[7] 5 (1965), 113–35.

1967 D.G. Sellwood, 'The Parthian "Dark Age" in the light of "Susa" ', *NCirc.* 75 (1967), 293–4.

1969 D.G. Sellwood, 'A small hoard of Parthian drachms of the first century B.C.', *Seaby's Coin and Medal Bulletin* 1969, 227–32.

1971a D.G. Sellwood, 'Some politic alterations in the Parthian series', in *Mints, Dies and Currency. Essays Dedicated to the Memory of Albert Baldwin*, ed. R.A.G. Carson (London, 1971), 33–7.

1971b D.G. Sellwood, 'Deux notes sur les drachmes parthes', *RN*[6] 13 (1971), 154–9.

1976 D.G. Sellwood, 'The drachms of the Parthian "Dark Age" ', *Journal of the Royal Asiatic Society* 1976, 2–25.

1980 D.G. Sellwood, *The Coinage of Parthia* (2nd edn, London, 1980).

1989 D.G. Sellwood, 'New Parthian coin types', *NC* 149 (1989), 162–9.

SELTMAN 1921 C.T. Seltman, *The Temple Coins of Olympia* (Cambridge, 1921).

SEYRIG 1939 H. Seyrig, 'Antiquités syriennes 24. Les rois séleucides et la concession d'asylie', *Syria* 20 (1939), 35–9.

1950a H. Seyrig, *Notes on Syrian Coins* (NNM 119, New York, 1950).

1950b H. Seyrig, 'Antiquités syriennes 42. Sur les ères de quelques villes de Syrie: Antioche, Apamée, Aréthuse, Balanée, Epiphanée, Laodicée, Rhosos, Damas, Béryte, Tripolis, l'ère de Cléopâtre, Chalcis du Liban, Doliché', *Syria* 27 (1950), 5–50.

1951 H. Seyrig, 'Antiquités syriennes 49. Aradus et sa pérée sous les rois Séleucides', *Syria* 28 (1951), 206–20.

1958a H. Seyrig, 'Parion au 3e siècle avant notre ère', in *ANS Centennial Publication* (1958), 603–25.

1958b H. Seyrig, 'Antiquités syriennes 67. Monnaies contremarquées en Syrie', *Syria* 35 (1958), 187–97.

1962 H. Seyrig, 'Le monnayage de Ptolémaïs en Phénicie', *RN*[6] 4 (1962), 26–32.

1963 H. Seyrig, 'Monnaies hellénistiques, I–X', *RN*[6] 5 (1963), 7–64.

1964 H. Seyrig, 'Monnaies hellénistiques, XI–XIII', *RN*[6] 6 (1964), 7–67.

1968 H. Seyrig, 'Monnaies hellénistiques de Byzance et de Chalcédoine', in *Essays Robinson* (1968), 183–200.

1969 H. Seyrig, 'Monnaies hellénistiques, XIV–XVII', *RN*[6] 11 (1969), 36–52.

1971 H. Seyrig, 'Monnaies hellénistiques, XVIII–XXII', *RN*[6] 13 (1971), 7–25.

1973 H. Seyrig, *Trésors du Levant anciens et nouveaux* (Inst. français d'archéologie de Beyrouth, Bibl. arch. et hist. 94, Trésors monétaires séleucides 2, Paris, 1973).

1974 H. Seyrig, 'Un symbole monétaire de Tarse', in *Mélanges Mansel* (Ankara, 1974), I. 263–4.

SIMONETTA 1957 A. Simonetta, 'Notes on the Parthian and Indo-Parthian issues of the first century B.C.', in *INC Paris* (1957), II. 111–21.

1961 B. Simonetta, 'Notes on the coinage of the Cappadocian kings', NC^7 1 (1961), 9–50.

1964 B. Simonetta, 'Remarks on some Cappadocian problems', NC^7 4 (1964), 83–92.

1966 A.M. Simonetta, 'Some remarks on the Arsacid coinage of the period 90–57 B.C.', NC^7 6 (1966), 15–40.

1968 A.M. Simonetta, 'Le monetazione partica dal 247 al 122 a.C.', *RIN* 70 (1968), 11–64.

1973 B. Simonetta, 'Ariarathes IV o Ariarathes VI? Osservazioni su alcune rare monete di Cappadocia', *QT* 2 (1973), 37–42.

1974a B. Simonetta, 'Osservazioni su talune emissioni barbariche dei re di Cappadocia', *RIN* 76 (1974), 95–114.

1974b B. Simonetta, 'Problemi di numismatica partica. Tetradramma di Mitridate II o di "re ignoto"? Osservazioni sulle monete coniate fra il 90 ed il 70 A.C.', *RIN* 76 (1974), 115–38.

1975a B. Simonetta, 'Sulla prima monetazione di Ariarathes VI di Cappadocia', *SM* 25 (1975), 4–7.

1975b B. Simonetta, 'Raffronto tra alcuni stateri de Mazaeus a Tarsus e le dramme di Ariarathes I di Cappadocia', *SM* 25 (1975), 91–5.

1975c B. Simonetta, 'Un tetradramma inedito di Artabanus I de Parthia', *QT* 4 (1975), 151–6.

1975d B. Simonetta, 'Problemi di numismatica partica. Osservazioni sulle attribuzioni delle monete partiche coniate fra il 70 ed il 57 a.C.', *RSN* 54 (1975), 65–78.

1976a B. Simonetta, 'Sulla monetazione di Fraate IV e di Tiridate II di Parthia', *RIN* 77 (1976), 19–34.

1976b B. Simonetta, 'Sul probabile significato di un monogramma su alcune dramme partiche', *QT* 5 (1976), 103–6.

1977 B. Simonetta, *The Coins of the Cappadocian Kings* (Typos II, Fribourg, 1977).

1978a B. Simonetta, 'Considerazioni sull'inizio dell'anno partico nella monetazione di Seleucia sul Tigri', *SM* 28 (1978), 2–8.

1978b B. Simonetta, 'On some tetradrachms of Orodes II and the probable issues of Pacorus I', NC^7 18 (1978), 7–13.

SIMONETTA AND SELLWOOD 1978 A. Simonetta and D.G. Sellwood, 'Again on the Parthian coinage from Mithridates II to Orodes II', *QT* 7 (1978), 95–119.

SIMONETTA AND SIMONETTA 1949 B. and A. Simonetta, 'Le vicende di Fraate IV, re dei Parti, ricostruite con l'aiuto dei tetradrammi da lui coniati', *Numismatica* 15 (1949), 37–46.

SKEAT 1954 T.C. Skeat, *The Reigns of the Ptolemies* (Münchener Beiträge zur Papyrusforschung und antiken Rechtsgeschichte 39, Munich, 1954).

SORDI 1956 M. Sordi, 'La dracma di Aleuas e l'origine di un tipo monetario di Alessandro Magno', *AIIN* 3 (1956), 9–22.

SPAER 1971 A. Spaer, 'Monnaies de bronzes palestiniennes d'Antiochos VII', RN^6 13 (1971), 160–1.

1976 A. Spaer, 'Antiochus IV et Ake-Ptolemais', in *INC New York–Washington Proc.* (1976), 139–41.

1989 A. Spaer, 'More on the "Ptolemaic" coins of Aradus', in *KME* (1989), 267–73.

STÖCKLI 1975 W.E. Stöckli, 'Bemerkungen zur Chronologie von Victoriat, Denar, Quinar und Sesterz', *JNG* 25 (1975), 73–90.

STRAUSS 1971 P. Strauss, 'Un trésor de monnaies hellénistiques trouvé près de Suse (2e partie)', RN^6 13 (1971), 109–40. (See Houghton and Le Rider 1966 for an earlier part of this hoard.)

SULLIVAN 1973 R.D. Sullivan, 'Diadochic coinage in Commagene after Tigranes the Great', *NC*^{7} 13 (1973), 18–39.

1977 R.D. Sullivan, 'The dynasty of Commagene', in *ANRW* II.11.8 (1977), 732–98.

1980 R.D. Sullivan, 'Dynasts in Pontus', in *ANRW* II.7.2 (1980), 902–30.

SVORONOS 1890 J.N. Svoronos, *Numismatique de la Crète ancienne* (Mâcon, 1890).

1904–8 J.N. Svoronos, *Τὰ νομίσματα τοῦ κράτους τῶν Πτολεμαίων* (4 vols., Athens, 1904–8).

TARN 1951 W.W. Tarn, *The Greeks in Bactria and India* (2nd edn., Cambridge, 1951).

TASYÜREK 1975 A. Tasyürek, 'Die Münzprägung der Könige von Kommagene', *Antike Welt* 6 (Sondernummer: Kommagene), 42–3.

THOMPSON 1942 M. Thompson, 'Coins for the Eleusinia', *Hesperia* 11 (1942), 213–29.

1965 M. Thompson, 'A countermarked hoard from Büyükçekmece', *ANSMN* 6 (1954), 11–34.

1961 M. Thompson, *The New Style Silver Coinage of Athens* (NS 10, 2 vols., New York, 1961).

1962 M. Thompson, 'Athens again', *NC*^{7} 2 (1962), 301–33.

1968a M. Thompson, 'The mints of Lysimachus', in *Essays Robinson* (1968), 163–82.

1968b M. Thompson, *The Agrinion Hoard* (NNM 159, New York, 1968).

1981a M. Thompson, 'The Cavalla hoard (*IGCH* 450)', *ANSMN* 26 (1981), 33–49.

1981b M. Thompson, 'The Alexandrine mint of Mylasa', *QT* 10 (1981), 207–17.

1982 M. Thompson, 'Posthumous Philip II staters of Asia Minor', in *Studia Naster* (1982), 57–63.

1983 M. Thompson, *Alexander's Drachm Mints.* I: *Sardes and Miletus* (NS 16, New York, 1983).

1984 M. Thompson, 'Paying the mercenaries', in *Festschrift Mildenberg* (1984), 241–7.

1986 M. Thompson, 'The Armenak hoard (*IGCH* 1423)', *ANSMN* 31 (1986), 63–106.

THOMPSON AND BELLINGER 1955 M. Thompson and A.R. Bellinger, 'Greek coins in the Yale Collection, IV: A hoard of Alexander drachms', *YCS* 14 (1955), 3–45.

THOMSEN 1961 R. Thomsen, *Early Roman Coinage. A Study of the Chronology.* (3 vols., Copenhagen, 1957–61).

TOPALOV 1986 S. Topalov, 'Chronologie relative des tétradrachmes frappés à Cabylé', *Numismatica* 20.1 (1986), 34–41. (In Bulgarian, with French summary.)

TROXELL 1971 H.A. Troxell, 'The Peloponnesian Alexanders', *ANSMN* 17 (1971), 41–94.

1977 H.A. Troxell, 'Greek accessions: Asia Minor to India', *ANSMN* 22 (1977), 9–27.

1982 H.A. Troxell, *The Coinage of the Lycian League* (NNM 162, New York, 1982).

1983 H.A. Troxell, 'Arsinoe's non-era', *ANSMN* 28 (1983), 35–70.

VANDEGEERDE 1984 P.-Y. Vandegeerde, 'Portraits de rois séleucides', *Revue belge de philologie et d'histoire* 62 (1984), 59–78.

VAROUCHA-CHRISTODOULOPOULOU 1941 I. Varoucha-Christodoulopoulou, *Πτολεμαικὰ νομίσματα στὴν κυρίως Ἑλλάδα*', in *'Επιτύμβιον Χρήστου Τσούντα* (Athens, 1941), 668–79.

VIEDEBANTT 1923 O. Viedebantt, *Antike Gewichtsnormen und Münzfüsse* (Berlin, 1923).

VOEGTLI 1973 H. Voegtli, 'Der Schild des Philadelphos', *SM* 23 (1973), 86–9.

VOLKMANN 1924 H. Volkmann, 'Zur Münzprägung des Demetrios I und Alexander I von Syrien', *ZfN* 34 (1924), 51–66.

WAAGE 1952 D.B. Waage, *Greek, Roman, Byzantine and Crusaders' Coins* (= *Antioch on the Orontes,* IV. 2, Princeton, 1952).

WADDINGTON *et al.* 1902–12 W.H. Waddington, E. Babelon and T. Reinach, *Recueil général des monnaies grecques de l'Asie Mineure* (4 vols., Paris, 1902–12; repr. Hildesheim/New York, 1976). I.1: *Pont et Paphlagonie* (1904); I.2: *Bithynie (jusqu'à Juliopolis)* (1908); I.3: *Nicée et Nicomédie* (1910); I.4: *Prusa, Prusias, Tius* (1912).

WAGGONER 1969 N.M. Waggoner, 'The early Alexander coinage at Seleucia on the Tigris', *ANSMN* 15 (1969), 21–30.

1974 N.M. Waggoner, 'The coinage of Phraates III of Parthia: Addenda', in *Studies Miles* (1974), 15–26.

1979a N.M. Waggoner, 'Tetradrachms from Babylon', in *Essays Thompson* (1979), 269–80.

1979b N.M. Waggoner, 'The Propontis hoard (IGCH 888)', *RN*[6] 21 (1979), 7–29.

1982 N.M. Waggoner, 'Another Alexander tetradrachm of Audoleon', in *Studia Naster* (1982), 99–103.

1983 N.M. Waggoner, 'Further reflections on Audoleon and his Alexander mint', *RBN* 129 (1983), 5–21.

1986 N.M. Waggoner, 'Cassander in Babylon?', *SAN* 16.4 (1986), 68.

1989 N.M. Waggoner, 'A new wrinkle in the Hellenistic coinage of Antioch/Alabanda', in *KME* (1989), 283–90.

WALKER 1982 A.S. Walker, 'Some plated coins from the Agora at Athens', in *INC Berne Actes* (1982), 131–6.

WALKER AND KING 1976 D.R. Walker and C.E. King, *The Metrology of the Roman Silver Coinage*. I: *From Augustus to Domitian* (BAR Supplementary Series 5, Oxford, 1976).

WALLACE 1956 W.P. Wallace, *The Euboian League and its Coinage* (NNM 134, New York, 1956).

1968 W.P. Wallace, 'A tyrant of Karystos', in *Essays Robinson* (1968), 201–9.

1984 W.P. Wallace, 'The "Reduced Euboio-Attic" coin standard', in *Nickle Papers* (1984), 19–37.

WARREN 1968 J. Warren, 'The trihemidrachms of Corinth', in *Essays Robinson* (1968), 125–44.

1969 J. Warren, 'The earliest obols of Megalopolis', *ANSMN* 15 (1969), 31–40.

WARREN 1983, 1984, 1985 J.A.W. Warren, 'The autonomous bronze coinage of Sicyon', *NC* 143 (1983), 23–56; 144 (1984), 1–24; 145 (1985), 45–66.

WELLES 1970 C.B. Welles, *Alexander and the Hellenistic World* (Toronto, 1970).

WESTERMARK 1960 U. Westermark, *Das Bildnis des Philetairos von Pergamon. Corpus der Münzprägung* (Stockholm, 1960).

1980 U. Westermark, 'Notes on the Saida hoard (*IGCH* 1508)', *NNÅ* 1979–80, 22–35.

1981 U. Westermark, 'The portrait coin of Eumenes II', in *LAGOM. Festschrift für Peter Berghaus zum 60. Geburtstag* (Münster, 1981), 19–23.

WHITEHEAD 1943 R.B. Whitehead, 'The eastern satrap Sophytes', *NC*[6] 3 (1943), 60–72.

WILL 1975 E. Will, 'Les sources des métaux monnayés dans le monde grec', in *NAPM* (1975), 97–102.

1979 E. Will, *Histoire politique du monde hellénistique (323–30 av. J.-C.)* (2 vols., 2nd edn, Nancy, 1979).

WOLSKI 1959 J. Wolski, 'L'historicité d'Arsace Ier', *Historia* 8 (1959), 222–381.

1962 J. Wolski, 'Arsace II et le généalogie des premiers arsacides', *Historia* 11 (1962), 138–45.

WROTH 1900a W. Wroth, 'Otanes, and Phraates IV', *NC*[3] 20 (1900), 89–95.

1900b W. Wroth, 'On the rearrangement of Parthian coinage', *NC*[3] 20 (1900), 181–202.

1905 W. Wroth, 'The earliest Parthian coins: a reply to Sir Henry Howorth', *NC*[4] 5 (1905), 317–23.

YARKIN 1981 U. Yarkin, 'An unpublished coin of Ariarathes III for Cybistra in Cappodocia', *NC* 141 (1981), 144–5.

YOUROUKOVA 1976 J. Youroukova, *Coins of the Ancient Thracians* (BAR Supplementary Series 4, Oxford, 1976).

1982 J. Youroukova, 'La présence des monnaies de bronze des premiers Séleucides en Thrace. Leur importance historique', in *Studia Naster* (1982), 115–27.

ZAMBELLI 1968 M. Zambelli, 'Crisi monetaria e separitismo municipale durante il regno di Antioco IV Epifane', in *Seconda Miscellanea Greca e Romana* (Studi pubblicati dall'Istituto Italiano per la Storia Antica 19, Rome, 1968), 293–333.

ZERVOS 1967 O.H. Zervos, 'Early tetradrachms of Ptolemy I', *ANSMN* 13 (1967), 1–16.

1976 O.H. Zervos, 'The Delta hoard of Ptolemaic Alexanders, 1896', *ANSMN* 21 (1976), 37–58.

1978 O.H. Zervos, 'A Ptolemaic hoard of "Athena" tetradrachms at ANS', *ANSMN* 23 (1978), 43–58.

1979 O.H. Zervos, 'Near Eastern elements in the tetradrachms of Alexander the Great: the eastern mints', in *Essays Thompson* (1979), 295–305.

1980 O.H. Zervos, 'Newell's manuscript of the Kuft hoard', *ANSMN* 25 (1980), 17–29.

1982 O.H. Zervos, 'The earliest coins of Alexander the Great. 1. Notes on a book by Gerhard Kleiner', *NC* 142 (1982), 166–79.

PLATES

PLATE CAPTIONS

The standard abbreviations for metals are used: AV (gold), AR (silver), AE (bronze). For other abbreviations see p. xxii (general) and pp. 209–11 (bibliographical).

I. PHILIP II AND ALEXANDER THE GREAT

Philip II (359–336)

1 *Pella, c.* 345/340–342/336. Stater, AV 8.55g. Stockholm (*SNG* 954). Le Rider 1977, 134.45a.
2 Same mint, *c.* 359–355/4. Tetradrachm, AR 14.43g. Stockholm (*SNG* 965). Le Rider 1977, 10.41a.
3 *Amphipolis, c.* 342/1–329/8. Tetradrachm, AR 14.06g. Copenhagen (*SNG* 554). Le Rider 1977, 109.388b.
4 *Uncertain mint.* AE 9.36g. Stockholm (*SNG* 978).

Alexander the Great (336–323)

5 *Aegae* or *Amphipolis, c.* 336. Tetradrachm, AR 14.42g. London (*PCG*, pl. 29.3). Pegan 1968, 107, pl.10.2.
6 As last, same types and date. Drachm, AR 4.29g. Copenhagen (*SNG* 692).
7 *Amphipolis, c.* 333/2. Distater, AV 17.21g. Stockholm (*SNG* 991). Cf. Newell 1923a, no. 254.
8 *Babylon.* Stater, AV 8.52g. Stockholm (*SNG* 1050).
9 *Amphipolis, c.* 324/3. Tetradrachm, AR 17.20g. Stockholm (*SNG* 996). Newell 1923a, no. 1344.
10 *Sardis, c.* 330–325. Drachm, AR 4.26g. Copenhagen (*SNG* –). Thompson 1983, nos. 43–9.
11 *Uncertain mint.* AE 5.86g. Stockholm (*SNG* 1085).
12 *Aegae.* Distater, AV 17.19g. Copenhagen (*SNG* 623). Noe 1950, 7.14b.
13 *Tarsus, c.* 323–319. Tetradrachm, AR 17.19g. Copenhagen (*SNG* 779). Newell 1923a, no. 2349.

Local issues

14 *Tarsus, c.* 327, with initial *I* (for Issus). Persic stater (= double siglos), AR 11.02g. London (*BMC, Lycaonia, etc.*, 173.65).
15 Same mint, with the name of Balacrus (satrap 333–323). Same denomination, AR 10.69g. *SNG von Aulock* 5963. Aulock 1964, 80, pl.5.2.

Alexander the Great

16 *Myriandrus, c.* 328–326. Tetradrachm, AR 16.92g. Copenhagen (*SNG* 788). Newell 1923a, no. 2796.
17 *Aradus, c.* 323–319. Tetradrachm, AR 17.25g. Copenhagen (*SNG* 796). Newell 1923a, no. 3303.

II. ALEXANDER THE GREAT AND CONTEMPORARY ISSUES

Alexander the Great (336–323)

18 *Byblus*, before 318. Tetradrachm, AR 17.28g. Copenhagen (*SNG* 804). Newell 1923a, no. 3587.
19 *Sidon*, *c*.323. Tetradrachm, AR 17.14g. Copenhagen (*SNG* 806). Newell 1916, 14.34.
20 *Ake*, dated 325. Tetradrachm, AR 17.17g. Copenhagen (*SNG* 808). Newell 1916, 43.14.
21 *Damascus*, *c*. 330–319. Tetradrachm, AR 17.15g. Copenhagen (*SNG* 792). Newell 1923a, no. 2919.
22 *Salamis*, *c*. 330–320. Tetradrachm, AR 16.92g. Copenhagen (*SNG* 783). Newell 1923a, no. 2445; Newell 1915, 308.7.

Local issues

23 *Byblus*, with Alexander types but initial of Ainel (*c*. 333) in Aramaic below throne. Tetradrachm, AR 17.02g. New York, ex Demanhur hoard (*IGCH* 1664), no. 3586. Newell 1923a, 122ff.
24 Same mint and ruler, issue in his own name. One-eighth shekel, AR 0.76g. Stockholm.
25 *Egypt: Memphis?*, with the name of Artaxerxes III (342–338) in Demotic. Imitation of Athenian tetradrachm, AR 17.06g. Copenhagen (*SNG*, *Ptolemies* 2). *CH* I (1975), find 38.
26 As last, with the name of Mazaces (satrap *c*. 333/2) in Aramaic. Imitation of Athenian tetradrachm, AR 17.08g. Stockholm. Nicolet-Pierre 1979, 227.28 (this coin).

Alexander the Great

27 *Babylon*, *c*. 326–324. Tetradrachm, AR 17.16g. Stockholm (*SNG* 1052). Newell 1923a, no. 4372.
28 *Babylon*, with the name of Mazaeus (331–328) in Aramaic. Stater, AR 17.13g. London (*BMC, Arabia, etc.*, 180.2, pl.20.15).
29 Same mint, *c*. 331–300. Double daric with Persian types, AV 17.67g. Stockholm.
30 Same mint, *c*. 327/6. Decadrachm, AR 41.76g. London, ex Bank Leu 13 (22.iv.1975), 129.

Local issues

31 Syria, *Manbog* (= Hierapolis-Bambyce), *c*.331–323, with the names of Hadad and Atargatis in Aramaic. Didrachm (Attic), AR 8.00g. Paris. Seyrig 1971, 20.6a.
32 Same mint and date, with the names of Atargatis and the high-priest Abdhadad in Aramaic. *Rev.* Abdhadad standing in front of altar. Didrachm, AR 8.47g. Copenhagen, ex Numismatica Ars Classica 2 (1990), 228. Cf. Seyrig 1971, 18.3d.
33 Same mint and date, with the name of Alexander in Aramaic. Didrachm, AR 8.38g. Paris. Seyrig 1971, 20.10.

III. PERIOD OF ALEXANDER THE GREAT AND PHILIP III

Alexander the Great (336–323)

34 *Sardis*, *c*. 330–325. Stater, AV 8.60g. Vienna, ex Saida hoard (*IGCH* 1508). Thompson 1983, no. 28.
35 Same mint, *c*. 322/1. Drachm, AR 4.12g. Stockholm (*SNG* 1037). Thompson 1983, no. 155. (See also **10**.)
36 *Colophon*, *c*. 325. Drachm, AR 4.26g. Stockholm (*SNG* 1016).
37 *Miletus*, *c*. 325–323. Drachm, AR 4.14g. Stockholm (*SNG* 1031).
38 Same mint, *c*. 323/2. Stater, AV 8.57g. Copenhagen (*SNG* 633). Thompson 1983, no. 128.
39 *Lampsacus*, *c*.322. Drachm, AR 4.19g. Stockholm (*SNG* 1008).
40 *Abydus*, *c*. 323. Tetradrachm, AR 17.22g. Copenhagen (*SNG* –).
41 *Citium*, *c*. 332–320. Tetradrachm, AR 17.20g. Copenhagen (*SNG* 786). Newell 1923a, nos. 2546ff.
42 *Alexandria*, *c*. 325. Tetradrachm, AR 17.16g. Copenhagen (*SNG* 863). Zervos 1967, p. 14 issue II.

43 *Side?*, *c.* 326/5–319/18. Tetradrachm, AR 17.03g. Copenhagen (*SNG* 764). Newell 1923a, no. 1819.

44 *Uncertain eastern mint*, *c.* 326–323. Porus decadrachm, AR 40.74g. Copenhagen (*SNG* –), Babylon hoard (= *CH* I (1975), 38). Price 1982a, 75.A-a(ii).

45 As last, *c.* 326–323. Tetradrachm, AR 14.72g. Bank Leu 13 (22.iv.1975), 131. Hollstein 1989, 6.1.

46 As last, same date. Tetradrachm, AR 15.97g. Bank Leu 13 (22.iv.1975), 132. Hollstein 1989, 6.3.

Philip III (323–317)

47 *Babylon*. Stater, AV 8.60g. Stockholm (*SNG* 1101).

48 *Aradus*. Tetradrachm, AR 16.77g. Stockholm (*SNG* 1103).

49 *Lampsacus*, *c.* 322. Drachm, AR 4.22g. Stockholm (*SNG* 1107).

50 *Colophon*, *c.* 319. Drachm, AR 4.20g. Copenhagen (*SNG* 1100).

IV. PERIOD OF PHILIP III

Philip III (323–317)

51 *Magnesia*, *c.* 320. Drachm, AR 4.28g. Copenhagen (*SNG* 1102).

52 *Sardis*, *c.* 321/20. Drachm, AR 4.16g. Copenhagen (*SNG* 1093).

53 *Miletus*, *c.* 320/19. AE 5.34g. Stockholm (*SNG* 1125). Thompson 1983, nos. 198–202.

54 *Susa*. Tetradrachm, AR 16.99g. Stockholm (*SNG* 1105).

55 *Pella*, posthumous issue with types of Philip II, *c.* 323–315. Stater, AV 8.56g. Copenhagen (*SNG* 527). Le Rider 1977, no. 528e.

56 *Colophon*, with same types, *c.* 323–317. Stater, AV 8.57g. Stockholm (*SNG* 963). Thompson 1982, no. 12.

Local issues

57 *Babylon area*, *c.* 323–316. Imitations of Athenian tetradrachm. AR. (a) 15.85g. Paris. (b) 16.45g. Paris. Le Rider 1972a, 5.7–8.

58 *Lapethus*, Praxippus (*c.* 320–312). AE. Athens. Cf. *BMC, Cyprus*, p. liv, pl.20.2; Babelon 1893, p. cliii, fig. 76.

59 *Marium*, Stasioecus II (before 315–312). Persic diobol, AR 1.23g. London (*BMC, Cyprus*, 34.5, pl.6.13).

60 *Citium*, Pumiathon (361–312), *c.* 320 (date off-flan). Hemistater (Attic), AV 4.10g. Stockholm. Cf. Babelon 1893, 710ff.

61 *Paphos*, Nicocles (*c.* 323–310/9), with Alexander's name on reverse and Nicocles in tiny letters on obverse, *c.* 323–319. Tetradrachm,. AR 16.92g. Copenhagen (*SNG* –). Mørkholm 1978a, pl.1.2.

62 Same mint and ruler, with his name on reverse, *c.* 315. Tetradrachm, AR 17.21g. Turin. *BMC, Cyprus*, p. lxxix, pl.22.10; Babelon 1893, p. cxlv, fig. 68 (cast in London).

63 *Salamis*, Nicocreon (332/1–311/10), after 323. Stater (Attic), AV 8.27g. Paris (de Luynes; Babelon 1910, II.2, p. 727.1188).

64 Same mint, ruler and date. Didrachm (Rhodian), AR 6.14g. Copenhagen (*SNG* 62).

65 Same mint, Menelaus (311/10–302). One-third stater, AV 2.72g. Paris. Babelon 1893, no. 640.

66 *Susiana*, issue with Alexander types in the name of the satrap Aspeisas, *c.* 316. Tetradrachm, AR 16.94g. London. Robinson 1921, 37–8, pl.3.1.

67 *Mylasa*, with Alexander types attributed to Eupolemus, *c.* 315–311. Drachm, AR 4.13g. New York, ex Armenak hoard (Thompson 1986, no. 549). Thompson 1981b, 207.3, pl.1.3.

68 Same mint, ruler and date, with his name on the reverse. AE 4.23g. Copenhagen (*SNG* 1168).

V. PERIOD OF THE DIADOCHI

Time of Cassander (316–297)

69 *Amphipolis*, with types of Alexander, *c.* 315–294. Tetradrachm, AR 17.13g. Copenhagen (*SNG* 702).

70 Same mint, with types of Philip II, *c.* 315–294. Tetradrachm, AR 13.52g. Stockholm (*SNG* 977). Le Rider 1977, 125, pl.48.2.

71 *Uncertain mint*, Cassander, *c.* 310–305. AE 4.22g. Copenhagen (*SNG* 1139).

72 As last, Cassander, *c.* 305–297. AE 7.74g. Stockholm (*SNG* 1116).

73 *Miletus* ('anonymous bronze'), *c.* 297–294. AE 4.89g. Stockholm (*SNG* 1110). Liampi 1986, no. 223 (late 4th century).

74 *Uranopolis*, Alexander types, *c.* 316–297. Tetradrachm, AR 17.03g. Copenhagen (*SNG* 704).

75 Same mint and date. *Rev.* Aphrodite Urania seated on globe. AE 3.71g. Stockholm (*SNG, Forbat* 233).

Lysimachus (306–281)

76 *Lysimachia*, first series, with the names of Philip (II) and Lysimachus *ΛΥ*, *c.* 306/5–301/300. Tetrobol, AR 2.48g. New York. Thompson 1968a, 168.1, pl.16.1.

77 Same mint, series, types and date. AE 4.86g. New York. Thompson 1968a, 168.2, pl.16.2.

78 Same mint, second series, with *ΛΥ*, same date. AR 2.26g. New York. Thompson 1968a, 168.3, pl.16.3.

79 Same mint, same series, but with *ΒΑΣΙΛΕΩΣ ΛΥ*, same date. AE 4.02g. New York. Thompson 1968a, 168.4, pl.16.4.

Antigonus I Monophthalmus (king 306–301)

80 *Lampsacus*, *c.* 306. Drachm, AR 4.06g. Stockholm (*SNG* 1010).

81 *Abydus*, *c.* 310. Drachm, AR 4.12g. Stockholm (*SNG* 1011).

82 *Aradus*, *c.* 310–301. Tetradrachm, AR 16.78g. Copenhagen (*SNG* 790). *WSM*, p. 194.

83 *Carrhae*, *c.* 310–302. Tetradrachm, AR 17.08g. Copenhagen (*SNG* 851). *WSM* 9.

84 *Tyre*, *c.* 307. Tetradrachm, AR 16.96g. Copenhagen (*SNG* 812). Newell 1923c, 3–4.

85 *Antigonea*, *c.* 306–301. Tetradrachm, AR 17.10g. Copenhagen (*SNG* 845). *WSM*, 84.2.

86 *Corinth*, *c.* 303–287/6. Tetradrachm, AR 17.12g. Copenhagen (*SNG* 734). Noe 1950, 22.2b.

Seleucus I (312–281)

87 *Ecbatana*, *c.* 303–293. Tetradrachm, AR 16.96g. Copenhagen (*SNG* 850). Cf. *ESM* 473.

88 Same mint, *c.* 311–303. Hemidrachm, AR 1.98g. Copenhagen (*SNG* 1015). *ESM* 430.

89 Same mint and date. Hemiobol, AR 0.22g. Copenhagen (*SNG* 1017). *ESM* 432.

VI. PTOLEMY I AND CYRENAICA

Ptolemy I (323–283/2, king from 305)

90 *Alexandria*, with head of Alexander the Great wearing elephant's scalp, *c.* 319–315. Tetradrachm, AR 16.92g. Copenhagen (*SNG* 11). Zervos 1967, issue B IX.

91 Same mint and date. Same type but wears scaly *aegis*. Tetradrachm, AR 16.03g. Copenhagen (*SNG* 12). Zervos 1967, issue XII.

92 Same mint and date. Tetradrachm (Attic), AR 16.78 g. New York. Zervos 1967, issue XIII.

93 Same mint, *c.* 310–305. Tetradrachm (reduced), AR 15.66g. Testmark on obverse. Stockholm. Jenkins 1960, 33, group b.

94 *Sidon*, dated 312/11. Tetradrachm (Attic), AR 16.15g. New York.

95 *Soli*, Eunostus, *c.* 313–310. Tetradrachm (Attic), AR 17.08g. New York, ex Abu Hommos hoard (*IGCH* 1667). Baldwin Brett 1938, 26, pl.4.8.

96 *Alexandria*, with portrait of Ptolemy I, *c.* 304–298. Stater (Ptolemaic), AV 7.03g. Stockholm.

97 Same mint, *c.* 300–283. Tetradrachm (Ptolemaic), AR 14.87g. Copenhagen (*SNG* 47).

98 *Uncertain mint*, same date. Pentadrachm, AV 17.69g. London (*BMC, Ptolemies*, 16.27).

99 *Alexandria*, same date. AE 8.24g. Stockholm. Svoronos 1904–8, no. 303.

100 Same mint and date. Octodrachm, AR 28.02g. London (*BMC* –). Svoronos 1904–8, no. 198*β*.

101 Same mint and date. Hemidrachm (= triobol), AV 1.78g. Stockholm. Svoronos 1904–8, no. 232.

Cyrenaica

102 *Cyrene*, *c.* 331–323. Stater (Attic), AV 8.58g. Stockholm. Naville 1951, no. 26h.

103 Same mint and date. Drachm, AV 4.23g. Copenhagen (*SNG* 1199). Naville 1951, no. 37c.

104 Same mint and date. Hemidrachm, AV 2.11g. Stockholm. Naville 1951, no. 111h.

105 Same mint and date. One-tenth stater, AV 0.86g. Stockholm. Naville 1951, no. 16e.

106 Same mint and date. Tetradrachm (Asiatic), AR 12.87g. Copenhagen (*SNG* 1189).

VII. CYRENAICA AND JUDAEA

107 *Cyrene*, *c.* 331–323. Drachm (Asiatic), AR 3.24g. Copenhagen (*SNG* 1208).

108 Same mint, Thibron (323–322). AE 8.51g. New York. Newell 1938b, 4, pl.1.2.

109 Same mint and ruler. AE 4.70g. Paris. Robert 1955, 170–1, pl.40.7–8.

110 Same mint, Alexander types, *c.* 314/13. Stater (Attic), AV 8.59g. London (*BMC, Cyrenaica*, 39.170). Mørkholm 1980b, 149.4, pl.1.3.

111 Same mint and date. Didrachm (Attic), AR 8.19g. Copenhagen (*SNG, Alex.–Cyr.* 1215). Mørkholm 1980b, 149.10, pl.1.9.

112A Same mint and date. Didrachm, AR. Leningrad (after Naville 1951, 54, fig. 1).

112B Same mint and date. Struck from same obverse die as **112A**, but with *silphium* reverse. AR 8.42g. Paris (= *BMC* no. 170c, pl.17.5). Mørkholm 1980b, 148.1, pl.1.1.

113 Same mint, *c.* 313/12. Didrachm, AR 8.42g. London (*BMC*, 40.172). Mørkholm 1980b, 150.11, pl.1.5.

114 Same mint, attributed to Governor Ophellas, *c.* 312–309. Hemistater, AV. Present location unknown (cast in the British Museum). Naville 1951, no. 144. Mørkholm 1980b, 151.21, pl.1.11.

115 Same mint, governor (?) and date. Didrachm, AR 8.07g. London (*BMC*, 40.173). Mørkholm 1980b, 151.22, pl.1.8.

116 Same mint, *c.* 308–304. Didrachm (reduced Ptolemaic), AR 7.60g. Copenhagen (*SNG, Alex.–Cyr.* 1235). Mørkholm 1980b, 152, pl.2.1.

117 Same mint, *c.* 300–298. Tetradrachm (reduced), AR 14.44g. London (*BMC*, 50.226).

118 Same mint, *c.* 305–300. Tetradrachm, AR 17.09g. Copenhagen (*SNG, Macedonia II.* 857 and *SNG, Ptolemies.* 425). Mørkholm 1980b, 153, pl.2.6.

119 Same mint, *c.* 308–306. One-eleventh stater, AV. (a) 0.77g. Paris. (b) 0.78g. Paris. Naville 1951, nos. 149–50.

120 Same mint, *c.* 305–300. Tetrobol (Attic), AV 2.81g. Stockholm. Naville 1951, no. 159b.

121 Same mint and date. Hemistater (Attic), AV 4.30g. Paris. Naville 1951, no. 237a. Mørkholm 1980b, 153.26, pl.2.7.

122 Same mint, *c.* 304–298. Royal types (cf. **96**). Stater, AV 7.11g. Copenhagen (*SNG, Ptolemies* 426). Mørkholm 1980b, 154, pl.2.9.

123 *Euhesperides*, with head of Ptolemy I, *c.* 290–280. Didrachm (light standard), AR 7.13g. Copenhagen (*SNG* –). Mørkholm 1980b, pl.2.14.

124 *Cyrene*, *c.* 300–298. Tetrobol (Attic), AV 2.81g. London. Naville 1951, no. 258d. Mørkholm 1980b, 154, pl.2.10.

125 Same mint, *c.* 295–285. *Obv.* head of Apollo Myrtous. Didrachm (reduced), AR 6.86g. London (*BMC*, 56.264). Mørkholm 1980b, 154, pl.2.13.

126 Same mint and date. Stater, AV 7.16g. Paris (unique). Naville 1951, no. 248a. Mørkholm 1980b, 154, pl.2.12.

127 Same mint, *c.* 300–280. AE 3.64g. London (*BMC*, 74.4 (*obv.*) and 5 (*rev.*)).
128 Same mint, *c.* 295–280. AE 5.88g. Copenhagen (*SNG, Alex.–Cyr.* 1261).
129 Same mint and date. AE 4.65g. Copenhagen (*SNG* 1268).

Judaea

130 *Judaea, c.* 300–283/2. Tetartemorion, AR 0.19g. Private collection. Mildenberg 1979, 195.25.
131 Same mint and date. Same denomination, AR 0.19g. Jerusalem, Spaer collection. Mildenberg 1979, 195.26.

VIII. SELEUCUS I AND THE EAST

Seleucus I (312–281)

132 *Seleucia on the Tigris, c.* 292/1. Tetradrachm, AR 16.45g. Stockholm. *ESM* 63d.
133 Same mint, *c.* 288/7. Drachm, AR 3.58g. Stockholm. *ESM* 91.
134 Same mint, *c.* 288–7. Stater, AV 8.32g. Stockholm. *ESM* 10.
135 *Susa, c.* 298–280. Tetradrachm, AR 16.98g. Numismatic Fine Arts (6.xii.1979), 256. *ESM* 316.
136 *Susa* or *Ecbatana, c.* 298–280. Stater, AV 8.57g. Berlin. *ESM* 331, pl.58.8. For the attribution see Le Rider 1965a, 31–2.
137 *Ecbatana, c.* 303–293. Double daric, AV 16.58g. London (*BMC, Arabia, etc.*, 191.62). *ESM* 460.
138 *Susa, c.* 298–280. Stater, AR 16.77g. New York. *ESM* 323.
139 Same mint, *c.* 300. Tetradrachm, AR 16.99g. Lisbon (Gulbenkian II.1020, ex Jameson 1342). *ESM* 424.
140 Same mint, types and date. Drachm, AR 4.05g. Stockholm. *ESM* 414.
141 *Ecbatana, c.* 293–280. Tetradrachm, AR 17.06g. Copenhagen (*SNG* 25). *ESM* 497*β*, pl.37.10.
142 Same mint and date. Drachm, AR 4.18g. Berlin. *ESM* 481, pl.36.9.
143 Same mint and date. Hemidrachm, AR 1.94g. London. *ESM* 482, pl.36.10.
144 *Seleucia on the Tigris*, with Alexander types in the name of Seleucus, *c.* 302/1. Tetradrachm, AR 17.04g. London (*BMC, Seleucid Kings*, 2.22). *ESM* 19.
145 *Bactra*, with the names of Seleucus (I) and Antiochus (I), *c.* 285–280. Tetradrachm (reduced), AR 13.78g. London, ex Oxus hoard (*IGCH* 1822). *ESM* 665.

Local issues

146 *Persis*, with name of priest-king Bagadates, *c.* 290–280. Tetradrachm, AR 16.58g. London (*BMC, Arabia, etc*, 195.1, pl.28.7).
147 Same mint, with name of priest-king Oborzos, same date. Drachm, AR 3.93g. London (*BMC*, 197.1, pl.28.10).
148 *Bactria* or *India*, Sophytes, *c.* 290–280. Drachm, AR 3.78g. London (*BMC, Greek and Scythic Kings*, 2.1, pl.1.3).

IX. SELEUCUS I

Seleucus I (312–281)

149 *Marathus*, Alexander types and name, *c.* 301–300. Tetradrachm, AR 17.14g. New York. *WSM* 1240*β*, pl.43.1.
150 Same mint, with Alexander types in the name of Philip (III). Same obverse die. Tetradrachm, AR 16.78g. New York. *WSM* 1241*γ*, pl.43.3.
151 Same mint, with Alexander types in the name of Seleucus (I). Same obverse die as **150**. Tetradrachm, AR 17.40g. New York. *WSM* 1242*γ*, pl.44.1.
152 *Laodicea ad Mare*, with Alexander types in the name of Seleucus (I), *c.* 300. Tetradrachm, AR 16.83g. New York. *WSM* 1202*β*, pl.39.1.
153 *Antioch*, municipal issue of the people of Antioch, *c.* 300–286. Bronze double, AE 7.19g. Berlin. *WSM* 913*β*, pl.16.8.
154 *Seleucia Pieria*, municipal issue of the people of Seleucia, *c.* 290–285. Bronze quadruple, AE 13.47g. Copenhagen (*SNG, Syria, Cities* 388). *WSM* 896.
155 *Tarsus, c.* 294–290. Tetradrachm, AR 17.16g. Stockholm. *WSM* 1290*δ*.

156 *Sardis*, *c.* 282–280. Tetradrachm, AR 17.06g. Stockholm. *WSM* 1350 (A1–P4), pl.53.4.
157 *Pergamum*, *c.* 281/80. Tetradrachm, AR 16.74g. New York. *WSM* 1528α, pl.68.9.
158 *Seleucia on the Tigris*, *c.* 284–283. Bronze quadruple, AE 10.76g. Copenhagen (*SNG* –). *WSM* 117 (var).
159 Same mint and date. Bronze double, AE 5.84g. Copenhagen (*SNG* –). *WSM* 118.
160 *Antioch*, *c.* 286–281. Bronze double, AE 6.06g. Stockholm. *WSM* 925.

X. DEMETRIUS POLIORCETES AND PYRRHUS

Demetrius Poliorcetes (306–283)

161 *Tyre*, with Alexander types in the name of Demetrius, *c.* 290–287. Tetradrachm, AR 17.11g. London. Newell 1927, no. 26. XXXIII–64, pl.3.9.
162 *Salamis*, *c.* 300–295. Tetradrachm, AR 17.19g. Copenhagen (*SNG* 1193). Newell 1927, no. 22.XXV–49, pl.2.18.
163 Same mint and date. Stater, AV 8.54g. Lisbon (Gulbenkian II. 876). Newell 1927, no. 21.G, rev.die var.
164 Same mint and date. AE 4.77g. Copenhagen (*SNG* 1194). Newell 1927, no. 20.
165 *Tarsus*, *c.* 298–294. Drachm, AR 4.16g. Copenhagen (*SNG* 1189). Newell 1927, no. 44.
166 Same mint and date. AE 2.04g. New York. Newell 1927, no. 34.
167 *Uncertain mint* (*Caria?*), after 290. AE 3.87g. Stockholm (*SNG* 1133).
168 *Miletus*, *c.* 300–294. Tetradrachm, AR 16.96g. London. Newell 1927, 48; Thompson 1983, no. 259.
169 *Ephesus*, with early portrait of Demetrius, *c.* 301–294. Drachm, AR 4.20g. Copenhagen (*SNG* 1184). Newell 1927, no. 54a, pl.6.3.
170 *Pella*, with Alexander types in the name of Demetrius, *c.* 290–89. Stater, AV 8.53g. Lisbon (Gulbenkian II. 879). Newell 1927, no. 69, pl.6.19 (this coin).
171 Same mint, *c.* 294–3. Tetradrachm, AR 16.49g. Copenhagen (*SNG* 1178). Newell 1927, no. 66, pl.6.15.
172 Same mint, with portrait of Demetrius, first type, *c.* 292–291. Tetradrachm, AR 16.67g. Copenhagen (*SNG* –). Newell 1927, no. 75.
173 *Amphipolis*, with portrait of later, idealized type, *c.* 289/8. Tetradrachm, AR 17.32g. Stockholm (*SNG* 1129). Newell 1927, 123.
174 *Pella*, *c.* 293–288. Stater, AV 8.65g. Lisbon (Gulbenkian II. 880). Newell 1927, no. 83.

Pyrrhus (287–285)

175 *Pella*. AE 3.28g. Copenhagen (*SNG* 1195).

XI. LYSIMACHUS AND PATRAEUS OF PAEONIA

Lysimachus (306–281)

176 *Sardis*, with Alexander types in the name of Lysimachus, *c.* 299/8. Tetradrachm, AR 16.92g. London. Thompson 1968a, no. 80; Thompson 1983, no. 410e.
177 *Colophon*, same types, *c.* 299/8–297/6. Tetradrachm, AR 16.68g. Copenhagen (*SNG* –), Thompson 1068a, no. 123.
178 *Amphipolis*, with head of deified Alexander, *c.* 288/7–282/1. Tetradrachm, AR 17.07g. Copenhagen (*SNG* –). Thompson 1968a, no. 193.
179 *Lampsacus*, same types, *c.* 297/6–282/1. Tetradrachm, AR 14.63g. Stockholm (*SNG* 843). Cf. Thompson 1968a, no. 61.
180 Same mint, *c.* 299/8–297/6. Drachm, AR 4.26g. Stockholm (*SNG* 850). Thompson 1968a, no. 37.
181 *Pella*, *c.* 286/5–282/1. Stater, AV 8.57g. Stockholm (*SNG* 834). Cf. Thompson 1968a, no. 240.
182 *Smyrna*, *c.* 287/6–282/1. Tetradrachm, AR 17.01g. Stockholm (*SNG* –). Thompson 1968a, no. 237.
183 *Uncertain mint*, uncertain date. Bronze unit, AE 4.81g. Stockholm (*SNG* 854).
184 As last. Bronze half, AE 2.00g. Stockholm (*SNG* 859).

Paeonia

185 Patraeus (340–315). Stater (local standard), AR 12.23g. Copenhagen (*SNG* 1389).
186 Same ruler and date. Stater, AR. 12.94g. Berlin. Gaebler 1935, 202.3, pl.37.16.
187 Same ruler and date. Stater, AR 12.37g. Paris. Gaebler 1935, 201.1, pl.37.19.
188 Same ruler and date. Drachm, AR 3.10g. Copenhagen (*SNG* 1391).
189 Same ruler and date. Tetrobol, AR 2.09g. Copenhagen (*SNG* 1394).

XII. DYNASTS AND GREEK CITIES

190 Audoleon (*c*. 315–286), king of *Paeonia*. Stater (local standard), AR 12.50g. Copenhagen (*SNG* 1399).
191 Same ruler, with Alexander types, after 305. Tetradrachm, AR 16.79g. New York. Waggoner 1982, pl.14.1.
192 Seuthes III, ruler of the *Odrysian Thracians* (*c*. 330–300). AE 5.13g. New York. Cf. Youroukova 1976, no. 68.
193 Monunius, ruler of the *Dardanian Illyrians*, with types of Dyrrhachium, *c*. 300. Stater, AR 10.25g. Copenhagen (*SNG* 528).
194 *Dyrrhachium*, *c*. 300–280. Drachm, AR 2.25g. Copenhagen (*SNG* 433).
195 *Corcyra*, same date. Didrachm, AR 4.98g. Copenhagen (*SNG*, *Epirus–Acarnania* 170).
196 *Epirus*, Pyrrhus (297–272). AE 8.76g. Copenhagen (*SNG* 100). Franke 1961, pl.55.11.
197 *Epirote symmachia*, *c*. 297–270. AE 9.00g. Copenhagen (*SNG* 85) (Pandosia). Franke 1961, 127.23.1, pl.13.
198 As last, *c*. 280–235. AE 3.24g. Copenhagen (*SNG* 106). Franke 1961, 133.96.1, pl.16.
199 *Philippi*, first series, *c*. 350–330. Tetradrachm (light Thraco-Macedonian), AR 13.23g. Copenhagen (*SNG* 292). Bellinger 1964, 31.4.
200 Same mint, series and date. Hemidrachm, AR 1.63g. Copenhagen (*SNG* 294).
201 Same mint, second series, *c*. 330–323. Stater (Attic), AV 8.58g. Copenhagen (*SNG* 291). Bellinger 1964, 33.15.
202 *Larissa*, *c*. 336. *Obv*. facing head of Aleuas. Drachm (Aeginetan), AR 5.99g. London (*BMC*, *Thessaly*, 29.53, pl.5.12).
203 Same mint, *c*. 340–330. Drachm (Aeginetan), AR 6.08g. Stockholm (*SNG* 1217).
204 *Delphi*, Amphictyonic Council, *c*. 336–334. Stater (Aeginetan), AR 12.27g. Bank Leu 20 (25.iv.1978), 86. Kinns 1983, 3.11, pl.1.11.
205 As last. Hemidrachm, AR 2.95g. New York (*SNG Berry* 585). Kinns 1983, 5.1, pl.3.1.
206 *Thebes*, *c*. 288/7. Tetradrachm (Attic), AR 17.12g. Lisbon (Gulbenkian II.922, ex Jameson 2065 and Weber 3303).

XIII. GREEK AND CRETAN CITIES

207 *Athens*, *c*. 350–294. *Pi*-style tetradrachm, AR 17.14g. Stockholm (*SNG* 1476).
208 Same mint, *c*. 297–294. Stater, AV 8.58g. Copenhagen (*SNG* 83).
209 Same mint, *c*. 350–330. *Obv*. head of Athena in Attic helmet; *rev*. double-bodied owl. AE 1.80g. Stockholm (*SNG* 1512). Kroll 1979, variety Ab.
210 Same mint and date. *Rev*. two owls confronted. AE 2.07g. Stockholm (*SNG* 1514). Kroll 1979, variety D.
211 Same mint, *c*. 322–300. *Obv*. head of Athena in Corinthian helmet. AE 4.77g. Copenhagen (*SNG* 94). Kroll 1979, variety F.
212 *Eleusis*, *c*. 350–300. AE 5.00g. Stockholm (*SNG* 1546). Kroll 1979, p. 142, variety K.
213 *Corinth*, *c*. 350–307. Stater, AR 8.50g. Stockholm (*SNG* 1586). Ravel 1948, 5th period, 3rd series, no. 1014.
214 Same mint, *c*. 330. Trihemidrachm, AR 3.89g. Copenhagen (*SNG* 101). Warren 1968, 128.A.1.1(c).
215 *Sicyon*, 4th century. Stater (Aeginetan), AR 12.00g. Stockholm (*SNG* 1619).
216 *Elis*, *Zeus mint of Olympia*, *c*. 343–325. Stater (Aeginetan), AR 11.02g. Stockholm (*SNG* 1676). Seltman 1921, group H, no. 205 (same obv. die).

Crete

217 *Gortyn*, *c.* 330–280/270. Stater (Aeginetan), AR 11.45g. Copenhagen (*SNG* 443).
218 *Phaestus*, same date. Stater, AR 11.80g. Copenhagen (*SNG* 510).
219 Same mint and date. Stater, AR 11.41g. Copenhagen (*SNG* 516).
220 Same mint and date. Stater, AR 11.76g. London (*BMC, Crete*, 62.11, pl.15.6).
221 Same mint and date. Stater, AR 11.57g. London (*BMC*, 64.20, pl.15.10).
222 Same mint and date. Stater, AR 11.54g. London (*BMC*, 64.20, pl.15.11).
223 *Knossos*, same date. Stater, AR 11.06g. Copenhagen (*SNG* 373).
224 Same mint and date. Drachm, AR 4.87g. London (*BMC*, 21.28, pl.5.14).

XIV. CRETE AND RHODES

Crete

225 *Olus*, same date. Stater, AR 10.63g. London (*BMC*, 60.1, pl.14.12).
226 *Chersonesus*, same date. Stater, AR 11.16g; London (*BMC* –).
227 Same mint and date. Stater, AR 10.64g. London (*BMC*, 16.3, pl.4.3).
228 *Stymphalus* (Arcadia), *c.* 365. Stater, AR 11.54g. Copenhagen (*SNG* 287).
229 *Sybrita*, *c.* 320–280/270. Stater, AR 11.45g. Paris. Babelon 1914, II. 3, no. 1710, pl.259.4.
230 Same mint, *c.* 300–280/270. Stater, AR 10.76g. New York.
231 Same mint and date. Stater, AR 11.26g. London (*BMC* –). Svoronos 1890, 315.4.
232 *Eleutherna*, *c.* 310–280/270. Stater, AR 11.13g. London (*BMC*, 33.3, pl.8.7).
233 *Hierapytna*, same date. Stater, AR 10.89g. London (*BMC* 48.1, pl.12.1).
234 *Uncertain mint*, same date. Stater, AR 11.40g. Hess-Leu (7.iv. 1960), 197.

Rhodes

235 *Rhodes*, *c.* 333/2–323. Stater (Attic), AV 8.59g. London (*BMC, Caria*, 231.10, pl.36.5).
236 Same mint and date. Tetradrachm (reduced Chian), AR 15.19g. *SNG Berry* 1121.
237 Same mint and date. Didrachm (same standard), AR 6.93g. Stockholm. Ashton 1988a, series 1a, cf. p. 88.21.
238 Same mint, *c.* 304–265. Didrachm (Rhodian), AR 6.64g. Stockholm. Ashton 1988a, series 2, cf. p.88.27.
239 Same mint, *c.* 250–230. Didrachm (same standard), AR 6.74g. Stockholm. Ashton 1988a, series 4, cf. p.89.62.

XV. GREEK LEAGUES AND CITIES

240 *Tenos*, *c.* 320. Tetradrachm (Attic), AR 16.43g. London (*BMC, Crete*, 127.1, pl.28.10).
241 *Chalcis*, *c.* 338–305. Drachm (Chalcidian ?), AR 3.54g. Stockholm (*SNG* 1424). Picard 1979, issue 3.9-f.
242 Same mint and date. AE 1.87g. New York. Picard 1979, issue 15.
243 *Carystus*, *c.* 338–305. Drachm (Chalcidian), AR 3.83g. Copenhagen (*SNG* 418).
244 *Histiaea*, same date. Drachm (same standard), AR 3.33g. Copenhagen (*SNG* 516).
245 *Euboean League* (*Chalcis?*), *c.* 304–290/285. Drachm (same standard), AR 3.43g. Stockholm (*SNG* 1432). Wallace 1956, 144.48 (= Picard 1979, 155, issue 8.2b).
246 *Chalcis*, Alexander type, first issue, *c.* 304–300. Tetradrachm, AR 17.35g. Paris. Picard 1979, 54, issue 23.1-a.
247 Same mint, types and date, second issue, *c.* 290. Tetradrachm, AR 16.94g. London. Picard 1979, 54, issue 24.2-b.
248 *Erythrae*, *c.* 350–315. Tetradrachm (reduced Chian), AR 14.98g. London (*BMC, Ionia*, 122.42, pl.15.9).
249 Same mint, *c.* 310–297. Drachm (Attic), AR 4.18g. London (*BMC*, 134.147, pl.16.1).

250 Same mint, *c.* 297–294. One-third stater (Attic), AV 2.82g. London (*BMC*, 139.197, pl.16.4).

251 Same mint, *c.* 325–295. AE 11.90g. Copenhagen (*SNG* 623).

252 *Colophon*, *c.* 310–290. Drachm (reduced Rhodian (?)), AR 3.20g. Copenhagen (*SNG* 143). Milne 1941, no. 67e.

253 Same mint and date. AE 3.68g. Stockholm. Milne 1941, 69, group D.

254 Same mint and date. AE 1.42g. Stockholm. Milne 1941, 74, group C.

255 *Ephesus*, *c.* 386–336/334. Tetradrachm (reduced Chian), AR 14.98g. Stockholm (*SNG, Gustaf VI Adolf* 90).

256 Same mint, *c.* 301–295/4. Octobol (Attic), AR 5.19g. Copenhagen (*SNG* 257).

257 *Arsinoea*, *c.* 289/8–280. Octobol (Attic), AR 5.32g. London (*BMC, Ionia*, 55.71, pl.10.5).

258 Same mint and date. AE 3.89g. Copenhagen (*SNG* 258).

XVI. GREEK CITIES

259 *Samos*, *c.* 310–300. Didrachm (reduced Rhodian), AR 6.62g. Copenhagen (*SNG* 697). Barron 1966, 215.13 HA.

260 Same mint and date. Hemidrachm, AR 1.30g. Copenhagen (*SNG* 1702). Barron 1966, 217.2c.

261 Same mint and date. Trihemiobol, AR 0.63g. Paris. Barron 1966, 217.2.

262 *Miletus*, same date. Didrachm, AR 6.66g. Copenhagen (*SNG* 978). Deppert-Lippitz 1984, period III.467.

263 Same mint, *c.* 350–300. AE 1.02g. Stockholm. Deppert-Lippitz 1984, period II, series V.

264 Same mint, civic issue, with Alexander types, *c.* 294–280. Tetradrachm, AR 16.91g. London. Newell 1927, p. 60, cf. pl.4.23; Deppert-Lippitz 1984, 68, cf. no. 6, pl.33.1.

265 *Mylasa*, Alexander types, *c.* 300–280. Tetradrachm, AR 16.87g. London. Thompson 1981b, 208 n. 6.

266 *Cius*, *c.* 334–323. Stater (Attic), AV 8.55g. London, ex Saida hoard (*IGCH* 1508) (*BMC, Bithynia*, no. 1). Westermark 1980, 26.28.

267 Same mint, *c.* 340–315. Persian quarter-drachm, AR 1.26g. Stockholm.

268 *Pergamum*, *c.* 334–323. Stater (Attic), AV 8.32g. Berlin (Fox), ex Saida hoard (*IGCH* 1508). Westermark 1980, 28.36.

269 *Panticapaeum*, so-called Scythian style, *c.* 320. Stater (Attic), AV 8.54g. London. Jenkins 1972, fig. 243.

270 *Byzantium*, *c.* 340–300. Persian hemidrachm, AR 2.47g. Stockholm (*SNG* 750).

271 *Chalcedon*, same date. Same denomination, AR 2.19g. Copenhagen (*SNG* 349).

272 *Thracian Chersonese*, same date. Same denomination, AR 2.36g. Stockholm (*SNG* 794).

273 *Parium*, same date. Same denomination, AR 2.39g. Stockholm (*SNG* –).

274 *Cyzicus*, *c.* 300. Staters (uncertain standard), AR. (a) 13.48g Paris. Fritze 1914, no. 29, pl.6.5 (b) 10.60g. London.

XVII. ASIA MINOR; EGYPT AND CYRENAICA

Asia Minor

275 *Heraclea Pontica*, tyrant Dionysius (337–305). Stater (local standard), AR 9.68g. Copenhagen (*SNG* 422). Cf. *Recueil* I.2, 351.38.

276 Same mint, Queen Amastris, but in the name of the city, *c.* 305–302. Same denomination, AR 9.71g. London (*BMC* –). Cf. *Recueil* I.2, 351.42–3.

277 Same mint, struck under Lysimachus, *c.* 302–288/7. Same denomination, AR 9.80g. Stockholm (*SNG* 1943). Cf. *Recueil* I.2,351.44.

278 Same mint, types and date. Tetradrachm (Attic), AR 16.49g. London (*BMC, Bithynia*, 143.33, pl.30.8). *Recueil* I.2, 352.45.

279 *Amastris*, Queen Amastris, *c.* 300–288/7. Staters (local standard), AR. (a) 9.40g. Paris. *Recueil* I.1, 172.2, pl.18.2. (b) 9.31g. Berlin (Prokesch-Osten). Cf. *Recueil* I.1, 173.2a.

280 Same mint and types but in the name of the city, *c.* 288–280. Same denomination, AR 9.00g. Stockholm (*SNG* 1868). Cf. *Recueil* I.1, 173.5.

281 *Sinope*, second half of 4th century. Drachm (Aeginetan), AR 6.05g. Copenhagen (*SNG* 278).
282 Same mint, with the name of Ariarathes, satrap of Cappadocia, in Aramaic script, *c.* 341–333. Persian shekel, AR 5.09g. London (*BMC, Pontus, etc.*, 96.9. pl.22.1).
283 *Gaziura* (Pontus), same satrap, *c.* 333–322. Same denomination, AR 5.10g. London (*BMC, Galatia–Cappadocia, etc.*, 29.1, pl.6.1).

Egypt

284 *Alexandria*, Ptolemy II (285–246). Tetradrachm, AR 13.92g. Copenhagen (*SNG* 105).
285 Same mint and ruler, with letter *I* (=9) between legs of eagle. AE 15.28g. Stockholm (*SNG, Forbat* 527). Cf. Svoronos 1904–8, 576; Le Rider 1969b, p. 29, 26–31.

Cyrenaica

286 *Cyrene*, Governor Magas (*c.* 277–250). Didrachm, AR 6.46g. Copenhagen (*SNG, Ptolemies* 428).
287 Same mint, governor and date, with the portrait and name of Berenice I. Didrachm, AR 6.55g. Copenhagen (*SNG, Ptolemies* 429).
288 Same mint, governor and date, with the portrait of Ptolemy I. AE 5.82g. London (*BMC, Cyrenaica*, 81.33, pl.6.8).

XVIII. CYRENAICA AND PTOLEMY II

Cyrenaica

289 *Cyrene, koinon*, *c.* 250. Didrachm (reduced Chian), AR 7.54g. Copenhagen (*SNG, Alex.–Cyr.* 1275).
290 As last, same date. AE 7.75g. Copenhagen (*SNG, Alex.–Cyr.* 1280).

Ptolemy II (285–246)

291 *Alexandria*. Tetradrachm, AR 13.29g. Copenhagen (*SNG, Ptolemies* 137).
292 *Tyre*, year 30 (=256/5). Tetradrachm, AR 14.17g. Copenhagen (*SNG* 488).
293 *Sidon*, year 30 (=256/5). Tetradrachm, AR 14.26g. Copenhagen (*SNG* 512).
294 *Alexandria*, with portrait of Arsinoe II, after 270. Decadrachm, AR 34.14g. Copenhagen (*SNG* 136).
295 Same mint and types, *c.* 261/60–240. Octodrachm, AV 27.80g. Copenhagen (*SNG* 134).
296 Same mint, portrait and date. Tetradrachm, AR 13.47g. Copenhagen (*SNG* 140).
297 Same mint and date. *Obv.* jugate busts of Ptolemy II and Arsinoe II; *rev.* Ptolemy I and Berenice I. Octodrachm (*mnaeion*), AV 27.71g. Copenhagen (*SNG* 132).
298 Same mint, types and date. Tetradrachm, AV 13.84g. Copenhagen (*SNG* 133).
299 *Tyre*, with head of Arsinoe II struck under Ptolemy III, dated year 4 (=244/3). Octodrachm, AV 27.70g. London (*BMC, Ptolemies*, 42.4, pl.8.2).
300 *Alexandria*, struck during earlier part of the reign. AE 13.80g. Copenhagen (*SNG* 91).

XIX. EGYPT: PTOLEMY II AND PTOLEMY III

Ptolemy II (285–246), cont.

301 *Alexandria*, issue of later series, introduced *c.* 260. Denomination A, AE 91.41g. Copenhagen (*SNG* 141).
302 Same mint, series and date. Denomination B, AE 61.35g. Copenhagen (*SNG* 144).
303 Same mint, series and date. Denomination C, AE 42.34g. Copenhagen (*SNG* 153).
304 Same mint, series and date. Denomination D, AE 22.78g. Copenhagen (*SNG* 155).
305 Same mint, series and date. Denomination F, AE 7.20g. Copenhagen (*SNG* 159).

306 Same mint, series and date. Denomination G, AE 4.39g. Copenhagen (*SNG* 164).

Ptolemy III (246–222)

307 Same mint, with portrait of Berenice II. Decadrachm (Attic), AV 42.72g. Bank Leu 20 (25.iv.1978), 176.

308 Same mint, with head of Arsinoe II. Double octodrachm (Ptolemaic), AV 55.50g. Bank Leu 20 (25.iv.1978), 174.

XX. EGYPT, ETC.: PTOLEMY III AND PTOLEMY IV

Ptolemy III (246–222), cont.

309 *Alexandria*, issue of the new lighter series introduced by Ptolemy III. Denomination C, AE 33.84g. Copenhagen (*SNG* 174).

310 Same mint (?), issue struck for circulation in Greece. AE 6.55g. Copenhagen (*SNG* 194).

311 *Cyprus*, issue probably struck for circulation in Cyprus. AE 10.99g. London (*BMC, Ptolemies*, 52.59, pl.11.1).

312 *Tarsus*. Tetradrachm, AR 12.95g. New York. *WSM* pl.49B.

313 *Ephesus*, with head of Berenice II. Octodrachm, AV 27.80g. Bank Leu 20 (25.iv.1978), 175.

314 *Alexandria*, *c.* 230–222. Tetradrachm, AR 13.79g. Copenhagen (*SNG* 167).

315 *Tyre*, dated 243/2. Tetradrachm, AR 14.03g. Copenhagen (*SNG* 501).

Ptolemy IV (222–205)

316 *Alexandria*, with head of Ptolemy III. Octodrachm, AV 27.75g. Copenhagen (*SNG* 196).

317 Same mint. *Obv.* jugate busts of Sarapis and Isis. Tetradrachm, AR 14.12g. Copenhagen (*SNG* 197).

318 Same mint. AE 34.08g. Copenhagen (*SNG* 202).

XXI. EGYPT AND PHOENICIA: PTOLEMY V

Ptolemy V (205–180)

319 *Joppa*, with portrait head, year 5 (=201/200). Tetradrachm, AR 13.53g. Copenhagen (*SNG* 466).

320 *Dora*, same types, *c.* 205–199. Tetradrachm, AR 13.74g. Copenhagen (*SNG* –). Mørkholm 1981, 8.1.

321 *Alexandria*, with bust of Ptolemy IV, *c.* 204/3. Octodrachm, AV 27.75g. London (*BMC, Ptolemies*, 65.33, pl.15.1).

322 Same mint with bust of Arsinoe III, same date. Octodrachm, AV 27.73g. London (*BMC*, 67.1, pl.15.6).

323 Same mint and date, but with radiate bust of Ptolemy V. Octodrachm, AV 27.77g. London (*BMC*, 72.51, pl.17.2).

324 *Uncertain Phoenician mint*, with portrait head, *c.* 205–199. Tetradrachm, AR 14.23g. Copenhagen (*SNG* 530).

325 *Sidon*, with bust of Ptolemy IV, same date. Tetradrachm, AR 14.03g. London (*BMC, Ptolemies*, 64.23, pl.14.9).

326 *Uncertain Phoenician mint*, year 3 (=203/2). AE 17.49g. London (*BMC, Ptolemies*, 62.6, pl.14.3).

327 As last, with jugate busts as **297**, *c.* 205–199. Octodrachm, AV 27.71g. London (*BMC*, 40.8, pl.7.5).

328 As last, with head of Ptolemy I, same date. Tetradrachm, AR 13.53g. Copenhagen (*SNG* 528).

329 As last, with portrait head, same date. Tetradrachm, AR 13.24g. Copenhagen (*SNG* 527).

XXII. THE SELEUCIDS: CENTRAL AND EASTERN MINTS

330 *Antioch on the Orontes*, Antiochus I (281–261), *c.* 278–268. Tetradrachm, AR 16.94g. Copenhagen (*SNG* 66). *WSM* 940α.

331 *Apamea*, Antiochus II (261–246), *c.* 261–252. Tetradrachm, AR 16.79g. Stockholm. *WSM* 1135 (this coin).

332 *Antioch on the Orontes*, Seleucus II (246–226/5). Stater, AV 8.54g. Copenhagen (*SNG* 109). *WSM* –.

333 Same mint and ruler, *c.* 232–228. Tetradrachm, AR 16.47g. Copenhagen (*SNG* 111). *WSM* 1013.

334 *Ecbatana*, Seleucus II, *c.* 232–228. Drachm, AR 4.10g. Copenhagen (*SNG* 104). *WSM* 547A.

335 '*Apamea*', Interregnum, with portait of Antiochus I, *c.* 246–244. Tetradrachm, AR 17.04g. London (*BMC, Seleucid Kings*, 10.22, pl.3.7). *WSM* 1144β.

336 Same mint, Interregnum, with portrait of Antiochus I, *c.* 246–244. Octodrachm, AV 34.35g. Ankara, ex Gordion hoard no. 7. Cox 1966, 52.5. Obverse die as *WSM* 1144 F-θ.

337 *Antioch on the Orontes* or *Apamea*, Seleucus III (226–223), with portrait head. Tetradrachm, AR 17.06g. London (*BMC, Seleucid Kings*, 22.5, pl.7.7). *WSM* 1028.

338 *Antioch on the Orontes*, Seleucus III, *c.* 226–223. Octodrachm, AV 34.35g. Houghton collection 58. Obverse die as *WSM* 1029 *X–ββ* (= AR tetradrachms).

339 Same mint, Antiochus III (223–187), *c.* 208–200. Octodrachm, AV 33.88g. London (*BMC, Seleucid Kings*, 25.1). *WSM* 1097β.

340 *Apamea* (or *Antioch?*), Antiochus III, *c.* 223–200. Tetradrachm, AR 17.09g. Copenhagen (*SNG* 164). *WSM* 1186. Cf. Waage 1952, 7.

341 As last, Seleucus II, *c.* 244–226. Bronze unit, AE 3.64g. London (*BMC, Seleucid Kings*, 19.39, pl.6.16). *WSM* 1167β. Cf. Waage 1952, 8.65.

342 *Apamea*, Seleucus II, *c.* 244–226. Bronze octuple, AE 19.18g. London (*PCG* V.A.11, pl.32). *WSM* 1162δ.

XXIII. THE SELEUCIDS: CENTRAL MINTS

343 *Laodicea ad Mare*, Antiochus III (223–187), *c.* 223–215. Tetradrachm, AR 16.65g. Houghton collection 445. Cf. *WSM* 1230–1.

344 *Tarsus*, Antiochus I (281–261), *c.* 278–261. Tetradrachm, AR 17.14g. Copenhagen (*SNG* 75). *WSM* 1297α.

345 Same mint, Antiochus III, *c.* 201–197. Tetradrachm, AR 17.22g. Stockholm. *WSM* 1255.

346 *Soli*, Antiochus III, *c.* 197–187. Tetradrachm, AR 16.83g. London, ex Dunne's Hoard (*IGCH* 1769). *WSM* 1284, pl.47.3. Reattributed to Soli by Mørkholm (1964a, 58–62).

347 *Simyra* (Phoenicia), Seleucus III (226/5–223), with Phoenician date 35 (= 225/4). Tetradrachm, AR 16.60g. Paris. Seyrig 1971, p.8, fig. 1; Seyrig 1973, hoard 1, no. 101.

348 *Antioch*, Antiochus III, *c.* 223–213. Bronze quadruple, AE 10.12g. London (*BMC, Seleucid Kings*, 28.50, pl.9.9). *WSM* 1060ζ, pl.27.13.

349 Same mint, Antiochus I, *c.* 278–268. Bronze double, AE 6.47g. Copenhagen (*SNG* 71). *WSM* 953.

350 Same mint, Seleucus I (312–281), *c.* 300–286. Bronze unit, AE 3.59g. Copenhagen (*SNG* 35). Cf. *WSM* 921.

351 Same mint, Antiochus I, *c.* 280–278. Bronze half, AE 1.37g. Copenhagen (*SNG* 65). *WSM* 935.

352 *Tarsus*, Antiochus II (261–246). Bronze double, AE 10.75g. Copenhagen (*SNG* 87). *WSM* 1313.

353 *Antioch*, Antiochus III, *c.* 208–200. Bronze double, AE 7.67g. London (*BMC, Seleucid Kings*, 27.41). *WSM* 1107α.

354A *Carrhae*, Antiochus I, but in the name of Seleucus (I), *c.* 280–261. Stater, AV 8.55g. London (*BMC, Seleucid Kings*, 3.24, pl.1.6; *PCG* IV.A.12). *WSM* 784, pl.6.2.

354B Same mint, ruler, types and date. Tetradrachm, AR 16.18g. London (*BMC* –). *WSM* 785, pl.6.4.

355 *Nisibis*, Seleucus II (246–226/5), *c.* 244–240. Bronze double, AE 5.18g. New York. *WSM* 807, pl.7.9.

XXIV. THE SELEUCIDS: EASTERN MINTS

356 *Nisibis*, Seleucus II (246–226/5), *c*. 240–230. Tetradrachm, AR 16.41g. Stockholm. *WSM* 818α.

357 Same mint, Antiochus III (223–187), *c*. 204–200. Tetradrachm, AR 16.84g. Bank Leu 20 (25.iv.1978), 162 (= Münzen und Medaillen 19 (1959), 535), ex Seyrig 1973, hoard 8, no. 156 (*IGCH* 1413). *ESM* 628 (Ecbatana); Houghton 1986, 109.8, pl.27.

358 Same mint, ruler and types, *c*. 199–196. Tetradrachm, AR 16.91g. Houghton collection 903. Houghton 1986, 114.99, pl.29.

359 Same mint, ruler and date. Drachm, AR 4.23g. Stockholm. *WSM* 853γ (this coin). Houghton 1986, 114.109.

360 *Seleucia on the Tigris*, Antiochus I (281–261), with elderly portrait of Antiochus I, *c*. 264/3. Tetradrachm, AR 17.09g. Copenhagen (*SNG* 50). *ESM* 149.

361 Same mint, Molon, (222–221). Bronze double, AE 6.59g. Copenhagen (*SNG* –). *ESM* 227.

362 Same mint, Antiochus II (261–246), *c*. 261–256. Bronze quadruple, AE 16.47g. Copenhagen (*SNG* –). *ESM* 182.

363 *Susa*, Antiochus III, *c*. 223–220. Bronze quadruple, AE 14.50g. Paris. *ESM* 382, pl.29.5.

364 *Ecbatana*, Antiochus III, *c*. 200–187. Drachm, AR 4.03g. Stockholm. *ESM* 647A (this coin).

365 Same mint and ruler, *c*. 215–209. Hemidrachm, AR 1.95g. New York. *ESM* 589, pl.43.1.

366 Same mint, ruler and date. Obol, AR 0.66g. London. *ESM* 590γ, pl.43.2.

367 Same mint and ruler, *c*. 209–205. Bronze octuple, AE 27.17g. Copenhagen (*SNG* 142). Cf. *ESM* 622.

368 Same mint, Seleucus II, *c*. 246–226/5. Bronze double, portrait head with pointed beard. AE 4.94g. London (*BMC, Seleucid Kings*, 19.38, pl.6.15). *ESM* 564*F*, pl.41.9.

369 Same mint, Antiochus III, *c*. 200–187. Bronze double, AE 7.69g. Copenhagen (*SNG* –). *ESM* 650.

370 *Hecatompylus*?, Seleucus II, *c*. 246–226. Tetradrachm, AR 16.37g. Copenhagen (*SNG* 108). Cf. *ESM* 744.

371 *Bactra*, Antiochus I, *c*. 280–268. Stater, AV 8.57g. London (*BMC* –). *ESM* 676, pl.51.1.

372 Same mint, ruler and date. Drachm, AR 4.20g. Stockholm. *ESM* 688α.

373 Same mint, ruler and date. Tetradrachm, AR 16.59g. Stockholm. *ESM* 687γ.

XXV. THE SELEUCIDS AND THEIR EASTERN NEIGHBOURS

374 *Bactra*, issue in the name of Antiochus (II) but with head of Diodotus (I), governor of Bactria, *c*. 255–246. Tetradrachm, AR 16.43g. Stockholm. *ESM* 717δ. Mitchiner 1975, 1.39, type 64.

375 Same mint, issue in the name of Antiochus (II) but with head of Diodotus (II?), same date. Stater, AV 8.37g. London. *ESM* 723β, pl.53.15. Mitchiner 1975, 1.40, type 66α.

376 *Persis*, Artaxerxes, *c*. 280–250. Drachm, AR 3.60g. London (*BMC, Arabia, etc.*, 198.2, pl.29.2).

377 Same mint, Autophradates I, same date. Tetradrachm, AR 16.83g. London (*BMC*, 201.3, pl.29.7).

378 *Parthia*, Andragoras, *c*. 245–240. Stater, AV 8.55g. London (*BMC, Arabia, etc.*, 193.1, pl.28.1).

379 Same mint, ruler and date. Tetradrachm, AR 16.56g. London (*BMC*, 193.2, pl.28.2).

380 *Bactra*, Diodotus I–II, in the name of Diodotus (II?) and with his portrait (cf. **375**), *c*. 250–230. Tetradrachm, AR 16.66g. London (*BMC, Greek and Scythic Kings*, 3.3, pl.1.6). Mitchiner 1975, 1.42, type 74α.

381 Same mint, rulers and date. AE 6.47g. London (*BMC* –). Mitchiner 1975, 1.44, type 79α.

382 Same mint, rulers and date. AE 9.00g. London (*BMC, Greek and Scythic Kings, etc.*, 4.7, pl.1.9).

383 Same mint, Euthydemus (*c*. 230–200), youthful portrait. Tetradrachm, AR 16.31g. Copenhagen (*SNG, Parthia–India* 252). Mitchiner 1975, 1.51, type 85e.

384 Same mint, ruler and date, elderly portrait. Tetradrachm, AR 16.63g. London (*BMC*, 5.13, pl.2.5). Mitchiner 1975, 1.54, type 94a.

385 Same mint, ruler and date. Stater, AV 8.36g. London (*BMC*, 4.2, pl.1.10). Mitchiner 1975, 1.51, type 84a.

386 Same mint, ruler and date. Octodrachm, AV 32.73g. Paris (Le Rider 1969a, 26.15, pl.2.15). Mitchiner 1975, I.52, type 89i,a.

387 Same mint, ruler and date. Dichalkon, AE 7.53g. Stockholm. Mitchiner 1975, I.52, type 87.

XXVI. THE SELEUCIDS: WESTERN MINTS

388 *Sardis*, Antiochus I (281–261), but with head of Seleucus I, *c.* 280–278. Tetradrachm, AR 16.28g. Glasgow (Hunter III,11.1). *WSM* 1359, pl.54.1.

389 Same mint and ruler, but with head of Seleucus I, *c.* 277–272. Tetradrachm, AR 16.05g. Stockholm. *WSM* 1363α.

390 Same mint, Antiochus II (261–246) but with head of Antiochus I, *c.* 261–250. Tetradrachm, AR 17.12g. Stockholm. *WSM* 1387β.

391 Same mint, Antiochus I, *c.* 277–272. Bronze unit, AE 5.24g. Copenhagen (*SNG* 76). Cf. *WSM* 1369.

392 Same mint, Antiochus II, *c.* 261–250. Bronze unit, AE 4.27g. Stockholm. *WSM* 1389.

393 *Magnesia ad Sipylum*?, Antiochus I, end of reign, *c.* 260. Tetradrachm, AR 17.07g. Copenhagen (*SNG* 79). *WSM* 1456.

394 *Lysimachia*, Antiochus II, but with portrait of Antiochus I, *c.* 250? Tetradrachm, AR 16.99g. New York. *WSM* 1611β, pl.77.9.

395 *Sardis*, same ruler, issue with his own portrait, *c.* 250–246. Tetradrachm, AR 17.15g. Glasgow (Hunter III, 20.5). *WSM* 1406δ, pl.57.8.

396 Same mint, Seleucus II (246–226/5), portrait head with long beard, *c.* 228–226. Tetradrachm, AR 15.87g. Copenhagen (*SNG* –). Mørkholm 1969a, 10.A1.–P4. Cf. *WSM* 1321–2.

397 *Alexandria Troas*, Antiochus Hierax (241–226), portrait head wearing winged diadem. Tetradrachm, AR 17.08g. Copenhagen (*SNG* 129). *WSM* 1576.

398 *Parium*, same ruler and date. Tetradrachm, AR 16.98g. Copenhagen (*SNG* 123). *WSM* 1464α, pl.61.12; Seyrig 1958a, 608.30.

399 *Lysimachia*, same ruler, issue from end of reign. Tetradrachm, AR. Copenhagen (*SNG* –). *WSM* 1614.

XXVII. THE SELEUCIDS: WESTERN MINTS; PERGAMUM

400 *Uncertain mint in Phrygia*, Seleucus III (226/5–223) issue with his own portrait. Tetradrachm, AR, 16.73g. Copenhagen (*SNG* –). Mørkholm 1969a, fig. 20.

401 As last, Antiochus III, with portrait of Seleucus III, *c.* 223/21. Struck from the same obverse die as **400**. Tetradrachm, AR 17.00g. London (*BMC, Seleucid Kings*, 25.12). *WSM* 1696, pl.84.10.

402 *Sardis*, Antiochus III (223–187), *c.* 222–220. Tetradrachm, AR 16.64g. Stockholm. *WSM* 1452, pl.60.13. Mørkholm 1969a, 12.A–P3.

403 Same mint, Achaeus (220–213), issue with his portrait. Tetradrachm, AR 15.48g. Lisbon (Gulbenkian II.1030, ex Jameson 1692). *WSM* 1440, pl.60.2.

404 Same mint, ruler and date. Bronze double, AE 5.07g. Copenhagen (*SNG* 168). Cf. *WSM* 1441.

405 Same mint, ruler and date. Bronze double, AE 5.20g. Copenhagen (*SNG* 169). Countermark: horse's head. *WSM* 1441.

406 Same mint, Antiochus III, of inferior style, *c.* 215/213–190. Tetradrachm, AR 16.95g. Stockholm. *WSM* 1695β; Mørkholm 1969a, p. 17 A4–P4.

Pergamum

407 *Pergamum*, Philetaerus (283–263), Alexander types in the name of Seleucus (I), *c.* 280–274. Tetradrachm, AR 16.83g. London (*BMC, Mysia*, 113.26, pl.23.11). Newell 1936b, 18.10α, pl.4.3.

408 Same ruler, but with portrait of Seleucus I, *c.* 274–263. Tetradrachm, AR 17.05g. Stockholm. Newell 1936b, 24.XIII–26.

409 Eumenes I (263–241), with head of Philetaerus.

Tetradrachm, AR 16.92g. Copenhagen (*SNG* –). Westermark 1960. V1-R2 (var.). Mørkholm 1984a, 183.4, pl.27.

410 Attalus I (241–197), issue from the earlier part of reign. Tetradrachm, AR 17.00g. Copenhagen (*SNG* 335). Westermark 1960, V43-R2.

XXVIII. LESSER KINGDOMS OF ASIA MINOR

Pergamum

411 *Pergamum*, Attalus I (241–197), Alexander types, *c.* 210–290. Tetradrachm, AR 16.87g. New York. Kleiner 1971, 97.F-12, pl.21.
412 Regal issue in the name of Philetaerus, 3rd century. AE 2.18g. Stockholm.
413 Municipal issue in the name of the city, 2nd century. AE 8.81g. Stockholm.

Bithynia

414 *Nicomedia*, Nicomedes I (*c.* 280–*c.* 250). Tetradrachm, AR 16.47g. London (*BMC* –).
415 Same mint, ruler and date. Drachm, AR 4.17g. London (*BMC, Bithynia*, 208.1, pl.37.1).
416 Same mint, Ziaelas (*c.* 250–*c.* 230). AE 5.53g. Berlin. *Recueil* 1.2, 219.8, pl.29.9.
417 Same mint, Prusias I (*c.* 230–187). Tetradrachm, AR 17.06g. Copenhagen (*SNG* 623).
418 Same mint, ruler and date. AE 5.45g. Berlin. *Recueil* 1.2, 222.14, pl.30.8.
419 Same mint, ruler and date. AE 36.24g. Bank Leu 30 (8.iv.1982), 157.

Pontus

420 Mithridates II (*c.* 255–220). Stater, AV 8.52g. *SNG von Aulock* 1.
421 Mithridates III (*c.* 220–*c.* 185). Tetradrachm, AR 17.13g. Copenhagen (*SNG* –). Bank Leu 20 (25.iv.1978), 109.

Cappadocia

422 *Uncertain mint*, Ariaramnes (*c.* 280–*c.* 230). AE 7.89g. Paris (Waddington 6830). Mørkholm 1969b, 21.1, pl.5.1.
423 *Tyana*, same ruler and date, with the name of the city on the reverse. AE 4.63g. Paris (Waddington 6800). Mørkholm 1969b, 22.4, pl.5.4.
424 Same mint, Ariarathes III (*c.* 230–*c.* 220). AE 5.25g. Paris. Mørkholm 1969b, 22.5, pl.5.5.
425 Same mint, ruler and date. AE 5.98g. *SNG von Aulock* 6258. Mørkholm 1969b, 22.6, pl.5.6.
426 *Morima*, same ruler and date. AE 3.49g. Berlin. Regling 1935, 9.10, pl.10.
427 *Uncertain mint*, Ariarathes IV (*c.* 220–163), issue struck before 188. AE 5.91g. Paris. Mørkholm 1969b, 22.7, pl.5.7.
428 *Uncertain mint*, same ruler and date. AE 1.94g. Paris. Mørkholm 1969b, 22.8, pl.5.8.

XXIX. MACEDON

429 *Amphipolis*, Antigonus II Gonatas (276–239), Alexander types, *c.* 273–271. Tetradrachm, AR 17.08g. Stockholm (*SNG* 1003). Mathisen 1981, 117, pl.18.14.
430 Same mint and ruler, *c.* 271–265. Pan head tetradrachm, AR 17.02g. Copenhagen (*SNG* 1202).
431 Same mint, ruler and date. Drachm, AR 3.60g. Copenhagen (*SNG* 1203).
432 *Uncertain mint*, same ruler and date. AE 3.94g. Copenhagen (*SNG* 1206).
433 *Uncertain mint* and ruler (Antigonus Gonatas or Antigonus III Doson (229–221)). AE 3.11g. Copenhagen (*SNG* 1214).
434 As last. AE 4.69g. Copenhagen (*SNG* 1223).
435 *Uncertain mint*, Demetrius II (239–229). AE 4.42g. Copenhagen (*SNG* 1224).
436 *Amphipolis*, Antigonus III Doson, *c.* 227. Tetradrachm, AR 16.27g. Stockholm (*SNG* 1143).
437 *Pella?*, same ruler, *c.* 223–221. Trident symbol. Tetradrachm, AR 17.02g. Berlin. Gaebler 1935, 187.4, pl.33.25.

438 *Pella?*, Philip V (221–179), *c.* 220–217. Tetradrachm, AR 16.99g. Lisbon (Gulbenkian II.888).
439 *Pella?*, same ruler, *c.* 214–197. *Obv.* head of the hero Perseus. Tetradrachm, AR 17.03g. London (*PCG* VI.B.10, pl.42). Boehringer 1972, pl.8.6.
440 *Pella*, *c.* 200. Stater, AV 8.50g. Paris. Gaebler 1935, pp. 189–90.1, pl.34.14; Boehringer 1972, pl.8.1.
441 *Uncertain mint*, same ruler, *c.* 221–197. AE 6.35g. Copenhagen (*SNG* 1234).
442 As last. AE 3.51g. Copenhagen (*SNG* 1244).
443 As last. AE 8.64g. Copenhagen (*SNG* 1237).
444 As last. AE 2.77g. Copenhagen (*SNG* 1247).
445 *Uncertain mint*, Titus Quinctius Flamininus, *c.* 196. Stater, AV 8.44g. London (*NC* 1959, pl.1.4).

XXX. POSTHUMOUS ALEXANDERS (I)

446 *Argos*, Alexander types, *c.* 270–260. Tetradrachm, AR 16.60g. Copenhagen (*SNG* –). Noe 1962, 38, pl.10.A–2 (same dies).
447 *Megalopolis*, same types and date. Tetradrachm, AR 16.97g. Copenhagen (*SNG* –). Noe 1962, 41, cf. pl.12. cf. C–8.
448 *Sicyon*, same types. *c.* 220–217. Tetradrachm, AR 16.77g. Athens, ex Patras hoard (*IGCH* 186) (cast in the ANS). Troxell 1971, 93.7, pl.17.7.
449 *Corinth*, same types and date. Tetradrachm, AR 17.06g. Athens, ex Patras hoard (*IGCH* 186) (cast in the ANS). Troxell 1971, 92.2, pl.17.2.
450 *Messene*, same types. *c.* 192–190? Tetradrachm, AR 15.44g. (broken). New York. Troxell 1971, 94.2, pl.20.2.
451 *Cabyle*, same types, last quarter of 3rd century. Tetradrachm, AR 16.55g. Copenhagen (*SNG* –).
452 *Heraclea Pontica*, same types, 3rd century. Tetradrachm, AR 16.62g. Copenhagen (*SNG* –). Cf. Olcay and Seyrig 1965, pl.2.33ff.
453 *Sinope*, same types and date. Tetradrachm, AR 16.61g. New York. Newell 1918b, 120.12, pl.1.
454 Same mint, Alexander types, *c.* 290–230. Stater, AV 8.48g. London (cast in the ANS). Newell 1918b, 120.14, pl.1.
455 Same mint, autonomous types, *c.* 225. Tetradrachm, AR 16.96g. Lisbon (Gulbenkian II.955).
456 Same mint and types, *c.* 200. Tetradrachm (local standard), AR 13.35g. *Obv.* countermark: head of Helios; *rev.* countermark: head of Athena. London (*BMC* –).
457 Same mint and date. Didrachm (local standard), AR 7.30g. *Obv.* same countermark as **456**; *rev.* countermark: head of Zeus. Stockholm (*SNG* 1922).

XXXI. POSTHUMOUS ALEXANDERS (II)

458 *Parium*, second issue, *c.* 230–220. Tetradrachm, AR 16.38g. Paris. Seyrig 1958a, pl.42.37.
459 *Lampsacus*, *c.* 280–250. Tetradrachm, AR 17.00g. Copenhagen (*SNG* –, ex Kress 131 (16.xi. 1964), 205). Cf. Baldwin 1924, pl.7.11.
460 Same mint, *c.* 229. Stater, AV. Paris. Seyrig 1969, 39, fig. 3.
461 *Alexandria Troas*, second issue, *c.* 228–220. Tetradrachm, AR 16.97g. Copenhagen (*SNG* –). Cf. Bellinger 1961, pl.16, A127–A132.
462 *Cyzicus?*, mid 3rd century. Tetradrachm, AR 16.99g. Copenhagen (*SNG* –).
463 *Sardis*, *c.* 226–220. Rev. Zeus Lydius. Tetradrachm, AR 15.32g. Paris (de Luynes 2736). Seyrig 1963, 35.1, pl.3.5.
464 Same mint and date. Tetradrachm, AR 16.73g. London. Seyrig 1963, 36.2, pl.3.6.
465 Same mint and date. Drachm, AR 4.20g. London. Seyrig 1963, 36.4, pl.3.7.
466 *Chios*, period I, *c.* 280–270. Tetradrachm, AR 16.98g. New York. Bauslaugh 1979, 8.20–37, pl.3.
467 Same mint, period and date. Drachm, AR 4.09g. Copenhagen (*SNG* 901). Bauslaugh 1979, 3.3–9.
468 Same mint, period II, *c.* 270–220. Tetradrachm, AR 16.94g. Copenhagen (*SNG* –). Bauslaugh 1979, 15.39–79.
469 Same mint, period and date, or later. Stater, AV 8.48g. New York, Bauslaugh 1979, 17.52–95, pl.2.
470 Same mint, period III, *c.* 220–190. Tetradrachm, AR 16.21g. London. Bauslaugh 1979, 22.55–106, pl.9.

XXXII. POSTHUMOUS ALEXANDERS (III)

471 *Rhodes*, group I, *c.* 210–188. Tetradrachm, AR 16.31g. Copenhagen (*SNG* 761). Kleiner 1971, 106.I.–23.

472 Same mint, group II with magistrate's name Stasion, same date. Tetradrachm, AR 17.02g. Copenhagen (*SNG* 763). Kleiner 1971, 109.CC–96.

473 *Samos*, *c.* 205–189. Tetradrachm, AR 16.78g. Stockholm. Cf. Barron 1966, 222.8–12, but different dies.

474 *Miletus*, *c.* 225–190. Tetradrachm, AR 16.55g. Copenhagen (*SNG* –). Deppert-Lippitz 1984, 90, pl.33.4.

475 *Antioch/Alabanda*, with autonomous types, *c.* 197–190/88. Tetradrachm, AR 16.59g. London (*BMC, Caria*, 1.1, pl.I.1).

476 As last, same types and date. Drachm, AR 4.14g. London (*BMC*, 1.3, pl.I.2).

477 *Sillyum*, dated year 6 (=215/14?) of an uncertain Pamphylian era. Tetradrachm, AR 16.76g. Copenhagen (*SNG* –, ex Auctiones 8 (1978), 163, and *SNG von Aulock* 6660).

478 *Aspendus*, dated year 29 (=192/1?) of the same (?) Pamphylian era and with Seleucid countermark (anchor). Tetradrachm, AR 15.04g. Stockholm.

479 *Perge*, dated year 18 (=203/2?) of the same (?) era. Tetradrachm, AR 16.78g. Stockholm.

480 *Phaselis*, dated year 14 (=207/6?) of the same (?) era. Tetradrachm, AR 16.05g. Copenhagen (*SNG* –).

XXXIII. POSTHUMOUS ALEXANDERS (IV) AND LYSIMACHI; LOCAL ISSUES

481 *Side*, autonomous types, *c.* 200–175. Tetradrachm, AR 16.94g. Copenhagen (*SNG* 390).

482 *Perge*, autonomous types, *c.* 255–240. Tetradrachm, AR 16.69g. London (*BMC, Lycia, etc.*, 119.1, pl.24.1).

483 *Aradus*, Alexander types, dated year 18 (=242/1) in Phoenician numerals. Tetradrachm, AR 16.96g. London. Cf. Seyrig 1973, hoard 5, no. 1 (same obv. die).

484 Same mint, similar types, dated year 60 (= 199) in Greek numerals. Tetradrachm, AR 17.04g. London.

485 *Aradus?*, issue with pseudo-Ptolemaic types, dated year 48 (=212/11). Tetradrachm, AR 14.07g. Copenhagen (*SNG, Ptolemies* 540). Mørkholm 1976, no. 11.

486 *Gerrha* (Arabia), local imitation of Alexander types, *c.* 220–210. Tetradrachm, AR 15.20g. Kuwait, ex hoard from Failaka in the Persian Gulf (*IGCH* 1767). Mørkholm, 1979a, 221.7.

487 *Hagar* (Arabia), Abyal and Harithat, kings of Hagar, local imitation of an Alexander issue of Aradus, *c.* 230. Tetradrachm, AR. Bahrein, ex hoard from Bahrein (*IGCH* 1765). Mørkholm 1972, series II, 197.221.

488 *Uncertain mint in Arabia*, Abyatha, imitation of Alexander issue, *c.* 210. Tetradrachm, AR 15.40g. Kuwait, ex same Failaka hoard as **486**. Mørkholm 1979a, 220.10.

489 As last, same ruler, types and date. Drachm, AR 3.67g. Same location and hoard as **488**. Mørkholm 1979a, 220.15

490 *Aenus*, Scostocus, with types of Lysimachus and Scostocus' name in the exergue (partly off-flan), mid 3rd century. Tetradrachm, AR 16.50g. Stockholm (*SNG* 862). Cf. Youroukova 1976, 26–8 and pl.10.

491 *Byzantium*, Lysimachus types, *c.* 280–270. Tetradrachm, AR 16.85g. Copenhagen (*SNG* –). Cf. Seyrig 1968, 185, and Seyrig 1973, hoard 1, nos. 46–7, pl.3.

492 *Chalcedon*, same types and date, but with the name of the city. Tetradrachm, AR 15.79g. New York. Cf. Seyrig 1968, pl.24.21.

493 *Cyzicus*, Lysimachus types, same date? Tetradrachm, AR 16.70g. New York.

XXXIV. GREEK CITIES

494 *Byzantium*, Ptolemaic issue cmk by the city, *c.* 250. Tetradrachm, AR 13.94g. London (*BMC Thrace*, 110.1).

495 Same mint, *c.* 235–220. Tetradrachm (local standard), AR 13.67g. Copenhagen (*SNG* 486).

496 *Chalcedon*, same date. Tetradrachm (local standard), AR 13.97g. London (*BMC, Pontus*, etc., 126.19, pl.27.12).
497 Same mint and date. Drachm (Persian), AR 5.29g. London (*BMC*, 126.20, pl.27.13).
498 *Byzantium*, with Lysimachus types, after 205. Stater, AV 8.48g. Copenhagen (*SNG* 1086). Cf. Seyrig 1968, pl.24.14.
499 Same mint and types, *c.* 205–190. Tetradrachm, AR 16.92g. E. von Post collection, Lausanne. Cf. Olcay and Seyrig 1965, 123.
500 *Chalcedon*, same types, *c.* 190–155. Tetradrachm, AR 16.95g. E. von Post collection, Lausanne. Cf. Seyrig 1968, pl. 25.31.
501 *Athens*, *c.* 287–261. Tetradrachm, AR 17.14g. London (*BMC* –).
502 Same mint, late 3rd-early 2nd century. Tetradrachms, AR. (a) 16.40g. Paris. Nicolet-Pierre 1982, 108.10.1, pl.16; Price 1989, 238.225. (b) 16.50g. London. Nicolet-Pierre 1982, 108.8, pl.16; Price 1989, 238.230, pl.40. Both pieces ex Larissa (Sitochoro) hoard (*IGCH* 237).
503 *Sparta*, Alexander types in the name of Areus, *c.* 267–265. Tetradrachm, AR 16.67g. Paris. Grunauer von Hoerschelmann 1978, I. Gruppe, no. 1, pl.1.I.1.
504 Same mint, *c.* 265–250. Obol (reduced Aeginetan), AR 0.90g. London (*BMC, Peloponnesus*, 121.2). Grunauer von Hoerschelmann 1978, II. Gruppe, no. 2, pl.1.II.2.
505 Same mint, Cleomenes III, *c.* 226–222. Tetradrachm, AR 16.77g. Copenhagen (*SNG* 551). Grunauer von Hoerschelmann 1978, III. Gruppe, no. 8.1, pl.2.III.8.
506 Same mint and ruler, *c.* 226–223. AE 11.84g. Copenhagen (*SNG* 552). Grunauer von Hoerschelmann 1978. IV. Gruppe, no. 11.1, pl.3.IV.11.
507 Same mint and ruler, *c.* 223. AE 4.54g. Copenhagen (*SNG* 554). Grunauer von Hoerschelmann 1978, V. Gruppe, no. 1.1, pl.3.V.1.
508 Same mint, *c.* 219–196. Hemidrachm (reduced Aeginetan), AR 2.37g. Copenhagen (*SNG* 559). Grunauer von Hoerschelmann 1978, VIII. Gruppe, series 17, no. 101.1, pl.5.VIII.101.

XXXV. GREEK CITIES AND LEAGUES

509 *Sparta*, Nabis, *c.* 206–197. Tetradrachm, AR 13.40g. Berlin. Grunauer von Hoerschelmann 1978, IX. Gruppe, series 1, no. 5.1, pl.6.IX.5.
510 Same mint, ruler and date. Same types but with the name of Nabis on the reverse. Tetradrachm, AR 16.93g. Berlin. Grunauer von Hoerschelmann 1978, IX. Gruppe, series 4, no. 16.1, pl.6.IX.16.
511 Same mint and ruler, with portrait of the king, *c.* 196. Tetradrachm, AR 17.09g. London (*PCG* V.B.20). Grunauer von Hoerschelmann 1978, IX. Gruppe, series 5, no. 17.1, pl.6.IX.17.
512 *Messene*, *c.* 280–250. Tetradrachm, AR 16.68g. Copenhagen (*SNG* 504).
513 *Aetolian League*, *c.* 220–189. Stater (Attic), AV 8.48g. Copenhagen (*SNG* 1).
514 As last, same date. Tetradrachm (same standard), AR 16.88g. Stockholm (*SNG* 1370).
515 As last, same date. Drachm (same standard), AV 4.29g. London (*BMC, Thessaly, etc.*, 194.3, pl.30.4).
516 As last, same date. Stater (didrachm) (Corcyrean), AR 10.70g. Copenhagen (*SNG* 4).
517 As last, same date. Drachm (same standard), AR 5.14g. Copenhagen (*SNG* 8).
518 As last, same date. Hemidrachm (same standard), AR 1.39g. Copenhagen (*SNG* 14).
519 As last, same date. AE 5.15g. Stockholm (*SNG* 1371).
520 *Acarnanian League*, *c.* 220–205. Stater (Corcyrean), AR 9.18g. Copenhagen (*SNG* 418).
521 As last, same date. Drachm (same standard), AR 4.90g. Copenhagen (*SNG* 420).
522 *Epirote League*, *c.* 234/3–168. Stater (Corcyrean), AR 10.03g. London (*BMC, Thessaly, etc.*, 89.10, pl.17.5; *PCG* V.B.10, pl.35). Franke 1961, I. Gruppe, 1st series, 162.4.1, pl.17.
523 As last, same date. Drachm (same standard), AR 5.18g. Copenhagen (*SNG* 109). Franke 1961, II. Gruppe, 36th series, 178.182.1, pl.26.
524 As last, same date. AE 4.76g. Copenhagen (*SNG* 131). Franke 1961, V. Gruppe, 1st series, 196.4.

XXXVI. GREEK CITIES AND LEAGUES; CRETE

525 *Corcyra*, *c.* 229–200. Drachm (Corcyrean), AR 4.32g. Stockholm (*SNG* 1333).
526 As last, same date. Drachm, AR 2.89g. Copenhagen (*SNG*, *Epirus–Acarnania* 203).
527 *Apollonia*, *c.* 240–160. Drachm (Rhodian ?), AR 3.43g. Stockholm (*SNG* 1273).
528 *Dyrrhachium*, same date. Drachm (same standard), AR 3.18g. Stockholm (*SNG* 1286).
529 Same mint, *c.* 150–100. Hemidrachm (same standard), AR 1.63g. Copenhagen (*SNG*, *Thessaly–Illyricum* 452).
530 *Boeotia*, *c.* 250–220. Drachm (Corcyrean or reduced Aeginetan), AR 5.06g. Stockholm (*SNG* 1417).
531 *Elis*, *c.* 230–190. Drachm (uncertain standard), AR 4.79g. Copenhagen (*SNG* 427).
532 *Achaean League*, anepigraphic type, *c.* 200. Hemidrachm (reduced Aeginetan standard), AR 2.76g. Copenhagen (*SNG* 227).
533 As last, *Patras*, *c.* 195–168. Same denomination and standard, AR 2.38g. Copenhagen (*SNG* 274). For the date see Thompson 1968b, 116.
534 As last, *Messene*, same date. Same denomination and standard, AR 2.42g. Copenhagen (*SNG* 314).
535 Arcadian League types, *Megalopolis*, period I, *c.* 195–182 or earlier. Hemidrachm (reduced Aeginetan), AR 2.83g. Stockholm (*SNG* 1732), Dengate 1967, 61.2ff.
536 As last, period II, *c.* 182–168. Same denomination and standard, AR 2.40g. Stockholm (*SNG* 1733). Dengate 1967, 66.2g.
537 As last, *c.* 151–146. Same denomination and standard, AR 2.40g. Stockholm (*SNG* 1736). Dengate 1967, 84.40b.

Crete

538 *Gortyn*, *c.* 260. Drachm (Rhodian), AR 6.44g. Copenhagen (*SNG* 446).
539 Same mint, *c.* 250. AE 5.79g. Copenhagen (*SNG* 447).
540 Same mint, late 3rd century. AE 7.98g. Copenhagen (*SNG* 458).
541 Same mint and date. Stater, AV. Present location unknown (cast in New York).
542 Same mint and date. Drachm, AR 4.80g. London (*BMC*, *Crete, etc.*, 44.57).
543 Same mint, types and date. Hemidrachm, AR 2.36g. London (*BMC* –).
544 *Knossos*, same date. AE 3.82g. Copenhagen (*SNG* 378).
545 *Polyrhenium*, with portrait of Philip V of Macedon (221–179). Tetradrachm, AR 15.51g. London (*BMC*, 68.18, pl.17.1.).
546 *Arsinoea*, *c.* 222–205. AE 1.65g. Stockholm (*SNG* 1741).

XXXVII. GREEK CITIES

547 *Rhodes*, struck for circulation in Crete *c.* 200. Didrachm (uncertain standard), AR 4.40g. Copenhagen (*SNG* 864). *Obv.* countermark: winged head.
548 Same mint, *c.* 290–280; Didrachm (Rhodian), AR 6.11g. Copenhagen (*SNG* 734). Ashton 1986a, 77.9.A5–P5.
549 Same mint, *c.* 265–250. Hemidrachm (same standard), AR 1.38g. Helsinki, Keckmann collection. Cf. Ashton 1988a, 89.71.
550 Same mint, *c.* 250–225. Diobol (same standard), AR 0.92g. Stockholm. Cf. Ashton 1988a, 90.77–8.
551 Same mint, after 225. Tetradrachm (reduced), AR 13.50g. Stockholm (*SNG*, *Gustaf VI Adolf* 98).
552 Same mint, *c.* 229–226. AE 5.76g. Stockholm. Ashton 1986, group 3.
553 Same mint and date. AE 2.71g. Ashton collection. Ashton 1986, group 1.4.
554 Same mint and date. AE 3.00g. Stockholm. Ashton 1986, group 2.
555 Same mint, late 3rd century. AE 1.25g. Stockholm.
556 Same mint, *c.* 205–188. Drachm, AR 2.40g. Helsinki, Keckmann collection.
557 *Cos*, 3rd century. Didrachm (Rhodian), AR 6.71g. Stockholm.
558 *Melos*, end of 3rd century. Tetradrachm (Chian), AR 14.29g. Paris.
559 *Paros*, same period. Tetradrachm (Chian), AR 15.55g. London (*BMC*, *Crete, etc.*, 114.16, pl.26.10).
560 Same mint and date, Didrachm (same standard), AR 7.69g. London (*BMC*, 115.17, pl.26.11).

561 *Naxos*, same date. Didrachm (same standard), AR 7.60g. London (*BMC* –).
562 Same mint and date. Didrachm (same standard), AR 7.42g. Paris.
563 *Carystus*, *c*. 253/2–245. Didrachm (Ptolemaic), AR 7.03g. New York, ex Karystos 1930 hoard (*IGCH* 210). Wallace 1968, 202, Group 1, Ie, pl.26.
564 Same mint and date, issue of group 2 with portrait head. Didrachm (same standard), AR 6.85g. Stockholm (*SNG* 1452). Cf. Wallace 1968, group 2, IIIff.
565 *Histiaea*, 3rd–2nd centuries. Tetrobol, AR 2.34g. Stockholm (*SNG* 1437).

XXXVIII. GREEK CITIES

566 *Ephesus*, *c*. 250–200. Rhodian trihemidrachm (?), AR 4.87g. London (*BMC, Ionia*, 57.77, pl.10.8).
567 *Priene*, *c*. 250–200. Uncertain denomination and standard, AR 4.93g. London (*BMC*, 229.3, pl.24.3). Regling 1927, no.13.2.
568 *Miletus*, same date. Hemidrachm (Persian?), AR 2.61g. Copenhagen (*SNG* 988). Deppert-Lippitz 1984, no. 532.
569 *Samos*, *c*. 270–240. Octobol (Ptolemaic), AR 4.20g. Copenhagen (*SNG* 1711). Barron 1966, 220.28.
570 *Ephesus*, *c*. 200. Didrachm (Rhodian), AR 6.51g. Copenhagen (*SNG* 276).
571 *Miletus*, same date. Drachm (Persian?), AR 5.00g. Copenhagen (*SNG* 987). Deppert-Lippitz 1984, no. 643.
572 *Priene*, same date. Didrachm (Ptolemaic), AR 6.93g. Copenhagen (*SNG* 1081). Regling 1927, no. 15.
573 *Samos*, same date. Tetrobol (Attic), AR 2.96g. Stockholm. Barron 1966, 226.46a.
574 Same mint and date. Diobol (same standard), AR 1.45g. London (*BMC*, 367.184, pl.36.8).
575 *Cnidus*, *c*. 300–225. Diobol or reduced Rhodian hemidrachm, AR 1.14g. Copenhagen (*SNG* 303). Nordbø 1972, no. 513.
576 Same mint, *c*. 250–210. Drachm (reduced Rhodian), AR 2.56g. Copenhagen (*SNG* 292). Nordbø 1972, no. 714.
577 Same mint. Didrachm (reduced Rhodian), *c*. 210–185. AR 4.90g. Copenhagen (*SNG* 320). Nordbø 1972, no. 1024, fig. 257.
578 *Phaselis*, *c*. 300–250. Stater (Persic), AR 10.32g. Stockholm.
579 *Aspendus*, same date. Stater (same standard), AR 10.96g. Copenhagen (*SNG* 211).
580 *Selge*, same date. Stater (same standard), AR 8.02g Stockholm.
581 Same mint, *c*. 280–260. Stater (same standard), AR 9.40g. *SNG von Aulock* 5269.

XXXIX. MACEDONIA

Philip V (*221–179*)

582 *Amphipolis*(?), with portrait of Philip V as hero, Perseus, *c*. 188/7–179. Tetradrachm, AR 16.97g. Paris (*de Luynes* 1702). Boehringer (1972, 124) attributes all silver coins of Philip V and Perseus to *Pella*.
583 Same mint and date, with portrait of Philip V, diademed. Didrachm, AR 8.17g. Stockholm (*SNG* 1144).
584 *Uncertain mint*, same date. AE 7.48g. Stockholm (*SNG* 1145).
585 As last, same date. AE 4.57g. Copenhagen (*SNG* 1309).
586 As last, end of reign. AE 12.58g. Copenhagen (*SNG* 1259).
587 As last, same period. AE 4.55g. Copenhagen (*SNG* 1261).

Perseus (*179–168*)

588 *Amphipolis?*, signed by Zoilus, *c*. 179/8. Tetradrachm, AR 16.81g. London (*PCG* VI.3.7, pl.42.7). Boehringer 1972, 101, pl.7.5.
589 Same mint, no signature, *c*. 178–173. Tetradrachm, AR 16.75g. Copenhagen (*SNG* 1267).
590A Same mint and date. Didrachm, AR 7.63g. Paris (*de Luynes* 1714). Gaebler 1935, 195.4.

590B Same mint, similar portrait, same date. Drachm, AR 2.81g (sic). Copenhagen (*SNG* 1268).

591 *Uncertain mint*, 179–168. AE 5.13g. Copenhagen (*SNG* 1280).

Regional issues, c. *187–168*

592 *Amphipolis*, time of Philip V.Tetrobol (Attic), AR 2.40g. Stockholm (*SNG* 1154).

593 Same mint, time of Perseus. Same denomination, AR 1.92g. Stockholm (*SNG* 1155).

594 Same mint, and period. Same denomination, AR 2.26g. Copenhagen (*SNG* 1292).

595 Same mint, time of Philip V. AE 12.72g. Copenhagen (*SNG* 1294).

596 *Thessalonica* (for Amphaxitis), time of Perseus. AE 7.24g. Stockholm (*SNG* 1158).

XL. MACEDONIA AND NEIGHBOURING MINTS

597 *Pella* (for the district of Bottiaea), time of Philip V, *c.* 187–180. Tetrobol (Attic), AR 2.85g. Copenhagen (*SNG* 137).

598 Same mint and date. AE 9.50g. Copenhagen (*SNG* 139). Gaebler 1906, 48.132.3.

599 *Amphipolis?*, issue of the Roman *quaestor* Lucius Fulcinius, 168/7(?). AE 9.67g. Stockholm (*SNG* 1168). Gaebler 1906, 65.197–201.

600 *Pella* (for the district of Bottiaea), issue of the Roman *quaestor* Gaius Publilius, same date as **599**. AE 11.34g. Stockholm (*SNG* 1169). Gaebler 1906, 68.209–10.

601 *Uncertain Macedonian mint*, *c.* 166/5(?). AE 11.61g. Stockholm (*SNG* 1170). Gaebler 1906, 69.212.

602 *Amphipolis*, First Meris (district), *c.* 168–7. Tetradrachm, AR 16.82g. Bank Leu 22 (8.v.1979), 84.

603 As last, *c.* 160/158–50. Tetradrachm, AR 17.87g. Copenhagen (*SNG* 1310).

604 As last, *c.* 148/7 or *c.* 85–80. Tetradrachm, AR 16.61g. Copenhagen (*SNG* 1317). MacKay 1968b, 17.Bd. For the date cf. Burnett 1985, 54–8.

605 As last, Aesillas, Roman *quaestor*, *c.* 94–88 or later. Tetradrachm, AR 16.87g. Copenhagen (*SNG* 1328). For a date in the 70s see Burnett 1985, 54–8.

606 *Thasos*, after 180. Tetradrachm, AR 16.94g. Stockholm (*SNG* 826).

607 *Maroneia*, same date. Tetradrachm, AR 16.40g. Stockholm (*SNG* 770). Schönert-Geiss 1987, no. 1157.2, pl.53.

608 *Samothrace*, *c.* 200–150. Didrachm, AR 7.86g. Copenhagen (*SNG* 992).

XLI. GREEK CITIES; KINGDOM OF PERGAMUM

609 *Athens*, early monogram issue, first half of 2nd century. Tetradrachm, AR 16.76g. Stockholm (*SNG* 1501). Thompson 1961, no. 55.

610 Same mint, issue of later type, signed by two magistrates, second half of 2nd century. Tetradrachm, AR 16.34g. Stockholm (*SNG* 1502). Thompson 1961, no. 323g.

611 Same mint, issue signed by three magistrates, with letter *Z* on amphora (= month 7), first century. Drachm, AR 4.11g. Stockholm (*SNG* 1507). Cf. Thompson 1961, no. 800c.

612 *Eretria*, *c.* 170–160. Tetradrachm, AR 16.85g. Bank Leu 28 (5.v.1981), 108.

613 Same mint and date. Octobol, AR 5.53g. Copenhagen (*SNG* 497).

614 *Pergamum*, Eumenes II (197–158) with his portrait, *c.* 175–165. Tetradrachm, AR 16.62g. Paris, ex Bank Leu 33 (5.v.1983), 364. Nicolet-Pierre 1989, pl.47.1.

615 Same mint, *c.* 181. Tetradrachm, AR 16.75g. Copenhagen (*SNG* –). Mørkholm 1984a, 187.9, pl.27.9.

616 Same mint, *c.* 166–161 or earlier. Cistophoric tetradrachm, AR 12.42g. Copenhagen (*SNG* 413). Kleiner and Noe 1977, series 1b, no. 1-a, pl.1.6.

617 *Ephesus*, *c.* 160–150. Same denomination, AR 11.70g. Stockholm. Kleiner and Noe 1977, series 13, no. 12-a.

618 *Cyzicus*, *c.* 160–145. Tetradrachm, AR 16.86g. Copenhagen (*SNG* 66).

619 *Cyme*, same date. Tetradrachm, AR 16.05g. Stockholm (*SNG* 2288). Oakley 1982, issue 22i.

XLII. KINGDOMS OF ASIA MINOR; SYRIA

620 *Myrina*, *c.* 160–150. Tetradrachm, AR 16.05g. Stockholm (*SNG* 2216). Sacks 1985, issue 18.13r (same dies).

621 *Bithynia*, Nicomedes III (127–94), dated year 188 (= 110/9). Tetradrachm, AR 15.34g. Copenhagen (*SNG* 649). Glew 1987, 48, no. 45.6.

622 *Cappadocia*, Ariarathes VII Philometor (116–101). Drachm, AR 4.03g. Stockholm. Simonetta 1977, 35.3.

623 *Pontus*, Pharnaces I (*c.* 185–170). Tetradrachm, AR 16.90g. Lisbon (Gulbenkian II.934).

624 Same mint, Mithridates IV Philopator (*c.* 170–150), with jugate busts of the king and Queen Laodice. Tetradrachm, AR 16.02g. *SNG von Aulock* 1675, ex Jameson 1365.

625 Same mint, Mithridates VI (*c.* 120–63), dated year 209 (= 89/8). Tetradrachm, AR 16.38g. Stockholm.

626 *Antioch*, Tigranes II of Armenia (97–56). Tetradrachm, AR 15.42g. Stockholm. Bedoukian 1978, no. 17.

627 Same mint, Antiochus IV (175–164), series III, *c.* 169/8–164. Tetradrachm, AR 16.78g. Copenhagen (*SNG* –, ex *SNG Lockett* 3128). Mørkholm 1963, 14.A22–P91.

628 Same mint, ruler and date, with same types but a more idealized Zeus head. Tetradrachm, AR 16.58g. Copenhagen (*SNG* –). Mørkholm 1963, 14.A.25–P104, pl.5.

XLIII. SYRIA AND PARTHIA

629 *Ake-Ptolemais*, Antiochus IV (175–164), series I, with realistic portrait, *c.* 170–168. Tetradrachm, AR 17.03g. Lisbon (Gulbenkian II.1042). Cf. Mørkholm 1963, 46.3 (obv. die A2 but different rev. die).

630 *Antioch*, Antiochus IV, series II, with idealized portrait, *c.* 173/2–169/8. Tetradrachm, AR 16.53g. Copenhagen (*SNG* 187, ex Jameson 1697). Mørkholm 1963, 7.A10–P43, pl.3.

631 Same mint, Antiochus VI (145–142/1), dated year 170 of the Seleucid era (143/2). Tetradrachm, AR 16.77g. Stockholm.

632 Same mint and ruler, 145–142/1. Serrated edge. AE 7.49g. Stockholm.

633 *Tyre*, Antiochus VII (138–129), dated year 178 (135/4). Tetradrachm, AR 16.59g. Stockholm, ex Naville 10 (15.vi.1925), 1283. Rogers 1927, 32.127.

634 *Tarsus*, Demetrius II, second reign (129–126/5). Tetradrachm, AR 16.69g. Stockholm. Houghton 1979b, group D.A4–P9 (this coin).

635 *Sidon*, Cleopatra Thea and Antiochus VIII (126/5–96), with jugate heads, dated year 191 (= 122/1). Tetradrachm, AR 13.40g. Stockholm. Cf. Houghton collection 721.

636 *Ake-Ptolemais*, Antiochus VIII, *c.* 120–117. Tetradrachm, AR 16.61g. Private coll., Stockholm. Newell 1939, 25.28.

637 *Parthia*, Mithridates I (*c.* 171–138/7). Drachm, AR 3.88g. Stockholm (*SNG, Forbat* 519).

638 Same mint, Mithridates II (123/2–88/7). Drachm, AR 4.11g. Stockholm (*SNG, Forbat* 520).

XLIV. BACTRIA, ETC.; PHOENICIA, PALESTINE AND EGYPT

639 *Bactria*, Eucratides I (*c.* 170–*c.* 145). Tetradrachm, AR 16.85g. Stockholm. Mitchiner 1975, I, type 177dd (*Pushkalāvati*).

640 As last, same ruler and date. Tetradrachm, AR 16.86g. Bank Leu 28 (5.v.1981), 212. Mitchiner 1975, I, type 179a (*Merv*).

641 *India*, Menander (*c.* 155–*c.* 130), with bilingual inscription in Greek and Kharoshthi. Tetradrachm (local standard), AR 9.75g. Copenhagen (*SNG* –). Mitchiner 1975, 2I, type 217f (*Pushkalāvati*).

642 *Elymais: Susa*, Kamnaskires I (*c.* 163). Tetradrachm, AR 15.78g. Copenhagen (*SNG* –).

643 *Characene*, Tiraios II (*c.* 78/7–*c.* 49/8), dated year 243 of the Seleucid era (= 69/8). Tetradrachm, AR 14.20g. Stockholm. Le Rider 1959, 244.14–17.

644 *Aradus*, dated year 198 of the Phoenician era

(= 61/60). Tetradrachm, AR 14.43g. Stockholm. Kromann 1988, 108.46.

645 *Tyre*, dated year 4 of the second era of Tyre (= 123/2). Shekel, AR 13.75g. Stockholm.

646 *Alexandria*, Cleopatra VII (51–30), with her portrait. AE 19.38g. Stockholm.

647 *Judaea*, Alexander Jannaeus (103–76). AE 1.06g. Stockholm. Meshorer 1967, 119.10.

648 As last, John II (69, 63–57). AE 2.42g. Stockholm. Meshorer 1967, 121.18ff.

XLV. THE HELLENISTIC AGE: REMARKABLE TYPES

649 *Lampsacus*, *c.* 160. *Obv.* archaizing head of Dionysus; *rev.* Apollo Kitharoidos. Tetradrachm, AR 16.89g. Copenhagen (*SNG* –).

650 *Mytilene*, *c.* 160. *Obv.* head of Zeus Ammon; *rev.* herm of Dionysus. Tetradrachm, AR 16.43g. Copenhagen (*SNG* –) (*CH* 6 (1981), 37).

651 *Leucas*, 2nd century. *Obv.* statue of Artemis; *rev.* prow decorated with laurel. Stater, AR 8.12g. Copenhagen (*SNG, Epirus–Acarnania* 380).

652 *Ilium*, issued in the name of the deity, *c.* 97–87. *Obv.* head of Athena, *rev.* cult image of Athena Ilias. Tetradrachm, AR 15.93g. Copenhagen (*SNG, Troas* 362). Regling 1927, 122.XXII. Bellinger 1961, T99.

653 *Antioch* (Antiochus IV), special issue of 166. *Obv.* head of Apollo; *rev.* cult statue of Apollo Kitharoidos by Bryaxis at the sanctuary of Daphne. Tetradrachm, AR 16.11g. Lisbon (Gulbenkian II.1041, ex Jameson 1699). Mørkholm 1963, series III.A55–P206.

654 *Heraclea* (Ionia), *c.* 160–150. *Obv.* head of Athena Parthenos; *rev.* club in wreath. Tetradrachm, AR 17.05g. Stockholm.

655 *Cappadocia*, Orophernes (159–157), with his portrait. Tetradrachm, AR 16.59g. Lisbon (Gulbenkian II.1019, ex Jameson 1635), found at Priene in 1870 (= *IGCH* 1323). Regling 1927, 44–5.

656 *Alexandria Troas*, with representation of Apollo Smintheus, issued in the name of the city and the deity, *c.* 164 (undated). Tetradrachm, AR 16.67g. Bank Leu 28 (5.V.1981), 138. Cf. Bellinger 1961, A133.

657 *Ephesus*, dated year 9 (= 126/5). *Obv.* head of Artemis; *rev.* cult image of Artemis Ephesia. Stater, AV 8.30g. Lisbon (Gulbenkian II.987). For the date see Jenkins 1987, 185.

I PHILIP II AND ALEXANDER THE GREAT

1 2 3 4 5 6

7 8 9 10 11 12

13 14 15 16 17

18 19 20 21 22

23 25 26 27 28

24

29

31 32 33

30

III PERIOD OF ALEXANDER THE GREAT AND PHILIP III

34 35 36 37 38 39

40 41 42 43 44

45 46 47 48 49 50

51
52
53
54
55
56
57a
57b
58
59
60
61
62
63
64
65
66
67
68

69 70 71 72 73 74

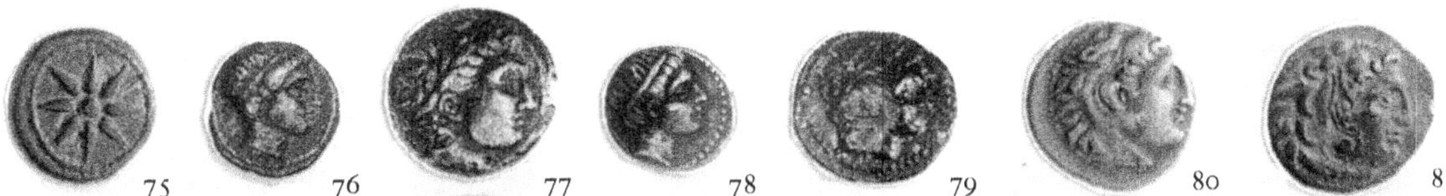

75 76 77 78 79 80 81

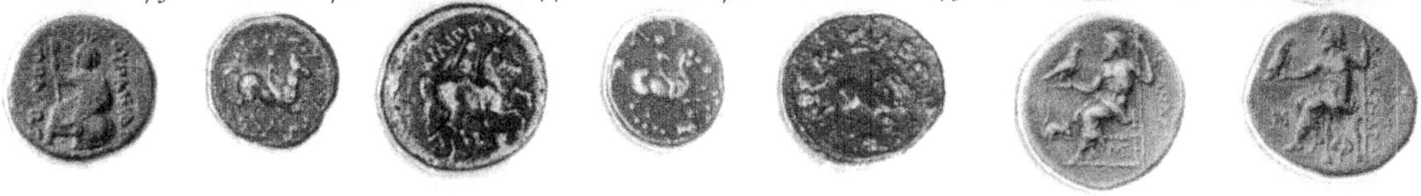

82

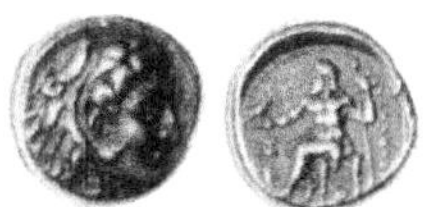

88

89

83 84 85 86 87

90 91 92 93 94

95 96 97 98 99

100 101 102 103 104 105 106

107 108 109 110 111 112A 112B

113 114 115 116 117 118

a 119 b

120 122 123 124 125 126

121

130 (× 2)

127 128 129

131 (× 2)

132 133 134 135 136 137

138 139 140 141 142 143

144 145 146 147 148

149

150

151

152

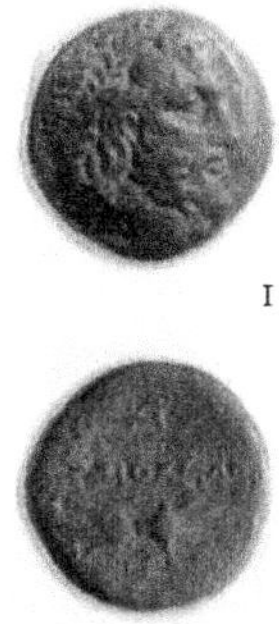

153

154

155

156

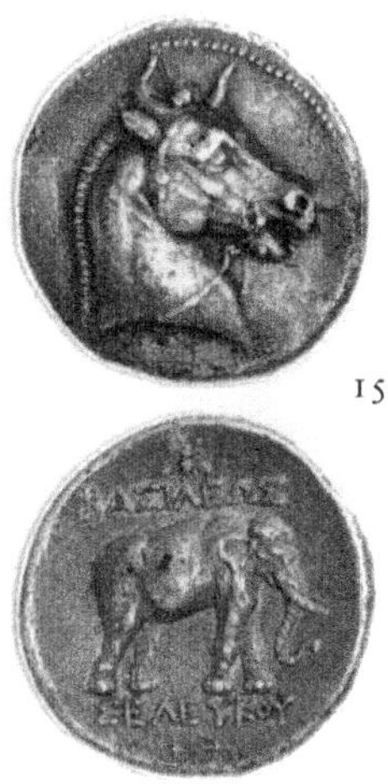

157

158

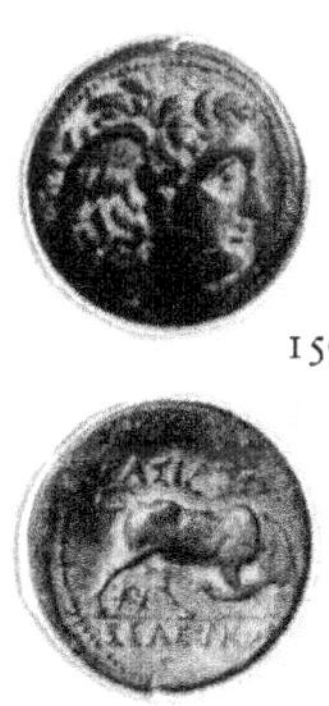

159

160

161 162 163 164 165 166

167 168 169 170 171

172 173 174 175

XI LYSIMACHUS AND PATRAEUS OF PAEONIA

176 177 178 179

180 181 182 183 184

185 186 187 188

189

XII DYNASTS AND GREEK CITIES

190 191 192 193 194 195

196 197 198 199 200 201

202 203 204 205 206

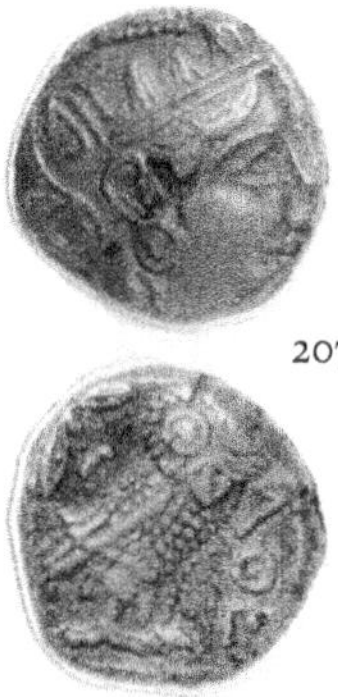
207

208

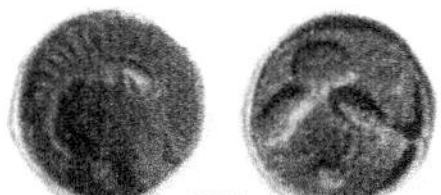
209

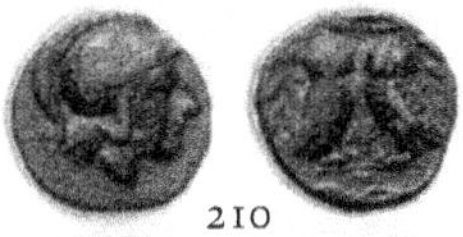
210

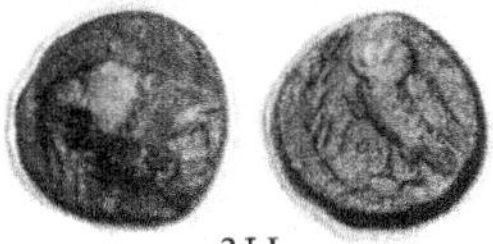
211

212

213

214

215

216

217

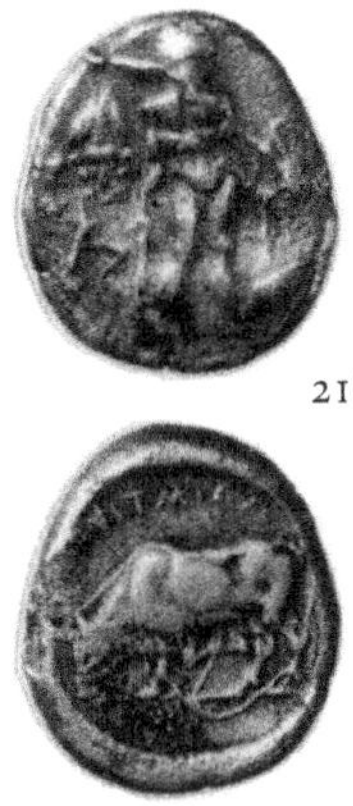
218

219

220

221

222

223

224

XIV CRETE AND RHODES

225 226 227 228 229

230 231 232 233 234

235 236 237 238 239

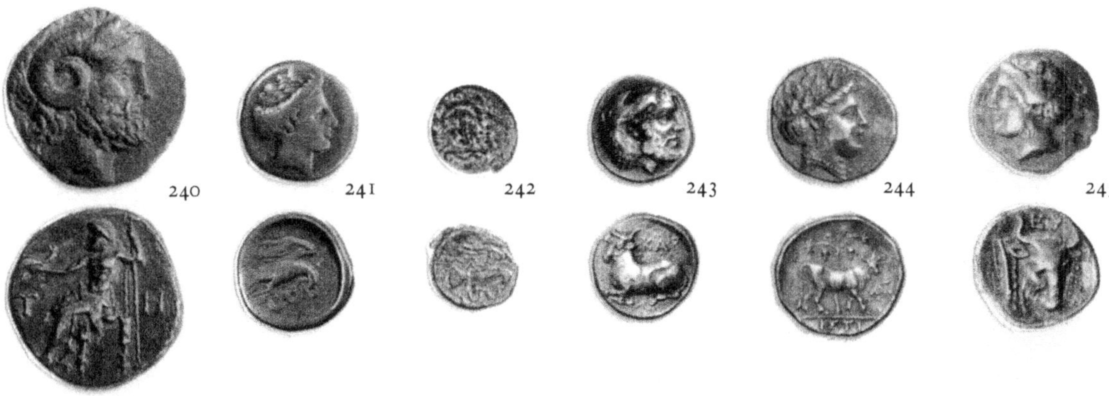

240 241 242 243 244 245

246 247 248 249 250 251

252 253 254 255 256 257 258

259 260 261 262 263 264

265 266 267 268 269

270 271 272 273 274a 274b

XVII ASIA MINOR DYNASTS; EGYPT AND CYRENAICA

275 276 277 278 279a

279b 280 281 282 283

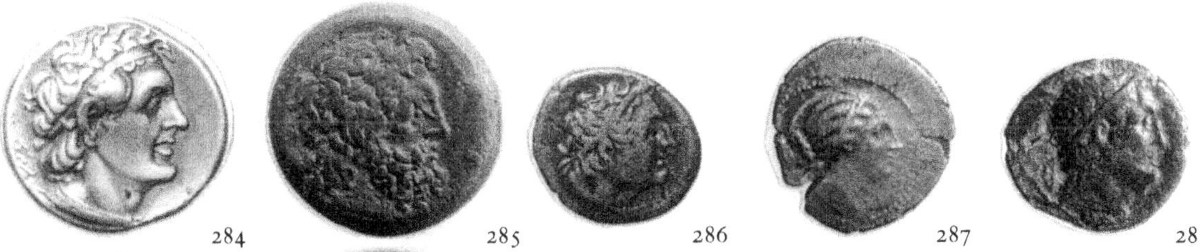

284 285 286 287 288

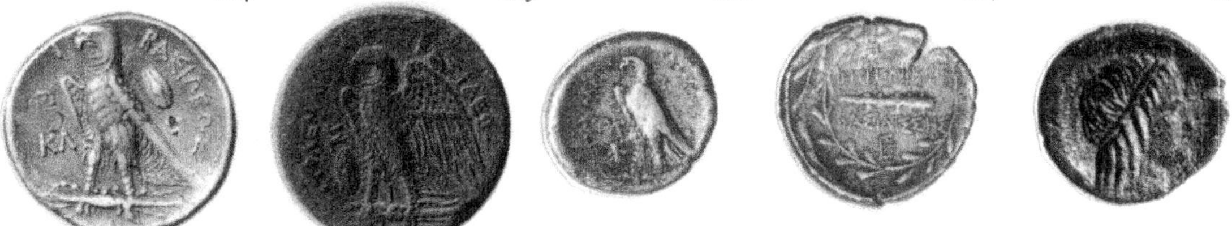

289

290

291

292

293

294

295

296

297

298

299

300

301

302

303

304

305

306

307

308

309

310

311

312

313

314

315

316

317

318

319 320 321 322

323 324 325 326

327 328 329

330

331

332

334

333

335

336

337

338

339

340

341

343 344 345 346

347 348 349 350 351 352

353 354A 354B 355

356

357

358

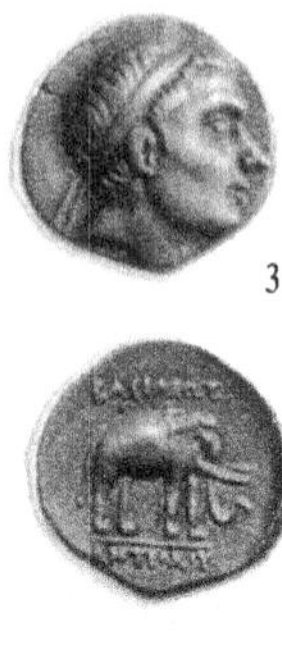
359

360

361

362

363

364

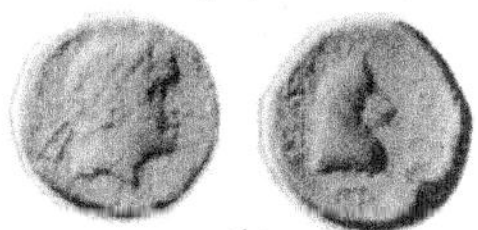
365

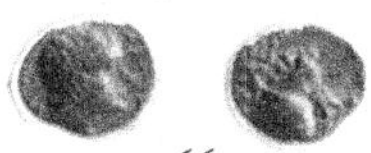
366

367

368

369

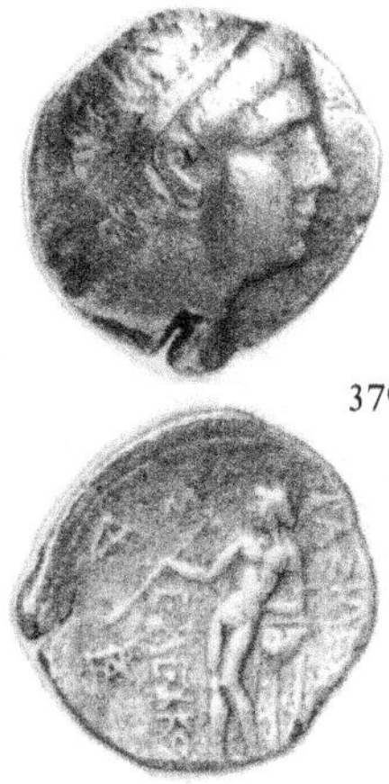
370

371

372

373

374 375 376 377

378 379 380 381 382

383 384 385 386 387

388

389

390

391

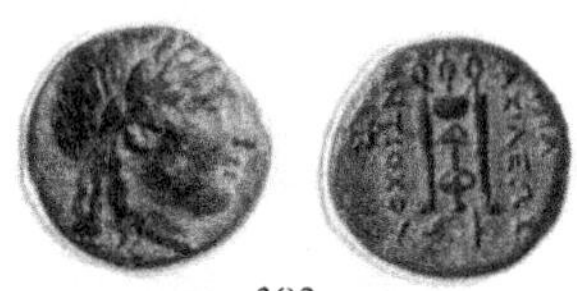

392

393

394

395

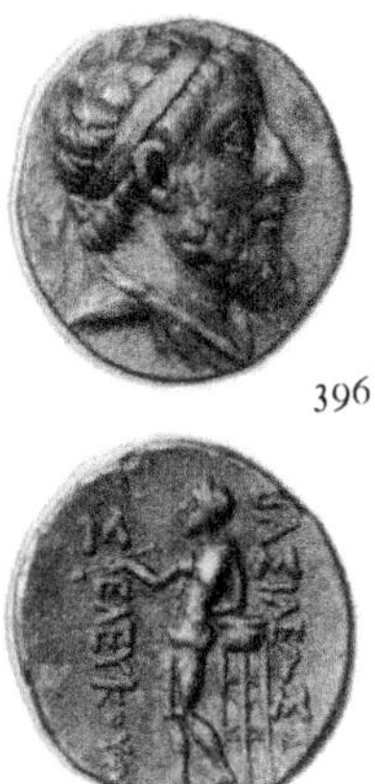

396

397

398

399

400

401

402

403

404

405

406

407

408

409

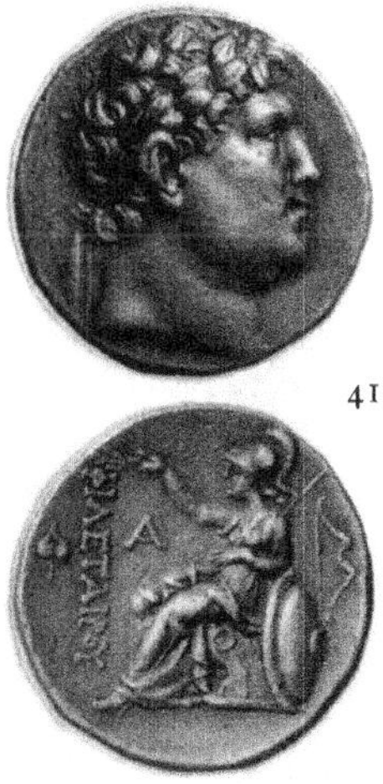

410

411 412 413 414 415 416

417 418 419 420 421

422 423 424 425 426 427 428

429

430

431

432

433

434

435

436

437

438

439

440

441

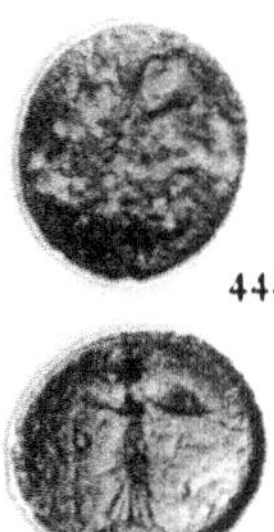
442

443

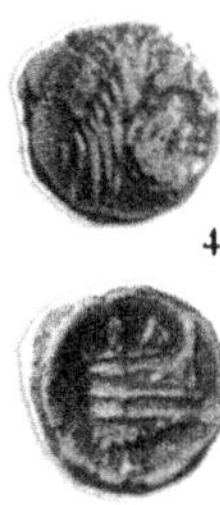
444

445

XXX POSTHUMOUS ALEXANDERS (I)

446 447 448 449

450 451 452 453

454 455 456 457

458

459

460

461

462

463

464

465

466

467

468

469

470

471

472

473

474

475

476

477

478

479

480

481
482
483
484
485
486
487
488
489
490
491
492
493

494
495
496
497
498
499
500
501
502a
502b
503
504
505
506
507
508

509 510 511 512 513

514 515 516 517 518 519

520 521 522 523 524

525 526 527 528 529 530

531 532 533 534 535 536 537

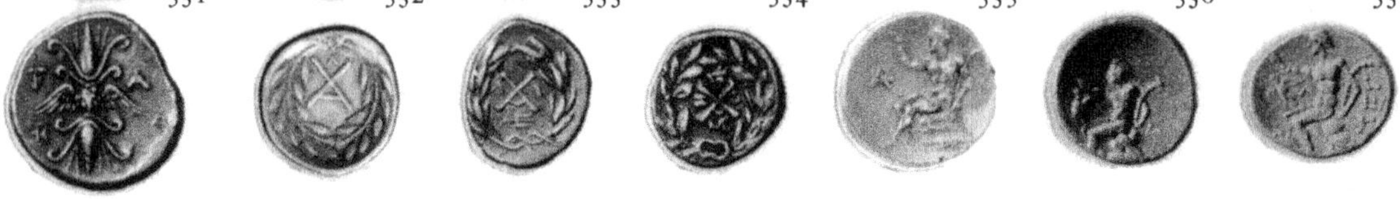

538 539 540 541 542 543

544

545

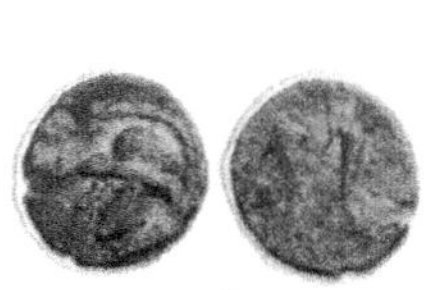

546

547

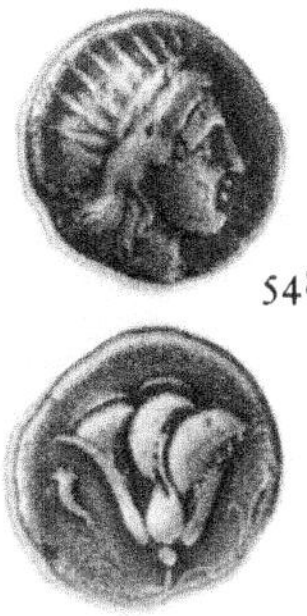

548

549

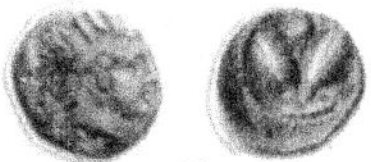

550

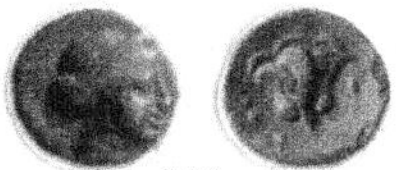

555

551

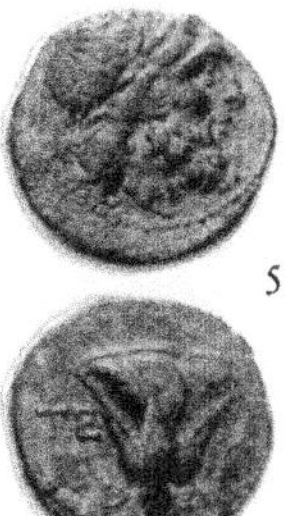

552

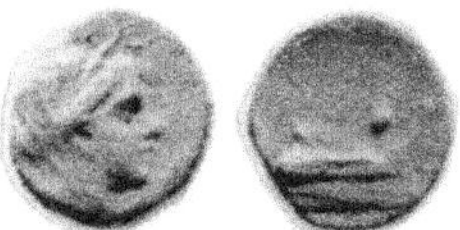

553

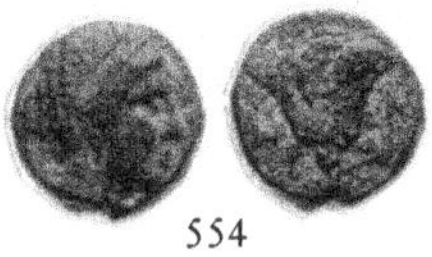

554

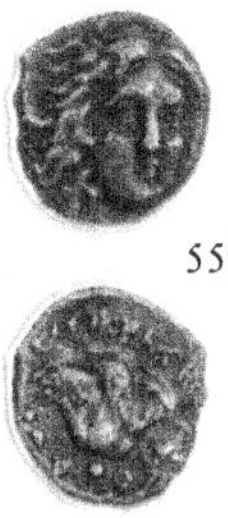

556

557

558

559

560

561

562

563

564

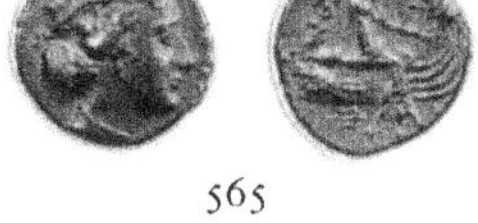

565

566
567
568
569
570
571
572
573
574
575
576
577
578
579
580
581

582 583 584 585 586

587 588 589 590A 590B

591 592 593 594 595 596

597

598

599

600

601

602

603

604

605

606

607

608

609 610 611 612 613

614 615 616 617

618 619

620

621

622

623

624

625

626

627

628

629

630

631

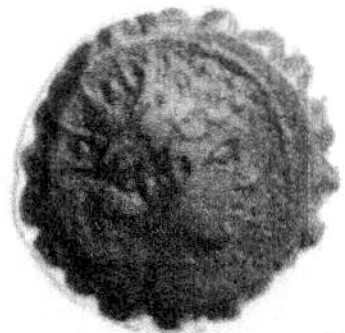
632

633

634

635

636

637

638

639

640

641

642

643

644

645

646

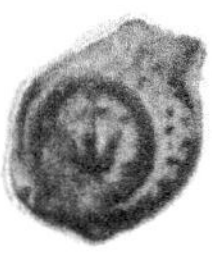

647

648

649

650

651

652

653

654

655

656

657

656

INDEX

Numbers in italic type refer to the maps, with *FEP* and *BEP* standing for *Front* and *Back endpaper* respectively. Numbers in bold type are those of the coin illustrations and serve as an index to names occurring in the captions on pp. 243–66. Since the book is not a coin catalogue, types and legends are indexed only where they are unusual or are specifically discussed in the text or notes. The indexing of the list of rulers and the glossary is likewise selective.

'Abdhadad of Manbog, 49; **31–2**
Abyal of Hagar, 145; **487**
Abyatha, Arab ruler, 145; **487–8**
'Abyati of Manbog, 49
Abydus, Troas (*1, 3, 5, 6*), 50, 61, 81, 82, 84, 123–5, 147; **40, 81**; mines near, 3
Acarnania, Greece (*5*), Acarnanian League, 87, 151–3; **520–1**
Achaea, Peloponnese (*5*), Achaean League, 9, 98, 138, 150, 154, 170, 199, 200; **532–4**
Achaemenids, 49, 96, 203
Achaeus, usurper in Asia Minor, 125–6, 189, 201; **403–5**
Actium, Acarnania (*5*), 152, 169
Aegae, Macedonia (*1, 5*), 42, 44–5, 122–3, 197; **5–6, 12**
Aenianes, Thessaly, 27
Aenus, Thrace (*5*), 82, 100, 108, 145; **490**
Aeolis, Asia Minor (*6*), 122
Aesillas, Roman *quaestor*, 167–8; **605**
Aetolia, Greece (*5*), Aetolian League, 9, 98, 135, 150–2, 171, 199, 201; **513–19**; *see also* weight standards
Afghanistan, 195–6
Agathocles, Indo-Greek king, 27, 181, 196
Agathocles of Syracuse, 68
Agrinion, Aetolia (*5*), hoard, 154 n. 55
Ahura-Mazda, as coin type, 119
Ai Khanum, Bactria (*BEP*), hoard, 181–2
Ainel of Byblus, 47; **23–4**
Ake (Ptolemais), Phoenicia (*1, 2, 3*), 56, 61, 101, 102, 108, 110; **20, 629, 636**
Alabanda (Antioch on the Chrysaoreis), Caria (*6*), 10, 23, 142–3; **475–6**
Aleuas, Thessalian hero, 85; **202**
Alexander III the Great, 3, 4, 8, 23, 40–55, 63–4, 67, 74, 89, 95, 187, 197; coins, 12, 15, 19, 40–54; **5–13, 16–22, 27–30, 34–46**; portraiture, 27–8, 32, 65, 72; titles, 29, 51; *see also* Alexanders, posthumous
Alexander IV of Macedon, 55, 56, 58, 59, 187, 190, 197–8
Alexander V of Macedon, 79, 187, 198–9
Alexander I Balas, Seleucid, 10, 25, 177, 178, 183, 189
Alexander II, Seleucid, 178
Alexander, son of Craterus, 158
Alexander Jannaeus, 183; **647**
Alexanders, posthumous, 21, 22, 23, 35–6, 56–7, 59–62, 69, 71, 73, 75, 77, 78, 79, 81, 91, 93–4, 113, 122, 132, 134, 137–45, 148; **61, 66–7, 69, 74, 82–8, 90–5, 144, 149–56, 161, 168, 176–82, 191, 199–201, 246–7, 264–5, 429, 446–54, 458–74, 477–80, 483–4, 486–9, 503, 514–15**
Alexandria, Egypt (*FEP, 1, 2, 3, BEP*), 48, 56, 59, 61, 197, 198; coins of, 15, 52, 63–7, 101–9, 184, 191; **42, 90–3, 96–7, 99–101, 284–5, 291, 294–8, 300–10, 314, 316–18, 646**
Alexandria Margiana (mod. Merv) (*4*), 179
Alexandria, Troas (*3*), 29, 81, 82, 123, 124, 139; **397, 461, 656**
Alexandria Kapisa, Bactria (*BEP*), 181
Alexarchus, brother of Cassander, 60
Amastris of Bithynia, 95–6; **276, 279**
Amastris, Paphlagonia (*BEP*), 96; **279–80**
Amathus, Cyprus (*1, 3*), 51, 58
Ambracia, Epirus (*5*), 84
Ammon, Zeus, *see* Siwah
Amphaxitis, Macedonia (*5*), 165, 166; **596**
Amphictyonic Council, 41, 85–6; **204–5**
Amphilocus/Argos, Acarnania (*5*), 87, 88
Amphipolis, Macedonia (*1, 5*), 41–52 *passim*, 56, 57, 59–60, 79–80, 82, 132–4, 163–8; **3, 5–7, 9, 69–70, 173, 178, 429–31, 436, 582–3, 588–90B, 592–5, 599, 602–5**
Amyntas, Indo-Greek king, 181, 196
Anactorium, Acarnania (*5*), 87, 152
Anadol, Ukraine, nr Odessa, hoard, 138
Anaitis, deity, 96
Andragoras, satrap of Parthia, 119–20, 194; **378–9**
Andriscus, Macedonian usurper, 135, 167, 169
Andritsaena, Elis (*1*), hoard, 44 n. 6
Andros, Aegean island (*5*), 135
Anisa, Cappadocia (mod. Kanish) (*3*), 132
Anthedon, Euboea (*5*), hoard, 171
Anthela, nr Thermopylae (*5*), 85
Antigonea, Syria (*3*), 61, 74–5; **85**
Antigonus I Monophthalmus, 55, 58, 59, 60–1, 72, 73, 77, 87, 157, 187, 197–8; **80–6**
Antigonus II (Gonatas) of Macedon, 26, 61, 81, 91, 132–5, 137, 151, 188, 199–200; **429–34**
Antigonus III (Doson) of Macedon, 13, 134–5, 138, 142, 149, 151, 188, 200–1; **433–4, 436–7**
Antimachus I of Bactria, 181, 196
Antioch on the Erythrean Sea (*4*), 178
Antioch on the Orontes, Syria (*2, 3, BEP*), 6, 8, 26, 28, 74, 76, 113, 114–15, 176, 178, 184; **153–60, 330, 332–3, 337–41, 348–51, 353, 626–8, 630–2, 653**; coins found at, 22
Antiochus I (Soter), Seleucid, 28, 30, 58, 73, 113–19, 122–4, 128, 130, 145, 188, 199–200; **145, 330, 335–6, 344, 349, 351, 354–5, 366, 371–3, 388–91, 393–4**

Antiochus II (Theos), 113–20, 122–4, 188, 200; **331, 352, 362, 374–5, 390, 392, 394–5**

Antiochus III (the Great), 25, 26, 28, 30, 98, 109, 114–19, 121, 124–7, 132, 141, 142–3, 151, 169, 171, 177, 179, 201–2; **339–40, 343, 345–6, 348, 353, 357–9, 363–7, 369, 401–2, 406**

Antiochus IV (Epiphanes), 11, 76, 177, 178, 179, 182, 189; **627–30, 653**

Antiochus VI (Epiphanes), 13, 177, 189; **631–2**

Antiochus VII (Sidetes), 180, 183, 189; **633**

Antiochus VIII (Grypus), 177, 178, 183, 189; **635–6**

Antiochus IX (Philopator, Cyzicenus), 177, 189

Antiochus IV of Commagene, 176

Antiochus Hierax, usurper in Asia Minor, 120, 123–5, 139, 146, 188, 200; **397–9**

Antipater of Macedon, regent, 55, 56, 63, 85, 187, 190, 197–8

Antipater I, king of Macedon, son of Cassander, 79, 187, 188, 199

Apamea, Phrygia (*3, 6*), 113, 114, 115, 118 n. 15, 173; peace of, 98, 132, 202

Apamea, Syria (*2, 3*), 75; **331, 335–7, 340–2**

Apelles, painter, 53

Aphytis, Chalcidice (*5*), 165

Apollo, as coin type, 25, 26, 29

Apollonia, Cyrenaica (*BEP*), 102

Apollonia, Illyria (*5*), 83–4, 152–3, **527**

Apollonia Mygdoniae, Macedonia (*5*), 165

Apollonia Pontica, Thrace (*5*), 26

Apollonius, finance minister of Ptolemy II, 104

Aradus, Phoenicia (*1, 2, 3*), 33, 46, 47, 56, 61, 74, 115, 144, 145, 179; **17, 48, 82, 483–5, 487, 644**

Aramaic, *see* coin inscriptions

Aratus of Sicyon, 200–1

Araxes (*4*), river, 175

Arbela, *see* Gaugamela

Arcadia, Peloponnese (*5*), Arcadian League, 89, 154; **228, 535–7**

Archebius, Indo-Greek king, 181, 196

Archilochus, poet, as coin type, 157

Areus of Sparta, 149, 200–1

Argos, Acarnania, *see* Amphilocus

Argos, Peloponnese (*5*), 9, 88, 137, 138, 154, 199; **446**

Ariaramnes of Cappadocia, 131, 193; **422–3**

Ariarathes I of Cappadocia, 96, 131, 174, 193; **282–3**

Ariarathes III, 131, 193; **424–6**

Ariarathes IV (Eusebes), 132, 174, 175, 193; **427–8**

Ariarathes VI (Epiphanes), 175, 193

Ariarathes VII (Philometor), 193; **622**

Ariarathes IX, 175, 194

Aristobulus, Rhodian magistrate, 157

Aristonicus, *see* Eumenes III

Aristotle, 23

Armenia (*FEP, 1, 4, BEP*), 175–6

Arsaces (Arshak) III of Parthia, 120, 179, 180, 194, 195, 200

Arsacids, 194–5

Arsinoe I, wife of Ptolemy II, 30, 93, 190

Arsinoe II, sister-wife of Ptolemy II, 33, 102–5, 190, 200; **294–9, 327–8**; supposed era of, 33, 103

Arsinoe III, sister-wife of Ptolemy IV, 109, 156, 190; **322**

Arsinoea (Crete), *see* Rhithymna

Artacoana, Bactria (*4*), 118, 120

Artemis, as coin type, 25, 26, 30

Ascalon, Judaea (*2, 3*), 109

Ashton, R. H. J.: on Rhodian coinage, 90, 156–7

Aspadana, Media (*BEP*), 182

Aspeisas, satrap, 58; **66**

Aspendus, Pamphylia (*6*), 9, 23, 143, 159–60; **478, 579**

Assos, Troas (*5*), 141

Astarte, goddess, 132

Astavene, Khurasan (*4*), 120

Atargatis, deity, 49; **31–2**

Athena, as coin type, 25, 26, 30

Athens, Attica (*FEP, 5, BEP*), 7, 41, 43, 44, 79, 80, 134, 137, 148–9, 168, 200; **207–11, 501–2, 609–11**; 'owls', 47, 86–7, 91; copies of, 57; **25–6, 57**; New Style coins of, 16, 17, 32, 33, 165, 170–1; **609–11**; coin flans found at, 13; coins found at, 86

Attalids of Pergamum, 23, 28, 191–2, 200–1

Attalus I of Pergamum, 123, 124, 126, 129, 139, 191; **410–11**

Attalus II, 192

Attalus III, 172, 174, 192

Attalus, father of Philetaerus, 191

Attic, *see* weight standards

Audoleon of Paeonia, 83; **190–1**

Autophradates I of Persis, 119; **377**

Axios, Macedonia (*5*), river, 82, 165

Ayaz-In, Phrygia (*3*), hoard, 141 n. 25

Ba'al, 43, 46, 48

Ba'altarz, 45, 46

Babylon, Babylonia, Mesopotamia (*FEP, 1, 4, BEP*), 40, 44, 48, 49, 51–6, 63, 70, 177, 179, 180, 182, 188, 194–5, 197; **8, 27–30, 47, 57**; coins found at, 52–3; **44**; weight standards, 7

Bactra, Bactria (*FEP, 4, BEP*), 3, 27, 28, 30, 71, 73, 98, 114, 118–19, 120–2, 179, 180–2, 194–6, 197; **145, 148, 371–3, 374–5, 380–7, 639–40**

Bagadates of Persis, 73–4, 119; **146**

Bakërr, *see* Apollonia/Illyria

Balacrus, satrap, 46; **15**

Bargylia, Caria (*3*), 126

bashlik, *see kyrbasia*

basileus, on coins of Alexander, 51

Bedoukian, P. Z.: on early Armenian coinage, 176

Berenice I, wife of Ptolemy I, 28, 70, 102, 103, 106, 107, 190, 199; **287, 297–8, 327–8**

Berenice II, wife of Ptolemy III, 106–8, 157, 190; **307–8, 313**

Berytus, Phoenicia (*1, 2*), 30, 51, 109, 110

Bithynia, Asia Minor (*3, 6, BEP*), 30, 33, 98, 130, 132, 173–4, 192, 193, 199; **414–19, 621**

Bivar, A. D. H.: on Bactrian coins, 180 n. 35

Boeotia, Greece (*5*), 9, 86, 154; **530**

Bopearachchi, O.: on Bactrian rulers, ix, 196

Bosphorus, Cimmerian (Crimea), 147

Bottiaea, Macedonia (*5*), 165, 166; **597–8, 600**

Brahmi, *see* coin inscriptions

Brettius Sura, *see* Sura

bronze: use in coinage, 6, 10–11

Bryaxis, sculptor, 26; **653**

Bucephalus, 73

Burnett, A.: on Macedonian coinage, 167–8

Büyükçekmece, Thrace (*3*), hoard, 146

Byblus, Phoenicia (*1, 2*), 30, 46, 47, 51, 55, 109; **18, 23–4**

Byzantium, Thrace (*3, 6*), 20, 23, 94–5, 98, 137, 138, 145–7, 157, 160; **270, 491, 494–5, 498–9**; *see also* weight standard

Cabyle, Thrace (*6*), 122, 138; **451**

Caesar, L. Julius, 167–8

Caesarea, *see* Mazaca

Calchedon, *see* Chalcedon

Callatis, Moesia (*6*), 138

Cappadocia, Asia Minor (*1, 3, BEP*), 3, 28, 30, 33, 75, 96, 98, 131–2, 173–5, 176, 193–4; **282, 422–8, 622, 655**

Caria, Asia Minor (*3, 6*), 59, 141, 173; **167**

Carmania (*4, BEP*), 4, 53

Carne, Phoenicia (*1*), 51, 144

Carrhae, Mesopotamia (*1, 3*), 61, 73, 74, 116, 122; **83, 354A–B**

Carthage, Carthaginians, 4, 29, 68, 198

Carystus, Euboea (*5*), 90–1, 157; **243, 563–4**

Cassander of Macedon, 55, 58, 59, 60, 79, 83, 86, 87, 187, 198; **69–75**
Cavarus, Celtic king in Thrace, 138
Celts, in Danubian region, 43
Chaeronea, Boeotia (*5*), battle, 41, 86, 87, 90
Chalcedon, Bithynia (*6*), 20, 95, 145–7; **271, 492, 496–7, 500**
Chalcidice, Macedonia (*5*), 60, 165
Chalcidian League, 41
Chalcis, Euboea (*5*), 80, 81, 90, 91, 137, 158; **241–2, 245–7**
Chalcis, Syria (*2, 3*), 61, 171
Chandragupta, Indian king, 71, 198
Characene, Iran (*6*), 20, 178, 179, 182; **643**
Chersonese, Thrace (*6*), 95; **272**
Chersonesus, Crete (*5*), 88; **226–7**
Chiliomodi, Argolis (*1*), hoard, 65, 87 n. 25
Chios, Aegean island (*3, 5, 6*), 10, 141–2, 201; **466–70**; *see also* weight standards
Chremonidean War, 105, 200
Chremonides, Athenian politician, 200
Cibyra, Lycia (*6*), 10, 173
Cilicia, Asia Minor (*1, 2, 3*), 3, 30, 45–6, 56, 75, 77, 78, 114, 131, 177, 178, 183, 197, 198, 199
Cimon, die cutter, 85
cistophori, 36–7, 171–2; *see also* weight standards
Citium, Cyprus (*1, 2, 3*), 15, 17, 30, 31, 47, 51, 56, 57, 58, 104; **41, 60**
Cius, Bithynia (*6*), 82, 94, 145, 192; **266–7**
Clazomenae, Ionia (*6*), 141, 142, 145
Cleomenes III of Sparta, 137, 149, 200–1; **505–7**
Cleopatra VII, dau. of Ptolemy XII, 5 n. 10, 35, 184, 191; **646**
Cleopatra Thea, queen of Syria, 177, 189; **635**
Cnidus, Caria (*6*), 159; **575–7**
coin: blanks, 12–13; circulation, 19–20; dates on, 17, 33–5, 46, 57–8; dies, *see* dies; finds and hoards, 20–2; inscriptions, *see* coin inscriptions; making of, 12–19; output, 85–6; portraiture, 25–9, 65, 74, 79, 80, 83, 102–3, 112, 120–1, 123–4, 128–32, 135–6, 164, 174–82, 184; types, 25–9; *see also* countermarking
coin inscriptions, 29–35; Aramaic, 46, 47, 48, 49, 57, 70, 74, 96, 122, 182; **23–4, 31–3**; Brahmi, 181; Demotic, 47; **25–6**; Hebrew, 70, 183; **131–2, 647–8**; Kharoshthi, 181
Colophon, Ionia (*1, 6*), 50, 57, 61, 81, 92–3, 141, 173; **36, 50, 56, 177, 252–4**
Commagene (*BEP*), 175–6
Corcyra, Adriatic island (*5*), 9, 84, 152–3; **195, 525–6**; *see also* weight standards
Corinth, Peloponnese (*1, 5*), 9, 61, 65, 79, 80, 81, 87–8, 100, 135, 137, 154, 169, 171, 198; **86, 213–14, 449**; hoard from, 148
Corinthian League, 41, 45, 50–1, 61, 87
Corone, Peloponnese (*5*), 154
Corupedium, Lydia (*6*), battle, 75, 82, 132, 199
Cos, Aegean island (*6*), 157, 173, 200; **557**
counterfeiting, 5–6
countermarking, 19–20, 92, 122, 126; **478**
Craterus, Macedonian general, 55, 197
Crete (*5, BEP*), 8, 13, 67, 88–90, 155–6; mercenaries, 13, 67–8
Crimea, 147, 175
Cybistra, Cappadocia (*3, BEP*), 132
Cyclades, Aegean islands (*5*), 90, 157, 200
Cyme, Aeolis (*3*), 122, 141, 173; **619**
Cynoscephalae, Thessaly (*5*), battle, 136, 163, 169, 201
Cyprus (*1, 2, 3, BEP*), 4, 15, 17, 46, 51, 55, 56, 57–8, 59, 61–2, 77, 78, 106, 108, 184, 191, 198, 199, 201; **311**; *see also* mines
Cyrenaica, Africa (*BEP*), 4, 5, 12, 13, 67–9, 101–2, 198, 199, 200; **102–29**
Cyrene, Africa (*1, BEP*), 64, 65–70, 100, 101–2, 190, 198, 200; **107–22, 124–9, 286–90**
Cyzicus, Mysia (*3, 6*), 20, 94, 95, 98, 139, 145, 147, 173; **274, 462, 493, 618**

Dacia (*BEP*), 168
Damascus, Coele-Syria (*1, 2, 3, BEP*), 15, 46, 47, 49, 51, 55, 109, 176; **21**
Damastion, Illyria (*5*), 82
Daphne, suburb of Antioch (Syria), 26; **653**
Dardania, Illyria (*5*), 83; **193**
Darius III, 28, 46, 49, 53, 197
debasement, 4–5
deben, Egyptian weight, 11, 105
decadrachms, 48, 52–4; **30, 49, 307**
deification, 79, 118
Delos, Aegean island (*5*), 171
Delphi, Greece (*5*), 85, 150; **204–5**
Demanhur, Egypt (*1*), hoard, 44–5, 51, 56; **23**
Demetrias, Thessaly (*5*), 80
Demetrius I, Bactrian king, 180, 196
Demetrius II, Bactrian king, 181, 196
Demetrius I Poliorcetes, 15, 26, 29, 57, 59, 61, 75, 77–81, 86, 87, 90, 92, 93, 132, 136, 146, 157, 188, 198–9; **161–74**; portraits, 27, 79
Demetrius II of Macedon, 135, 165, 188, 200
Demetrius I (Soter), Seleucid, 13, 189
Demetrius II (Nicator), Seleucid, 177, 183, 189; **435, 634**
Demophanes, philosopher, 102
dies, 14–19; adjusted (die axes), 15–16, 46, 91; life of, 16–18; linking, 16; recutting, 14–15
Diodotus I/II of Bactria, 120–1, 180, 194; **374–5, 380–2**
Dionysius of Heraclea Pontica, 95; **75**
Dionysopolis, Moesia (*6*), 138
Dodona, Epirus (*5*), 136, 152
Doedalses, sculptor, 130
Dora, Phoenicia (*2*), 109
Drama, Macedonia (*1*), hoard, 84
Dura-Europos, Assyria (*BEP*), coins found at, 6, 22
Dyrrhachium, Illyria (*5*), 83–4, 152–3; **193–4, 528–9**

Ecbatana, Media (mod. Hamadan) (*1, 4, BEP*), 15, 35, 49, 62, 71–2, 76, 118, 177, 178, 179; **87, 89, 137, 141–3, 334, 364–9**
Ecdemus, philosopher, 102
Edessa, Mesopotamia (*3*), 116
Egypt, 4, 5, 10–11, 19, 20, 27, 30, 33, 46, 47, 55, 98, 178, 183–4, 197ff.
electrum, 4, 94–5
Eleusis, Attica (*5*), 87; **212**
Eleutherna, Crete (*5*), 89; **232**
Elis, Greece (*5*), 9, 88, 154; **216, 531**
Elymais or Susiana (*BEP*), 178, 179, 182, 202; **642**
Ephesus, Ionia (*1, 3, 6*), 25, 26, 53, 78–9, 81–2, 93, 100, 108, 123, 141, 158–9, 173; **169, 255–6, 313, 566, 570, 617, 657**; called Arsinoea, 93
Epidaurus, Argos (*5*), 154
Epirote *symmachia*, 9, 152; **197–8, 522–4**
Epirus (*5, BEP*), 80, 83, 84, 136, 152, 153, 199, 200; **196**
epithets of rulers, 30–1
Eretria, Euboea (*5*), 90, 91, 158, 171; **612–13**
Erythrae, Ionia (*6*), 92, 141–2; **248–51**
Euboea, Greece (*5*), 80, 90–1, 134, 157–8, 171
Euboean League, 16, 90, 91, 158; **245**
Eucratides I of Bactria, 181, 196; **639–40**
Euhesperides, Cyrenaica (*BEP*), 69, 100; **123**
Eumenes I of Pergamum, 128–9, 191, 200; **409**
Eumenes II of Pergamum, 129, 171–2, 192; **614–16**
Eumenes III (Aristonicus) of Pergamum, 172, 192
Eumenes, Macedonian general, 55, 58, 198
Eunostus of Soli (Cyprus), 65; **15**

Eupolemus, general, 59; **67–8**
Euthydemus I of Bactria, 28, 121–2, 180, 196; **383–7**

finds, *see* coin finds
fire-temple, 74, 119
Flamininus, Roman general, 136–7, 169, 201; **445**
fratarak, title, 74
frequency tables, 7–8
Fulcinius, Lucius, 166; **599**

Gabala, Phoenicia (*3*), 144
Gaius Publilius, *see* Publilius
Galatians, 129, 130, 141, 142; *see also* Gauls
Gaugamela (Arbela) (*FEP, 1*), battle, 48, 197
Gauls, 98, 130, 132, 134, 150, 171, 199, 200; *see also* Galatians
Gaza, Judaea (*FEP, 1, 2*), 46, 65, 102, 108, 198
Gaziura, Pontus (*BEP*), 6; **283**
Gerrha, Arabia (*BEP*), 145; **486**
Gilgamesh, deity, 43
gold–silver ratios, 4–5, 43, 66–7
Gordium, Galatia (*FEP, 1, 3*), 45; hoards from, 114, 141 n. 25
Gortyn, Crete (*5*), 13, 67, 88, 155; **217, 538–43**
Grynaeum, Aeolis (*3*), 173
Grzybek, E.: on Ptolemaic chronology, 190
Gülnar, Cilicia (*3*), hoard, 125 n. 33

Hadad, deity, 49; **31**
Hagar, Arabia (*BEP*), 145; **487**
Harithat of Hagar, 145; **487**
harpa, 163, 164, 205
Hasmoneans of Judaea, 183
Head, B. V.: on style, 37; on Thessalian coinage, 84
Hebrew, *see* coin inscriptions
Hecatompylus, Hyrcania (*4*), 118, 120, 179; **370**
Heraclea, Ionia (*6*), 27; **654**
Heraclea Pontica, Bithynia (*6*), 82, 95–6, 138, 147; **275–8, 452**
Heracles, as coin type, 43
Hermaeus, Indo-Greek king, 195
Hermione, Argos (*5*), 137, 154
Hierapolis-Bambyce (Manbog), Syria (*1*), 48–9, 51; **31–3**
Hierapytna, Crete (*5*), 89; **233**
Himerus, usurper in Babylonia, 195
Histiaea, Euboea (*5*), 90–1, 158, 164–5, 168; **244, 565**
hoard, *see* coin finds and hoards; *see also* under names of individual hoards
hubbing, 14

Hyspaosines of Characene, 178, 182
Hyrcania (*FEP, 4*), 120, 179

Iconium, Lycaonia (*3*), 132
Ilium (Troy), Troas (*3, 5, 6*), 25, 29, 123–5, 147; **652**
Illyria, Illyrians (*5*), 83, 153; **193**
imitation coinages, 35–7; *see* Alexanders, Lysimachi, Philip II
immobilization (of coin types or legends), 35–7
India, 26, 49, 53–4, 180–2, 195–6; **148, 641**
Indo-Greeks, 28, 30, 180–2, 195–6
Ionia, Asia Minor (*3, 6*), 122, 141
Ipsus, Phrygia (*3*), battle, 29, 59, 61, 72, 74, 77, 78, 79, 81, 191, 198
Isis, goddess, 109; **317**
issues, size of, 16–17
Issus, Cilicia (*FEP, 1, 3*), 47; **14**; battle, 46, 47
Istakhr, Persis (*4*), 73, 119, 182; **376–7**
Istrus, Moesia (*6*), 138

Jerusalem, Judaea (*2, BEP*), 178, 183
Jewish coinage, 70, 183; **130–1, 647–8**
John I Hyrcanus, 183
John II Hyrcanus, 183; **648**
Joppa, Judaea (*2*), 102, 108, 109, 111
Judas I (or II?) of Judaea, 183
jugate busts, 28, 177; **297–8, 317, 327, 635**
Justin, historian, 119, 181

Kamnaskires of Elymais, 178, 181; **642**
Kanish, *see* Anisa
kausia, 41
Kharoshthi, *see* coin inscriptions
Kinns, P.: on Amphictyonic coinage, 85–6; on mints in Asia Minor, 92, 141 n. 28
Kleiner, F. S.: on cistophori, 172
Knossos, Crete (*5*), 88–9, 155; **223–4, 544**
Kyparissia, Peloponnese (*1*), hoard, 44 n. 6
kyrbasia, 42, 74, 203

L, as indicating 'year', 33, 111
Lachares of Athens, 86
Laconia, Peloponnese (*5*), 150
Lagids, *see* Ptolemies
Lamian War, 85, 88
Lampsacus, Mysia (*1, 3, 6*), 25, 31, 50, 61, 81, 82, 94, 123–5, 139, 147, 148, 173; **37, 49, 80, 179–80, 459–60, 649**; mines near, 3
Laodice, queen of Pontus, 175
Laodicea ad Mare, Syria (*2, 3*), 18, 75, 113, 114 n. 6, 118, 128, 173; **152, 343**
Lapethus, Cyprus (*2, 3*), 57; **58**

Larissa, Thessaly (*5*), 85, 148; **202–3**; *see also* Sitochoro
Laurion, Attica (*5*), mines, 3
Le Rider, G.: on Cretan coinage, 88–9; on Macedonian coinage, 42, 44 n. 6; on coinage of Susa, 118
Lebedus, Ionia (*6*), 93
Lesbos, Aegean island (*5, 6*), 81, 141
Leucas, Acarnania (*5*), 87, 152; **151**
Leucon II, Crimean king, 147
Lewis, D. M.: on Athenian New Style coinage, 170
Livy, 163 n. 1, 172
Lucius Fulcinius, *see* Fulcinius
Lycia, Asia Minor (*3, 6*), 55, 159
Lycurgus of Sparta, 150
Lysimachi, posthumous, 20, 22, 23, 35–6, 145–8, 157; **490–3, 498–500**
Lysimachia, Thrace (*3, 6*), 81, 82, 122, 123, 126, 134, 145, 147, 188, 199; **76–9**
Lysimachus, 19, 27, 55, 58, 59, 60–1, 75, 79–82, 83, 93, 95, 128, 132, 146, 188, 190, 191, 192, 197–9; **76–9, 176–84, 287–8, 394–9**; *see also* Lysimachi, posthumous
Lysippus, sculptor, 89, 176
Lyttian War, 155
Lyttus, Crete (*5*), 155

Ma, goddess, 132
Ma'ar'et en Nu'man, Syria, hoard, 172 n. 9
Macedon, 6, 26, 27, 41ff., 58, 79, 98, 132–7, 148, 150–1, 163–8, 187–8, 199ff.
Macedonia, 60, 79, 80, 163–8, 171; mines in, 3, 4, 166
Macedonian Wars, 98, 173, 201
Machanidas of Sparta, 150
Magas of Cyrene, 69, 101–2, 106, 190, 198–200; **286–8**
magistrates, initials or marks of, 31–2
Magnesia on the Maeander, Ionia (*1, 3, 6*), 50, 57, 61, 75, 76, 81, 82, 122, 141, 173; **51**
Magnesia ad Sipylum, Lydia (*3, 6*), 122–3, 125; **395**; battle, 169, 202
Mallus, Cilicia (*1*), 46, 179
Manbog, *see* Hierapolis-Bambyce
Mantinea, Peloponnese (*5*), 150
Marathus, Phoenicia (*1, 2, 3*), 56, 61, 74, 144; **149–51**
Margiana, *see* Alexandria Margiana
Marium, Cyprus (*1, 3*), 51, 57; **59**
Mark Antony, 184, 194
Maroneia, Thrace (*5*), 168; **607**
Mauryas, Indian dynasty, 73, 180
Mazaca, later Caesarea, Cappadocia (*3, BEP*), 174
Mazaces, satrap, 47, 57; **26**
Mazaeus, satrap, 45, 48, 96; **28**

Media (*FEP, BEP*), 177, 179
Megalopolis, Peloponnese (*5*), 9, 137, 154; **447, 535–7**
Mektepini, Phrygia (*6*), hoard, 141 n. 25, 147
Meleager of Macedon, 188, 199
Melos, Aegean island (*5*), 157; **558**
Melqart, deity, 43
Memphis, Egypt (*1, 2, BEP*), 47, 52 n. 17, 63, 198; **25–6**
Menander I (Soter), Indo-Greek king, 26, 180 n. 35, 181, 196; **641**
Menelaus, governor of Cyprus, 58, 61–2; **65**
mercenaries, 36, 89
Merv, *see* Alexandria Margiana
Mesembria, Thrace (*6*), 138
Mesopotamia (*FEP, 1, 4*), 61, 198, 201
Messene, Peloponnese (*5*), 137–8, 150, 154; **450, 512, 534**
metals, sources of, *see* mines
Methymna, Lesbos (*6*), 141
metrology, coin, 7–8
Miletus, Ionia (*1, 3, 6*), 15, 50, 56, 57, 61, 78, 93–4, 123, 137, 141, 142, 158–9, 173; **37–8, 53, 73, 168, 262–4, 474, 568, 571**
mina, 7
mines, 3–4, 41, 82, 106, 119
minting, right of, 36, 85, 165; *see also* coins, minting of
Mitchiner, M.: on Bactrian coinage, 120 n. 21, 122 n. 24
Mithridates I of Parthia, 177, 178, 179, 180, 189, 192, 193, 194, 195; **637**
Mithridates II of Parthia, 180, 182, 194, 195; **638**
Mithridates II of Pontus, 131, 139, 193; **420**
Mithridates III of Pontus, 131, 139, 175, 193; **421**
Mithridates IV (Philopator) of Pontus, 175, 193; **624**
Mithridates VI the Great (Eupator), 33, 175, 193; **625**
mnaion, 104; **297, 299**
Molon, usurper in Mesopotamia, 116, 118, 189, 201; **361**
Molossia, Molossians, Epirus (*5*), 80, 152
monograms, 31, 32, 34, 47, 52, 69, 101, 103, 145, 154
Monunius of Illyria, 83–4; **193**
Mopsus, Cilicia (*3*), 179
Morima, Cappadocia, 132; **426**
Mørkholm, O.: on Athenian New Style coinage, 170; on Bithynia, 130; on Cappadocia, 175; on cistophori, 172; on Parthia, 120; on portraits, *see* coin portraits; on Roman expansion, 169
Mygdonia, Macedonia (*5*), 165
Mylasa, Caria (*6*), 59, 93–4, 137, 141, 142; **67–8, 265**
Myonessus (*5*), island, 202
Myriandrus (= Alexandria ad Issum), Cilicia (*1*), 29, 46, 47, 51, 56; **16**
Myrina, Aeolis (*3*), 122, 141, 173; **620**
Mytilene, Lesbos (*5*), 25, 81, 82, 94, 141, 145; **650**

Nabis of Sparta, 150, 201–2; **509–11**
Nagasena, Buddhist sage, 181
Nagidus, Cilicia (*1*), 51
Narain, A. K.: on Indo-Greek coins, 181
Naucratis, Egypt (*BEP*), 178
Naupactus, Greece (*5*), peace of, 201
Naxos, Aegean island (*5*), 157; **561–2**
New Style (Athenian) coinage, *see* Athens
Newell, E. T.: on Macedonian coinage, 44, 47; on Seleucid coinage, 31, 61, 71 n. 1, 72, 76, 113ff.
Nicocles of Paphos, 58; **61–2**
Nicocreon of Salamis, 58, 62; **63–4**
Nicomedes I of Bithynia, 130, 174, 199–200; **414–15**
Nicomedes II, 174, 192
Nicomedes III, 174, 192; **621**
Nicomedia, Bithynia (*3, 6*), 130, 200
Nike, as coin type, 43–4
Nike of Samothrace, 78
Nisa (mod. Ashkabad) (*4, BEP*), 179
Nisibis, Mesopotamia (*4*), 116, 126, 178, 179; **355, 356–9**
Nisyros, Caria (*6*), 141
Noe, S. P.: on cistophori, 172
numerals, on coins, 32–5

Oborzos of Persis, 73–4, 119, 182; **147**
Odessus, Thrace (*6*), 19, 138
Odrysae, Thrace (*5*), 83; **192**
officinae, 32
Olus, Crete, 88; **225**
Olympia, Elis (*5*), 88; **216**
Olympias, mother of Alexander the Great, 55, 198
Ophellas, general, 68, 198; **114–15**
Opis, Babylonia (*1, 4*), 53
Orodes of Elymais, 182
Orodes II of Parthia, 33, 195
Orophernes, usurper in Cappadocia, 28, 193; **655**
overstriking, 13, 64–5, 67, 83, 89–90
'owls', Athenian, *see* Athens
Oxus (*FEP, 4, BEP*), river, hoard, 145

Paeonia, Macedonia (*5*), 83, 165; **185–91**
Palestine (*2, 3*), 179, 183, 198
Pamphylia, Asia Minor (*3, 6*), 55, 56, 143, 148, 159–60
Pan, deity, 134, 154
Panium, Phoenicia (*2*), 111; battle, 201
Panticapaeum, Tauric Chersonese (*1*), 94; **269**
Paphos, Cyprus (*1, 2*), 17, 31, 51, 58, 67, 104; **61–2**; coins found at, 12
Parium, Mysia (*3*), 82, 95, 125, 139, 145, 148; **273, 398, 458**
Parni, 120
Paroreia, Macedonia (*5*), 165
Paros, Aegean island (*5*), 157; **559–60**
Parthia, Parthians (*FEP, 4, BEP*), 4, 28, 30, 31, 33, 98, 119, 120–1, 177, 179–80, 194–5, 200; **378–9, 637–8**; court mint, 18
Patraeus of Paeonia, 42, 83; **185–9**
Patras, Achaea (*5*), 154; **533**
pegasi, of Corinth, 87
Pella, Macedonia (*FEP, 1, 5*), 42, 44, 45, 51, 56, 57, 59, 79–80, 82, 84, 134–5, 165, 181; **1–2, 55, 170–2, 174–5, 181, 437, 440, 597–8, 600**
Pellene, Achaea (*5*), 137
Peloponnese, southern Greece, 58, 137–8, 148, 198, 200; coins found in, 107
Perdiccas, Macedonian general, 55, 56, 58, 63, 96, 193, 197
Pergamum, Mysia (*3, 6, BEP*), 3, 10, 20, 26, 28, 30, 36, 75, 82, 94, 98, 126, 128–30, 137, 139, 146, 148, 169, 171–3, 174, 175, 191–2, 200, 201, 202; **157, 268, 407–13, 614–16**
Perge, Pamphylia (*6*), 23, 30, 37, 143, 160; **479, 482**
Perinthus, Thrace (*6*), 82, 145
Persepolis, Persis (*FEP, 4, BEP*), 49, 182, 197; coin find, 73
Perseus, hero, 135–6, 163; **582**
Perseus of Macedon, 136, 164–6, 171, 173, 188; **588–91, 593–4**
Persian, *see* weight standard
Persis (*FEP, 4, BEP*), 73–4, 119, 179, 182–3; **146–7, 376–7**
Phaestus, Crete (*5*), 13, 67, 88, 160; **218–22**
Pharnaces I of Pontus, 28, 139, 175, 193; **623**
Phaselis, Lycia (*1, 6*), 9, 23, 52, 143, 159; **480, 578**
Pheidias, sculptor, 26, 43, 170
Philetaerus of Pergamum, 28, 75, 128–30, 171, 172, 191, 200; **407–10, 412**
Philip II of Macedon, 3, 8, 19, 41, 86, 187, 197; **1–14**; imitations, 43; posthumous imitations, 50, 57, 59–60, 79, 142; **55–6, 70, 76–9**
Philip III (Arrhidaeus) of Macedon, 55–7, 74–5, 79, 187, 197–8; **51–6**
Philip IV of Macedon, 3, 79, 187, 199
Philip V of Macedon, 98, 135–6, 138,

Philip V of Macedon—*contd.*
142, 151, 155, 163–5, 171, 188, 201–2; **438–44, 582–7, 592, 595–6**
Philip VI (Andriscus), supposed king of Macedon, 135
Philippi, Macedonia (*5*), 84, 85; **199–201**
Philopoemon, 150
Phocaea, Ionia (*3*), 94, 122–3, 141
Phoenicia (*2, 3*), 10, 30, 46–7, 56, 77, 98, 101–2, 111, 115, 144, 178, 179, 183, 184, 197, 198
Phraates I of Parthia, 179, 195
Phraates of Elymais, 182
Phrygia, Asia Minor (*3, 6*), 55, 125–6, 197; **400–1**
Picard, O.: on Euboean coinage, 91, 158
Piraeus, Attica (*5*), 80, 86
Pleistarchus, satrap of Cilicia, 78, 198
plinthophoroi, 173
Plutarch, 167
Polyaenus, historian, 74
Polybius, historian, 4, 154, 171, 174
Polyperchon, regent of Macedon, 55, 58, 198
Polyrhenium, Crete (*5*), 155–6; **545**
Pontus, Asia Minor (*3, BEP*), 28, 30, 33, 98, 131, 132, 173–5, 192–3; **283, 420–1, 623–5**; mines in, 3
portraiture, *see* coin portraiture
Porus, Indian king, 28, 53–4; **44**
Poseidon, 78
posthumous coinages, 35–7; *see also* Alexanders, Lysimachi, Philip II
Praxippus of Lapethus, 57; **58**
Price, M. J.: on Macedonian coinage, 42
Priene, Ionia (*6*), 141, 158–9; **567, 572**; coin found at, **655**
Prusias I, II of Bithynia, 130, 174, 192; **417–19**
Ptolemaic weight standard, *see* weight standard
Ptolemais, *see* Ake (Ptolemais)
Ptolemies (Lagids), 4, 23, 190–1
Ptolemy I (Soter), 8, 10, 26, 27, 29, 30, 55, 56, 58, 59, 61–2, 63–70, 72, 77, 78, 80, 90, 100, 101, 102, 103, 132, 137, 190, 197–9; **90–101, 123, 297, 327–9**; portraits, 27, 65
Ptolemy II (Philadelphus), 10, 28, 30, 70 n. 11, 101–102, 146, 148, 190, 199–200; **284–5, 291–306, 327**
Ptolemy III (Euergetes I), 100–8, 114, 119, 149, 184, 190, 200–1; **307–15**
Ptolemy IV (Philopator), 98, 100, 108–9, 156, 190, 201; **316–18, 321, 325**
Ptolemy V (Epiphanes), 26, 27, 33, 98, 109–11, 183, 190; **319–29**
Ptolemy VI (Philometor), 177, 190
Ptolemy VIII (Euergetes II, Physcon), 184, 191
Ptolemy XII (Neos Dionysus, Auletes), 5 n. 10, 184, 191
Ptolemy Ceraunus, 75, 132, 188, 190, 199
Ptolemy of Commagene, 176
Publilius, Gaius, 166; **600**
Pumiathon of Citium, 47, 57, 58; **60**
punch marks on coins, 19
Punjab (India), 180–1, 195–6
Pushkalāvati, India (*BEP*), 181
Pydna, Macedonia (*5*), 166, 169
Pyrrhus of Epirus, 80, 82, 132, 153, 188, 199; **175, 196**

queens, Ptolemaic, *see* Arsinoe, Berenice, Cleopatra; *see also* Amastris, Laodice
Qunduz (Khisht Tepe), Bactria (*BEP*), hoard, 181

Raphia, Palestine (*2*), battle, 201
Ravel, O.: on Corinthian coinage, 87
Rawalpindi, India (*BEP*), 120
Reinach, T.: on Cappadocian coins, 174
Rhagae, Media (mod. Tehran) (*4*), 179
Rhithymna (Arsinoea), Crete (*5*), 156; **257–8, 546**
Rhodes, Aegean island (*3, 6*), 10, 20, 23, 31, 36, 90, 98, 138, 139, 141–2, 147, 148, 156–7, 158–9, 166, 171, 173, 198, 201, 202; **235–9, 471–2, 547–56**; *see also* weight standards
Robert, L.: on *taurophoroi*, 171
Robinson, E. S. G.: on cistophori, 172
Rome, Romans, 31, 35, 98, 116, 127, 129, 135, 138, 151, 153, 163–8, 169, 170, 171, 172, 174, 176

Sabaces, satrap, 47 n. 10
Sacas, 179, 195
Saida (Sidon), hoard, 84–5, 90
Salamis, Cyprus (*1, 2*), 17, 31, 46, 47, 49, 55, 56, 58, 61, 77, 104; **22, 63–5, 162–4**; sea battle, 29, 59, 77, 78, 198
Samos, Aegean island (*5, 6*), 93, 141, 142, 158–9; **259–61, 473, 569, 573–4**
Samos of Commagene, 176
Samosata, Commagene (*BEP*), 175–6
Samothrace, Aegean island (*5*), **608**
Sandan, deity, 46, 178
Sarapis, deity, 109; **317**
Sardis, Lydia (*FEP, 1, 3, 6*), 50, 56, 61, 75, 76, 81, 82, 115, 122–4, 126, 141, 173, 201; **10, 34–5, 52, 156, 176, 388–92, 395–6, 402–6, 463–5**; coins found at, 141
Scepsis, Aeolis (*6*), 124
Scostocus of Thrace (Aenus), 145; **490**
Scythians, 36
Seleucia on the Calycadnus, Cilicia (*2, 3*), 115, 131, 178
Seleucia on the Tigris, Mesopotamia (*4, BEP*), 20, 33, 35, 71, 73, 76, 116, 118, 178, 179; **132–4, 158–9, 360–2**; coins found at, 6, 22
Seleucia Pieria, Syria (*2, 3*), 113, 178; **154**
Seleucus I (Nicator), 15, 27, 29, 55, 58–9, 61, 62, 71–6, 78, 79, 80, 82, 115, 116, 122, 128, 132, 178, 188, 197–9; **87–9, 132–45, 149–52, 155–60, 350, 354–5, 388–9, 407–8**; portraits, 28
Seleucus II (Callinicus, Pogon), 4, 28, 102, 113–19, 123–4, 189, 200–1; **332–4, 336, 341–2, 354B, 368, 370, 396**
Seleucus III (Soter, Ceraunus), 125, 189, 201; **337–8, 347, 400–1**
Seleucus IV (Philopator), 13, 177, 189
Seleucus V, 177, 189
Selge, Pisidia (*6*), 160; **580–1**
Sellasia, Peloponnese (*5*), battle, 149, 201
Sellwood, D. G.: on Parthian dating, 194–5
Seltman, C.: on coins of Elis, 88
Sentius, C., 168
serrated edges of coins, 13, 164–5
Sestus, Thrace (*3*), 6, 81, 82
Seuthes III of Thrace, 83; **192**
Seyrig, H.: on Byzantine coinage, 20, 145–7; on Paeonian coinage, 83; on Parium, 125
Shamash, deity, 144
shield, varieties of, 207; Celtic, 10, 101; Macedonian, 163, 167
Sicyon, Peloponnese (*1, 5*), 9, 45 n. 7, 61, 86 n. 4, 88, 137–8, 171; **215, 448**
Side, Pamphylia (*1, 6*), 31, 52, 56, 143, 154; **43, 481**
Sidon, Phoenicia (mod. Saida) (*FEP, 1, 2, 3*), 30, 31, 33, 46, 48, 51, 52, 56, 61, 65, 77, 78, 101, 102, 108, 109, 110, 183, 199; **19, 94, 293, 635**; *see also* Saida
Sigeum, Troas (*3*), 124
signatures, of die cutters, 35
Sillyum, Pamphylia (*6*), 143; **477**
silphium, 67–9, 101–2
silver, supplies of, *see* mines
Simonetta, B., on Cappadocia, 131, 174–5, 193
Simyra, Phoenicia (*2, 3*), 115, 144; **247**
Sinope, Paphlagonia (*BEP*), 96, 138–9, 192; **281–2, 453–7**
Sitochoro (near Larissa), Thessaly (*5*), hoard, 148–9; **502**
Siwah, Egypt (*FEP, 1*), oasis, sanctuary of Zeus Ammon, 48, 81, 197, 203
Skeat, T. C.: on Ptolemaic chronology, 190
Smyrna, Ionia (*3, 6*), 20, 82, 93, 123, 141, 173; **182**; called Eurydicea, 93
Sogdiana (*FEP, 4*), 122, 197

Soli, Cilicia (*1, 2, 3*), 51, 115; **346**
Soli, Cyprus (*2, 3*), 46, 51, 58, 65; **95**
Sophene (*BEP*), 175–6
Sophytes, Indian king, 73; **148**
Sosthenes of Macedon, 188, 199
Sparta, Laconia (*5*), 9, 25, 137, 148–50, 200, 201; **503–11**; hoard from, 150
Spasinou Charax, Characene (*6*), 182
square coins, 13
Stasioecus II of Marium, 57; **59**
Stasion, Rhodian magistrate, **472**
statistics, in numismatics, 16–17
statues, as coin types, 25–7, 78, 108, 176, 178; **162, 268, 502, 609–11, 615, 650–3, 657**
stephanophoroi, 170
stolos, prow ornament, 77
Stratonice, mother of Demetrius Poliorcetes, 77
style, in coinage, 27–8
stylis, 43–4, 77
Stymphalus, Arcadia (*5*), 88; **228**
Sura, Brettius, 167–8
Susa, Susiana (*FEP, 1, 4, BEP*), 49, 53, 56, 58, 62, 71–2, 76, 118, 128, 178, 179, 182, 197; **54, 66, 135–6, 138–40, 144, 363, 642**; coins found at, 21, 22, 118, 182
Susiana/Elymais (*4*), 6, 58
Svoronos, J. N.: on Ptolemaic coinage, 101ff.
Sybrita, Crete (*5*), 88; **229–31**
Syene, Egypt (*FEP, 1*), 47 n. 10
Synnada, Phrygia (*6*), 173
Syracuse, Sicily (*FEP*), 35, 85; *see also* Agathocles
Syria, 5, 11, 30, 46ff., 176, 198
Syrian Wars: First, 200; Second, 123, 200; Third (War of Laodice), 102, 114, 119, 123, 200; Fourth, 201; Fifth, 98, 101, 109, 110, 115, 201

tagos, ruler of Thessaly, 85
Talon, giant, 88
Tarn, W. W.: on Bactria, 181
Tarsus, Cilicia (*1, 2, 3*), 45–6, 48, 49, 51, 56, 61, 75, 78, 100, 108, 113, 114–15, 124, 178; **13–15, 155, 165–6, 312, 344–5, 352, 634**
taurophoroi, 171
Taurus Mts, Asia Minor (*FEP, 3*), 3, 75, 122, 131
Taxila, India (*BEP*), 181
Taxiles, Indian prince, 53–4
Telephus, hero, 172
Temenids, 59, 187
Temnus, Aeolis (*6*), 20, 23, 141
Tenedos, Aegean island (*5*), 147
Tenos, Aegean island (*5*), 60; **240**
Teos, Ionia (*1, 6*), 50, 61, 81, 92–3, 141
tetrapolis, Syrian, 74, 113, 179
Thalia, P. Juventius, 167
Thasos, Aegean island (*5*), 168; **606**
Thebes, Boeotia (*5*), 80, 86; **206**
Theoi Adelphoi coins, 104, 109, 110
Thermopylae, Locris (*5*), 85, 201
Thessalian League, 26
Thessalonica, Macedonia (*5*), 165–7; **596**
Thessaly (*1, 5*), 41, 84, 85, 91
Thibron of Cyrene, 67–8, 89; **208–9**
Thompson, M.: on Athenian New Style coinage, 170; on drachm coins of Asia Minor, 50 n. 15
Thorikos, Attica (*5*), hoard, 86
Thrace, Thracians (*FEP, 1, 3, 5, 6, BEP*), 55, 83, 168, 197, 199; **192**; mines, 3
Thyrrhaeum, Acarnania (*5*), 87
Tigraios of Elymais, 182
Tigranes I of Armenia, 176
Tigranes II (the Great), 176, 178, 189; **626**
Timarchus, usurper, 13
Tiraios II of Characene, **643**
Tomis, Moesia (*6*), 138

trace elements, 6–7
Tralles, Lydia (*6*), 173
trikhryson, 67, 104
Triparadeisus, Syria, 55, 63, 197
Tripolis, Phoenicia (*2*), 109, 110
Triptolemus, Greek hero, 110
Trogus, historian, 181
Troxell, H. A.: on the coinage of Arsinoe, 103
Troy, *see* Ilium
Tryphon, pretender, 20, 177, 189
Tyana, Cappadocia (*3*), 131, 132, 174; **423–5**
Tyche, of Antioch, 176
Tyre, Phoenicia (*FEP, 1, 2, 3, BEP*), 10, 15, 30, 33, 46, 66, 77, 78, 101, 102, 104, 108, 109, 110, 115, 179, 183, 197, 199; **84, 161, 292, 299, 315, 633, 645**

Uranopolis, Chalcidice (*5*), 60, 84; **74–5**

value, marks of, 33, 35
Velchanos, Cretan hero, 88
Vulso, Cn. Manlius, Roman general, 141

Wallace, W. P.: on Euboean coinage, 91, 158
weight standards, 7–10; Aeginetan, 8, 85, 91, 165; Aetolian, 8–9; Asiatic, 67; Attic, 8, 9, 10, 40–3, 64–6, 77, 91, 92, 94; Babylonian, 7; Byzantine, 9; Chian, 9, 10, 90, 91, 102; cistophoric, 9, 10; Corcyrean, 9, 83; Macedonian, 40, 42; Persian, 9; Ptolemaic, 9, 64–9; Rhodian, 9, 10, 58, 68, 90, 91, 92, 166
Wolski, J.: on Parthian chronology, 194

Zenon archive, 104
Zeus, as coin type, 25, 43; *see also* Siwah
Ziaelas of Bithynia, 130, 192; **416**
Zoilus, mint official, 164, 165

DACIA
R. Danube
THRACE
Black Sea
(Euxine)
MACEDON
EPIRUS
Amastris
Sinope
PONTUS
Gaziura
BITHYNIA
PERGAMUM
Aegean
Sea
ARMENIA
CAPPADOCIA
Mazaca
Lake Van
Athens
Cybistra
COMMAGENE
Samosata
SOPHENE
KINGDOM OF THE SELEU
R. Tigris
Lake Urm
Mediterranean Sea
CRETE
Antioch
SYRIA
R. Euphrates
CYPRUS
Dura Europos
Cyrene
Apollonia
Damascus
Euhesperides
CYRENAICA
Tyre
Seleucia
Babylon
Alexandria
Jerusalem
KINGDOM
Naucratis
N
Memphis
OF THE
PTOLEMIES
R. Nile
Red Sea
ARABIA
Boundaries of the kingdoms were subject to frequent change. Those shown on this map are approximate.
Kingdom of the Seleucids
Former Seleucid provinces
Kingdom of the Ptolemies
Kingdom of Macedon

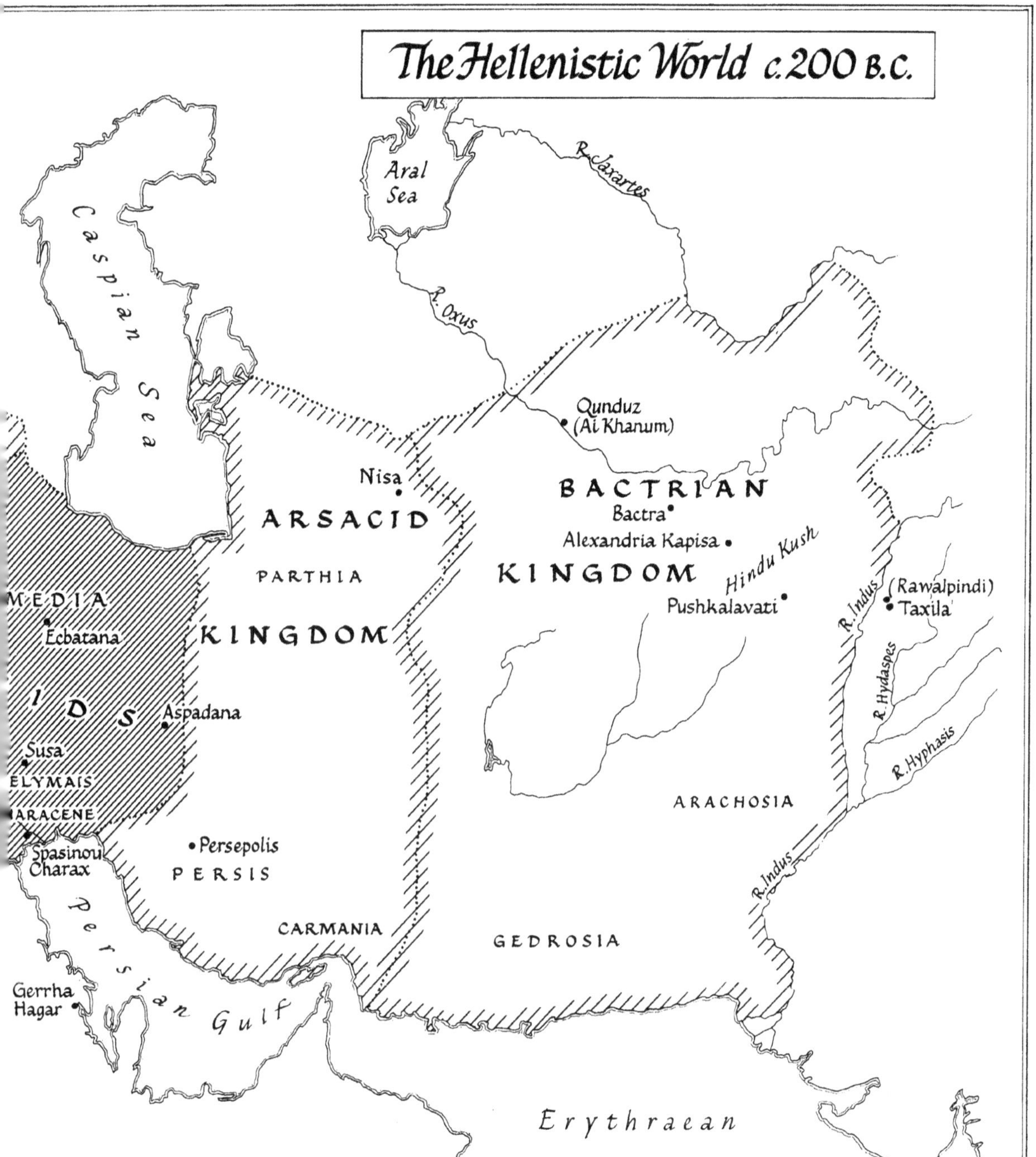
The Hellenistic World c. 200 B.C.
Aral Sea
R. Jaxartes
Caspian Sea
R. Oxus
Qunduz
(Ai Khanum)
Nisa
BACTRIAN
Bactra
ARSACID
Alexandria Kapisa
PARTHIA
Hindu Kush
KINGDOM
KINGDOM
MEDIA
Pushkalavati
(Rawalpindi)
Taxila
R. Indus
Ecbatana
R. Hydaspes
Aspadana
Susa
R. Hyphasis
ELYMAIS
ARACHOSIA
ARACENE
Persepolis
Spasinou Charax
PERSIS
R. Indus
Persian Gulf
CARMANIA
GEDROSIA
Gerrha Hagar
Erythraean Sea
0
500 km
0
500 miles

Lightning Source UK Ltd.
Milton Keynes UK
UKOW05n1802041217
313874UK00013B/120/P